All about making –

GEOMETRICAL BUCKS POINT LACE

by Alexandra Stillwell

Dedication
In memory of Mrs Vi Bullard

Previous books by the author
The Technique of Teneriffe Lace, Batsford, 1980, reprinted 1987
Laced with Laughs, Lace Guild, 1984
Drafting Torchon Lace Patterns, Dryad, 1986, reprinted Batsford 1992
Cassell Illustrated Dictionary of Lace, Cassell, 1996

First published in the UK 2006 by
Salex Publishing
26 Willow Park, Haywards Heath, West Sussex, RH16 3UA

Text, photographs and illustrations by Alexandra Stillwell 2006
The right of Alexandra Stillwell to be identified as
the author of this work has been asserted by her in
accordance with the provisions of the UK Copyright,
Design and Patent Act 1988

All rights reserved
The patterns and grids may be reproduced for personal
use only, but no other part of this book may be reproduced or
transmitted in any form or by any means, electronic or
mechanical, including photocopying, recording or any
information storage or retrieval system,
without prior permission in writing from the author.

ISBN

Cover designed by John Wilson
Printed and bound in Great Britain by Ditchling Press Ltd.

ISBN
978-0-9554694-0-4

All about making -

GEOMETRICAL BUCKS POINT LACE

CONTENTS

	Introduction
Chapter 01	History and Development
Chapter 02	Materials and Basic Skills
Chapter 03	Project 01 Rosette Brooch
Chapter 04	Project 02 Jabot
Chapter 05	Project 03 Handkerchief sachet
Chapter 06	Project 04 Globe candleholder
Chapter 07	Project 05 Hexagonal motif for handbag mirror
	Project 06 Pentagonal motif for handbag mirror
Chapter 08	Project 07 Handkerchief/Jabot
Chapter 09	Project 08 Mounted circular edging
	Project 09 Large UFO Candleholder with coloured gimps
	Project 10 Large UFO Candleholder with beads
	Project 11 Small UFO Candleholder with coloured beads
Chapter 10	Project 12 Small oval motif
	Project 13 Brush back insert
	Project 14 Ruler insert
Chapter 11	Project 15 Wedding garter
	Project 16 Ring pillow
	Project 17 Photo frame trim
	Project 18 Handkerchief edging
Chapter 12	Project 19 Bookmark fillings sampler
Chapter 13	Project 20 Fingerplate
Chapter 14	Project 21 Glass cover
	Project 22 Tray motif
	Project 23 Plate motif
	Project 24 Wine coaster motif
Chapter 15	Project 25 Clock
Chapter 16	Project 26 Lid motif made in white for crystal bowl
	Project 27 Lid motif made in black for satin finished bowl
Chapter 17	Project 28 Camisole
	Project 29 Half-slip
	Project 30 French knickers
Chapter 18	Copying, adapting and designing Bucks Point patterns
	Bibliography
	Index

INTRODUCTION

This Manual started as 'Learn how to make Bucks Point lace in easy stages'. However, while researching old lace to check that the techniques I was describing were correct, I discovered that a many more techniques had been used in the past, some of the techniques being restricted to specific areas of the country. I believe that many of these were lost during the period between the Second World War and the revival in the 1970s, the time when crafts went 'out of fashion' and the making of Bucks Point was only carried on by a handful of dedicated ladies. There is also material that I have come across since I started lacemaking; some I discovered for myself; some has come from other lacemakers. Other information has come from historians and from experts in other fields and much of this information has not previously been written down. My study of lacemaking has spanned the last 40 years. When I started lacemaking there was no one in my area from whom I could learn so I had to learn from books, of which there were very few available at the time, and those that I could obtain were not particularly easy to follow. Having a maths/science background I found the techniques intriguing. Lacemaking relies heavily on visio-spatial ability. Because there were few patterns available when I started I used my skills to work out how to draft the patterns and have been drafting, designing and teaching pattern drafting and designing ever since. The modern pieces in this book are my own designs; the idea for overlapping the snowflakes in Chapter 14 was originally developed by Jane Partridge and is in her 'Hearts and Snowflake' pattern. The antique lace and pattern are from Joan Tyler-Smith's Collection.

The first chapter describes the development of lace and the emergence of the Bucks Point family; the second describes the materials and equipment required and explains the basic skills and basic stitches. These are followed by a series of projects, describing how to make different items in Bucks Point, with the series following a progression of steps that allow the lacemaker to master the different techniques. Most lacemakers progress faster and enjoy lacemaking more when they can concentrate on a few new techniques at a time. Information is also included for drafting the patterns and finishing, joining and/or mounting the lace as required for each project.

Additional information about techniques, in depth explanations, techniques that can be used as alternatives to the ones described in the main text, and extra information are included as 'End Notes' when appropriate. Occasionally I have included techniques that, while they may not have been in use before 1900, can achieve a better result than the former technique. Once a standard technique has been mastered try an alternative technique. It is useful to mark the pricking or a copy or tie a coloured thread round one of the lace threads to indicate when you change technique, so you can compare the results. Some alternative techniques make a substantial difference; sometimes hardly any difference at all. Sometimes the choice may be affected by the situation; the thickness of thread or the way a particular lacemaker handles the bobbins. In many cases it comes down to personal preference. The more techniques you understand the greater your ability to make and design good quality lace. The choice of technique is yours. Crafts rarely reach the point where nothing can be improved and much of the enjoyment is achieving the best possible result within the integrity of the subject.

Today lacemaking is a hobby and time is not of the essence, so very fine lace can be made using the very best, if time consuming, techniques. Since the revival of lace, as with the revival of many other crafts, I keep hearing people say that 'lacemaking must develop or die'. Mankind has been drawing for thousands of years and art teaching still covers very primitive methods such as charcoal drawing and pen and ink. We do not hear the same clamour for these to change. There are, and should always be, those who will experiment and develop the craft. However, the constant insistence that we should all be concentrating on change, devalues the very beautiful pieces made in fine white thread in traditional style. Our traditional techniques are the building blocks of our craft. Lace, whatever methods used to make it, whether traditional or innovative, white or coloured, should be valued according to the design and quality of workmanship. Our treasury of techniques needs to be carefully examined and preserved, while at the same time encouraging innovation and experimentation.

Writing this book has not been easy, and my thanks go to all those who have supported and encouraged me. I would especially like to thank Barbara Underwood for reading through my manuscript, Ann Day for giving me the benefit of her expertise concerning history and dating, Pat Norman for her skills in needlework and for machine stitching the lingerie, Phyllis Hadden for her critical eye regarding design, Ian A. Morgan and Glen K. Morgan, non-lacemakers, for carefully checking the wording of the manuscript, Carol McFazdean for sharing her experiences in publishing, Lindsay Norris for helping me sort out problems with my computer and Ditchling Press for their help and patience. Above all my thanks go to Maureen Philpott and Jean Eke, who were relatively new to Bucks Point, and who have painstakingly worked through all the projects, pointing out my mistakes and shortcomings so that I could correct them and thank you Jean for proof reading, no mean task in itself. They say 'the proof of the pudding is in the eating'. As Maureen returned my last chapter, with its corrections, she presented me with the pricking for a square adapted from the wide lingerie edging, with the comment that it was working up without any problems. Congratulations Maureen, your square is in chapter 18. Every effort has been made to ensure that the prickings are as accurate as possible. However, my computer has its own inbuilt parameters and cannot work in increments of less than 1%, so it has been impossible to be 100% accurate. Also, in a work of this size there are bound to be errors that slipped through the net; for these I apologise and hope they do not detract from your enjoyment.

Providing the lace looks good and is structurally sound, the final decisions regarding design and the techniques you select are yours. Above all ENJOY!

Chapter 1
HISTORY AND DEVELOPMENT

Lace developed and became popular during the 16th century when trading became lucrative and the emerging, very wealthy merchant class, wished to parade its success before the world. Lace became a symbol of this success, as it would be on show wherever the wearer went; it was expensive, beautiful and, since it served no practical function, totally frivolous. The early needle made laces, of the late 15th and early 16th centuries, were stiff and worn flat or pleated into ruffs, and as the fine bobbin laces developed they were also worn flat. In the early 18th century fashion changed and fine laces with gathering and draping qualities were required. The stiffer laces with fussy all over designs were superseded by softer laces, with more open designs and larger expanses of open ground (the net connecting the motifs), where gathers could occur e.g. Alençon, a needle lace (figure 1), and Mechlin, a bobbin lace (figure 2).

Figure 1 Alençon

Figure 2 Mechlin (18th century)

Chapter 1

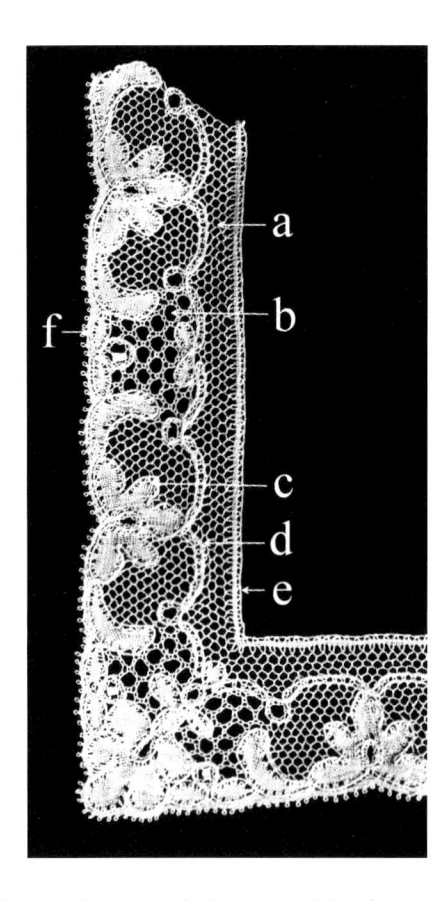

Characteristics of point lace
a Point ground is the net background of the lace (figure 7).
b Honeycomb stitch is the most popular of the decorated grounds, usually called fillings, which are used to provide the lighter areas of texture that enliven the design.
c The motifs are the more solid decorative shapes that provide the dense areas of the design. They are usually of 'cloth stitch' when made in white and off white, and 'half stitch' when made in black.
d The gimp is the thicker, often shiny, thread that surrounds the motifs and gives them greater definition.
e The footside is the reinforced edge by which lace is attached to fabric or another piece of lace.
f The headside is the free unattached edge of the lace. It often undulates, or is Vandyked, and is usually edged with a line of small picots.

Figure 7 (right) Bucks point lace

These characteristics provide the essential building blocks for well-balanced Bucks Point designs. There are many other fillings that can be very effective for adding interest to the design, but they must be used with care. Too many different fillings used in the same piece of lace can cause the finished item to look fussy and confused. This piece, (figure 7) is floral Bucks; the design is free flowing and unconstrained by the geometry of the ground, whereas the designs for geometrical Bucks follow the geometry of the ground, as in the designs for the projects in this book.

It is interesting to compare a piece of lace, made using Bucks Point techniques (figure 7), with a similar Alençon piece (figure 1). The grounds have a similar appearance as the top stitching of the needle lace and the gimp of the bobbin lace perform the same function in the design. Both have picots, although those of the bobbin lace are confined to the edge, whereas they are also used to embellish the top stitching, within the design, in the needle lace. Honeycomb stitch is very similar in appearance to pea stitch in needle lace. It is also interesting to find that many pieces of Alençon lace have grounds with angles from 52° to 58° to the 'footside'. It raises the question, did the Bucks point family of laces copy the angle from Alençon lace, or do they use the same angles because they give the most pleasing results?

The angle to the footside
The 'angle to the footside' is the angle the diagonal row of pinholes or diagonal thread makes with the footside (figure 8). In practice it is measured within the ground (figure 9), as the footside row of pins and the adjacent row are off-set and are not pricked in line with those of the ground. The angle to the footside can be any measurement between 45° and 70° with 52° to 58° being the most

popular for point ground and most fillings The angle to the footside measured for an antique piece of lace may not be that at which it was made. The lace may have been stretched when wound on a card before selling, during washing or ironing. This would distort the angle. There are some prickings where ground and fillings have different angles. These may have been the result of a lace maker taking a pricking for the grid from one pattern and the pricking for the filling from another. Usually it gives a better result when both have the same angle to the footside.

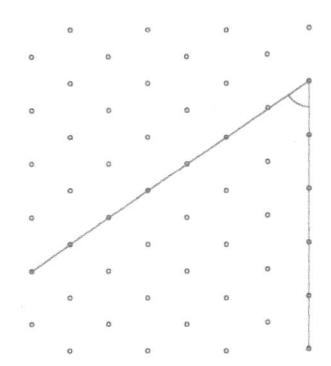

Figure 8 The angle to the footside

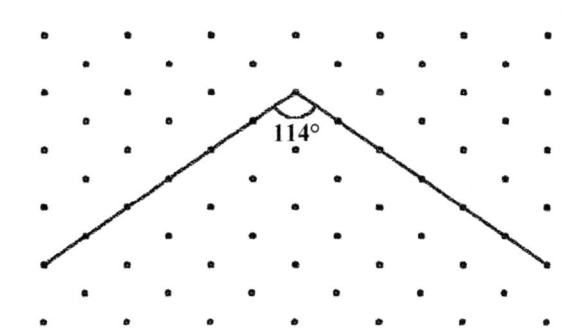

Effect of Changing the Angle to the Footside for Point Ground
When the same pattern is made using different angles, the effect of changing the angle becomes apparent (figure 10). For point ground, as the angle between the footside and the ground increases from 45° the squat, oval holes become more round, 55° producing the nearest to the circular. Then they become a more elongated '0' as the angle increases to 70°. The holes in honeycomb vary in a similar way, the closest to the circular being at 60°. At 45° the cloth stitched diamond has right angled corners and the fabric has a close even texture. As the angle increases the shape becomes elongated. The passives become more widely spaced and the workers closer. Thus the density of the clothwork changes very little as the angle increases.

Measuring the angle to the footside
Measuring the angle using the footpins and a diagonal line from the footpins does not give an accurate result since the footside is offset. A more accurate measurement is obtained by measuring the angle between the two sets of diagonal rows, or lines of pins, i.e. one working towards the left, the other to the right (figure 9). Since the footside is parallel to the vertical line through the centre point, the angle will be double the angle to the footside. Therefore halve the angle measured.

Figure 9 Measuring the angle to the footside

In this case the angle measured is 114°
and the angle to the footside is half of that
i.e. 57°

Copying Prickings
Traditionally lace patterns were designed by the few trained designers and supplied to lacemakers by lace dealers and teachers. Lacemakers would use a pattern until it became so torn or the holes so enlarged that it was unusable. They would then pin a new, transparent piece of parchment over the original and prick through. The exact positions of the original holes within the enlarged spaces would be difficult to reproduce, and the positions of the new pricked holes would vary from the original. After repeated repricking the arrangement of the holes would become very irregular (figure 11). Since the positions of the pins determine the positions of the threads, and the positions of the pins are governed by the holes in the pricking, a piece of lace can only be as regular and

Chapter 1

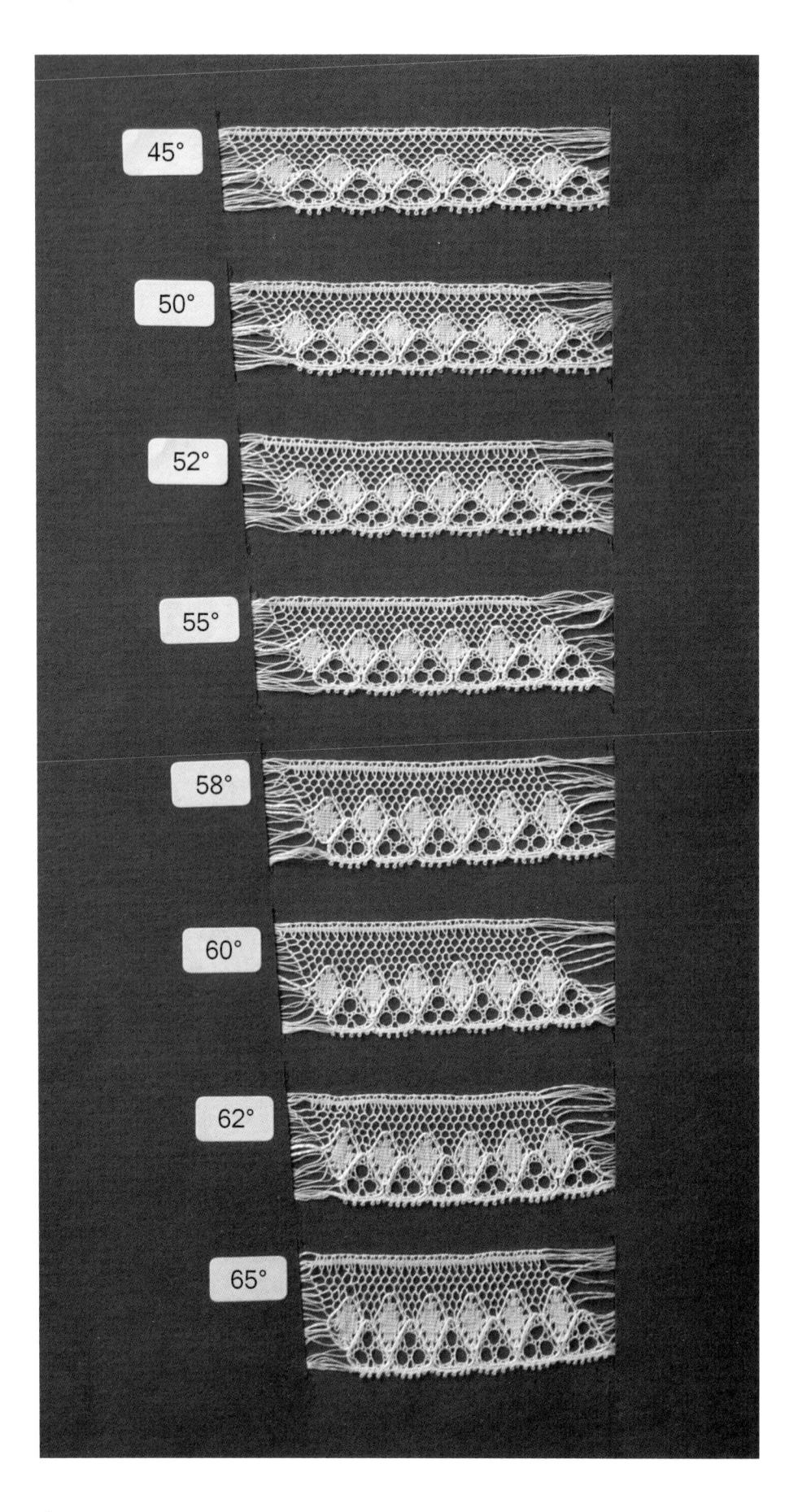

Figure 10 Changing the angle of the point ground

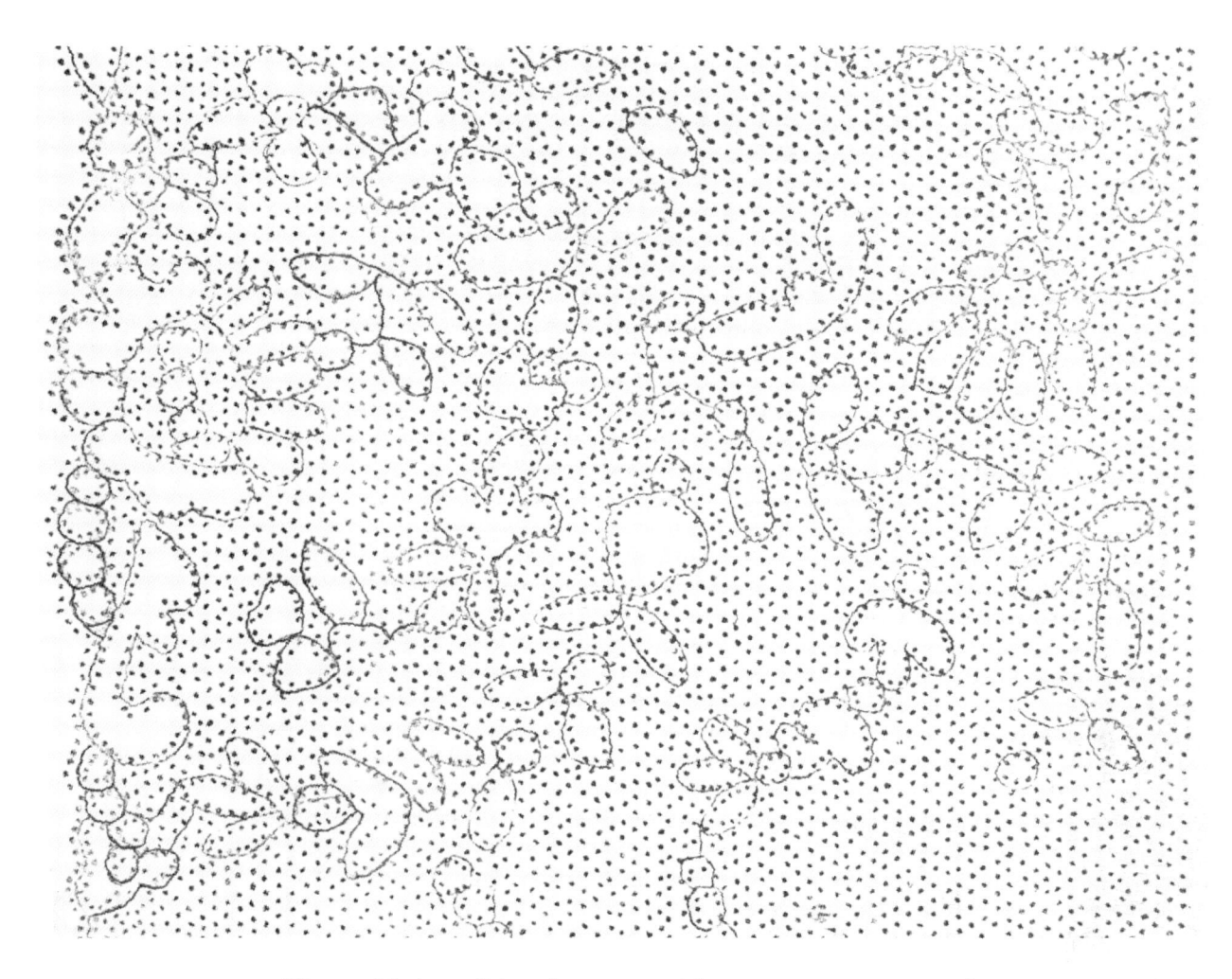

Figure 11 A traditional pattern with a very uneven ground

accurate as the pricking it is made on. Traditionally copies of prickings were made by placing a piece of paper over the reverse side of a pricking (the card being raised around the holes) and rubbing with heel-ball (black or brown wax sticks used by shoe menders to colour shoe heels after repair), the process being the same as making a brass rubbing. If you try this, use tracing paper and do not forget to turn the paper, over before pricking, or it will be 'back to front'.

END NOTES

1 The Bucks Point family
The Bucks Point family includes Bayeux, Beverse, Blonde Catalana, Blonde de Caen, , Bucks point, Chantilly, Downton, Erzgebirge, Fond Clair de Neuchâtel, Geraadsbergse Chantilly, Libenau, Lille, Malmsbury, Merletto aquilano, Point Clair de marche-en-Femenne, Rijslse, Tønder, Tulle du Pays d'Enhaut Tylová cipka, Vanstena Finknyppling, Vanha Rauman Pitsi, Vlácka etc.

Chapter 2
MATERIALS REQUIRED FOR MAKING BUCKS POINT LACE

Bobbins

Traditionally East Midlands bobbins (figure 12) or South Bucks bobbins (figure 13) are used for making Bucks point (preferably keep to one type at a time, rather than mixing them). From my experience I believe lacemakers achieve the best results when using the bobbins with which they are most comfortable, keeping to the general rule that lighter bobbins are more appropriate for use with fine thread.

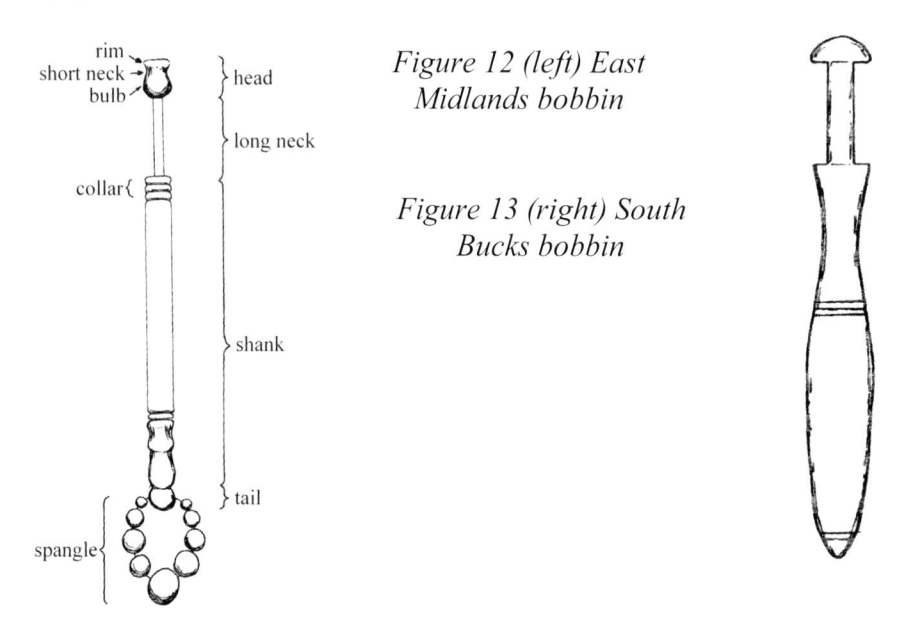

Figure 12 (left) East Midlands bobbin

Figure 13 (right) South Bucks bobbin

Spangle

The East Midlands bobbin's circle of beads provides the weight required for good tension.

Spangling with a Shackle

Mostly used in the southern parts of the lacemaking area - Southern Bedfordshire, parts of Buckinghamshire, Oxfordshire.

1. Arrange 7, 9, 11, or 13 beads in order, traditionally, so that they grade evenly from the largest, the bottom bead to the smallest on each side, the top beads.
2. Use fine nosed pliers to make a small loop at the end of the wire (figure 14), use 22 or 24 swg brass wire.

Figure 14 Wire loop

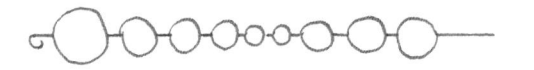

Figure 15 Threading beads on the wire

3. Thread the beads on the wire, starting with the bottom bead, working towards the smallest on one side, the top bead, then from the smallest on the other (figure 15).

4. Bend the wire and pass the end through the loop. Allow a bare 13mm (½in) of space past the beads and bend the wire against the loop. Allowing sufficient wire past the bend for another loop and cut off the remaining wire. Make the second loop interlocking with the first (figure 16).

8

If the hole in the adjacent bead is sufficiently large, push the join into it.

5. Make a loop at the end of another piece of wire. Thread the other end through the hole near the tail of the bobbin, the spangle of beads and through the loop at its other end. Allowing just sufficient wire for the spangle to clear the end of the bobbin, bend back, cut off and make a second loop interlocking with the first. Keep the join away from the hole to minimize wear (figure 17).

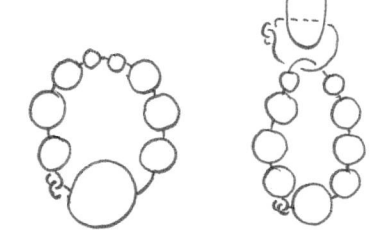

Figure 16 (above left) Spangle

Figure 17 (above right) Spangle with shackle

Spangling without a shackle
(Popular in northern parts of the lacemaking area - Northern Bedfordshire, Northamptonshire, Huntingdonshire.)

Follow points 1-4 for 'Spangling with a shackle' threading the wire through the bobbin between the two smallest beads (figure 18).

Figure 18 (left) Spangle without shackle

Wearing Out
If the spangle wire wears through the shank, resulting in the spangle falling out, cut the end off the bobbin through the damaged hole. Sandpaper the new end until smooth, drill another hole and respangle.

Pillow
Currently slightly domed mushroom pillows (figure 19) are most frequently used, but again the type that is the most comfortable for the lacemaker will result in the best lace being made. These pillows should be used at a slight angle, i.e. they need raising slightly at the back. A loosely filled beanbag is easy to adjust to achieve a comfortable height.

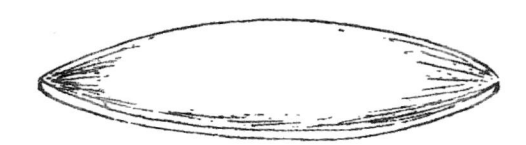

Figure 19 Mushroom pillow

Thread
Bucks point is usually made using very fine linen or cotton thread. The threads recommended for the projects may be substituted for a thread of similar thickness (see Chapter 18). Different brands vary slightly in thickness and texture; some work up softer, others give a more dense and stiffer finish.

Pins
Traditionally fine brass pins are used; these should be at least 2.5 cm (1 in) long with a diameter of about .55 mm. They are only inserted half way into the pattern. Fine stainless steel pins are also suitable and are less likely to corrode.

Pattern Draft
The paper pattern with dots for the holes, and lines to assist the lacemaker, from which the pricking is made.

Pricking card
Traditionally parchment was used, but now we use glazed manilla card 0.4 - 0.5 mm thick. It is strong, resists wear and is a suitable colour for the background when making white lace. Use a white or pastel coloured background when making black lace. The finer card can be used when designing floral Bucks as it can be 'pricked by eye' as you make the lace.

Pricker
The pricker is a handle with a needle clamped in the end. They come in many shapes of which the one illustrated (figure 20) is the most common. The needle should have the same diameter as the pins that are to be used for making the lace; a no 8 is suitable for the majority of pins, and the needle should protrude no more than 1cm (0.4 in). If the needle protrudes too far it will break easily, if it is too short the holes will be too small. Always try a pricker before purchasing as not all prickers suit all hands

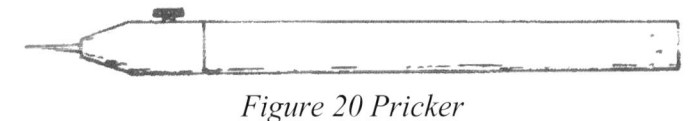

Figure 20 Pricker

Pricking Board
The firm support on which the pricking card is placed while the holes are being pricked. A cork mat, polystyrene sheet or several layers of corrugated cardboard are all suitable and 20cm x 35cm x 1cm thick is a suitable size. Ensure it is sufficiently thick, so that the pricker does not make contact with the surface beneath. Check cork for hard chips; these could deflect the pricker and cause irregular pricking. Pricking on a pillow is uncomfortable, it wears the pillow and does not always produce sufficiently accurate results.

Pricking
The pricking card pattern, with holes pricked through it, together with lines and other marks drawn with a fine felt tipped pen (0.1mm dia. tip). Traditionally black is used when working with white or pale threads and red when using black thread. Other colours are useful for corrections. Working black thread over black indicator lines can be confusing. Traditionally lines are drawn for the paths of the gimps, large black dots for tallies and crosses for mayflowers, but lacemakers have always invented their own reminders. Holes pricked incorrectly are ringed.

Making a Pricking (Making a card copy of a Pattern Draft)
1 Make a paper copy of the pattern or pattern draft and attach to a piece of pricking card using staples, transparent sticky tape, Blu-tac etc. so that the card and paper are securely fixed together. Staples or transparent sticky tape are probably the most secure methods.
2 Place the card, with the draft attached, on a pricking board and prick through all the dots, keeping the pricker vertical. Push the needle completely into the card at each hole, so that all holes are the full diameter of the needle. Lubricate the pricker by stabbing the needle into beeswax, or a wax candle, as required or rub a wax candle all over the paper pattern draft prior to pricking; the pricker will pick up sufficient wax as it passes through the paper.
3 The footside may be pricked by first pricking only the top and bottom footside holes. Insert a pin part way into each and hold a ruler tightly against these two pins. Prick the footside using the ruler as a guide. Do **not** use this method for pricking the ground as it produces 'tram lines' (figure 21), wider gaps between some adjacent rows showing as white streaks in the ground.

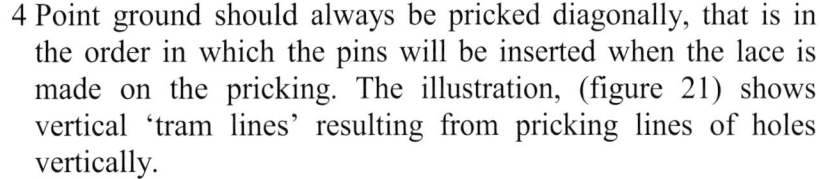

Chapter 2

4 Point ground should always be pricked diagonally, that is in the order in which the pins will be inserted when the lace is made on the pricking. The illustration, (figure 21) shows vertical 'tram lines' resulting from pricking lines of holes vertically.
5 Check that no dots have been missed by looking at the back of the card, and by holding it up to the light. Prick any dots that were missed and remove the Pattern Draft.
6 Use a pencil to transfer the indicators, the black lines and symbols drawn on the draft, onto the card pattern. Use a sharp HB pencil. Use the pencil gently to avoid making deep marks that may be difficult to remove with an eraser. When the lines and indicators have been correctly drawn go over them using a very fine felt tipped pen.
7 To avoid soiling the lace, remove the pencil marks using a soft eraser. Ring any holes pricked by mistake.
8 Cut out the pricking leaving a border of card about 1.5 cm (½ in) wide around the pricked holes.

Figure 21 'Tram lines'

When the gimps follow a complicated path, prick the pattern, then lift one side of the pattern draft and place a piece of 'non-smudge' carbon paper, 'business side' down between the paper and card Transfer the lines using a ballpoint pen or stylus. The carbon only leaves a faint line, which must be redrawn in pen. Finally remove any loose carbon using a soft eraser. Alternatively the pattern draft may be trimmed to size and covered with a suitably coloured sticky backed plastic. Stick the prepared pattern onto the card. Always prick all the pattern before starting to make the lace, (pricking 'as you go' does not give as good a result, except around the freestyle shapes in Floral Bucks). The paper pattern will remain on the card together with its indicator lines. The main drawback to this method is that the adhesive tends to 'grab' the pins, making them harder to insert and remove, and eventually make them sticky. If the plastic film is shiny remove the gloss using fine steel wool (without soap) or an abrasive scouring pad.

Truing Up a Pattern
The process of removing any distortions from a pattern. It requires a lot of work and is very time consuming. Chapter 1 figure 11 shows a very distorted pattern that has many areas that would be very difficult, if not impossible, to work well without some truing up beforehand.

Grids
Areas of specially prepared dots produced for pattern drafting (see Chapter 18).

Photocopying Prickings
Many photocopying machines are designed to distort, the copy being slightly narrower than the original, in order to avoid words close to the edges of the original being lost. After a copy has been copied and that copied and this repeated several times, the distortion becomes very obvious. This is one of the reasons why it is often impossible to match four photocopies to make a square border, or relocate lace after moving up or after a corner has been turned. Always check a pattern with a corner carefully before pricking; to make sure that the width of the lace is the same both sides of the corner. Pattern drafting is time consuming, and frequently exasperating, but it can be very

Chapter 2

rewarding. Apart from control over accuracy the actual drawing of the pattern gives an insight into the structure of the lace that will be produced on the pattern, and hence an insight into the techniques that will be required to make the lace. Experience in pattern drafting also leads to being able to adapt patterns and eventually to being able to design your own. First class lace cannot be made on a second rate pricking and it is worth the time spent mastering the art of pattern drafting in order to ensure that you always have an accurate pricking on which to make your lace.

Cover Cloths
Pieces of fabric that are used to protect the pillow and pattern from wear, and the lace from collecting dirt. One type of cover cloth, the Pillow Cloth covers the pillow, protecting it from becoming soiled and worn and keeps the lace clean. If it is rectangular or square it should be attached using strong pins. If it shaped to fit the pillow, it has elastic in a hem around the edge and should fit snugly over the pillow without needing any extra securing. Another, the Working Cloth, is used over the pattern to protect the pattern and to stop bobbins from catching on it. Another, the Hiller or Heller, is thrown over the whole pillow to keep the dust off when the pillow is left. As lace is made it should be protected by wrapping it in white fabric, the Lace Cloth. All cover cloths, apart from the lace cloth, should be of a smooth, dark, fabric and be at least as wide as the pillow. All cloths should be washed every time a piece of lace has been completed and lifted off the pillow.

Dressing a pillow
The arranging of cover cloths, and pinning on a pricking, in preparation for starting a piece of lace.
 1 Place the working cloth over the pillow or secure in place using strong pins.
2 Attach the pricking to the pillow by the two top corners only, using strong pins. The lower edge of the pricking does not need to be attached; it will be kept in place by the working cloth. The pricking should be positioned so that it starts as far from the lacemaker as is comfortable.
3 Fold under several inches of the upper edge of the worker/working cloth and pin across the pillow at right angles to the pricking and about 7 cm (3 ins) from the start of the pricking. Use strong pins and position them as far to the sides of the pillow as possible. Use a firm tension and angle the pins outwards for the best results. The worker cloth should be a little wider than the pillow and cover the lower edge at the front (figure 22).

Figure 22 (right) Pillow with pillow cloth, working cloth and pattern set in

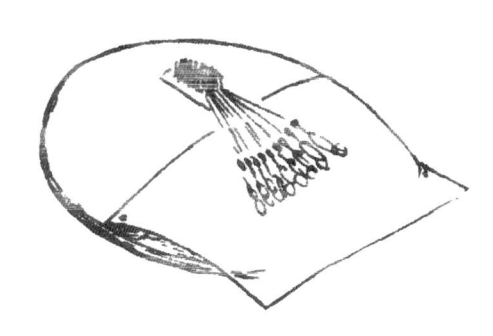

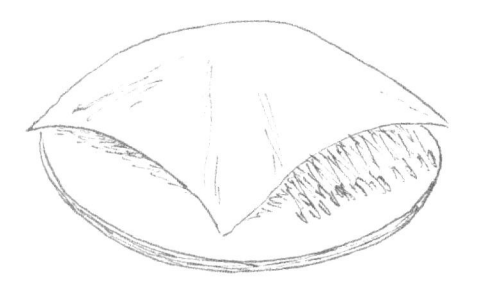

A loose cloth, the heller or hiller (figure 23) is a dust cover that is thrown over everything every time the pillow is left.

Figure 23 (left) Pillow with a hiller (heller) to protect it from dust.

Chapter 2

Winding bobbins

1 Hold the bobbin in the left hand. Place the lace thread along the neck with the tail pointing towards the head and hold in position with the left thumb (figure 24).

Figure 24 (right) Starting to wind a bobbin

2 Start winding the thread clockwise, when looking down on the head (figure 25). After a few turns, when the thread has stopped slipping, continue by rotating the bobbin anti-clockwise, first covering the ½ cm (¼ in) below the head (this helps to reduce slipping). If the thread is continually wound clockwise round the head the twists on the thread will be changed and this can lead to the thread weakening, shredding and even breaking.

Figure 25 Winding a bobbin

3 When sufficient thread has been wound secure with a half hitch. Hold the thread between thumb and middle finger, place the index finger in front of the thread and take it back and up under the thread to make a loop (figure 26).

Figure 26 (right) Starting the hitch

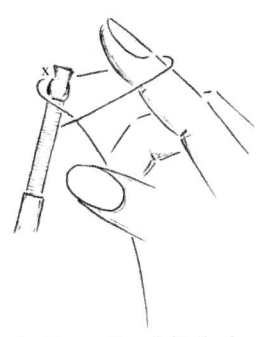

4 Place the bobbin head behind the thread held between the thumb and index finger and bring the bobbin forwards and up through the loop. The loop should sit in the short neck (figure 27). If the loop tends to slip off the head before it is tightened place the left index finger across the short neck at X, do not hold so tightly that the hitch cannot tighten.

Figure 27 (left) Passing the head through the loop

5 Check that the hitch has been correctly made. After winding, the thread should emerge to the right from the back of the bobbin, it doubles back behind the bobbin and emerges the other side, it crosses in front of the neck and passes from front to back through the loop (figure 28).

Figure 28 Hitch correctly made

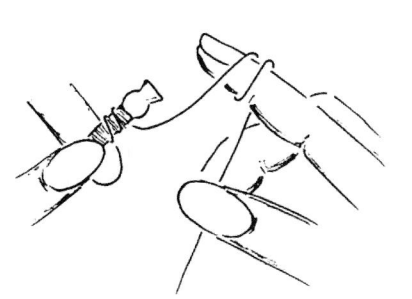

Figure 29 Making a hitch with two turns

When using very shiny bobbins, or when the hitch continually slips, a hitch with two turns may be used. Make the hitch as above passing the thread twice rounds the index finger (figure 29) before passing the head of the bobbin through both loops. There are many methods that can be used for making the hitch and all can be successful, providing the thread doubles back before passing around the neck and through the loop (figures 30 & 31).

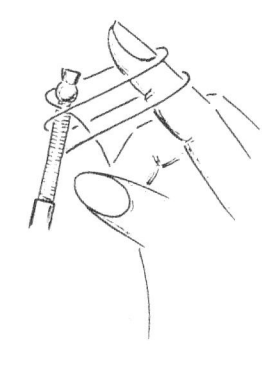

Chapter 2

Figure 30 (left) Passing the head through two loops

Figure 31 (above) Hitch with two turns

For extra difficult bobbins, and shiny thread, the hitch can be made with three turns. Wind the thread three times around the finger, and then pass the head through all three loops. However, this hitch holds the thread so securely that the bobbins need regular lengthening. It would appear that the hitch with two turns allows a restricted amount of 'slip' so that the bobbins keep pace with the lacemaker. It also appears that rotating the bobbin slightly, so as to keep the hitch at the correct tension, is a skill we acquire with experience.

Coupled Bobbins
When the starting edge of a piece of lace is to be seen, each pair of bobbins should be wound on a single piece of thread without using a knot. Wind one bobbin then, either continue overwinding sufficient thread for another bobbin or, take that amount of thread from the reel before cutting. Starting at the cut end, wind the second bobbin, as the first, transferring the extra thread from the first bobbin (figure 32) or using up the loose thread.

Figure 32 (right) Coupled bobbins

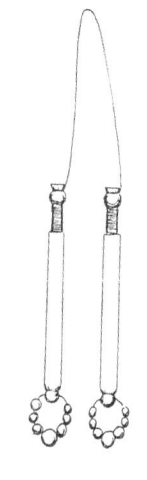

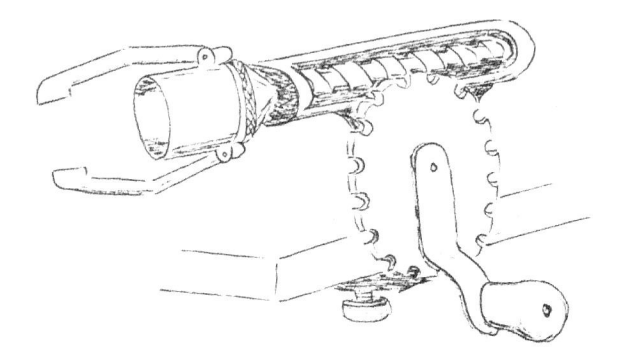

Bobbin Winder
There are many gadgets and machines, on the market, that speed up the process of winding bobbins figure 33). Always try out a winder before purchasing, as not all work successfully with East Midlands bobbins, and choice of a winder is frequently personal preference.

Figure 33 (left) Bobbin winder

Lengthening the bobbin thread
Hold the bobbin at right angles to the thread and unwind as required. Tighten the hitch by winding back against it (figure 34).

*Figure 34 (right)
Lengthening the bobbin thread*

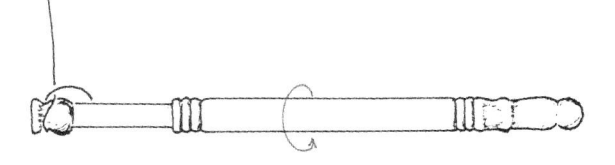

Chapter 2

Shortening the bobbin thread
Hold the bobbin at right angles to the thread, loosen the hitch with a pin and continue holding the loop of the hitch out while winding the bobbin as required. Release the loop and wind against the hitch to tighten it (figure 35).

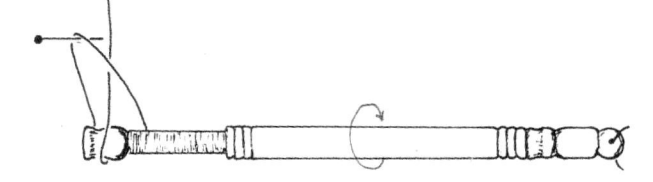

Figure 35 Shortening the bobbin thread

Numbering Bobbins and Pairs
Bobbins and pairs are always numbered from the left, unless instructions are given to count from the right or from the edge, which may be the left or right, according to the situation. Bobbins and pairs are renumbered after every movement.

Basic Movements
Almost all bobbin lacemaking is a mixture of twists and crosses.

When the right bobbin of a pair passes over the left bobbin, of the same pair, it makes a twist (figure 36).

When the centre two bobbins, of two pairs, pass left over right they make a cross (figure 37).

Figure 36 (left) Twist   Figure 37 (right) Cross

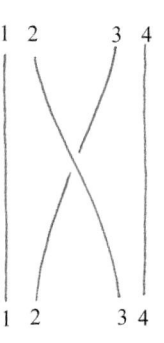

Cloth Stitch
Cloth stitch is the stitch that produces the woven areas in lace. The stitch is made using two pairs of bobbins that work cross, twist, cross, i.e. using four bobbins numbered 1-4
        pass 2 over 3 (figure 38) (renumber)
        pass 2 over 1 and 4 over 3 (bobbins 2 & 4 move together) (figure 39) (renumber)
        pass 2 over 3 (figure 40)

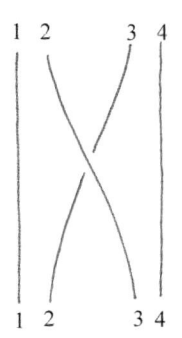

Figure 38 Cross
cross, twist & cross

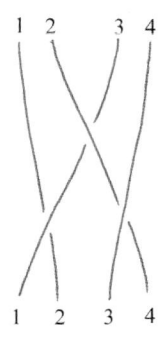

Figure 39 Cross & twist

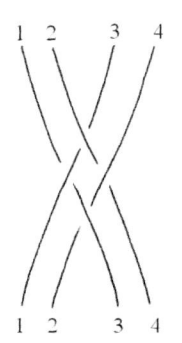

Figure 40 Cloth stitch

Chapter 2

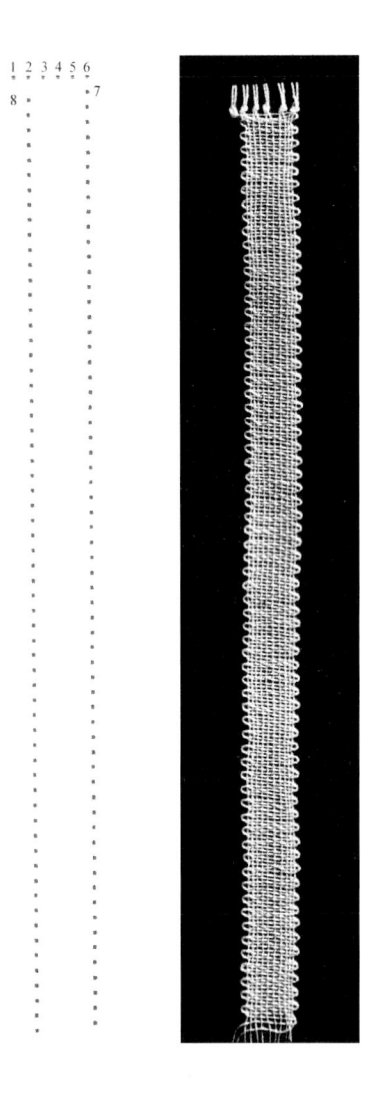

1 Make a pricking from the pattern draft (figure 41), dress the pillow and wind 6 pairs of bobbins in couples.
2 Place a pin in each hole across the top of the pricking and tie one pair of bobbins to each pin, pins 1-6. Adjust the bobbins so that they are all the same length, and that there is about the same length of thread between the pins and the bobbins as the length of the bobbin. The two bobbins of pair 1, that will work rows to and fro across the pricking, are called the workers. The pairs they work through are called the passives.
3 Work cloth stitch using pair 1 with each pair across the row, until the original pair 1 reaches the right hand side. Twist the workers twice (right over left). Place a pin in pinhole no. 7, the first hole below the top row of pins, between the workers (now pair 6) and pair 5.
4 Work back across the row with the workers making cloth stitches with each pair in turn, then twist the workers twice (right over left). The stitches are made exactly as before; they are not reversed when the direction of the row changes. Set up pin 8 between pairs 1 & 2 in the highest available hole on the left side (figure 41).
5 Continue making rows of cloth stitches until you are comfortable (figures 42 & 43).

Figure 41 (left) Pattern draft

Figure 42 (centre) Cloth stitch

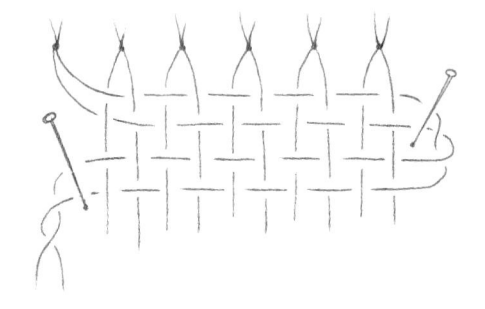

Figure 43 (right) Cloth stitch

Half stitch
Half stitch is made using two pairs of bobbins that work cross, twist, i.e. using four bobbins numbered 1-4
  pass 2 over 3 (figure 44)
  pass 2 over 1 and 4 over 3 (bobbins 2 & 4 move together) (figure 45)

16

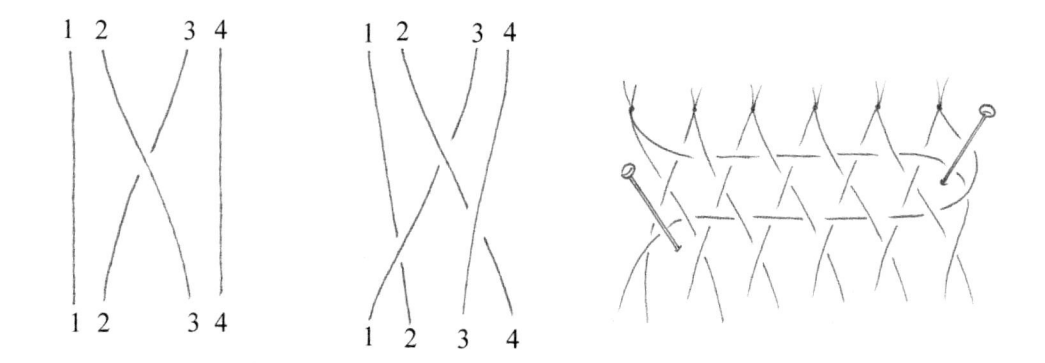

Figure 44 Cross   Figure 45 Half stitch (cross & twist)   Figure 46 Half stitch

Using the same pricking as for the cloth stitch sampler (figure 41) and start with freshly wound bobbins, or continue from the cloth stitch braid. Work rows as for cloth stitch but use half stitches (figure 46 & 47). This time only one thread of the original pair travels across the row; the other bobbin, making the pair changes as each stitch is made. The bobbin travelling across and its temporary partner, at any particular time, are known as the workers. Continue making rows of half stitches until they become comfortable.

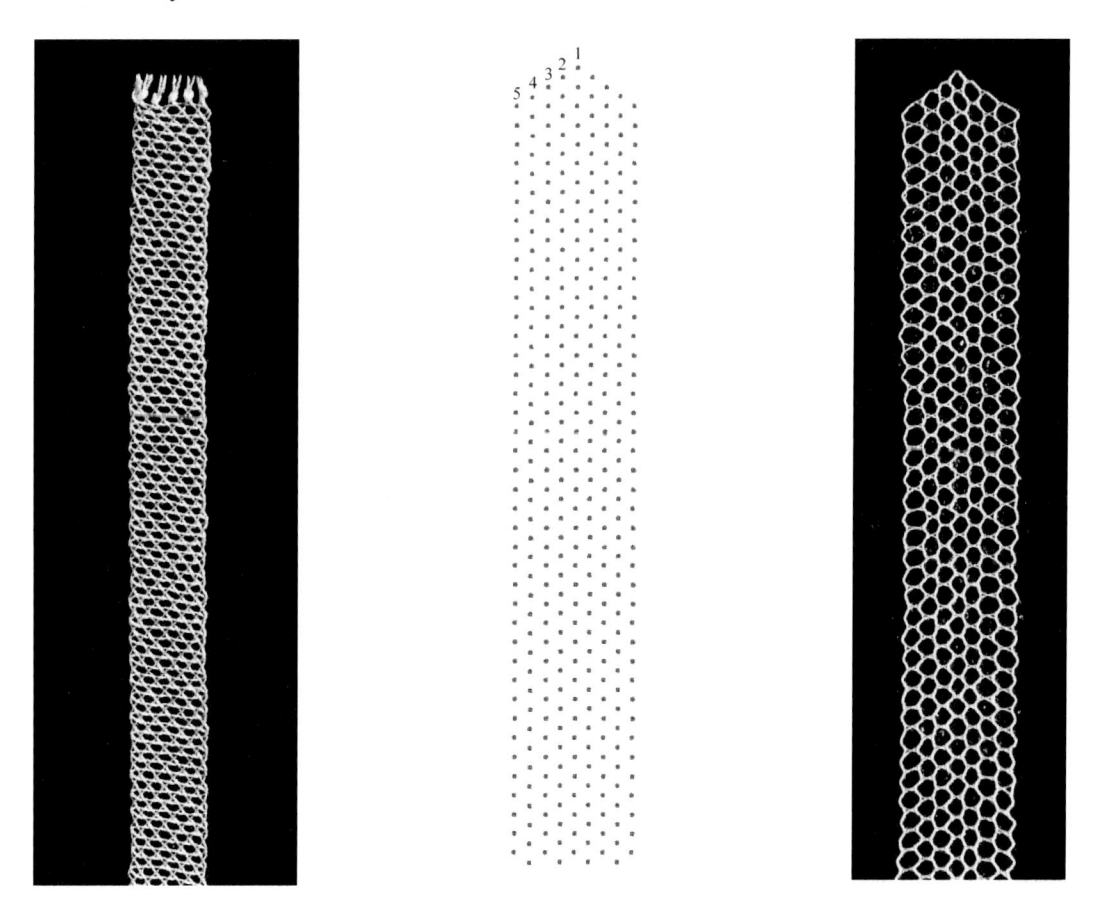

Figure 47 Half stitch   Figure 48 Pattern draft for point ground   Figure 49 Point ground

17

Chapter 2

Point ground
This is the typical ground and is found in the majority, but not all, Bucks point lace.

Setting In
Make a pricking of the pattern draft (figure 48), dress the pillow and wind 8 pairs of bobbins in couples.

Figure 50 (right) Point ground stitch

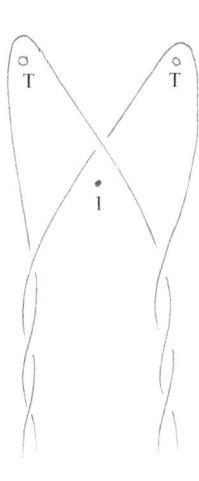

1 Place each pair of bobbins over a separate pin set in the pillow about 2.5cm (1 in) above the pricking, i.e. there will be a row of eight pins above the top of the pricking. These pins will only support the pairs until the lace has been started and are called temporary pins.
2 With the centre two pairs, on temporary pins T (figure 50), make a point ground stitch which is worked cross, twist three times (if a particular pair is not specified the twists apply to both) and set up pin 1 between the pairs. Remove the temporary pins, T, and allow the stitch to settle on pin 1. The point ground stitch is complete; there is no stitch covering the pin, i.e. the pin is left uncovered. Point ground is known as an 'uncovered ground'.

3 With the left pair from the stitch at pin 1 and the next pair on the left make a point ground stitch setting up pin 2 (figure 51).

Continue down the first diagonal line. At each pinhole use the left pair from the previous stitch with the next pair on the left, pins 3 and 4. Since this is a sampler of the ground only, there is no headside or footside. Set up pin 5 under the left most pair, without making a stitch, to bring the bobbins at the edge into the working position for the next row. Twist this pair three more times. 4 Start the next row making a point ground stitch with the right pair from pin 1

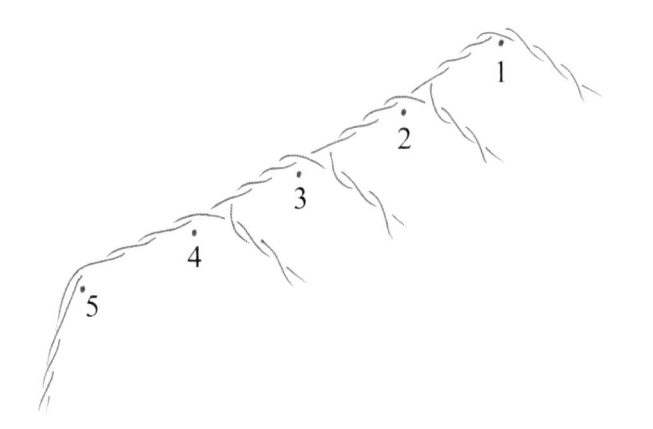

Figure 51 First row of point ground

and the next new pair on the right, and set up pin 6 (figure 52). *Using the left pair from this stitch and the next pair on the left make the next stitch of the row*, set up pin 7. Repeat *to* for the remaining stitches of the row, setting up pins 8, 9 and 10. Set up pin 11 under the left most pair and twist the pair three more times.
5 Start the next two rows using the last pair on the right with a new pair for the first stitch of the row.
6 Subsequent rows start by placing a pin under the right most pair and twisting this pair three times (figure 52).

18

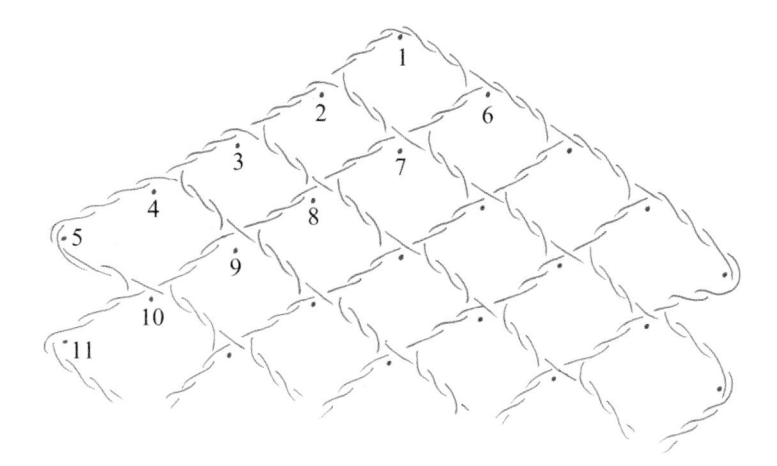

Figure 52 Point ground

Changing the direction of work
Work each row from right to left until you can work them easily, then try working left to right. For any row, the direction of work is diagonally towards you, never away from you. Always start a row of point ground at the unused pin nearest the back, using the pairs laying either side of the pin. After working a diagonal line A-J (figure 53) pin 1 is furthest from you, then pin 2. Complete the row diagonally towards the right, pin 3. The next row starts with pin 4 and travels diagonally towards the right to pin 6. The unused pinhole furthest from you is now pin 7.

(Note: The letter 'I' has not been used as it could be confused with the number '1'.)

Continue until you are working comfortably, and change direction again. The direction in which the rows are worked should have no effect on the final appearance of the ground.

Cut the bobbins off first, and then take care when removing the sample from the pillow. The edges are very weak and stretch easily.

Figure 53 (right) Changing working direction

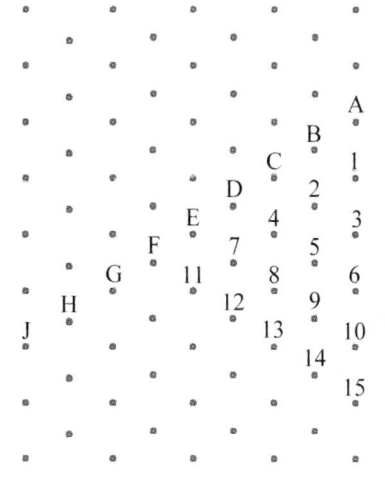

Chapter 3
PROJECT 1 ROSETTE BROOCH (Plate no 2)

Figure 54 Rosette brooch

New Techniques
whole stitch round a pin
starting at the footside
footside
Bucks point ground
catch-pin and catch-pin stitch
double picot
headside passives
joining end to beginning

Materials required
14 pairs Egyptian cotton no. 60[3]
pricking (figure 56)[1&2]
small ribbon rose
23 cms very narrow (3mm) ribbon
small safety pin

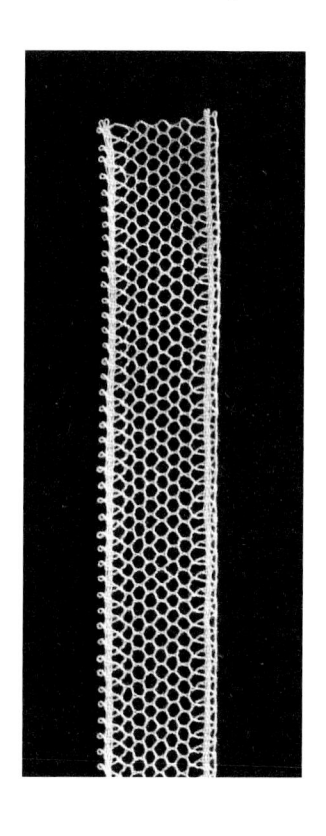

End Notes
1 the off-set footside picots
2 preparing a draft from a grid
3 threads
4 point ground
5 catch-pin and catch-pin stitch
6 footside
7 picots
8 firming up
9 preventing the footside curving
10 gathering lace

Figure 55(above) Lace

Figure 56 (right) Pattern draft

Chapter 3

For all projects it is assumed that all previous chapters have been read and understood.

Setting in horizontally
Make a pricking of the pattern draft[1] (figure 56), dress the pillow and wind 14 pairs of bobbins in couples.

Setting in the ground horizontally[4]

1 Place several pairs, side-by-side, on separate temporary pins above the pricking; adding more as required.
2 With pairs 1 & 2 make a point ground stitch, pin 1. Remove the temporary pins allowing the stitch to settle on the pin (figure 57).
3 Repeat for pinholes 2, 3 & 4.

Figure 57 (left) Setting in the ground

4 Using pairs 2 & 3 work a point ground stitch, placing the pin, between the pairs, in pinhole 5 just below them (figure 58). The pairs may slide around at first, but will stabilize after a few stitches have been worked.

Figure 58 (right) Setting in the ground

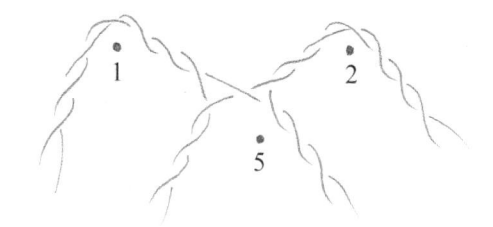

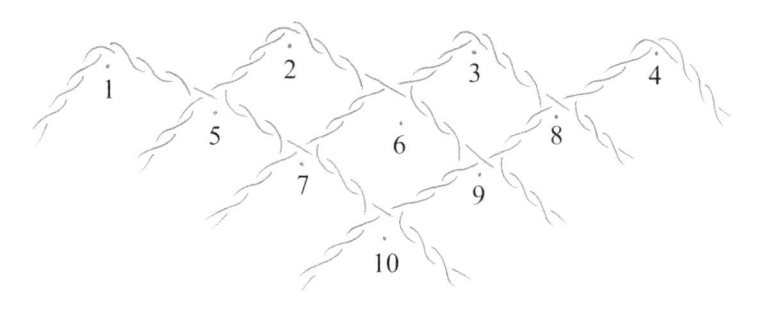

5 Start a new diagonal row with pairs 4 & 5, setting up the pin in hole 6, and work down the row setting up pin 7. At any time a stitch can only be made if both stitches at the pinholes diagonally above it have been made. Starting with pairs 6 & 7 work another row using pins 8, 9 & 10 (figure 59).

Figure 59 Working a triangle of ground

Setting in the Footside[5&6]
1 Place two pairs on temporary pins, T, (figure 60) above the pattern. At the top pin on the right hand side, pin 1, work a whole stitch round the pin, i.e. half stitch, pin, cross.

Figure 60 (right) Making a whole stitch round a pin

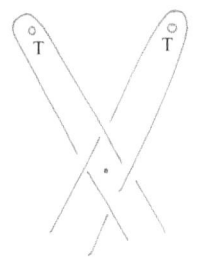

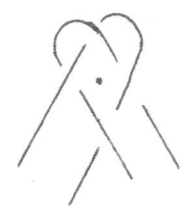

2 Take out the temporary pins and allow the threads to settle around the pin (figure 61) and you have a whole (cloth) stitch around the pin.

Figure 61 (left) Whole stitch round the pin completed

Chapter 3

3 Now twist both pairs three times[6]. The outer pair becomes the edge pair and the inner pair the footside workers.
4 Place two pairs, on separate temporary pins, T, above the pattern (figure 62), so that they lie to the left of the pairs making the whole stitch round the pin.
5 With the footside workers, cloth stitch through the two new pairs and twist the workers three times. The two pairs supported by the temporary pins become the footside passives.

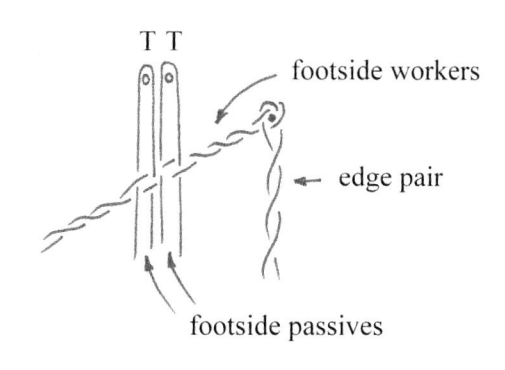

Figure 62 Setting in the footside passives

6 Place the catch-pin under the footside workers and make a point ground stitch with the footside workers and adjacent ground pair. This is the catch-pin stitch (figure 63). **Do NOT pin between these pairs.** The pin belonging to this stitch is the catch-pin and it is already in position to the right of the stitch.
7 Take the left pair from the catch-pin stitch and work a row of point ground down the edge of the triangle of ground.
8 Thread a support pin through the loops of the passive pairs and let these pairs down.

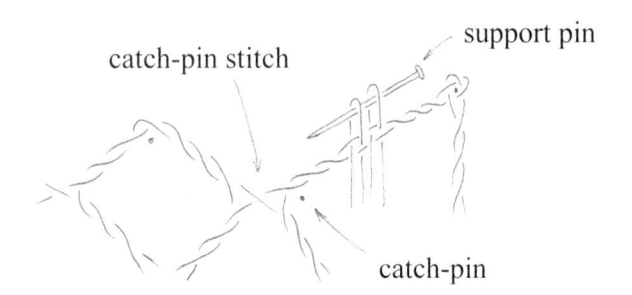

Figure 63 Catching the ground to the footside

Starting subsequent rows from the footside[5,6&8,]

1 Start the next line of point ground with the point ground pair next to the passives (the fourth pair from the right) and cloth stitch to the right through the passives (figure 64).
2 Twist the workers three times and set up the next footpin under them.
3 Cloth stitch the workers with the edge pair (the stitch about the pin).
4 Firm up the stitch by gently separating the pairs, taking up any slack on the threads, and slide the stitch into place next to the pin. Twist both pairs three times. The right pair is the new edge pair, the second from the right the new working pair.
5 Cloth stitch the workers, towards the left, through the passives and twist the workers three times. Set up the catch-pin beneath them.

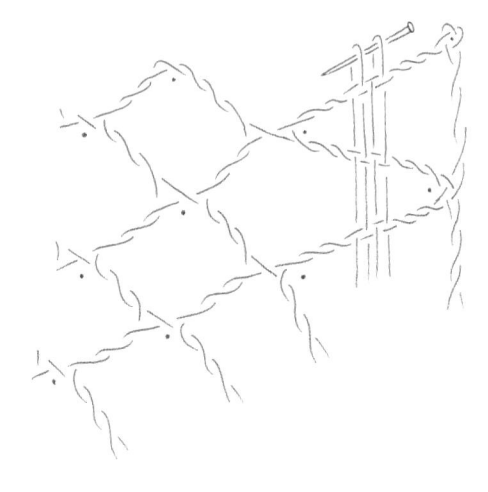

Figure 64 Starting subsequent point ground rows from the footside

6 With the workers and the next pair to the left to make the catch-pin stitch. **Do NOT pin between these pairs.** The pin belonging to this stitch, the catch-pin, is already in position to the right of the stitch.

Chapter 3

7 With the left pair from the catch-pin stitch and the next pair on the left make a point ground stitch and pin.
8 Continue the row of point ground diagonally, towards the left, pinning each stitch. Do not use the last pair of the previous row.
9 Work several rows, stopping one pair short of the previous row each time.

Setting in the headside[7&8]
1 Place two new pairs on separate temporary pins, T above the pattern (figure 65), so that they lie to the left of the bobbins currently in use, these will be the headside passives.
2 With the left most pair from the ground cloth stitch through the new pairs, make a double picot and return through the passives. Set up the catch-pin, make the catch-pin stitch and continue down the row of ground.

Figure 65 (right) Setting in the headside

Double Picot[7&8]
The decorative loop at the headside made using a single pair of bobbins
1 Twist the pair five times.
2 Hold a pin, with the point towards you, pass the point under the thread from the outside, and lift the outer thread. Pass the point of the pin over the same thread, towards the left, and insert the point into the pinhole, pin 11 (figure 66).
3 Reduce the size of the loop of twisted threads about the pin but **do not let it pull tight.** (Resting your wrist on the pillow to increases control).

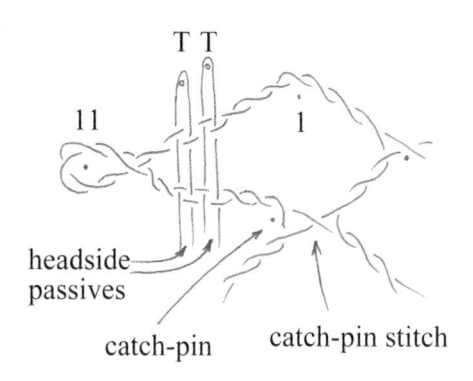

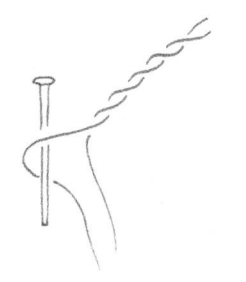

Figure 66 Inserting the pin for a picot

4 Pass the other thread around the pin in the same direction (clockwise).
5 Gently ease up the threads until they are evenly tensioned, ending with a gentle seesawing movement to tighten them about the pin[8].
6 Twist the pair twice (figure 67).
7 Make a cloth stitch with the next pair and firm it up.

Figure 67 (right) Completing a picot

Continue setting in the headside
3 Cloth stitch the picot pair back through the passives, twist the workers three times, set up the catch-pin, pin 12, (figure 67).
4 Make a catch-pin stitch with the next pair from the ground. **Do <u>NOT</u> pin between these pairs.** The pin belonging to this stitch is the catch-pin, and is already in position to the left of the stitch.
5 Continue the line of ground, down the diagonal.

Chapter 3

Starting Subsequent Rows from a Picot
1 Using the left pair from the catch-pin, pin 12 (the third pair from the left), cloth stitch through the passives (figure 68).
2 Make a picot, pin 13 and cloth stitch back through the passives, firming up after the first stitch. Twist the workers three times and set up the next catch-pin, pin 14, beneath them.
3 Make a catch-pin stitch with the next pair from the ground. **Do <u>NOT</u> pin between these pairs.** The pin belonging to this stitch is the catch-pin, pin 14, and is already in position to the left of the stitch. Work towards the right, down the ends of the rows that were worked from the footside, making a point ground stitch and pinning each pair in turn.

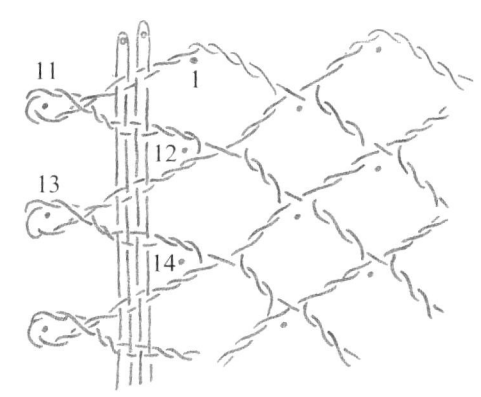

Figure 68 Starting subsequent rows from the headside

Work diagonal rows starting from both the footside and the headside, until working in both directions becomes comfortable, i.e. work a few rows in one direction and then a few in the other. The working direction makes no difference to the final appearance of the ground. Until you are completely confident working the ground, headside and footside, it is not advisable to work the headpins, footpins or catch-pins at the end of a diagonal row; always end rows within the ground itself. It is much easier to start rows at the headside or footside than to finish at these places. Continue working until the stitches come easily, without referring to the directions. The sample of point ground in Chapter 2 has an easier starting line, but it is not a good position to join end to start, as a join in this position is more difficult to conceal.

Continue making the lace
Continue making the edging in point ground with a footside on the right and picots on the left (figure 69). After about 7.5 cms (3 ins) pins may be removed from the back and reused. However the footside and headside pins should not be removed for at least 10 cms (4 ins). The untwisted passives will easily slip and the lace will gather[9]. If your lace tends to curve towards the footside, when removed from the pillow, pull less on the passives and/or keep more pins in the footside.

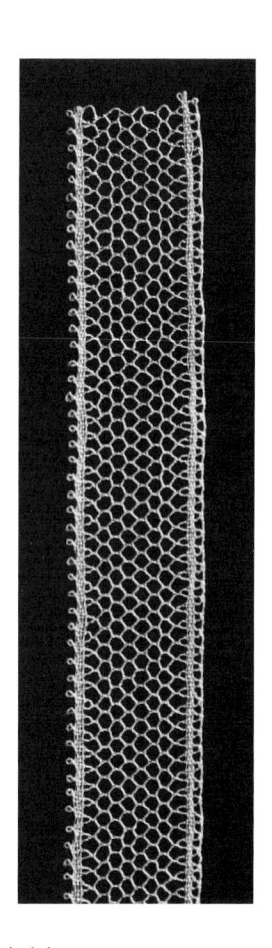

Figure 69 (right) Lace

Rosette Brooch
1 Continue until the strip measures 16.5 cms (6 ins) ending at the line on the pricking.
2 After making the last picot work the headside workers through the headside passives, twist and leave them ready for joining.
3 After working the last catch-pin stitch, cloth stitch the footside workers through the footside passives, twist and leave them ready for joining.
4 Complete the point ground as far as the line.

5 Let down the bobbins and cut off the passives leaving sufficient thread to sew with. Carefully remove all except the last 2.5cms (1 inch) of pins. Leaving a sewing length, cut remaining pairs off as required,

The join is tricky because the room for manoeuvre is restricted. Take care and work methodically.

6 Lift the starting edge of the lace over, place in position on the pricking immediately below the end and insert a few pins to hold it (figure 70).

Figure 70 (right) Joining end to start

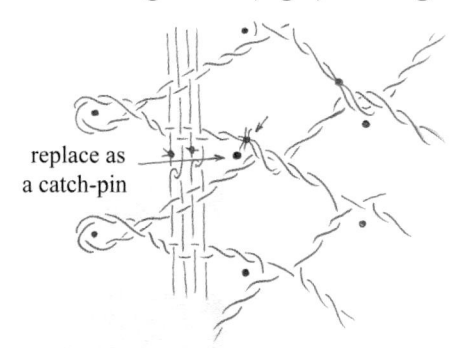

Figure 71 Joining the headside

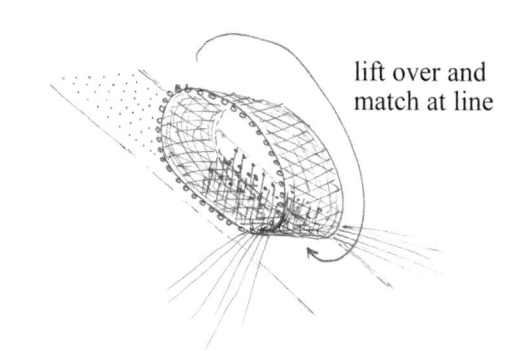

7 To join the headside passives use a needle to sew one passive thread through the corresponding support pin loop, remove the needle and tie the thread to its partner using a reef or square knot (figure 71).
8 Join the other headside passives similarly.
9 To join the headside workers, first remove the pin, and sew both workers through the loop of the ground pair (figure 73). Replace the pin, as though a catch-pin stitch has been made, and tie the reef knot.
10 At each pin across the point ground, sew both threads of a pair through the appropriate loop of the starting edge, replacing the pin if it was removed, and make a reef knot with the other pair. Settle the knot as close to the pin as possible and take care not to strain the ground (figure 72). Tie off the rest of the ground pairs the same way.

Figure 72 (right) Joining point ground

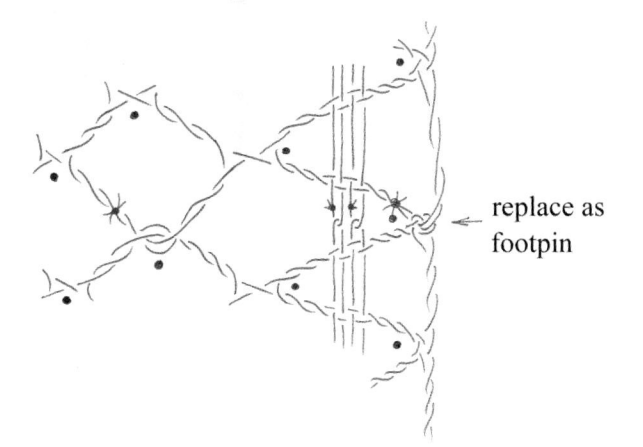

11 Join the footside passives the same way as the headside passives (figure 71).
12 Remove the edge pin and sew both threads of the edge pair through the whole stitch about the pin.
13 Replace the pin to the left of this join, as a footpin, and tie the edge pair and the footside workers as close to the pin as possible (figure 73).

Figure 73 (left) Joining the footside

Chapter 3

All the threads are now secure, all the pins can be removed and the ends hidden. The ends of the passive threads can be darned along the passives; two small stitches for each are sufficient. Since the threads are already secure, the purpose of these stitches is only to hide the ends. Do not trim the ends too early, since working next to a trimmed end can cause a short end to pop out.

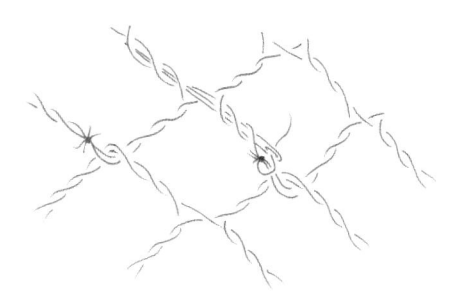

The two pairs at the footside can be hidden when the lace is attached for use. It is more difficult to hide ends in the ground but sliding a needle between the twists should be sufficient (figure 74). Do not trim the ends too early since working next to a trimmed end can cause it to pop undone.

Figure 74 (left) Sewing away a point ground pair

Making up the brooch
1 Using a sewing needle with double thread, make a line of small running stitches along the footside, gather up as tightly as possible and tie securely.
2 Sew a small ribbon flower or decorative button over the centre front, and a brooch pin (or safety pin) and doubled length of very narrow ribbon to the back (figure 75).
3 Arrange the gathers evenly, hiding the join.

Figure 75 (right) Adding the ribbon and pin

END NOTES

1 The Off-Set Footside
Unlike most other laces of this family, the rows of pinholes for the headside picots, footside and catch-pins for Bucks Point are placed slightly wider apart than the rows of point ground. Most point ground has one pin per pair, but there are two pairs between the catch-pin, and the adjacent point ground pin. Therefore, if the spacing of the pins is the same, the pairs would actually be closer and the row of ground closest to the footside would have a slightly smaller mesh (figure 76). To prevent this the catch-pin is off-set, i.e. placed slightly further away from the adjacent point ground pin, while keeping it diagonally in line with the point ground row (figure 77). The headside and footside both contain two pairs of passives, and therefore require slightly wider horizontal spacing than point ground. Since the arrangement of stitches and twists between the passives and the edge is the same above and below the pins, these pins are placed mid-way between the catch-pins. In practice the extra spacing may be very small.

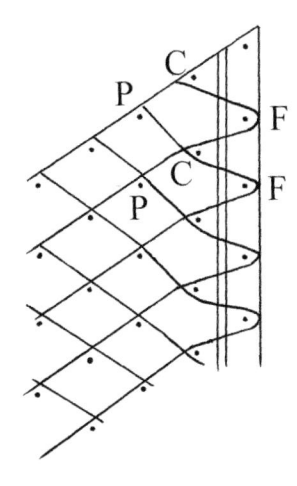

Figure 76 (left) Pins equally spaced, ground pairs unequally spaced

Figure 77 (right) Catch-pins offset, ground pairs equally spaced

C - catch-pin
F - footside
P - point ground

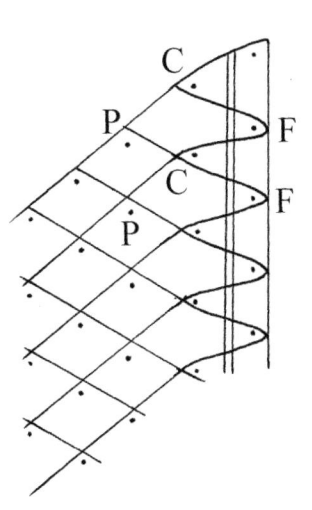

2 Preparing the draft from a grid

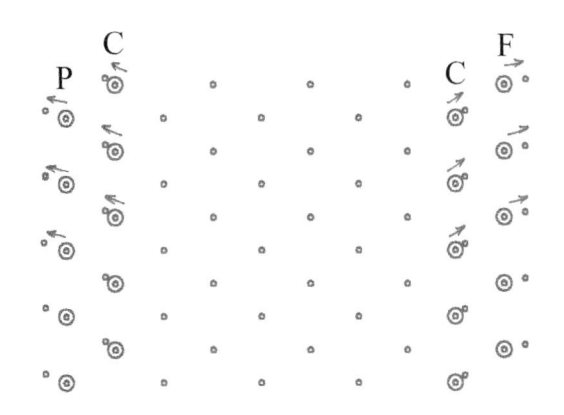

Figure 78 Preparing the pattern draft using a grid

1. Using Grid no. 1 (56°, 40 pins per 10 cm (4 ins) along the footside) prick all except the picots, footside and catch-pins. Point ground should be pricked diagonally across the pattern in the order in which it will be worked, **not** vertically down it. Pricking diagonally produces a more accurate pricking (see 'tram lines).
2. Prick the catch-pins, C, slightly further out, and slightly above, the grid dots to allow extra room for the extra catch-pin pair. The holes diagonally downward from the catch-pin through the ground remain in a straight line (figure 78).(The original dots that are now redundant are ringed.
3. The edge or footpins, F, are pricked slightly further out, than the normal vertical spacing of the point ground, to allow for the two pairs of passives. They remain mid-way between the holes for the catch-pins.
4. The picot pins are pricked slightly further out. than the normal vertical spacing of the point ground, to allow for the two pairs of passives.
5. Only the pinholes for the footside and straight headside may be pricked in lines vertically. Prick one hole at the top and another at the bottom of the vertical row. Place a ruler tightly against these two pins, and prick the row with the pricker touching the ruler. This does **not** work for the ground.

3 Threads

During the writing of this book the threads available have changed and, at first, new samples were made with the ones remaining. However, the rate of change is increasing and it is not practical to remake them all. The threads recommended for the items are those available when the book goes to press but, of course, no one can predict the future. If the recommended thread is unavailable choose a thread from the appropriate list in Chapter 18, or experiment with other threads you may have or new threads as they become available.

Chapter 3

4 Point ground[8]

In practice rows of point ground are usually started from the footside and worked in diagonal lines towards the left with the stitches being pinned as they are made. When new to making Bucks point it is useful to check your pinning at the end of a row. Counting from the right there should be an edge pair, two passive pairs hanging in the space between the edge pin and the catch-pin, and **two pairs** in the space between the catch-pin and the next pin on the left. The remaining spaces, between pins, have one pair each. Several stitches can be worked and the leading pair (the one at the far end, usually the left,) held while the pins are set. This increases speed but may result in a tighter or uneven tension. Our folklore says that the early lace makers would often make the ground without pins. There is some evidence for this, but very little. Pricking ground is so time consuming we should have many prickings where only the motifs, fillings and footside are pricked and the ground left unpricked. It is possible that the tradition may pre-date Bucks Point. Mechlin was certainly made in the East Midlands area and the ground for this is not, and has never been, pricked. I have only seen one pattern, in Luton Museum, that has a pricked line of motifs and a line of pinholes parallel to them; probably the footside, but no ground. However, this may be a Mechlin pattern.

5 The catch-pin and catch-pin stitch

The pin for the point ground stitch next to the footside is placed to the side of the stitch, rather than in the usual position between the pairs (figure 79), thus preventing the stitch from being pulled out of position by the stronger tension used on the worker pair as it passes through the passives; the pin and the stitch being called the catch-pin and catch-pin stitch respectively. In the sample, (figure 79) repeats 1-9 were worked without a without a catch-pin, i.e. the pin for the stitches adjacent to the footside passives was placed as for the rest of the ground, for repeats 10-18 catch-pins were used adjacent to the footside passives. (The tag at the footside indicates where the technique changed).

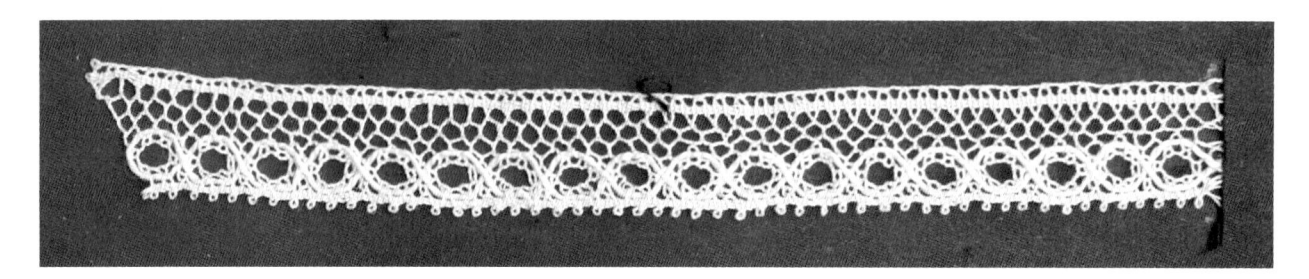

Figure 79 Catch-pin and catch-pin stitch

NB. The word 'catch' has several meanings, (1) to take hold of something that comes within reach e.g. catching a ball or a cold, (2) to 'catch' together means to secure two items together, (3) to 'catch out' means to surprise, usually unpleasantly. The word 'catch' in the context of 'catch-pin' and 'catch-pin stitch' is thought use the second meaning. That is, the stitch catching the footside to the ground. Although it could equally have its origin in the first meaning, that the catch-pin 'catches' the threads and holds them. However, it is very easy to put the pin in the wrong place, i.e. between the pairs of the catch-pin stitch instead of under both pairs. Hence it is easy to believe that the third meaning was the one intended!

Chapter 3

6[8] The footside

The footside used for Bucks point lace contains passive pair(s) to prevent the edge stretching during use. The ground pair reaching the passives passes through them in cloth stitch and twists before making a stitch, the stitch about the pin, with the existing edge pair. The two pairs exchange functions, the former ground pair becomes the edge pair and vice versa. Research has shown that the numbers of twists, stitches and pairs used for making the footside was more varied in the past. The following samples illustrate the different numbers of twists, stitches etc. that have been used.

6a Point ground footside as it is usually made today

The typical twists, stitches etc. as used today (figure 80) are.
- The stitch about the pin is a cloth stitch.
- The footside pair is twisted three times.
- There are three twists between the passives and the stitch about the pin.
- There are two pairs of passives of the lace thread.
- The passives are not twisted.
- There are three twists between the passives and the catch-pin.
- A catch-pin is used.
- The catch-pin stitch is a half stitch with two extra twists.

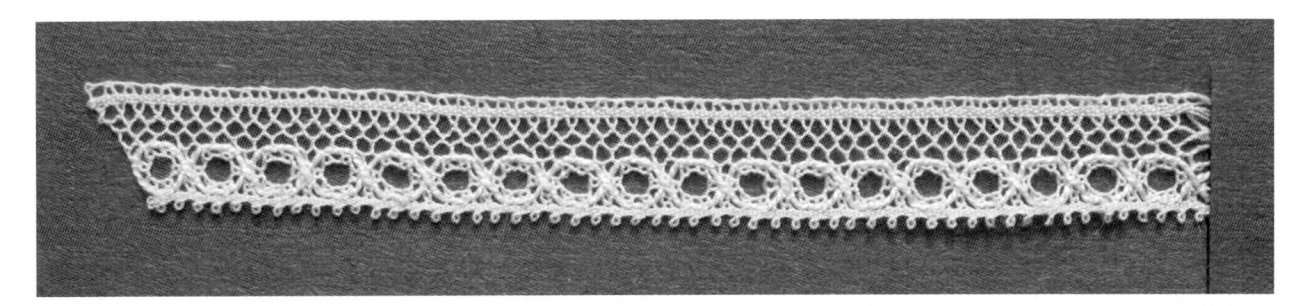

Figure 80 Footside as it is usually made today

6b Stitch about the pin

Today the stitch about the pin is invariably made as a cloth stitch, but a third of Bucks point made in the 19th century had a half stitch as the stitch about the pin. In the sample piece I made (figure 81) repeats 1-9 have a cloth stitch about the pin and repeats 10-18 have a half stitch about the pin.

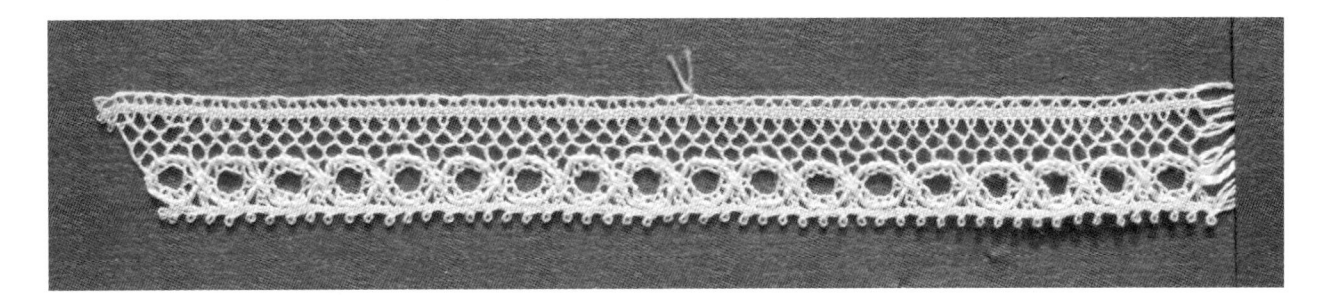

Figure 81 Stitch about the pin

29

Chapter 3

A half stitch is sometimes used for the stitch about the pin in the belief that it would help to counteract the tendency for the lace to curve[9]. It is also believed to make it easier to gather[10] the lace. However, an advantage it may have, is to reduce the bulk when two footsides are joined.

6c Twists on the edge pair
Bucks point is currently made with three twists on the edge pair, although pieces have always been made with one, two and four twists on the edge pair. The sample (figure 82) has repeats 1-4 worked with the edge pair twisted once, repeats 5-9 with it twisted twice, repeats 10-13 with it twisted three times and repeats 14-18 with it twisted four times.

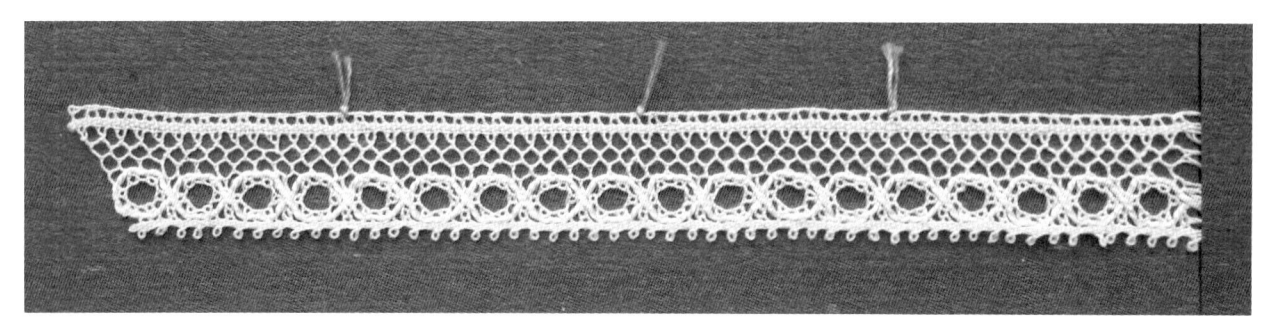

Figure 82 Twists on the edge pair

Today four twists are often used in the belief that it would help to counteract the tendency for the lace to curve[9].

6d Thick footside passives
Most Bucks point has been made using two pairs of passives of the lace thread left untwisted. However, some Bucks Point was made using one pair of a thicker thread, which in some pieces was twisted after every stitch. The sample (figure 83) shows one pair of passives of thicker thread. For repeats 1-9 it is untwisted, repeats 10-18 it is twisted once after each cloth stitch.

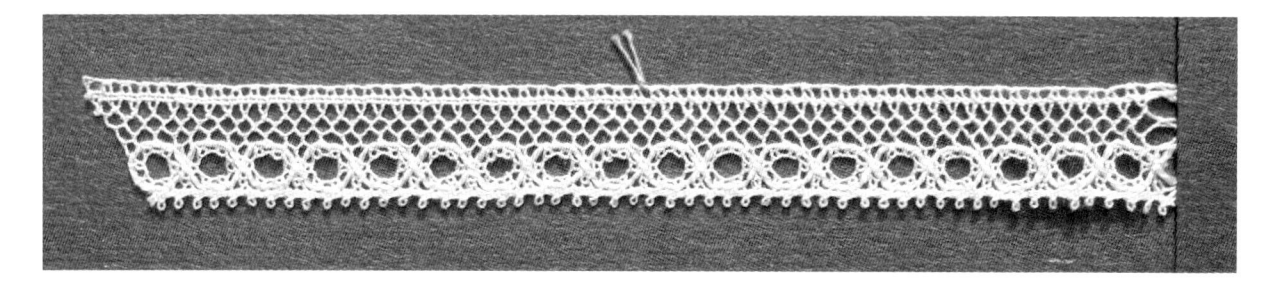

Figure 83 Thicker footside passives

Twisting the passives reduces the tendency for the lace to curve, and prevents the passives being used to gather up the lace.

6e Single footside passive pair
Bucks point is usually made using two pairs of passives of the lace thread that are untwisted. However, some Bucks Point was made using a single pair of lace thread twisted after every stitch.

30

Chapter 3

The sample (figure 84) shows a single passive pair untwisted for repeats 1-9 and twisted once after every cloth stitch for repeats 10-18.

Figure 84 Single passive untwisted and twisted

The footside passives in Bucks Point were occasionally used double. Since the lace studied was made for commercial reasons, it is possible that using the threads double was a means of saving time. However, although it was not common practice, using the threads double was found in over half the collections showing that, although only occasionally used, the technique may have been widely known in this country as there were examples in most of the collections studied. There were even fewer pieces with mixed single and double threads.

Although the majority of the pieces had untwisted passives there were a few that had the passives twisted once after each stitch in the footside, the norm for the footside adjacent to kat stitch.

6f Twists between footside passives and stitch about the pin
Today we usually twist the workers three times between the passives and the stitch about the pin. In 19th century the most popular number of twists between the passives and the stitch about the pin was two, although lace has always been made using one, two or three twists. In the sample (figure 85), repeats 1-6 have one twist, repeats 7-12, two twists and repeats 13-18 three twists.

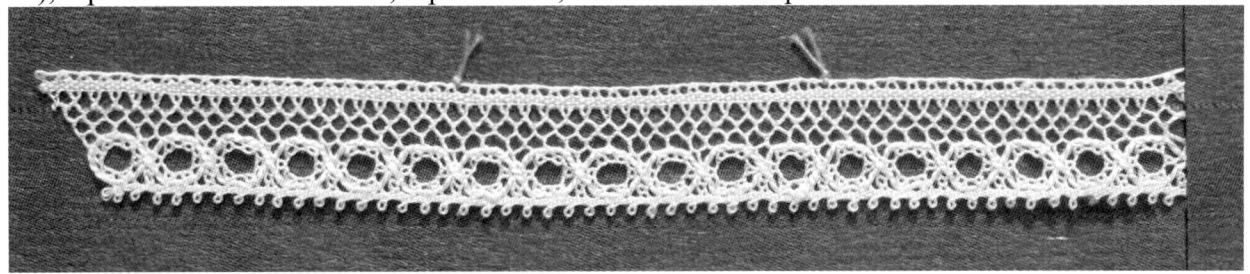

Figure 85 Twists between passives and stitch about the pin

6g Twists between footside passives and catch-pin stitch
Today we usually twist the workers three times between the passives and the catch-pin stitch. However, more 19th century Bucks Point was made with only two twists between the passives and the catch-pin than one or three. In the sample (figure 86), repeats 1-6 have one twist between the passives and catch-pin stitch, repeats 7-12 have two twists and repeats 13-18 have three twists.

31

Chapter 3

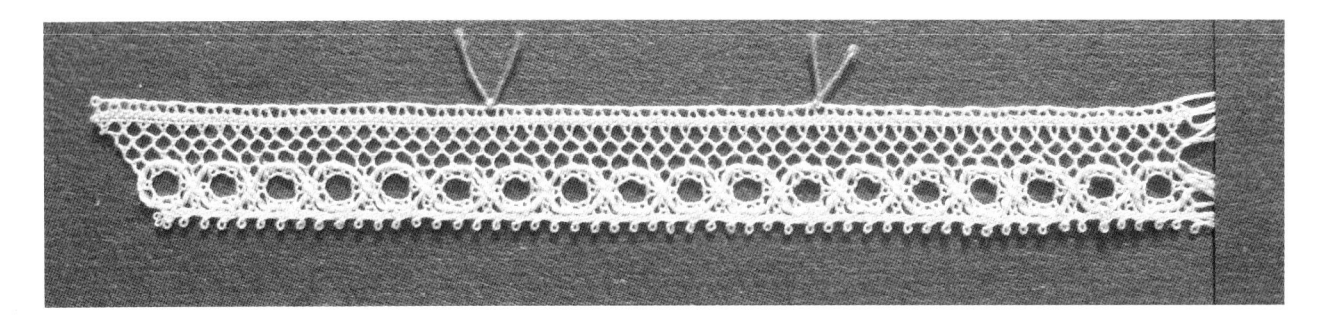

Figure 86 Twists between passives and catch-pin stitch

Nearly all the lace I examined was made with a half stitch for the catch-pin stitch. Occasionally during my research I came across pieces, that had been identified as Bucks Point, but which had the catch-pin stitch worked in cloth stitch. However, these pieces had been made with the footside pins in line with the ground, and not off-set, and I suspect they are probably not English but Lille.

7 Picots
If a very fine thread, e.g. Honiton thread, is used the number of twists before the pin is set is usually increased to seven. In the past some lace, made using coarser thread, had picots made with only three twists before the pin; but those picots tended to split. Picots have been made with three twists following making the loops round the pin, but this tends to show as a bar.

8 Firming up
Tension in lacemaking is assessed by eye rather than by feel. Watch the threads, and only take up the slack, do not keep pulling until you can feel the tension.

8a Point ground
Point ground should never be made with a tight tension as this destroys the rounded hole, making it more hexagonal and harsh in appearance. Ideally the tension should come from the weight of the bobbins and by allowing plenty of space for the bobbins to move from side to side while working; not by consciously pulling the bobbins. Push the bobbins not being used to the back of the pillow to create a wider working area and tension will improve.

8b The footside
The footside can be firmed up after working through the passives. Steady the passives by placing the free hand across them, and slide the working pair back. There is no need to pull. Set up the pin and then twist the workers. Work the stitch about the pin and, gently, swing the hands out sideways to slide the stitch up into place next to the pin. Then twist both pairs. Work the new workers back through the passives. Steady the passives, slide up the workers, and pin. Twist the workers. It is always better to tension before twisting pairs than after. When pairs are twisted, the twists hold the threads close together and more force is required to move the threads crossing the twisted pair. When threads are untwisted, they will be less closely packed and threads crossing them will move more easily and less force will be needed.

Watch the line that the footside pairs make and compensate for inaccurate holes in the pricking by leaning the pins. Lean the pin outwards to push the stitch about the pin out and vice versa. Try

Chapter 3

leaning a footpin first in then out, to see the effect it has on the line of the footside pair. It does not matter if the pins look uneven providing the lace is even.

8c The headside
The headside can be firmed up by steadying the passives and tensioning the workers as for firming up the footside. Twist the pair for the picot but do not let the twists become tight, leave a loop, just under 1 cm across, (¼-½ in), around the pin. Steady the hand holding the picot bobbins by placing the side of the hand, or wrist, on the pillow. Make the loop round the pin with the other bobbin; the first loop can be eased up slightly to bring the second thread round the pin. Only now can the threads be eased up evenly with a very small, gentle, see-sawing action, causing the twisted section to surround the pin. (If either thread tightens around the pin on its own, the twists are forced down to the section before the threads pass around the pin then, when the second thread passes round the pin, the two threads will lay separately. Hence the split picot.) Once the twisted threads are snug around the pin, twist the pair and make a cloth stitch with the first passive pair. Firm up this stitch by lifting and separating the pairs to move the stitch close to the pin, so completing tensioning the picot snugly around the pin. Compensate for inaccurately pricked holes by leaning the picot pins as for compensating for uneven pricking by leaning the foot pins.

9 Preventing edgings from curving
Many lacemakers find their lace curves towards the footside, when it is lifted from the pillow, and certain techniques are believed to counteract this tendency. In order to separate myth from truth I tried various combinations with the following results. Since the footside passives are there to stabilize the footside they were omitted from the test pieces so that any curvature would be more pronounced.

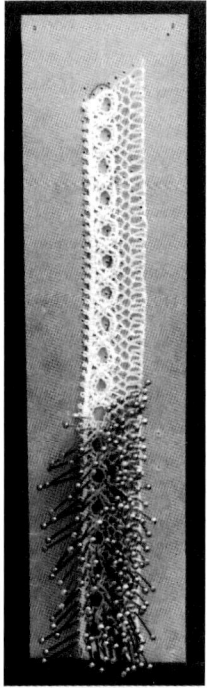

Figure 87
cloth stitch about the pin

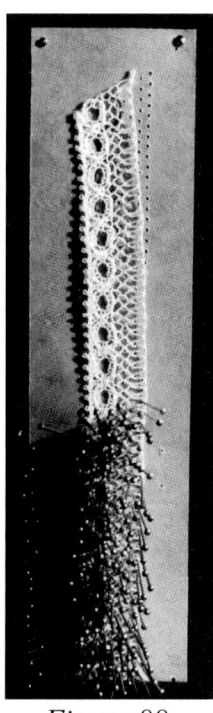

Figure 88
Half stitch about the pin

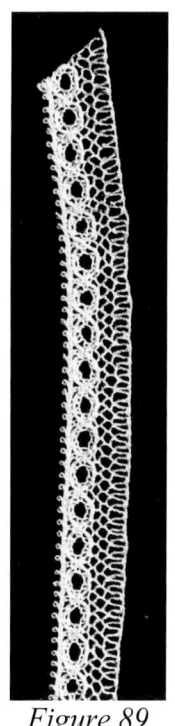

Figure 89
Cloth stitch about the pin, after lifting

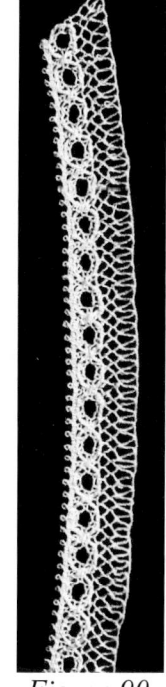

Figure 90
Half stitch about the pin, after lifting

33

Chapter 3

The first technique I looked at was the stitch about the pin. Figures 87 & 88 show pieces made using a cloth stitch and half stitch about the pin respectively. Neither piece curves towards the footside, in fact the piece with the half stitch at the footside curves slightly the other way.Figures 89 & 90 show the same pieces after they had been lifted from the pillow. Both curve in the wrong direction, i.e. away from the footside, but there is little to choose between them.

The second technique I investigated was the footside passives. Sample 2 (figure 91) was made as the first sample (figure 80). However, only a band of pins 10 deep was kept in use during its making. It is very obvious that the pulling up of the footside passives can cause the lace to curve. This can easily be remedied by using more pins. Even if some pins must be reused, always keep at least 10 cm (4 ins) of pins in use at the footside, and keep only a light tension on the passives.

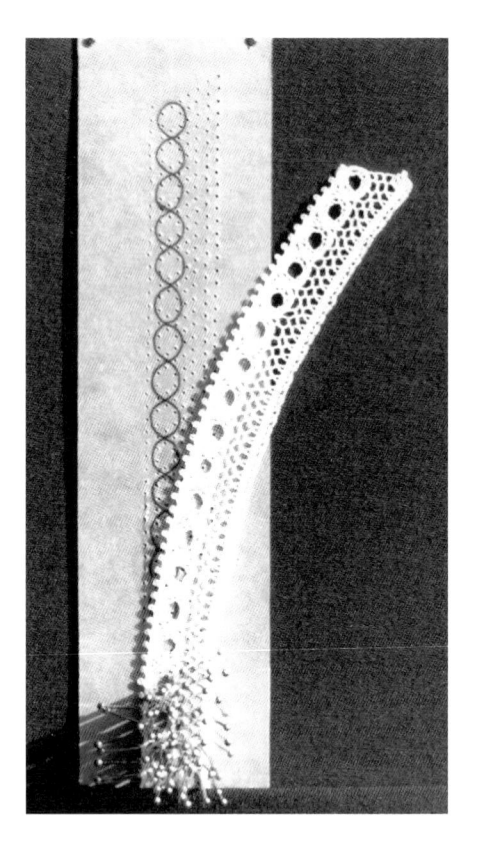

Figure 91 (right) Insufficient pins in use

10 Gathering lace
Sometimes we want lace to curve, and one of the reasons given for using a half stitch about the pin is that the lace gathers more easily. I made two samples, one with a cloth stitch about the pin (figure 92), and one with a half stitch about the pin (figure 93). They were both gathered the same way and both pulled up as tightly as possible. Unfortunately it made no difference at all.

Figure 92 Cloth stitch about the pin  *Figure 93 Half stitch about the pin*

Plate 1a Figure 249 Lace circle with coloured gimps and matching footside passives

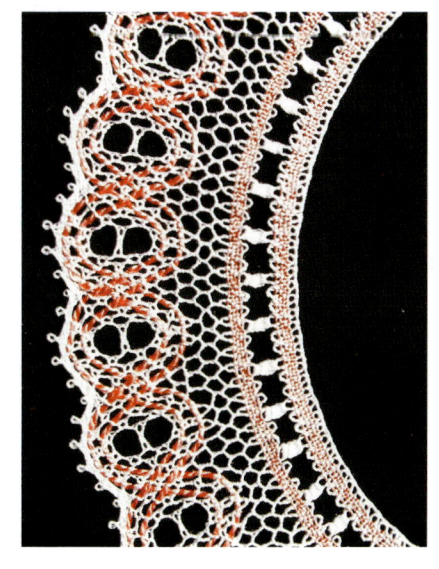

Plate 1b Figure 280 Lace threads not interfering

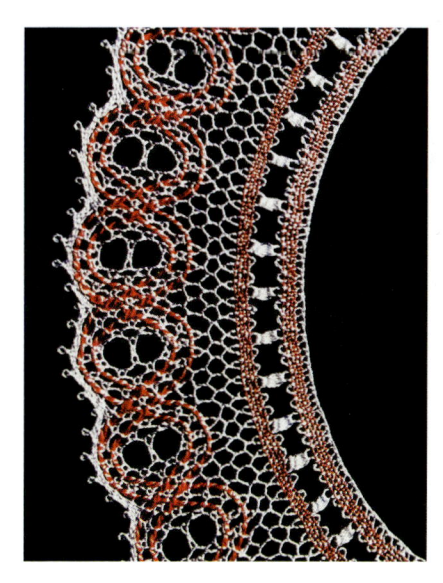

Plate 1c Figure 281 Lace threads interfering

Plate 2

Plate 3

Plate 4

Plate 5

Plate 6

Plate 7

Plate 8a

Plate 8b

Chapter 4
PROJECT 2 JABOT (Plate 6)

Figure 94 Jabot

New Techniques
- starting with a selvedge
- honeycomb ground
- twists before and after a gimp[3]
- gimps & crossing[4]
- honeycomb stitch within headside[5]
- finishing with a selvedge
- attaching lace using four-sided stitch[15]
- chain loops[17]

Materials required
- pricking[1] (figure 95), two pieces dovetailed[2]
- 16 pairs Egyptian cotton no. 60 (see Chapter 18)
- 1 pair perle thread, no 8
- 40cms x 40cms (16 in x 16 in) fine cotton or linen fabric
- ballpoint needle

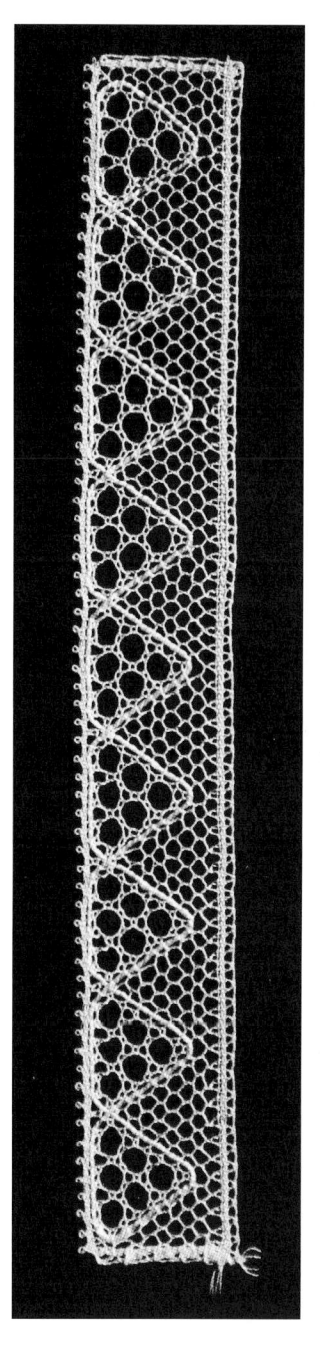

Figure 95 Pattern draft

Figure 96 Lace

Chapter 4

End Notes
1 drafting a pattern
2 dovetailing a pricking
3 twists adjacent to gimps
4 crossing gimps
5 alternative method of working honeycomb adjacent to a vertical gimp
6 blind spot
7 securing bobbins for transportation and lifting
8 setting up a pricking
9 replacing threads & gimps, faulty stitches and trimming ends
10 broken threads
11 weavers' knot
12 threads shredding
13 developing tension and speed
14 right & wrong side of Bucks Point
15 attaching lace to fabric
16 ballpoint needle
17 buttonholed loops

Setting in the selvedge from the footside
1 Place two temporary pins T1 & T2 (figure 97), above pinhole 1, with two pairs straddled (one pair outside the other) over the left temporary pin (T1) and a single pair over the other (T2). Pass the left thread from T2 over the right pair from T1. Set up pin 1 between the single thread and the pair. Pass the pair from T1 over the right thread from T2. Twist pair 1 twice and pairs 2 & 3 once. Remove the temporary pins and let down the pairs.

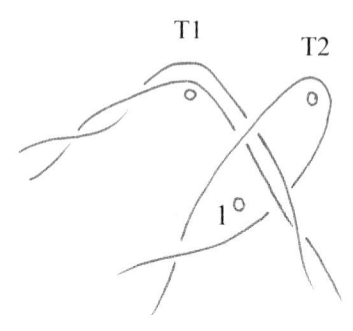

Figure 97 Setting in the footside

2 Place two temporary pins, T3 & T4 above the pricking, (figure 98), each supporting a single pair. Cloth stitch the left pair from pin 1, to the left, through these two pairs (the footside passives) and twist the workers twice. This pair is the top edge pair.
3 *Place two pairs straddled over another temporary pin, T5, to the left of the top edge pair. Cloth stitch the top edge pair with the nearest new pair, twist both twice and set up pin 2 between them, Twist the pair to the left

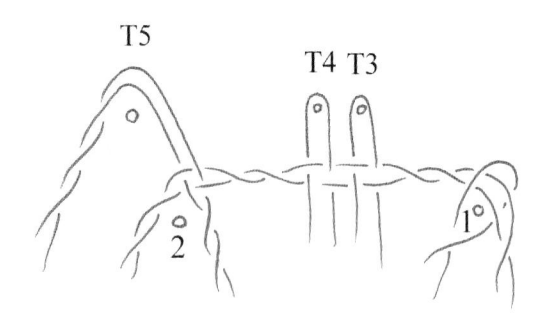

Figure 98 Setting in the footside passives

of pin 5, the new top edge pair, three times. Remove the temporary pin T5*. Repeat * to * for pins 3-6 (figures 99 & 100, pin 4 is not shown.). Slide a support pin through the loops on pins T3 & T4 and lay it flat on the pillow. Remove pins T3 & T4, one at a time, and gently ease these pairs down.
4 Using the pair lying on the left of pin 6 as workers (figure 99), cloth stitch to the right through all except the last two pairs. Twist the

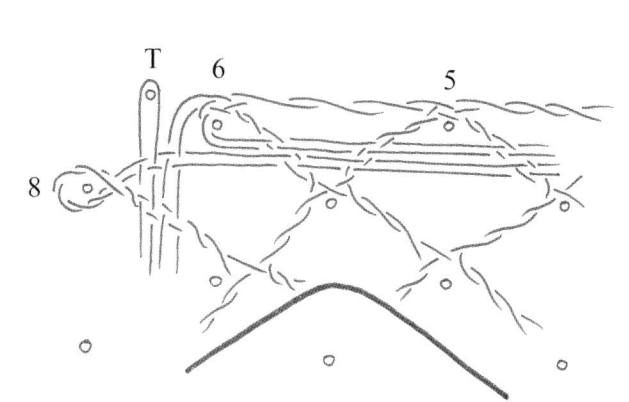

Figure 99 (right) The headside of the selvedge

Chapter 4

workers, cloth stitch the next pair, set up pin 7, (figure 100), under the workers and twist the workers again. Work the stitch about the pin, twist the new edge pair twice and the new workers once, and cloth stitch back through all the pairs.

5 Place a pair on a temporary pin to the left of all the pairs and cloth stitch the workers through them. Make a picot with the workers, pin 8 (figure 99). Cloth stitch back through the two headside passive pairs and set up the catch-pin. Twist all the pairs, lying between the two sets of passives, once. Place a support pin through the loop and let down the passive pair from the temporary pin.

6 Cloth stitch the second pair from the footside through the passives, set up the catch-pin, pin 9, and work the catch-pin stitch (figure 99). With the other pair from pin 2 and the adjacent pair from pin 3, work a point ground stitch, setting up pin 10. Continue across the row making and pinning point ground stitches with each two pairs.

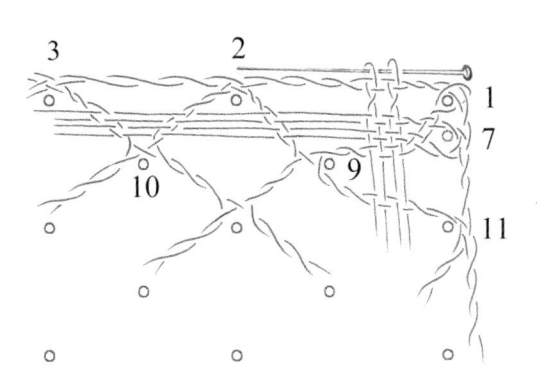

Figure 100 (left) The footside of the selvedge

Figure 101 (right) Detail of the selvedge

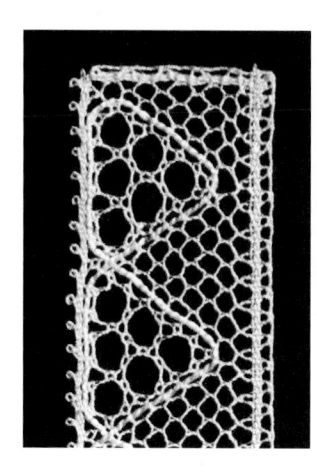

At the headside, work the catch-pin stitch and another picot, then work the footside and ground until the black line on the pricking, indicating the path of the gimp, is reached.

Setting in the gimp and passing it through[3]

1 Place the gimp pair on a temporary pin, above the pattern, laying the gimps between pairs 4 & 5. Pass the right gimp, to the right, through seven ground pairs by passing the gimp under the left bobbin and over the right of each pair. Twist each pair once (figure 102).

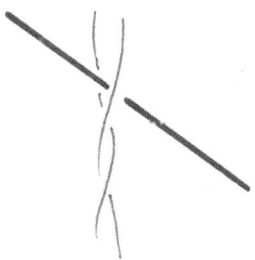

Figure 102 (right) Passing the gimp to the right

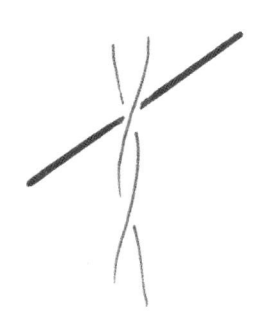

2 Pass the left gimp to the left through one ground pair and the picot pair, which has returned through the headside passives, by passing the gimp over the right bobbin and under the left bobbin of each pair. Twist each pair once (figure 103).

Figure 103 (left) Passing the gimp to the left

In figures 102 & 103 the pair may appear to have been twisted twice but the twist occurring across the gimp is the last of the three ground twists and there is only one following the passage of the gimp thread.

Chapter 4

Continuous row of honeycomb
3 With the first pair passing across the gimp from each side, i.e. pairs 4 & 5, work a honeycomb stitch, cross, twist twice, pin 1, cross, twist twice (figure 104). Remove the temporary pin from the gimp and ease the loop down. Discard the left pair and take the next pair on the right to make another honeycomb stitch. Continue working down the row until the gimp line on the pricking is reached, pins 1-7.

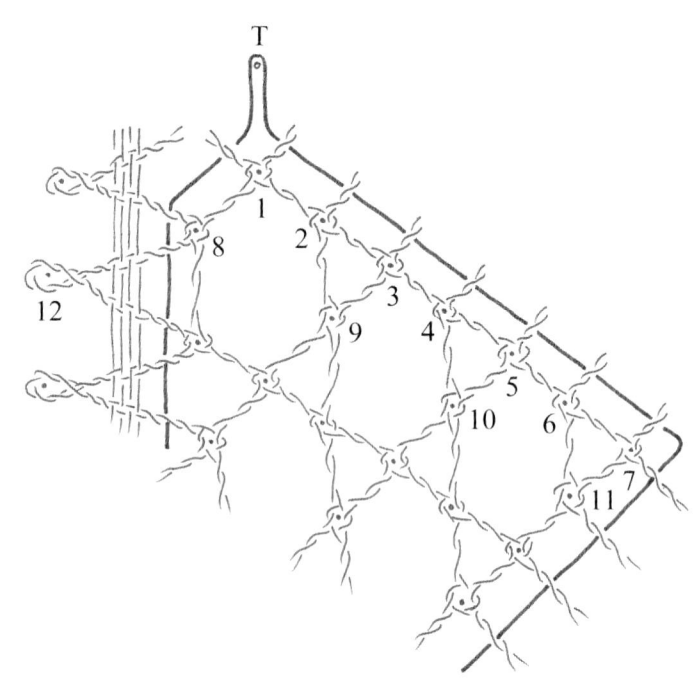

Figure 104 (right) Honeycomb ground

Gap row of honeycomb
4 The gap row starts by making a honeycomb stitch with the left pair from pin 1 and the next pair on the left (the picot pair that has returned through the headside passives and the gimp), pin 8 (figure 104). Discard these two pairs. *Take the next two pairs on the right to make the next honeycomb stitch and discard these pairs. Repeat from * until the gimp is reached, pins 9, 10 & 11.

The headside and honeycomb ground[5&6]
Pass the gimp through the left pair from pin 8 (figure 104), Cloth stitch this pair through the headside passives and make a picot, pin 12. Return the same pair through the headside passives, twist twice, pass the gimp through and twist the pair again. Use this pair to start the next continuous row of honeycomb stitch, stopping when the gimp line is reached. Start each row by taking the third pair across the gimp and through headside passives to make a picot, and return back through the passives and across the gimp. Continue making alternate continuous and gap rows of honeycomb stitches, each row stopping at the gimp line, until the honeycomb area is complete.

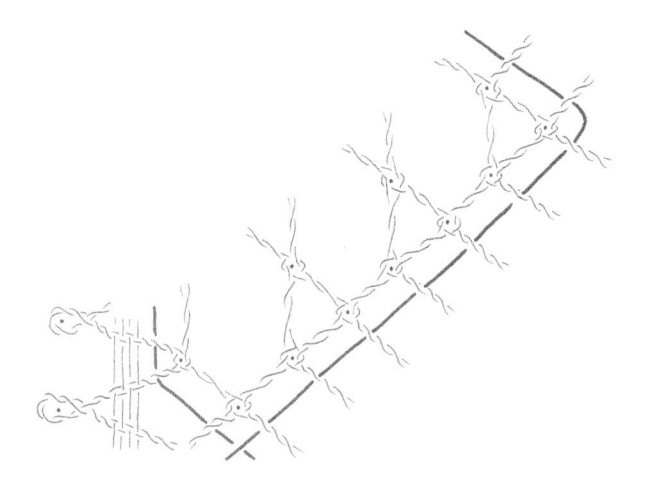

Crossing gimps[4]
When the honeycomb area is complete, pass the gimps through the pairs crossing the gimp line until the gimps meet, then cross the gimps right over left. Twist the pairs entering point ground twice, the others once (figure 105).

Figure 105 (left) Crossing the gimps

Chapter 4

The headside[5]
Using the pair next to the headside passives as workers, work the headside by cloth stitching through the passives, making a picot, and cloth stitching back through the passives. Twist the workers twice (figure 106).

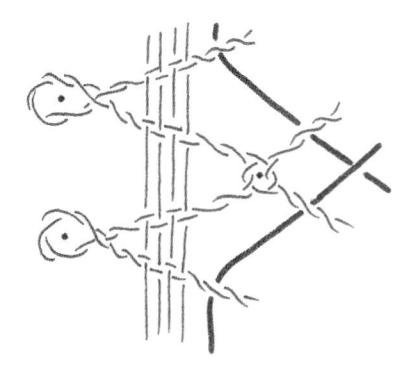

Honeycomb stitch within the headside
Make a honeycomb stitch with the pair that has worked back through the headside passives and the adjacent pair from the honeycomb ground. Use the left pair to work the headside, and pass the gimp through the pair from the honeycomb stitch and the pair from the headside (figure 106)

Continue working triangles of point ground, then the honeycomb areas, not forgetting the honeycomb stitch in the headside

Figure 106 (left) Honeycomb stitch within the headside

For the jabot[7-10]
Make 83 cms (33 ins) of lace, completing the last pattern repeat. Finish off the gimps by doubling up and finish with a selvedge.

Casting off gimps by doubling up
After completing the last honeycomb section pass the gimps through the pairs until they cross. Then, without twisting any of the pairs, take each gimp through another two pairs. Lay the gimps back over the pillow and twist the pairs twice (figure 107).

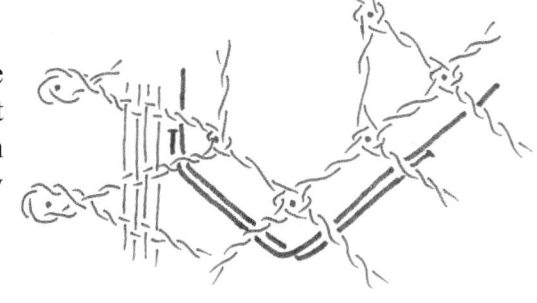

Figure 107 (right) Casting off gimps

Continue the footside, point ground until all pins along the horizontal row, starting with the picot below the gimps, have been completed.

Casting off along a selvedge
1 Reduce all twists on ground pairs to one each.
2 After making up the last footside pin, cloth stitch the workers back through the two passive pairs, make a reef knot and throw back out of the way over the pillow. This pair will not be used again (figure 108)

Figure 108 (left) Footside end of selvedge

Chapter 4

3 After making the last picot, cloth stitch the picot pair through the next three pairs and leave them where they are.
4 Cloth stitch the first passive pair (now pair number 1) through two pairs.
5 Twist the second passive pair and the first ground pair (now pairs 1 & 2) twice, work a cloth stitch with them and place a pin to the right of both pairs, pin 1 (figure 109)
6 Twist the new edge pair (now pair 1) three times, the other pair once and cloth stitch this pair (pair 2) towards the right through two pairs.

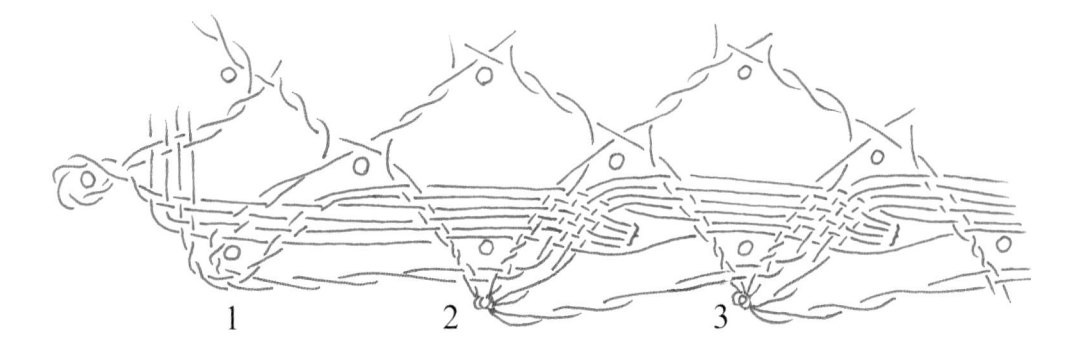

Figure 109 Picot end of the selvedge

7 *Cloth stitch the next two ground pairs (pairs 5 & 6) through the current passive pairs 4-2.
8 Twist both twice and set up pin (pin 2) between them.
9 Cloth stitch the edge pair (pair 1) through the two ground pairs (pairs 2 & 3).
10 Twist the former edge pair once and cloth stitch it through the passives (pairs 4-6).
11 Tie the former ground pairs (pairs 1& 2) in a reef knot. Twist the new edge pair (pair 1) three times and the other pair once and cloth stitch this pair (pair 2) through the passives (pairs 3-6).
12 From the passive pairs (pairs 2-5) throw back the 2nd, 3rd, 4th & 5th threads* (figure 109).
13 Repeat the process *to* three more times using the next three pinholes, taking into consideration that there are now three pairs of passives instead of two.
14 Return to the footside (figure 110) and cloth stitch the three remaining selvedge passive pairs through the footside passives. Throw out the four centre threads from the selvedge passives and tie the two remaining selvedge passives in a reef knot. These ends will be darned away.
15 Cloth stitch the edge pair through the footside passives and tie a reef knot with the passives.

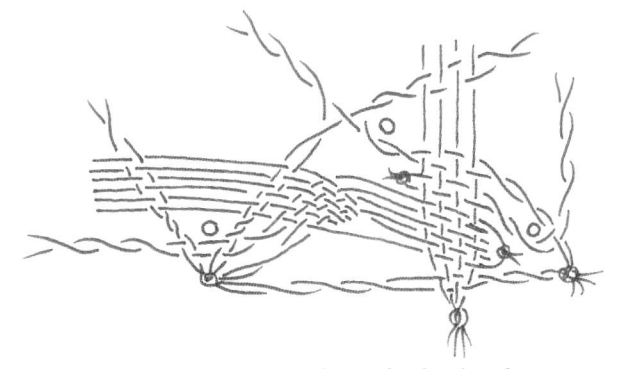

Figure 110 Footside end of selvedge

Chapter 4

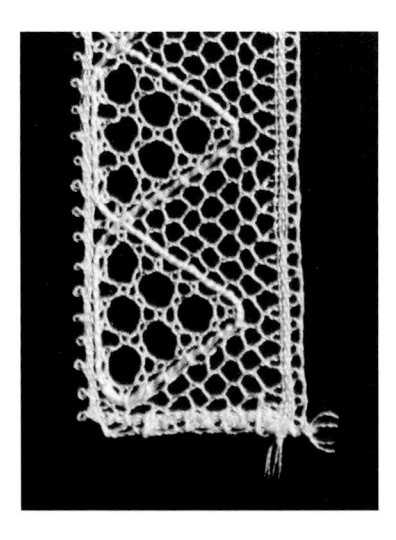

16 Twist the selvedge edge pair three times and untwist the footside edge pair. Tie a reef knot with these two pairs (figures 110 & 111).

17 The ends from the remaining two reef knots should be darned into the footside and selvedge passives, all other ends may be trimmed off closely.

18 Attach the lace to the fabric using four-sided stitch.

Figure 111 (left) The selvedge

Making up the jabot[14,15&16]

1 Make a paper pattern (figures 146 & 147). Fold the fabric diagonally across the grain and place line H-H of the pattern to the fold. Mark the positions of the pleats and cut out.

2 Pin, then tack, the wrong side[14] of the lace to the right side of the fabric along the edge from C to C, with the headside of the lace level with the edge of the fabric, easing in as required. Make a foundation row by oversewing the lace to the fabric, taking the needle through each footside hole, and also across each edge pair between footside holes (figure 112).

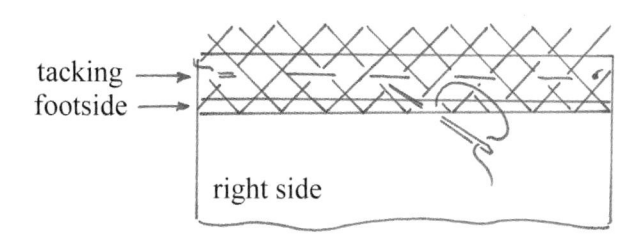

Figure 112 Foundation row

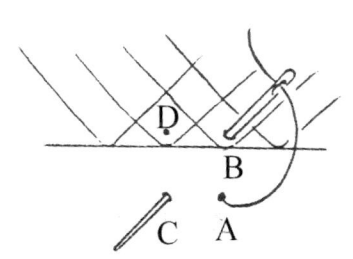

Four-sided stitch

1 (First row) Attach the thread to A, below a footside hole, insert the needle through the footside hole B to emerge at C below the next footside hole D (figure 113).

Figure 113 (left) Starting four-sided stitch

2 *Insert the needle through A to emerge through a footside hole at D (figure 114).

Figure 114 (right) The second stitch

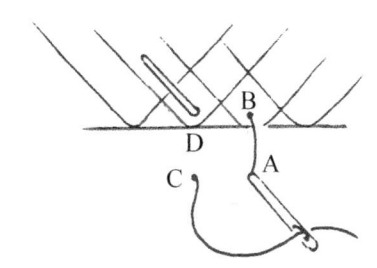

41

Chapter 4

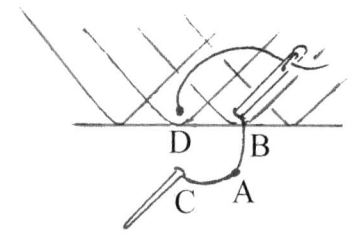

3 Insert the needle through B to emerge at C (figure 115).

Figure 115 (left) The third stitch

4 Rename C as A and D as B with the next two positions becoming C and D (figure 116). *Repeat *to** as required and fasten off the thread,

Figure 116 (right) The fourth stitch, which is the first stitch of the next set of four.

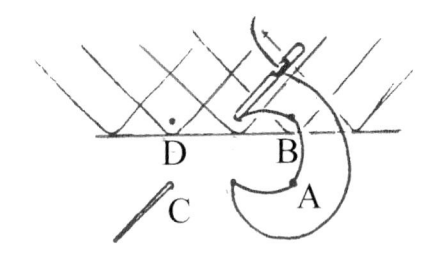

Four-sided stitch (second row)
Fold back the excess fabric close to the first row of stitching and tack. On the right side work a second row of stitches over the first row.

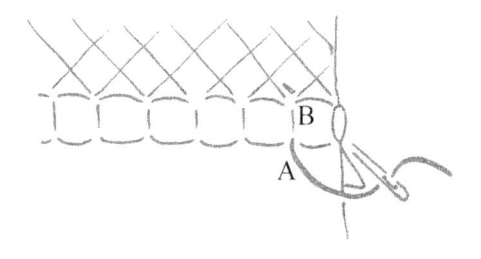

1 Fasten on the thread at the beginning of the row. Bring the thread through at A, then round the end of the fabric and through A again. Take the thread round the fabric to the back to come out through the footside of the lace at B (figure 117)

Figure 117 (left) First stitch of second row

2 Insert the needle at A and bring out at C (Figure 118)

Figure 118 (right) Second stitch of second row

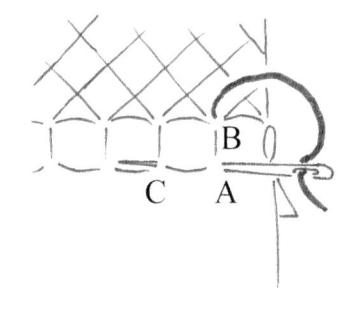

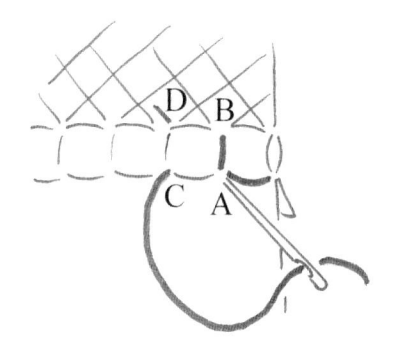

3 *Insert needle at A and bring out at D (figure 119)

Figure 119 (left) Third stitch of second row

42

4 Insert the needle at C and bring out at the next hole in the previous row * (Figure 120)

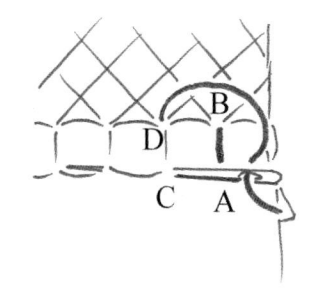

Figure 120 (right) Fourth stitch of second row

5 Repeat *to* as required and trim off excess fabric close to the stitching.

Four-sided stitch can also be used to neaten the two ends of the jabot, C-C on the jabot pattern.

Making up the Jabot
If you experience any problems folding the jabot, practice using the paper pattern, using paper clips to hold the folds in position. Once the paper jabot works, there should be no problems folding the fabric.
1 Pin and tack along all the folds as you go.
2 Fold back (wrong sides together) along D-D.
3 Make a pleat by folding E-E to F-F right sides together.
4 Make a pleat by folding G-G to H-H (centre front) right sides together.
5 Cut out the neckband (pattern figure 148) and fold over the long edges by 0.5cm (¼in) wrong sides together (figure 121). Tack and press.
6 Fold the neckband in half, long ways, with right sides together and seam across the ends, allowing a 0.5cm (¼ in) seam allowance Turn through and press.
7 Place the top edge of the jabot D-D between the long edges of the neck band, adjusting the pleats so that it takes up the full width, and stitch in place.
8 Make a chain stitch button loop at each end of the neckband and stitch two small buttons, in appropriate positions, under the collar of the blouse or shirt.

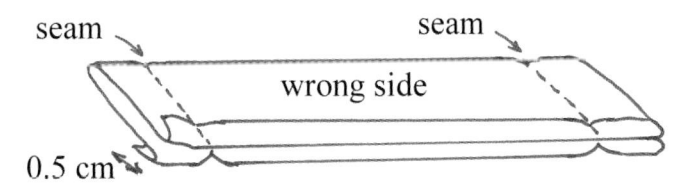

Figure 121 Neckband

Chain stitch button loops[17]
1 Fasten on a double sewing thread very securely at one corner of the neckband.
2 Take another stitch, in the same place, leaving a loop 5cm (2ins) long. Insert thumb and first finger through the loop and take hold of the free thread (figure 122). *Pull the free thread through the loop and continue pulling the thread until the loop fits snugly round the thread*.

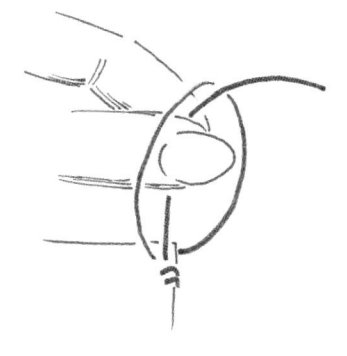

Figure 122 (right) Starting loop

Chapter 4

3 Insert first finger and thumb through the new loop. Repeat *to* as required (figure 123).
4 Fasten off the chain by passing the free end through the last loop (figure 124). Lay the chain along the short edge of the neckband and sew it securely in place using the free end of the chain thread.

Figure 123 Making a loop

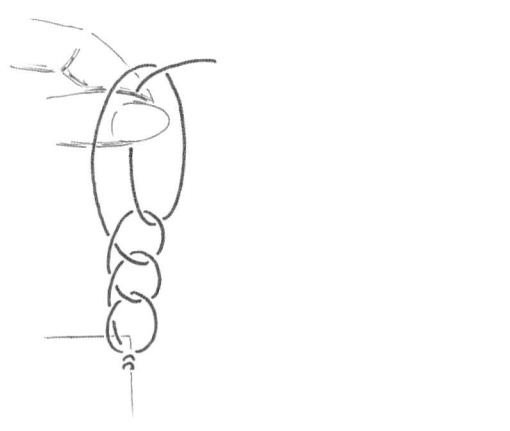

Figure 124 Fastening off the chain

END NOTES

1 Drafting the Pattern
Figures 125-127 have been enlarged for clarity.
1 Using Grid no. 1 (56°, 40 pins per 10 cm (4ins) along the footside) count from the footside of the printed pattern draft and mark key points within the honeycomb area (a-e). Draw the gimp line round these points. Repeat this several times down the grid (figure 125).
2 Within the honeycomb area use a very fine, white correction pen to remove alternate dots along alternate lines in both directions (figure 126 f-k).

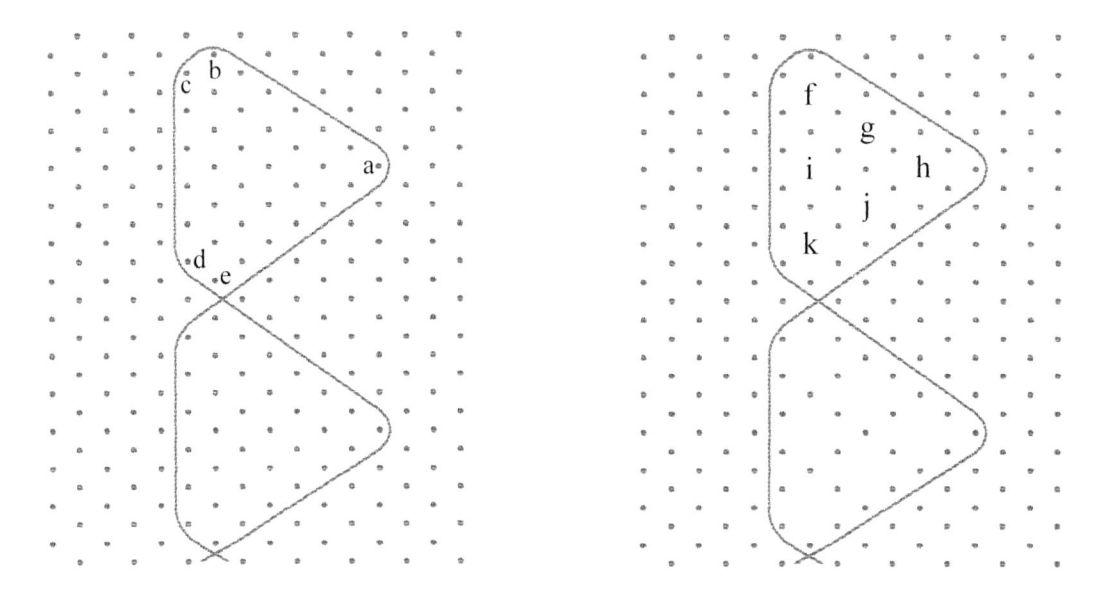

Figure 125 Draw in the gimps

Figure 126 Remove dots for honeycomb ground

Chapter 4

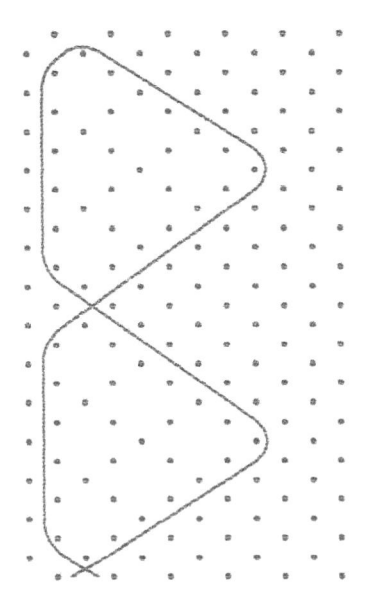

2 Allowing one line of dots for the headside, trim off the excess grid (figure 127). Adjust the pinholes for the headside and footside (figure 95).

Figure 127 (left) Excess grid removed, the headside and footside still require adjusting

2 Dovetailing a pricking
When the required length of lace is to be longer than can be made on the pricking, two pieces of pattern should be made and dovetailed. Cut a 'V' at the lower end of the first piece of pattern, so that no pinholes are cut. Place over the leading edge of the second piece of pattern, placing pins through matching positions that are easy to locate e.g. the pin between fans, the point of the fan etc. Scratch the second pattern piece along the edge of the first, and cut. A scratch, made using a pricker, is more accurate than using a pencil. (A pencil lead is much thicker, than a needle, and a pencil line will not be as close to the upper piece of card as a scratch). If more than two pieces of pattern are used mark with balance marks 'B' (figure 128). Dovetail the other ends of the pattern pieces, then the two can be used alternately down the pillow like 'stepping stones'.

Figure 128 (right) Dovetailed pricking with balance marks

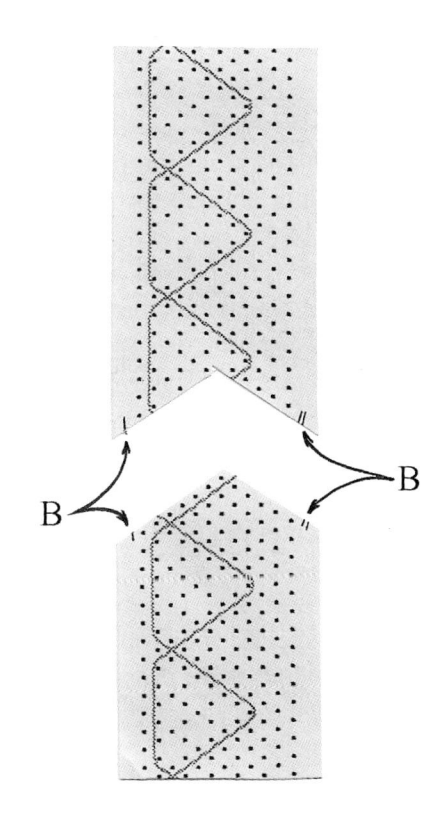

3 Twists adjacent to the gimp
In Bucks Point the gimp is passed between the threads of a pair by lifting the left bobbin of the pair, passing the gimp under it and replacing the bobbin in its former position. This works for passing the gimp to the left or to the right.

There are various theories regarding the 'correct' number of twists before and after the gimp in different situations. However, it must be remembered that when the gimp is passed under a thread, that has been twisted, the last twist is effectively 'lost', i.e. if the pair was twisted twice and the gimp passed through then there will effectively be only one twist before the gimp; the other twist occurs across the gimp. Thus if honeycomb has been made, and the gimp passed through a pair,

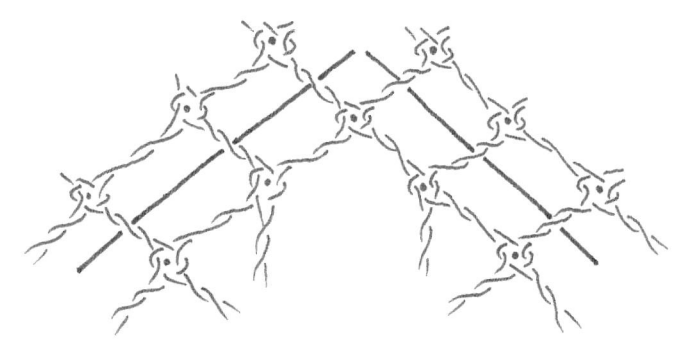

Figure 129 Twists in honeycomb adjacent to the gimp

there is effectively only one twist before the gimp. Therefore only one twist will be required after the gimp before working honeycomb to achieve a symmetrical result (figure 129). When studying antique lace I found a mixture of one twist before and two twists after the gimp by honeycomb stitch, suggesting that former lacemakers were not aware of the 'lost' twist and put two twists on the pair after a gimp when continuing in honeycomb. Unless otherwise stated, all samples are made with one twist following the gimp before continuing in honeycomb.

If point ground has been made, and the gimp passed through, there are effectively two twists before the gimp (the third occurs across the gimp). Therefore, to achieve a symmetrical result, only two twists will be required after the gimp before working point ground (figure 130). When studying antique lace I found a variety of numbers of twists between the ground and gimp, and different combinations of one, two and three, the most popular being two, In floral Bucks the number of twists tended to reflect the distance between the pins and the gimp. With evidence of so much variation in the past, the numbers of twists used adjacent to gimps, and the number does not appear to be crucial. They are matters of personal preference. Unless otherwise stated all samples are made with two twists following the gimp before continuing in point ground.

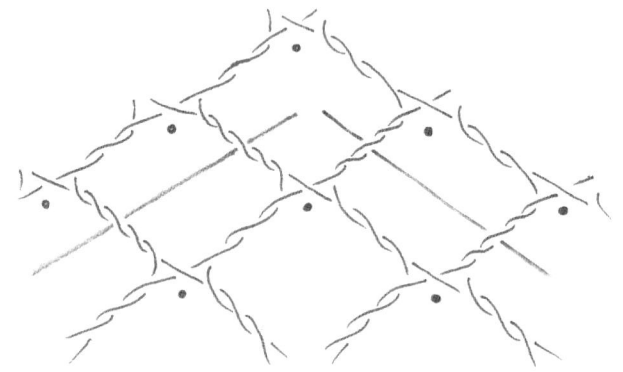

Figure 130 Twists adjacent to the gimp in point ground

4 Crossing gimps
In antique lace the most popular direction for crossing gimps was left over right, but nearly one third that number had them crossed right over left, and many contained crossings in both directions in the same piece. Also, where there were crossings in close proximity, the direction of the crossing was in sympathy the design.

5 Alternative method of working Honeycomb adjacent to the headside
The usual method of working the honeycomb results in gaps, between the pinholes adjacent to the gimp, where a pair has left the honeycomb to make a picot and returns (figure 103). However, there can be a continuous line of twisted pairs inside the gimp (figure 131). Instead of the pair leaving the honeycomb it travels straight down to make the next stitch directly below. The picot is made by working a blind spot.

Chapter 4

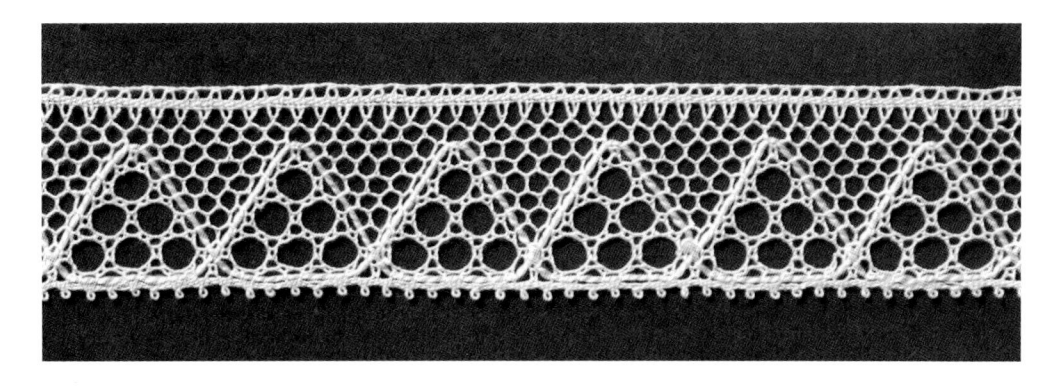

Figure 131 Alternative method for working honeycomb adjacent to the headside

6 Blind spot
When a pair is required to make a picot, but there is not one available, the second headside passive pair can be taken out to make the picot and returned back through at least one pair, preferably two (figure 132).

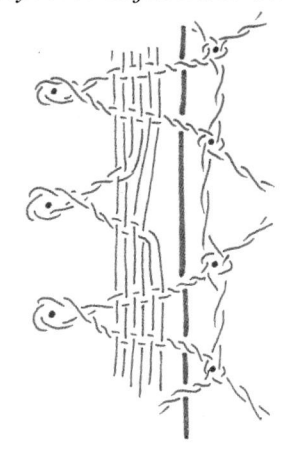

Figure 132 (right) Blind spot

7 Securing bobbins for lifting[8] and transportation

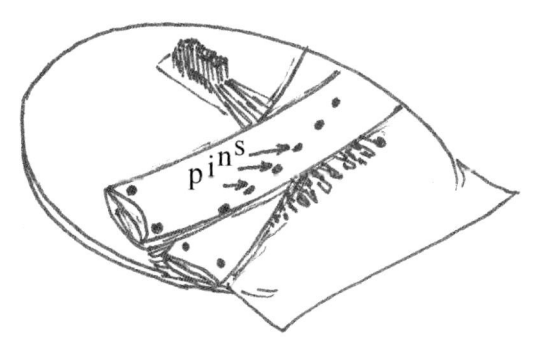

Figure 133 Securing bobbins for transportation and lifting

When a relatively small number of bobbins are in use they can be secured for transportation by pinning two large handkerchiefs, or two lengths of 2.5cm (1 in) elastic, across them. Fold the handkerchiefs in half twice, in the same direction, and pin across the bobbins, one diagonally one way and the other diagonally the other way. Use two glass headed pins in each end, pulling the second end tightly across the bobbins as the pins are inserted. Then insert a line of glass headed pins across between groups of bobbins (figure 133). Bobbins can be threaded onto stitch holders before being held down.

7a Stitch holders
Intended for knitters (some are like giant safety pins) these are useful to secure bobbins, especially where relatively large numbers of bobbins are concerned. The point of the holder is passed through the spangles of the bobbins and the bunches can then be secured to the pillow using handkerchiefs or a piece of wide elastic or folded into a bag for lifting (End Note 8a)

Chapter 4

8a Setting up (1) By lifting
1 Secure the bobbins by sliding the spangles onto stitch holders. Slip a large cover cloth, under the bunches held by the stitch holders, so that the top edge reaches to the heads of the bobbins. Bring the lower edge of the cloth up and over the bunches of bobbins, folding down the edge if necessary, so that the edge just reaches the heads of the bobbins, while the spangles are touching the fold of the fabric (figure 134)
2 Fold first one side over the bobbins, then the other, and pin closely to make a bag (figure 135).
3 Move the bag up slightly, to take any tension off the bobbins, and pin securely to the pillow using strong pins.
4 Remove all the pins from the pricking!
5 Holding the bag, remove the pins securing it to the pillow and, supporting the lace very gently, move them aside
6 Relocate the pricking, if necessary, and redress the pillow.

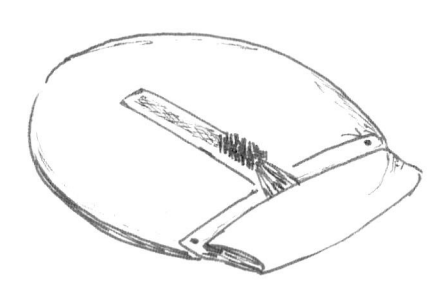

Figure 134 (left) Folding the cloth over the bobbins

Figure 135 (right) Making the bag

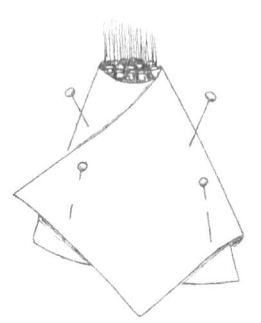

7 Holding the bag of bobbins, and supporting the lace very gently replace them on the pillow so that the last 5cms (2ins) or so, of the lace, lines up with a corresponding portion of the pricking at the top of the pillow. Move the bag up slightly so that there will be no tension on the bobbins and pin the bag securely to the pillow using strong pins.
8 Check that the lace is correctly in place and re-pin, taking care that sufficient pins have been replaced to prevent tension on the bobbins gathering up the lace, especially along the footside, straight headsides and where gimps change direction.
9 Unpin the bag, remove the stitch pins and continue making the lace, taking particular care not to pull the passives and gimps.

8b Setting up (2) Using a bridge
A bridge is a pad made up of a number of layers of felt each a little larger than the previous piece, with the smallest being as wide as the pricking. Before the pricking needs moving the bridge is placed, largest piece of felt uppermost, under the pricking. Continue making the lace onto the bridge and until the farthest end of the central area has been reached The bridge should be sufficiently thick so that the pins, across the centre square, enter the felt only and do not enter the pillow (figure 136) Follow points 1-3 for 'Setting up (1) By lifting'
4 Remove all pins except those in the centre square of the bridge.

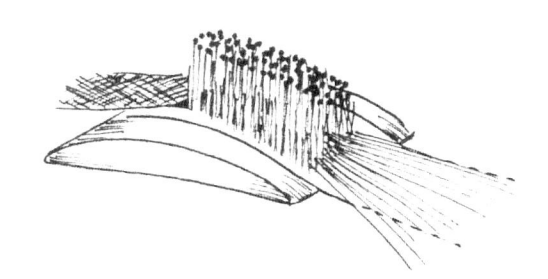

Figure 136 Using a bridge

5 Hold the bag and making sure there is no tension on the lace threads, lift the bridge and carefully relocate, without any tension on the threads.
6 Repin the bridge and bag to the pillow using strong pins. If necessary, replace some of the footpins and, when the headside is straight, some headpins,. Also replace any pins that are required to prevent gimps from pulling up.
7 Unpin the bag, remove the stitch pins, and continue making the lace, taking particular care not to pull the passives or gimps.

9a Joining threads
Bobbins only hold a limited amount of thread and therefore threads may need to be joined. It is best to avoid joining threads within the ground, as the join is more likely to show. A worker should never be joined, as doubling the worker causes thickening of the clothwork. Therefore plan ahead. Always exchange a worker for another thread, preferably one of the passives, by working a faulty stitch. (This is the correct term for the technique). The easiest threads to join are passives, preferably footside passives, but headside passives are also suitable.

9b Faulty stitch
When the thread running out meets a passive, or other suitable pair, select a bobbin of the other pair, usually the one with the most thread and, when these two bobbins meet, twist or cross them twice, then complete the stitch as usual. Figures 137-140 show the four different combinations. Figure 137 shows threads 1 & 3 exchanging. Figure 138 shows threads 1 & 4 exchanging, Figure 139 shows threads 2 & 3 exchanging, Figure 140 shows threads 2 & 4 exchanging. After the threads have exchanged continue working to stabilize them.

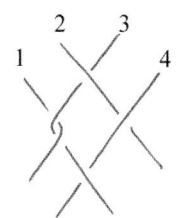

Figure 137 Twisting original 1 & 3 twice 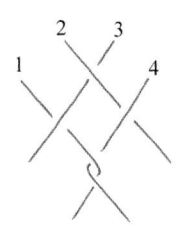   *Figure 138 Crossing original 1 & 4 twice* 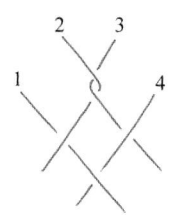   *Figure 139 Crossing original 2 & 3 twice* 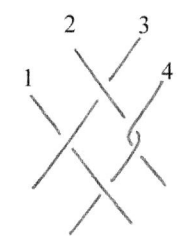   *Figure 140 Twisting original 2 & 4 twice*

9c Doubling threads to join them
This method can be used to join any thread except a clothwork worker. After making faulty stitch, work the threads for a few stitches to stabilize them before joining the thread. Wind a spare bobbin and attach to a pin at the side of the pattern. Pass the new thread through the pins so that it emerges from the pins on top of the thread that is running out. Twist the two bobbins 25 times. A small elastic band may be used to hold the bobbins together, (so that one does not go 'walk about' and end up in the wrong place), but make sure it is loose so that the bobbins can keep their individual tensions. After working about 2.5 cms (1 in) down the pattern remove the elastic band, if necessary, and untwist any remaining twists. Discard the empty bobbin by laying back over the work and continue working with the new thread. When removing the pins leave the head and footpins in, lift the cut ends with a slight tension and, keeping the scissors flat on the lace, trim the ends off closely. Then remove the remaining pins.

Chapter 4

9d Replacing a passive thread
Twist the pair containing the thread to be replaced and discard the unwanted bobbin by throwing back. Wind a spare bobbin and attach to a pin at the side of the pattern. Pass the new thread through the pins so that it emerges from the pins to lie to the left of the pair that was twisted. Twist the two threads once (figure 141) and continue lacemaking. Cut off the unwanted bobbin before removing the pins and trim the end closely after the pins have been removed.

Figure 141 (right) Replacing a passive thread

9e Replacing a thread at the footside.
When a thread that needs replacing reaches the stitch about the pin, exchange it with a new thread attached to a pin at the side of the pattern (figure 142). Cut off the unwanted bobbin before removing the pins and leave the ends to be sewn away when the lace is mounted.

Figure 142 Replacing a thread at the footside

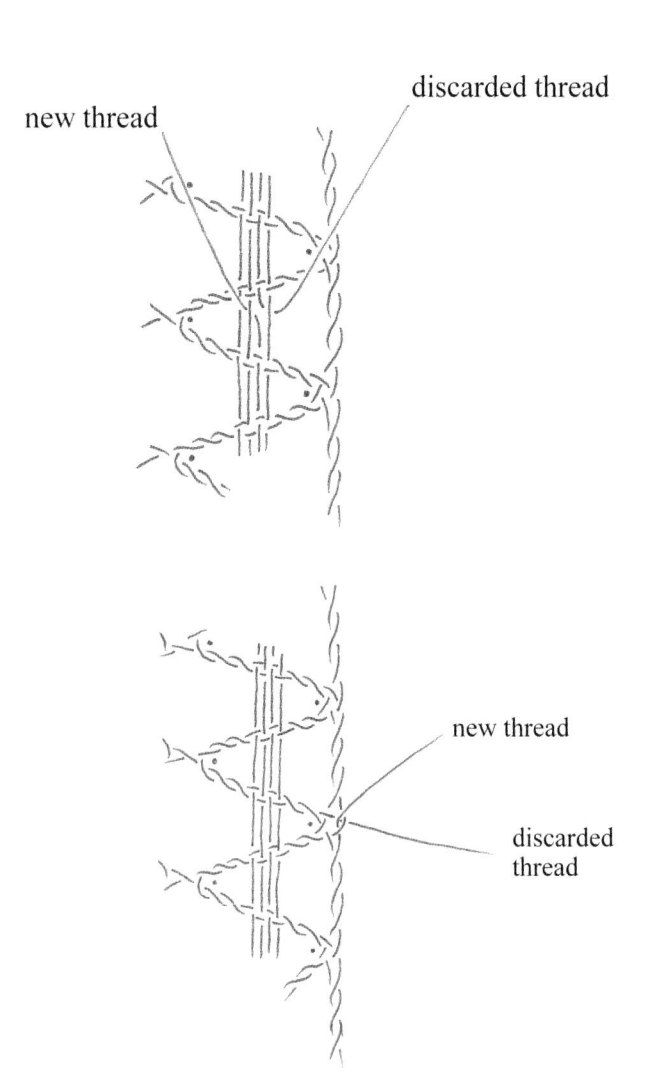

9f Replacing a gimp thread
When a gimp is running out, tie a full bobbin to the side of the pattern. Pass the new thread through the pins so that it emerges from the pins on top of the thread that is running out. The two threads should not be twisted but a small elastic band can be used to keep the bobbins together, (so that one does not go 'walk about' and end up in the wrong place,) but make sure it is loose so that the bobbins can keep their individual tensions. After working about 2.5cms (1in) remove the elastic band. Lay the empty bobbin back over the work and continue working with the new thread. After working a few more stitches on the new thread the empty bobbin can be cut off leaving at least 10 cms (4ins) of thread.

9g Trimming the ends of replaced threads & gimps
When a thread has been replaced, cut off the bobbin, leaving an end 10cms (4 ins) long, before the pins surrounding the replaced thread are removed. When the pins surrounding the remaining end have been removed, hold the end with a slight tension and, keeping the scissors flat on the lace, trim the ends off closely.

9h Removing pins
Lace is made under tension; therefore it will 'shrink' when pins are removed. Pins can only be removed when sufficient pins have been set, so that any tension cannot affect the lace. Always take

Chapter 4

pins out following a definite line and avoid leaving odd pins in place, as the lace will shrink away around them. When the pricking is sufficiently small, so that the lace can be completed without moving the lace or the pricking, pins can be removed from the centre, leaving the head and footpins in until the lace has been completed. Also, for small items that will not need moving and the end is to be joined to the beginning, leave sufficient pins in at the start so that the process of joining will not cause the lace to stretch.

10 Broken threads
Breaking a thread weakens individual fibres in it. These fibres may be up to 10 cms (4 ins) long, and therefore the broken end may be very fragile. If it is possible, remove this portion of the thread. **However, do not cut anything off short ends,** but treat them with care. If necessary, the lace should be unpicked until there is an end at least 2.5cm (1 in) long. Attach a piece of thread to the broken end using a weavers' knot[11]. If there is plenty of thread continue working until the knot is reached and replace using one of the usual methods. If the end is very short, immediately hang in a new bobbin, so that it lies on top of the broken end, and twist the two together. Continue working, watching that the two remain twisted.

11 Weavers' knot.
This knot, developed by weavers, has the property of staying secure when the ends are trimmed off closely. It can also be made very close to a short, broken end. Make a slip knot with the tail (the short end) as the running end (the end that slides through the knot to tighten the noose). Pass the noose over the end to which it is to be joined (figure 143) and gently pull the running end until no light can be seen through the knot. Hold the threads either side of the knot, one in each hand, and pull them apart. The end that passed through the noose should flip over as the knot locks (figure 144). This is only one of several methods for making this knot but it has the advantage that it can be made when there is only a short piece to join to. Unfortunately this knot does not lock every time and several attempts may have to be made. If you are having difficulty in making it lock, try passing the tail through the noose in the other direction.

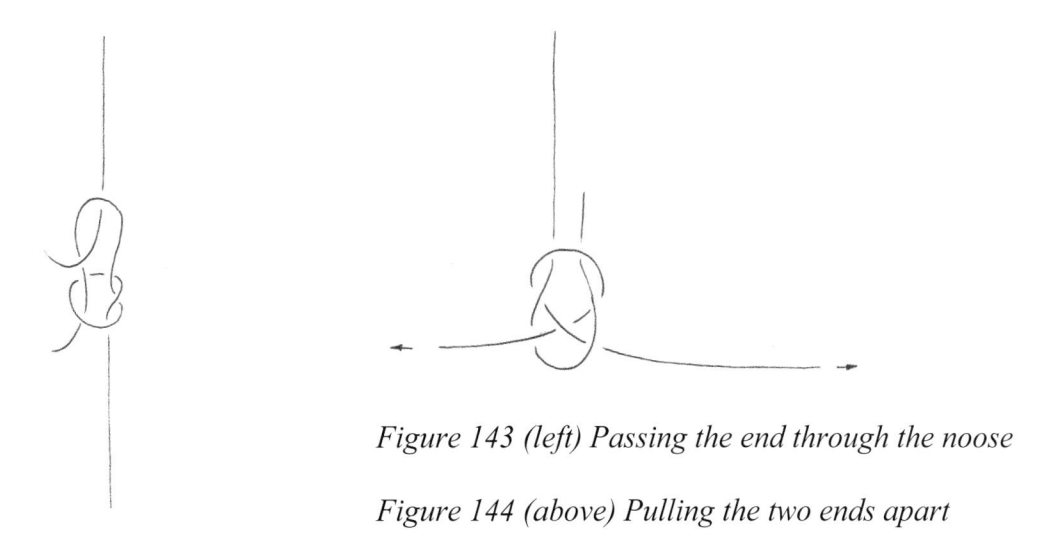

Figure 143 (left) Passing the end through the noose

Figure 144 (above) Pulling the two ends apart

12 Threads shredding
Sometimes a thread becomes untwisted and the plys separate, weaken and eventually part company. Should the thread appear to become untwisted then re-twisting it may be sufficient to

Chapter 4

address the problem. If the problem persists -
1. It may be a fault with that particular batch of thread. However, if this problem occurs with more than one batch of thread then there is probably another reason.
2. There may be friction between the thread and the cover cloth and the following may help.
    a) Press the crease where the top edge of the working cloth is folded over so that it is less likely to rub the threads.
    b) Try using a different fabric for the working cloth.
    c) Pin a strip of polythene across the pillow where the threads rub.
3. The twists on the threads may have been reduced by incorrect winding, After a few turns round the bobbin to secure the thread, rotate the bobbin, rather than winding the thread around it.

One of the theories for plys separating is static electricity created by the threads rubbing on the cover cloth. However, the force likely to be created is so infinitesimal it would only be able to make a very fine fibre wave in the air; it would not be able to move even a fibre that had both ends attached.

13 Developing tension and speed
Lacemakers would always make a yard (90cm approx.) of each pattern when they were learning; This tradition is as valid today in that practicing a piece beyond the stage of mastering the techniques allows the lacemaker to relax and develop good rhythm, tension and speed

14 Right and wrong sides of Bucks Point lace
The side of the lace that lies against the pillow when it is made is generally considered as the wrong side, as it is very flat, almost as though it had been pressed with an iron. The side that is uppermost, when it is made, is not as flat; the gimps stand proud and some tensioning techniques create slightly three-dimensional effects. These irregularities in the surface give 'life' to the lace, but unfortunately this is lost when the lace is pressed after washing.

15 Attaching lace to fabric[16]
Traditionally lace has always been attached to fabric by hand. However, poor attachment by hand can ruin the appearance of the lace and I prefer to see lace that has been successfully attached to fabric using a sewing machine, than lace that has been badly attached by hand. When attaching lace by machine, tack the lace to the fabric with small stitches along the footside passives using the same thread as the lace. The triple zigzag stitch usually gives good results and a length 1 and width 1 are suitable starting sizes, but adjust them to give the effect you are happy with. Practice using the lace thread, if it is suitable for the machine, and use the same fabric you are using for the item. Take care with corners, particularly the position of the needle when you rotate the fabric. For exhibitions and competitions lace should always be attached by hand.

16 Ballpoint needle
A ballpoint needle is used for sewing where the needle should avoid piercing the threads. A needle with a sharp point may spear the threads and so spoil the effect of some types of stitching e.g. hemstitching.

17 Buttonholed Loops

Another way of making loops at the ends of the neckband.

1 Fasten on a double thread at one corner of the neckband.
2 Lay a thread to the other corner of the short side and take a small stitch.
3 Return the thread to the starting point and make another small stitch.
4 Return the thread to the second corner and fasten the thread.
5 Make a line of closely worked buttonhole stitches across the three threads (figure 145) and fasten off securely.

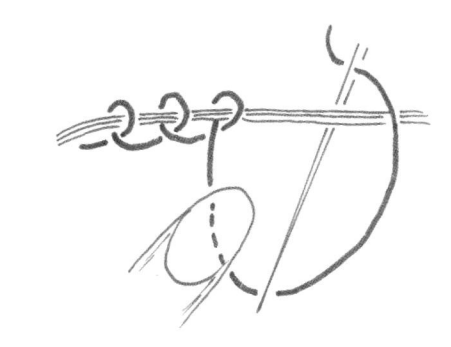

Figure 145 Buttonhole stitching a loop

Chapter 4

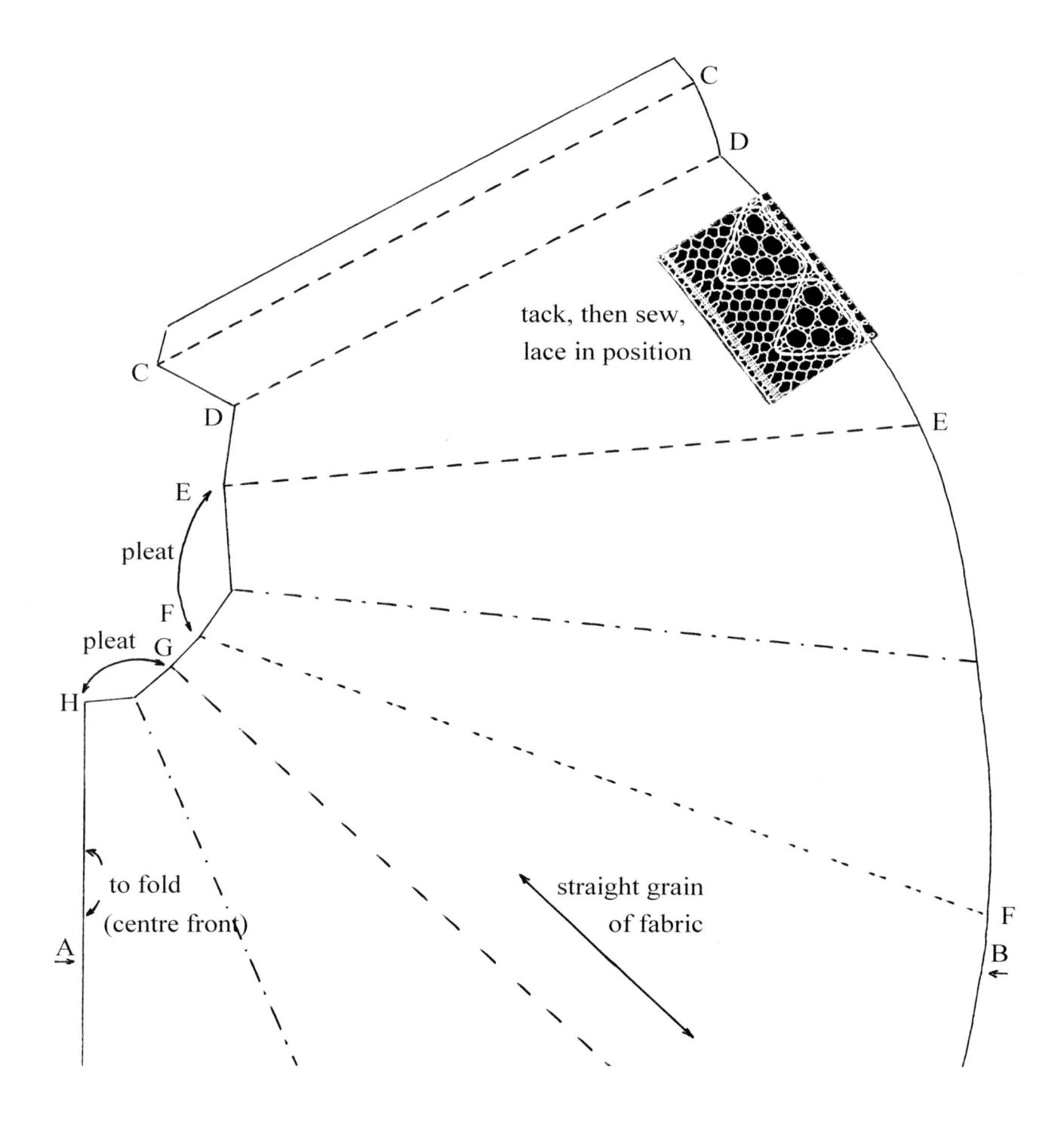

Figure 146 upper part of Jabot pattern

Cut out the jabot pattern pieces (figures 146 & 147), match the balance marks A-A and B-B and secure together.

54

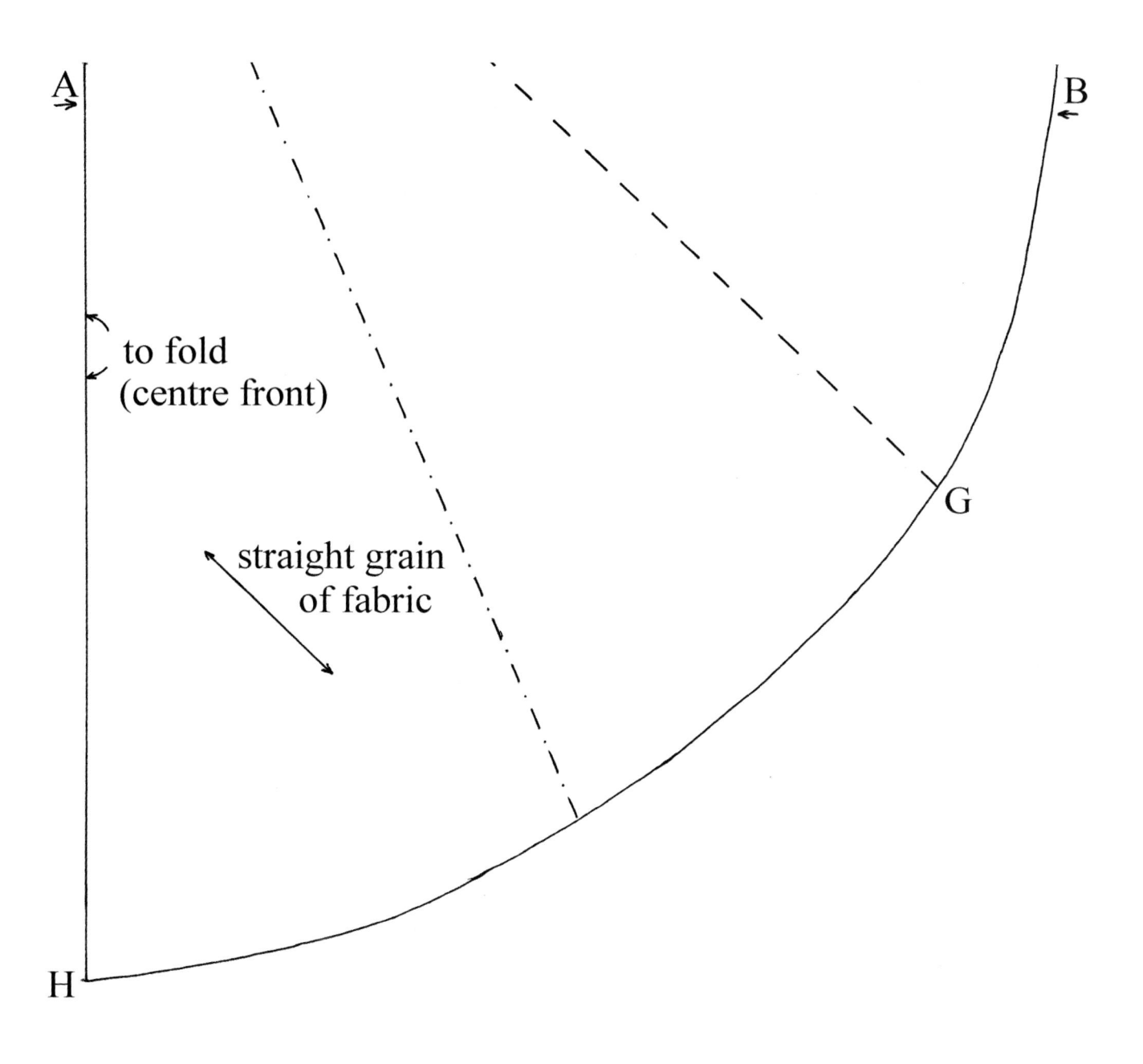

Chapter 4

Cut out the jabot pattern pieces (figures 146 & 147), match the balance marks A-A and B-B and secure together.

Figure 147 (above) Lower part of Jabot pattern

Figure 148 (right) Neckband pattern

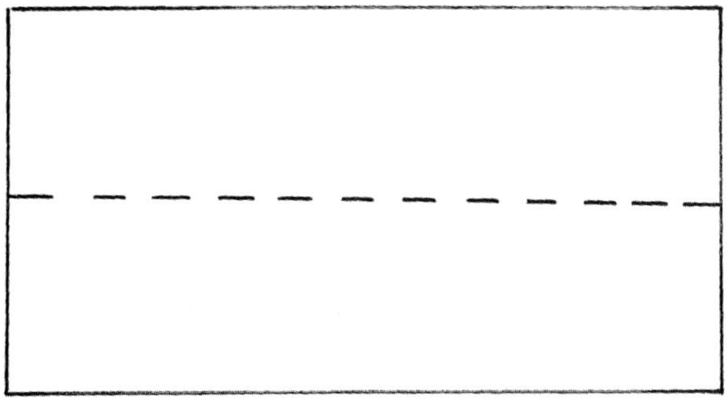

Chapter 5

PROJECT 3 TISSUE SACHET (Plates 2 & 3)

Figure 149 Tissue sachet

New Techniques
   starting from the footside on the diagonal
   cloth stitch diamond
   doubling gimps
   six-pin honeycomb ring

Materials required
   pricking (figure 150)[1]
   14 pairs Egyptian cotton no. 90
   1 pair cotton perle, no 12 (gimp)
   22cm x 14cm (8¾ ins x 5½ ins) fabric
      (this one is in needle cord)
   sewing thread to match fabric
   fabric bonding tape or powder
   tissues

End Notes
   1 drafting the pattern
   2 indicators
   3 twists between the gimp and clothwork
   4 catch-pin stitches adjacent to vertical gimps

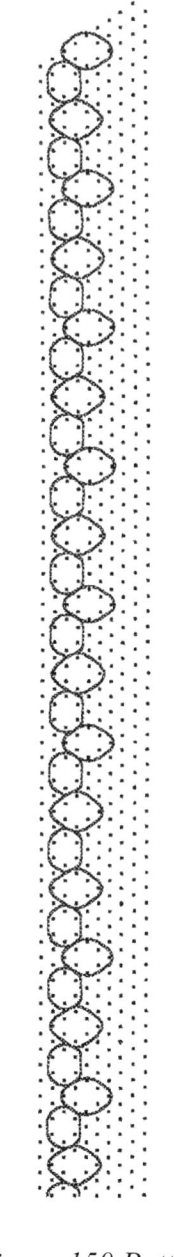

Figure 150 Pattern draft

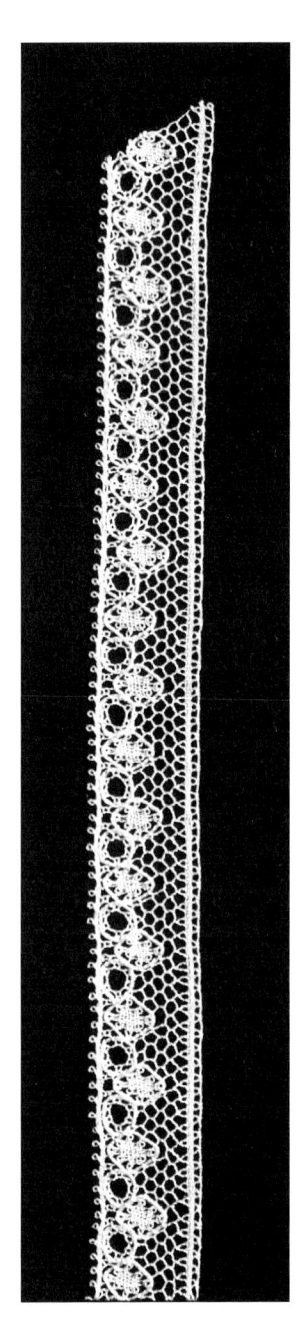

Figure 151 Lace

Setting In[1, 2&3]

Make a pricking of the pattern draft (figure 150) and mark in the indicators[2]. Dress the pillow and wind 14 pairs of bobbins, and one pair of gimps, in couples.

Setting in diagonally from the footside

1 Work a whole stitch round the pin at the top pin of the footside, work through the footside passives, twist the workers and set up the catch-pin.

2 Place four pairs on individual temporary pins above the pattern and to the left of the current pairs. With the workers, and a new pair, work the catch-pin stitch. *With the pair to the left of the pin, and the next new pair on the left, work a point ground stitch setting up a pin in the next pinhole diagonally below the previous pin (figure 152). *. Repeat *to* for the next two new pairs. Slip a support pin through the loops of the passives and the catch-pin pair, and let these pairs down.

Figure 152 Setting in the footside and point ground

3 Place the gimp pair on a temporary pin above the pattern, pass the right gimp through three pairs from the ground, and twist each pair[3]. Place three pairs on temporary pins to the left of the left gimp, pass the gimp through these pairs and twist the pairs.

4 Cloth stitch the first ground pair and a new pair and set up a pin at the top of the diamond. The pair on the left of the pin will be the workers so twist them twice, cover the pin and work through *one more pair to the right and set up the next pin down the right side of the diamond. Twist the workers twice. Return through these pairs and one more new pair, set up the next pin down the left side of the diamond, and twist the workers twice. Return through these pairs and one more pair from the ground and pin. Return and add another new pair at the widest part of the diamond. Slip a pin through the loops on the temporary pins, and let the pairs down[3] (figure 153).

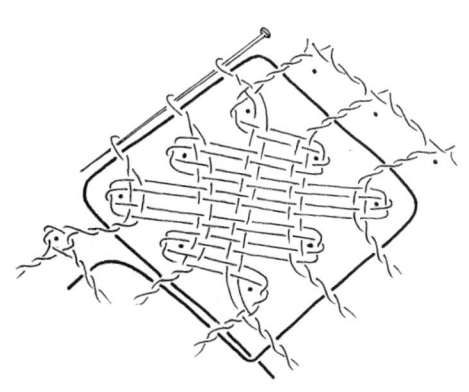

Figure 153 Adding pairs across a gimp and working a cloth stitch diamond

5 Return across the row except for the last pair, set up a pin and twist the workers twice. Continue, leaving off a pair at the end of each row until the last pin of the diamond has been set, and the workers twisted. Cover the pin with a cloth stitch. Twist all the pairs leaving the diamond, twice[3].

6 Starting from the footside work two rows of point ground as far as the gimp line,

7 Pass the right hand gimp through three pairs towards the left and twist the passives. Pass the left gimp through three pairs towards the right and only twist the left pair, leave the other two pairs untwisted.

8 With the pair from the left point of the diamond and a new pair, on a temporary pin, work the honeycomb stitch in the headside and let the pair down (figure 153)

9 Place two pairs, on temporary pins above, and to the left of the work. With the left pair, from the honeycomb stitch in the headside, cloth stitch through the two new pairs, the headside passives, make a picot, return through the passives, and twist in preparation for passing a gimp

Chapter 5

through them.
10 Cross the gimps, right over left, and pass the new left gimp through two pairs to the left so that it parallels the other gimp, (without twists between them) and then through the pairs from the honeycomb stitch and the picot. Twist these four pairs in preparation for working the honeycomb ring.
11 Work a row of point ground from the footside and through the pairs from the cloth stitch diamond.

Six-pin honeycomb ring[4]
With the pair from the honeycomb stitch, in the headside, and the adjacent pair from the diamond work a honeycomb stitch, pin 1. With the left pair from this stitch and the pair from the picot, work a honeycomb stitch, pin 2. Using the other pair from the top honeycomb stitch and the next pair from the diamond, work a honeycomb stitch, pin 3. These form the top three stitches of the honeycomb ring. Pass the outer pairs from the last two honeycomb stitches across the gimps to make a picot, pin 4, and a point ground stitch[4], pin 5, and return them across the gimp to make honeycomb stitches with the pairs dropping vertically, pins 6 & 7. Use the inner two pairs from these stitches to make the honeycomb stitch at the base of the ring, pin 8 (figure 154). Cross the gimps and double the gimp, now on right, through the next two pairs on the right in preparation for the next diamond.

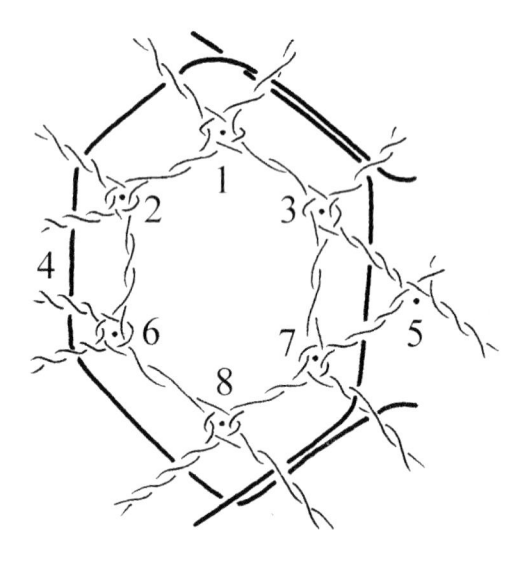

Figure 154 Honeycomb ring

(Note that the diamonds are not in the same position each time, alternate diamonds are one pin closer to the headside, and the gimps do not pass through the same number of pairs each time.)

Work the headside, the honeycomb stitch within the headside and the point ground as far as possible before passing the gimps through and working the next cloth stitch diamond.

Making the tissue sachet
1 Make two 15cm (6in) pieces of lace, (the length of the pattern). The ends do not need neatening but the pairs may be knotted together, two at a time, using reef knots. Trim off the bobbins before removing the pins.
2 Cut a piece of fabric 22 cms (8 $^{3}/_{4}$ inches) x 14 cms (5½ inches). Fold back 2 cms ($^{3}/_{4}$ inches), wrong sides together, along the 14 cm edges and press securely in place using fabric bonding (figure 155).

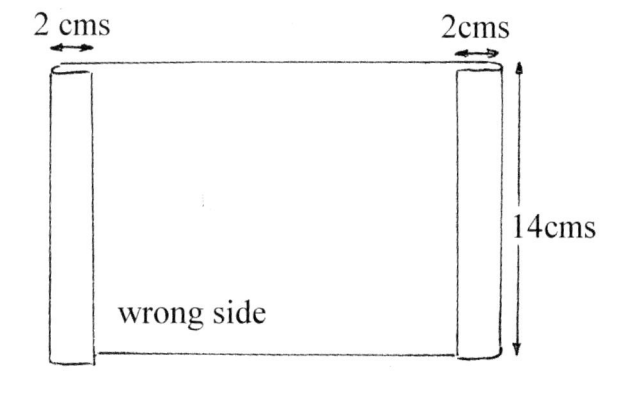

Figure 155 Turning in the edges

Chapter 5

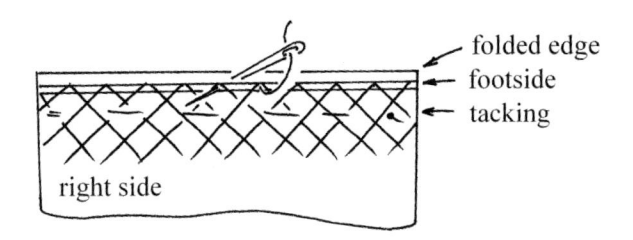

Figure 156 Attaching lace

3 Place the lace on the right side of the fabric close to these folds, tack, then stitch in place by oversewing through the footside holes of the lace (figure 156).

4 With right sides together fold the neatened edges together to meet in the centre and seam across the ends 1 cm, ($^3/_8$ in), seam allowance. Trim the ends and neaten using an overlocker or by over sewing (figure 157).
5 Turn right way out and insert tissues.

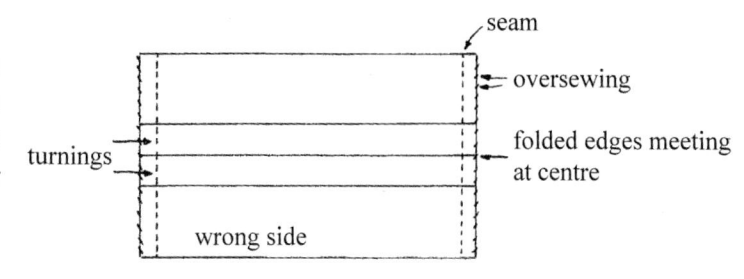

Figure157 Finishing the sachet

END NOTES

1 Drafting the pattern
1 Using Grid no. 2 (56°, 50 pins per 10 cm along the footside) count from the footside and mark the key points around the cloth stitch diamonds and the honeycomb rings.
2 Draw the gimp lines around them.
3 Repeat this down the pattern.

Note that the diamonds are not all in the same position relative to the headside; there are two positions that alternate. (figure 158).

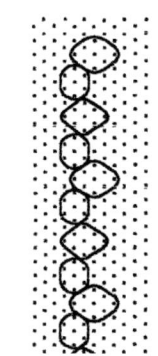

Figure 158 (right) Drawing in the gimps

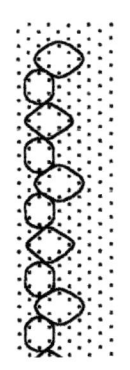

4 Allowing one line of dots for the headside, trim off the excess dots at the headside and block out unwanted dots within the honeycomb ring and diamonds (figure 159).
5 Adjust the pinholes for the headside and footside (figure 150).

Figure 159 (left) Unwanted pinholes removed

2 Indicators
The lines and symbols drawn on the pricking with a fine felt tipped pen that give guidance to interpreting the pricking. The black lines indicate the paths of the gimps, other symbols indicate other stitches etc. When new to making Bucks point lace it can be difficult to differentiate between

59

the honeycomb rings and cloth stitch diamonds. Traditionally Bucks point lacemakers do not use an indicator for cloth stitch. However, a cross can be used to indicate a cloth stitch diamond in honeycomb (see Chapter 12, Filling no. 1, Mayflower). Although not usual procedure, there is no reason why you cannot indicate the cloth stitch diamonds in this pattern with a cross, or even add any other symbols that assist you. It is useful to write an explanation on the pricking, so that such hieroglyphics can be interpreted in ten years time or by another lacemaker who may use the pricking.

3 Twists Between The Gimp and Clothwork
Today, when working cloth stitch, it is usual to twist pairs twice before and after the gimp has passed through them, resulting in two effective twists before and one after. Twisting only once after the gimp and twice before it will result in one effective twist in both cases. Surprisingly in antique lace the most popular number of twists between clothwork and gimp was none at all, followed by a mixture of one twist before the gimp (resulting in no effective twist, as the single twist occurres as the gimp passes through) and one twist after the gimp; then two twists before the gimp, giving one effective twist and one twist after the gimp.

4 Catch-pin stitches adjacent to vertical gimps
Catch-pin stitches are not confined to the footside; they are occasionally used adjacent to a vertical gimp. When point ground stitches, adjacent to a vertical gimp, are pinned in the usual manner enlarged holes sometimes form, particularly so when there are two or more such stitches one above the other. To counteract this the pin can be inserted to the side of the stitch forming a catch-pin stitch (figure 160).

Figure 160 (right) Catch-pin stitch adjacent vertical gimp

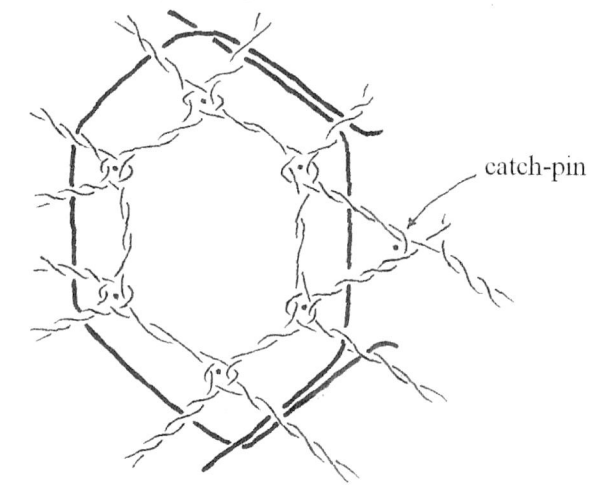

Chapter 6
PROJECT 4 GLOBE CANDLEHOLDER (Plate 6)

Figure 161 Candleholders

New Techniques
   coarse footside passive
   getting into & out of valleys
   stacking pairs
   valley pin
   new mayflower

Materials required
   pricking[1] (figure 163 or 164)[1]
   figure 163, 34½ pairs Egyptian cotton no. 60
   figure 164, 23½ pairs Egyptian cotton no. 60
   1 bobbin Madeira Tanne no 50
   1 bobbin Madeira Tanne no 30
   figure 163, 2 pairs perle thread, no 8
   figure 164, 1 pair perle thread, no 8
   candleholder & candle

Figure 162 Lace

End Notes
   1 drafting the pattern
   2 choosing a starting line
   3 valleys
   4 managing large numbers of bobbins

For this, and subsequent Projects, unless otherwise instructed it will be assumed that the usual twists will be made when the gimp is passed through.

Chapter 6

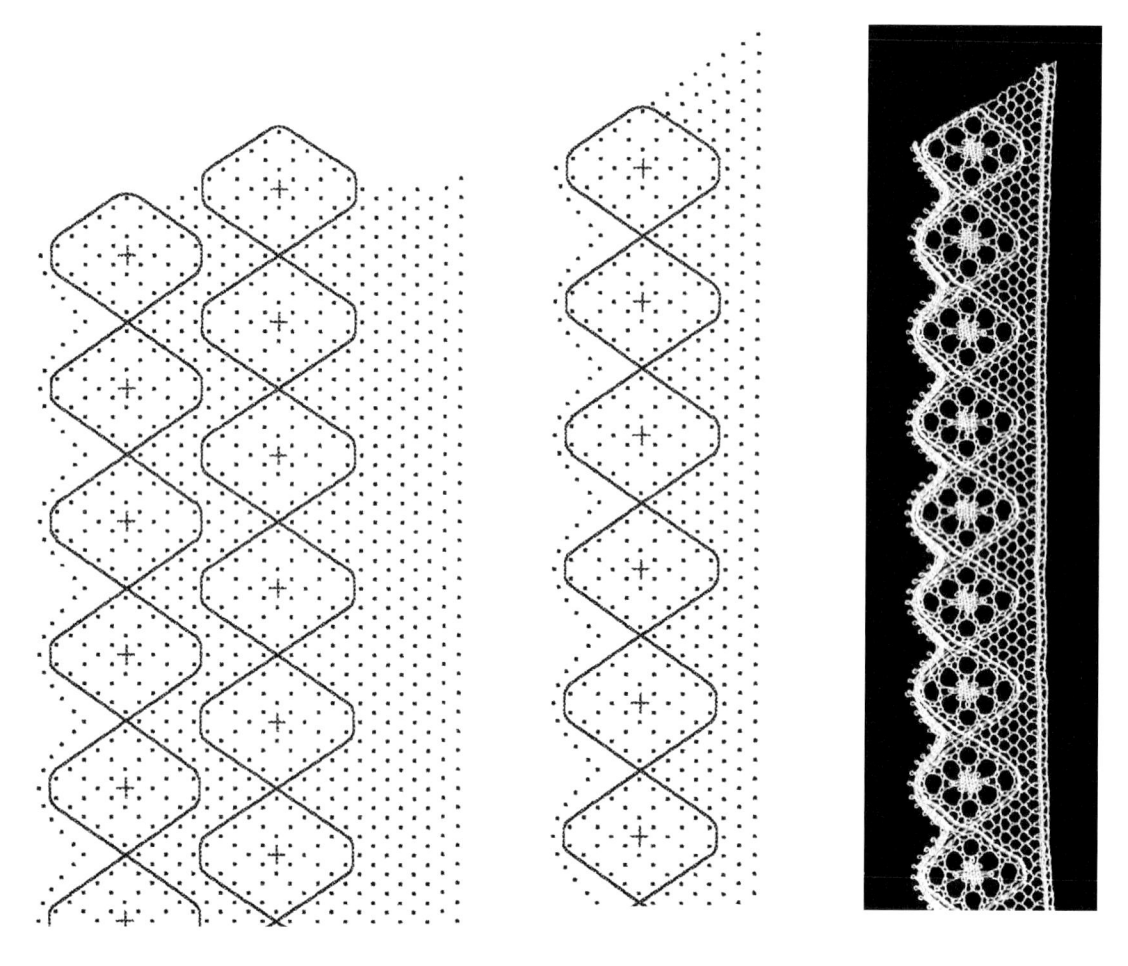

Figure 163 Pattern draft   *Figure 164 Pattern draft*   *Figure 165 Lace*

Pattern draft figure 163 is for the candleholder, figure 162, and draft figure 165 is for a narrower sample pattern (figure 165), covering the same techniques.

Before working the lace for the candleholder check the length required. Trace the pricking and make a test piece by cutting the shape out of net, or soft fabric, and try it in position in the candleholder (figure 166). Adjust until a suitable length is found. Note the number of pattern repeats that will be required and prepare the pricking.

Figure 166 (right) Assessing the number of repeats required

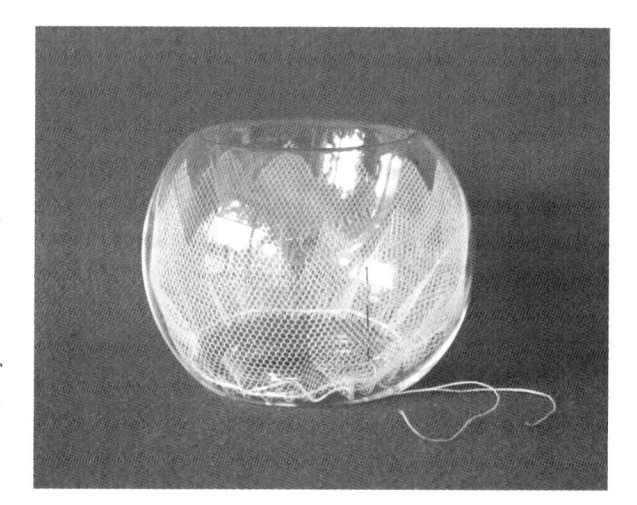

Chapter 6

Setting in the first area of honeycomb ground[2].
1 Start the honeycomb ground with a stitch at pin 1 using two pairs crossing the gimp (figure 167). Continue adding pairs down the continuous row to pin 2.
2 Pass the gimp through the leading pair from the row, make a catch-pin stitch at pin 3 with a new pair on temporary pin T, and return a pair back across the gimp to make a gap row honeycomb stitch. The pair on the temporary pin T should be supported.

Figure 167 (right) Adding a pair at a catch-pin stitch

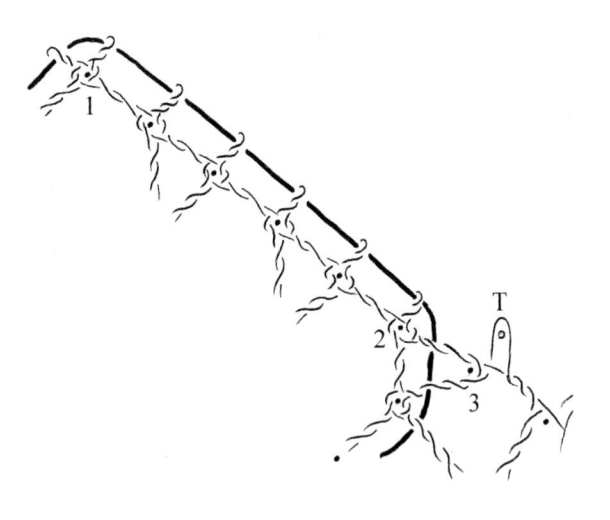

3 With the other pair from pin 1 work a continuous row to the left adding a pair across the gimp for each stitch. At the end of the row pass the gimp through the leading pair from the row, make a catch-pin with a new pair, and return a pair back across the gimp to make a gap row honeycomb stitch.
4 Complete the gap rows.

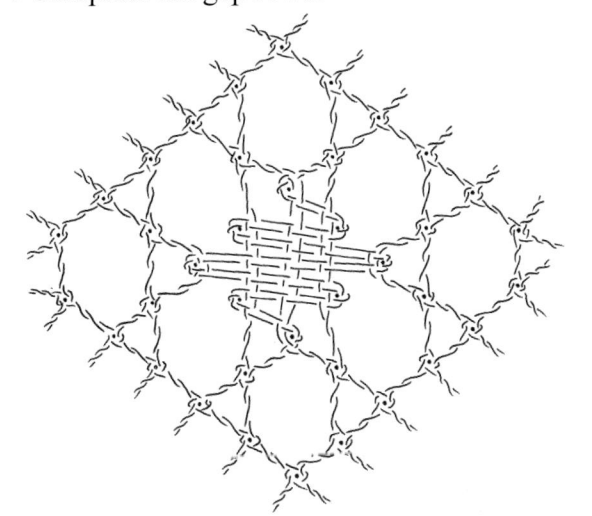

Figure 168 Mayflower

Mayflower
Traditionally the term 'Mayflower' was used for the filling that has a regular pattern of cloth stitch diamonds within honeycomb filling. However, the term is now also applied to a single diamond of cloth stitch within honeycomb. After working the first continuous and gap rows down each side of the honeycomb area, work the cloth stitch diamond starting with the two centre pairs (figure 168). Add a pair at the end of each row until the two pins at its widest are set up and then leave off a pair at the end of each row until the last pin is set up. Cover the last pin with a cloth stitch and twist all pairs, left out of the diamond, twice. The workers are twisted twice after setting up each pin. Work a gap row each side of the mayflower followed by a continuous row each side to complete the area. If problems are experienced, in selecting pairs to work the gap row, separate the two pairs that cover the last pin of the cloth stitch diamond. Work the first gap row honeycomb stitch on one side with one pair and the next pair from the same side. Continue working the gap row travelling 'up hill'. Then work the gap row on the other side of the diamond, again starting from the bottom and travelling 'up hill'. Gap rows in honeycomb are the exceptions to the rule that, in continuous laces, rows must be worked 'down hill' i.e. from the back of the pillow towards the front; down the slope. A gap row can be worked 'up hill' because of the 'gaps' which prevent a pair from travelling 'up the hill' and ending in the wrong place. Pass the gimps through the pairs, and cross them.

Chapter 6

Setting in the point ground and footside horizontally
1 Place two pairs, half straddled over pins 4 & 5, (i.e. place a pair over the pin, place a second pair on the same pin so that the bobbins occupy places 2 & 4), (figure 169), and twist the resulting pairs three times each. Starting with the left pair from pin 4, then the left pair from pin 5, work two rows of ground down the side of the honeycomb motif.
2 Set in the footside at pin 6 with a whole stitch round the pin.

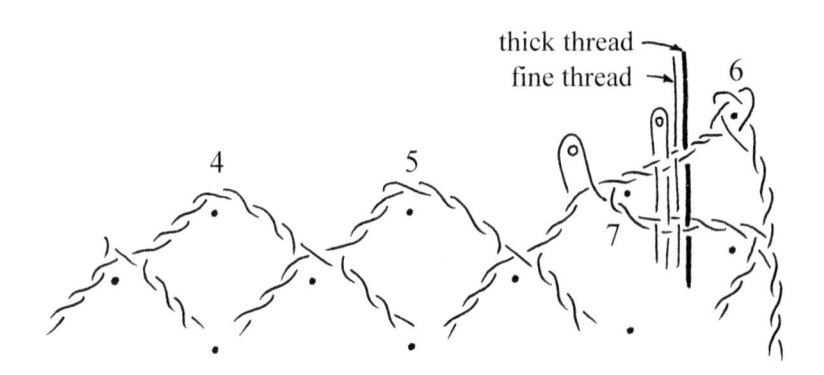

Figure 169 Setting in the point ground and footside

3 Tie the thick passive thread (Madeira Tanne no 30) and the single thread to a pin 7.5cm (3 in) above the pattern, with the thick thread closest to the footside partnered by the single fine thread. Place two pairs on temporary pins between the mixed pair and pin 5. From pin 6, work through the passives (one pair of mixed thickness and one new pair), and set up the catch-pin, pin 7. The passive pair and the pair added to make the catch-pin stitch will need supporting.
3 Work a triangle of ground as far as the gimp of the next honeycomb area.

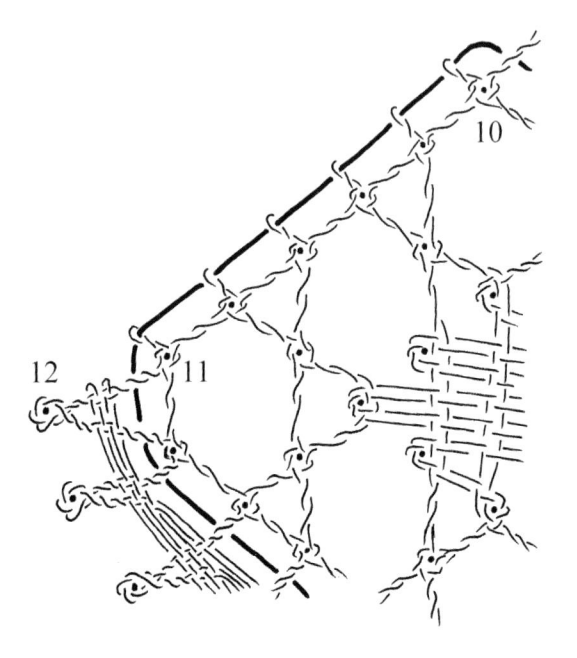

Setting in the second honeycomb area and headside
5 Support a new gimp to the left of the current work. Add new pairs, across this gimp and start the second honeycomb area at pin 10 (figure 170). Add a new pair for each stitch along the continuous row to pin 11. Use a pair from pin 11 to cross the gimp, add two headside passives before making the picot, pin 12, and return across the gimp. (The passives will need supporting.) Complete the honeycomb and mayflower, pass the gimps through the pairs leaving the honeycomb and cross the gimps.

Figure 170 (left) Setting in the honeycomb and headside

Stacking the pairs at the headside[3&3a]
For the valley, each of the pairs from pins 13-16 is cloth stitched, in turn, through the passives to make a picot and returned through two pairs to become the third pair of passives (picots 19-22) (figure 171). There are now six passive pairs.

The valley pin[3b]
The next pair entering the headside from the honeycomb area, pin 17, works the valley pin, pin 23 in the angle of the valley. A picot at this point will not lie comfortably, so the pair from pin 17 is twisted twice as it passes around the pin before returning through two pairs in cloth stitch to become the third pair of passives.

Working out of the valley[3c&d]
The first pin working out of the valley, pin 24, is opposite the third pin of the first continuous row of the next honeycomb area. Therefore the two innermost passive pairs will go to the first and second pins of this row.
1. Cloth stitch the pair from pin 18 through two passive pairs and pass the gimp through these two pairs.
2. Cloth stitch pair 2 towards the left through the edge passives and make a picot, pin 24. Return the picot pair through the passives, pass the gimp through and twist them.
3. Continue working pins 25-27, by cloth stitching the third pair through to the headside, making a picot and returning through the remaining passives, and the gimp, ready for working the next honeycomb area.

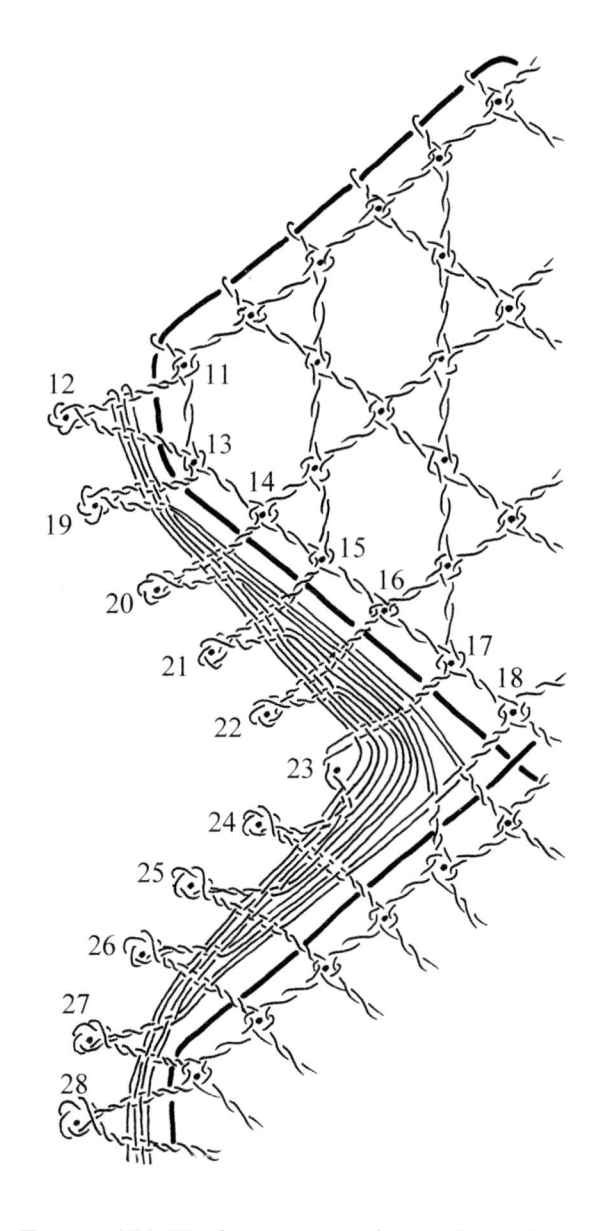

Figure 171 Working into and out of a valley

Work the length of lace required, flip the lace over and join end to start, except for the thick passive thread. Remove the pins and, except for the thick passive thread, darn the ends away. Using the thick passive thread, gather the footside to the size required so that the lace will sit just inside the lower rim of the candleholder. Knot the ends of the thick thread together and trim. Place the lace inside the candleholder.

For making the sample (figure 165), set in the footside at the top pinhole (pattern draft figure 164) and work the ground diagonally down from it. Introduce the gimp and continue adding pairs into the honeycomb area. Add the headside passives as described above.

Chapter 6

END NOTES

1 Drafting The Pattern

1 Using Grid no. 1 (56°, 40 pins per 10 cm along the footside) count from the footside and mark the positions of the gimps for the inner row of honeycomb areas (figure 172).

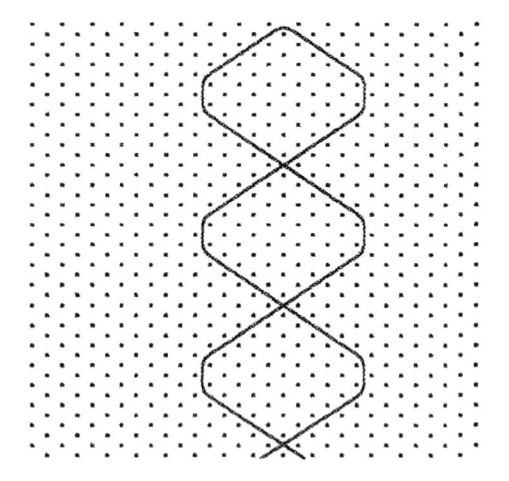

Figure 172 (right) The first line of gimps

2 Counting from the first line of gimps mark in the second line (figure 173).

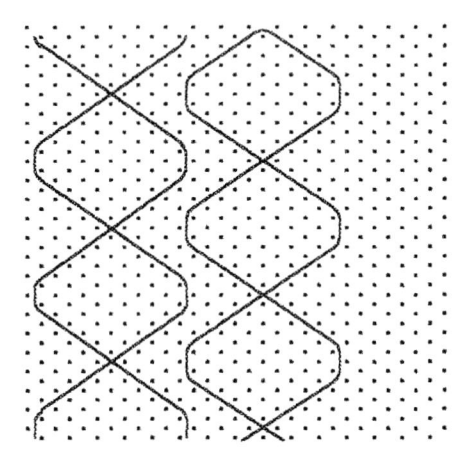

Figure 173 (left) The second line of gimps

3 Remove alternate dots from alternate rows to produce honeycomb areas (figure 174).

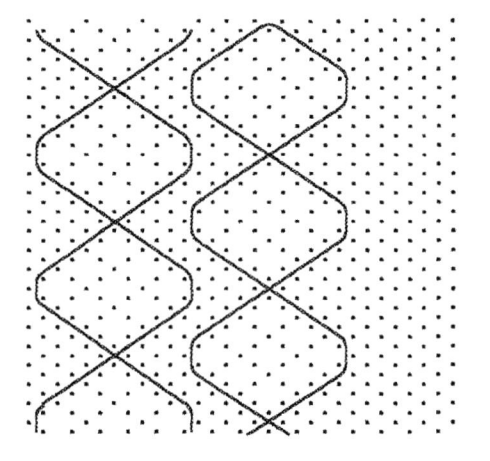

Figure 174 (right) Dots removed to produce honeycomb areas

4 Trim the dots away from the headside gimps and stick onto a piece of plain paper. The pinholes opposite the widest points need to be moved out slightly and allowance must be made for the stacked pairs in the angle of the valley. In this piece, the valley pinhole is in line with the third vertical row of honeycomb pinholes (figure 175)

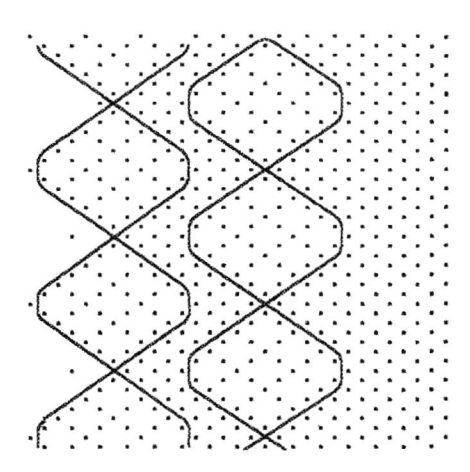

Figure 175 (left) Headside trimmed

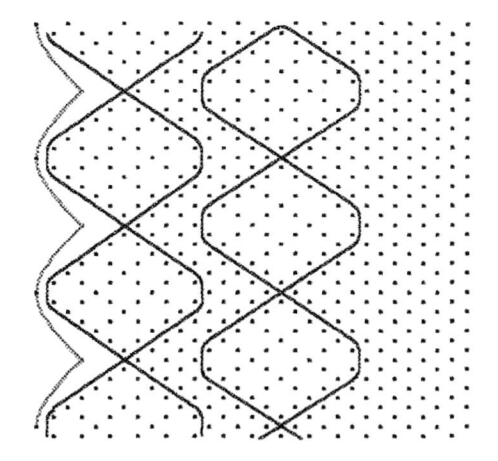

5 Draw a curve from one valley pin, through the centre at the headside to the next valley pin. Repeat for the valleys either side and adjust to get the best effect (figure 176)

Figure 176 (left) Headside curve added

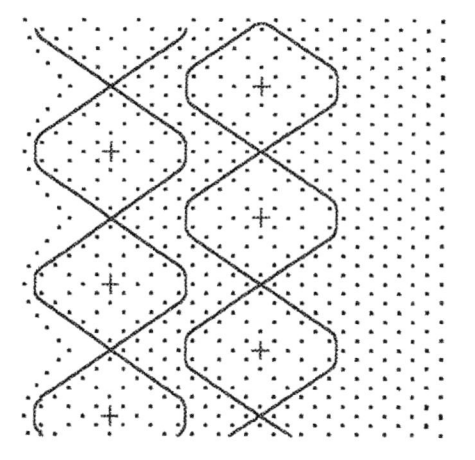

Figure 177 Headside pinholes and mayflower indicators

6 Mark four, equally spaced points, between the headside pinhole and the valley pinhole, and spend time getting this accurate. Place a piece of clear acetate over the headside, and prick from one centre headside pinhole to the valley pinhole. Flip the acetate over and pin through the matching centre headside and valley pinholes of the next section. Prick through the acetate holes to get make an exact repeat. Pin across each head in turn, and prick through the holes (figure 177).
8 Mark crosses in the centres of the honeycomb spaces to indicate the positions of the mayflowers
7 Adjust the footpins (figure 163).

2 Choosing a starting line

The best place for starting a piece, that is to be joined start to finish, is determined by the finishing requirements. The best place to darn away pairs is along a gimp, in clothwork or along passives. Also, from experience, I have found I darn pairs away into ground better from a horizontal start than the traditional diagonal start. A diagonal start is the most convenient position, from which to start, and was therefore favoured by lace workers who were earning a living. However, as this is not the present case, we do not have to start this way. Most patterns and books advise adding all pairs for the headside at the angle of the valley, but this means many pairs being knotted off close to each other with a rather untidy result. It is better to add the pairs across the gimp as the width of the lace increases, and have only two pairs of passives to add before the picot at the widest point. All the other pairs are joined at intervals along the gimp and can be darned away almost invisibly.

This piece was started -
  1 from the footside then horizontally across the ground,
  2 then the honeycomb was started diagonally, with the pairs added across the gimp,
  3 the next point ground stitches were added diagonally. As there are so few pairs added here they can be taken to the nearest gimp to darn them away,
  4 the next honeycomb area was started diagonally, with pairs added across the gimp,
  5 the last two pairs, the headside passives were added as the picot pair goes out.

To work out a starting line, draw a pencil line on the pattern and think through how to join across this line and where you may encounter problems. Then try thinking of two other starting lines, trying to avoid those problems without causing others. Consider which would finish the most successfully.

3 Getting into and out of valleys
When lace has a curved or Vandyked edge the width of the lace, excluding the headside, varies from the widest point of the outside of the curve to the lowest point of the dip between curves. Therefore less pairs will be needed as the lace narrows, and a process is needed in order to stack them tidily. The dip between curves is known as the valley and the pinhole where the lace is at its narrowest the valley pin.

There are many techniques that can be used when negotiating valleys and they fall into several categories that are independent and can be combined in many ways. The main categories are -
  a stacking pairs when working into the valley
  b the valley pin
  c negotiating the angle of the valley without leaving holes
  d taking pairs out of the stack when working out of the valley

3a Working into the valley and stacking pairs in the valley
At pin 12 (figure 171) the width of the lace, excluding the headside, is at its widest. At the valley pin, pin 23, where the gimps surrounding the honeycomb areas closest to the headside are crossed, the lace is at its narrowest, and therefore less pairs are needed. After completing the honeycomb area next to the headside and crossing the gimps below it, the pairs are hanging out past the gimp and they need to be stacked tidily.

In the following samples, each of the first four pairs from the honeycomb ground, is taken in turn through the passives in cloth stitch to make a picot and return through one or two pairs in cloth stitch before being left as the second or third pair of passives.

3b The valley pin
Headside pins are usually worked as picots however, if there is a valley that dips to an angle of less than 90°, a picot used at the valley pin will probably look unsightly because the two sides of the valley pinch it in.

Alternatives for the valley pin are
  i   workers twisted twice as they pass round the pin
  ii   honeycomb stitch worked using the edge pair and workers.
  iii if the angle of the valley is greater than 90° a picot should be suitable.

Chapter 6

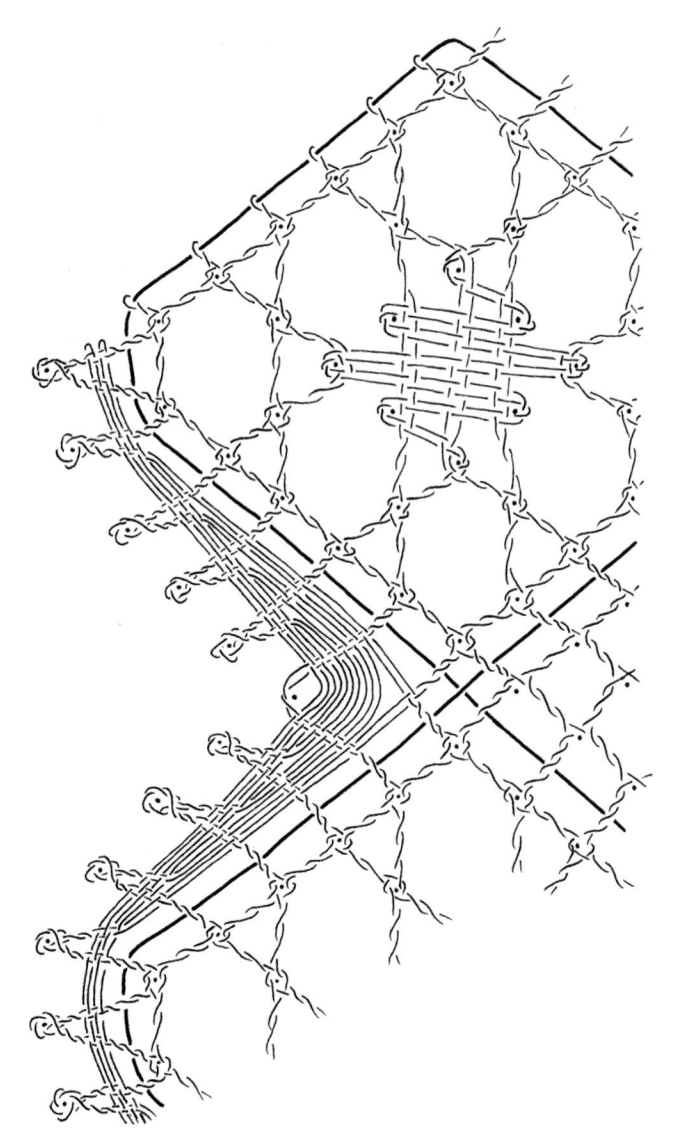

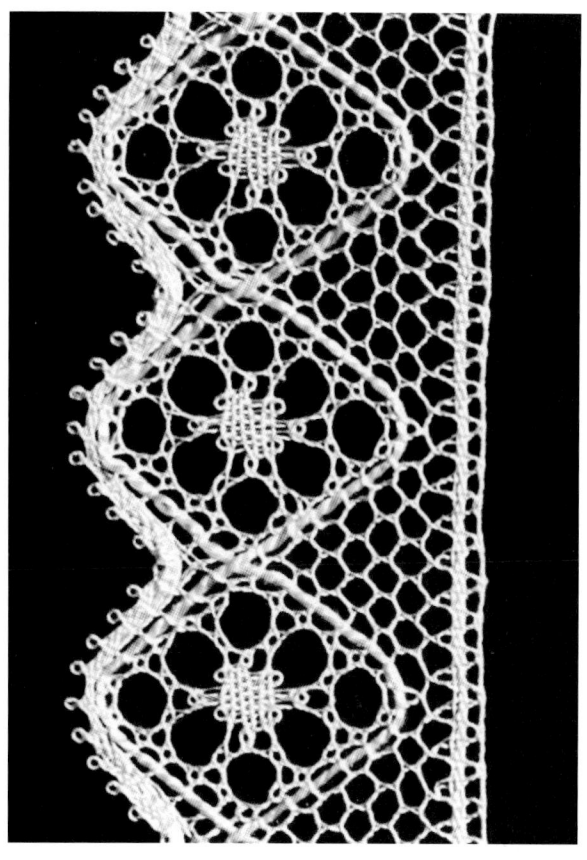

Figure 178 (left) thread diagram

Figure 179 (above) lace

a stacking through two pairs
b two twists around the valley pin
c symmetrical valley
d mayflower

3c Negotiating the valley without leaving holes
i When the valley is worked symmetrically as in (figures 178 & 179) the passive pairs tend to 'climb up' the valley pin because that is where the tension is taking them.
ii The last pair going into the valley from the honeycomb can be worked through the passives to make the first picot working out of the valley (figures 180 & 181). This helps to fill the angle of the valley but sometimes produces an unsightly 'dimple' in the edge of the passives where it starts working through them.
iii The pair working the valley pin cloth stitches back through two passive pairs, the second of which cloth stitches out to make the first picot working out of the valley (figures 182 & 183). This tends to fill the angle but has a weak spot where the pair that works the valley pin exchanges with the pair that works the first picot going out of the valley.

69

Chapter 6

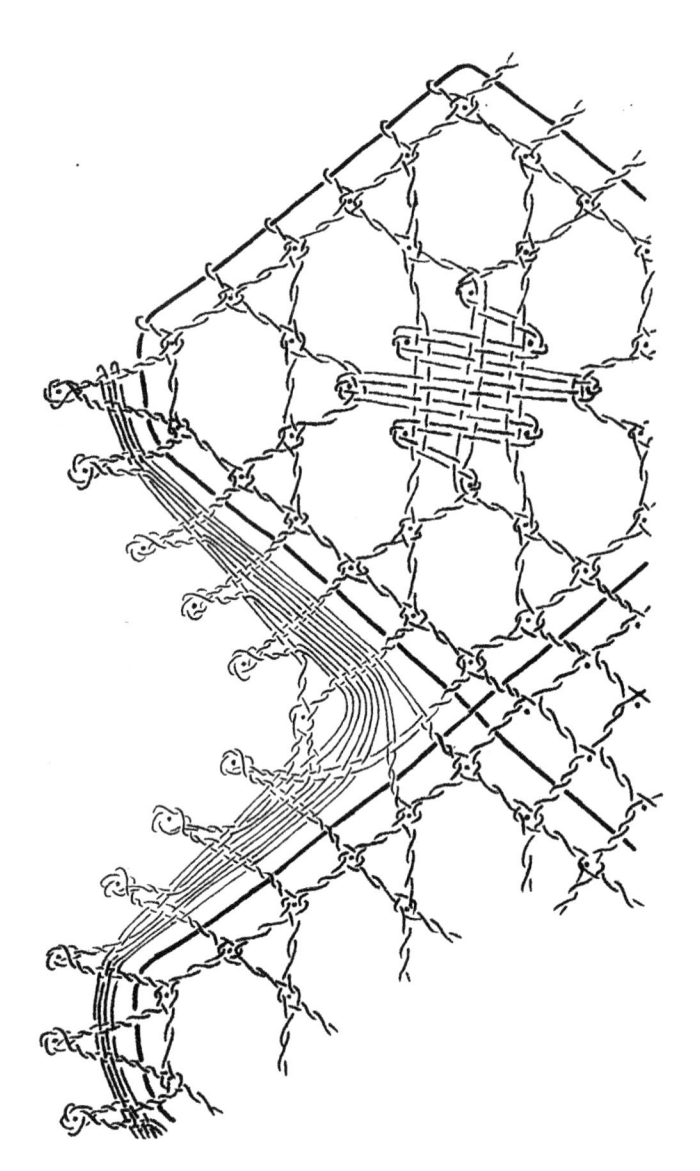

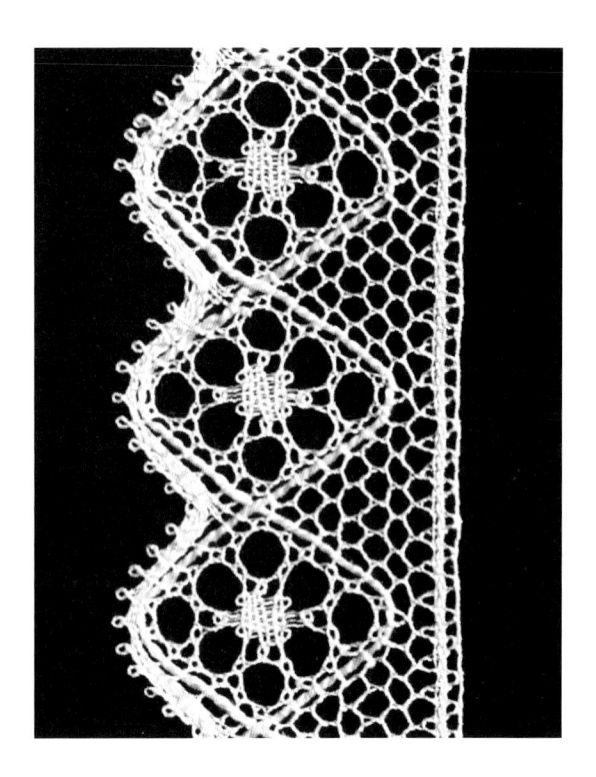

Figure 180 (left) thread diagram

Figure 181 (above) lace

a stacking through one pair
b honeycomb stitch around the valley pin
c working out of the valley, take last pair from honeycomb area to work 1st picot
d mayflowers

3d Working out of the valley
As the lace gets wider pairs are taken out of the stack, and made available for working the next area of honeycomb ground, by reversing the stacking process. If the picot pairs were stacked by cloth stitching through two pairs to become pair 3, then pair 3 will work through the passives to make the picot, then work back across the remaining passives to enter the honeycomb. If the picot pairs cloth stitch back through one pair to become pair 2 when stacking then, when working out of the valley, pair 2 will be used to make the picot, before cloth stitching across the remaining passives to enter the honeycomb.

Chapter 6

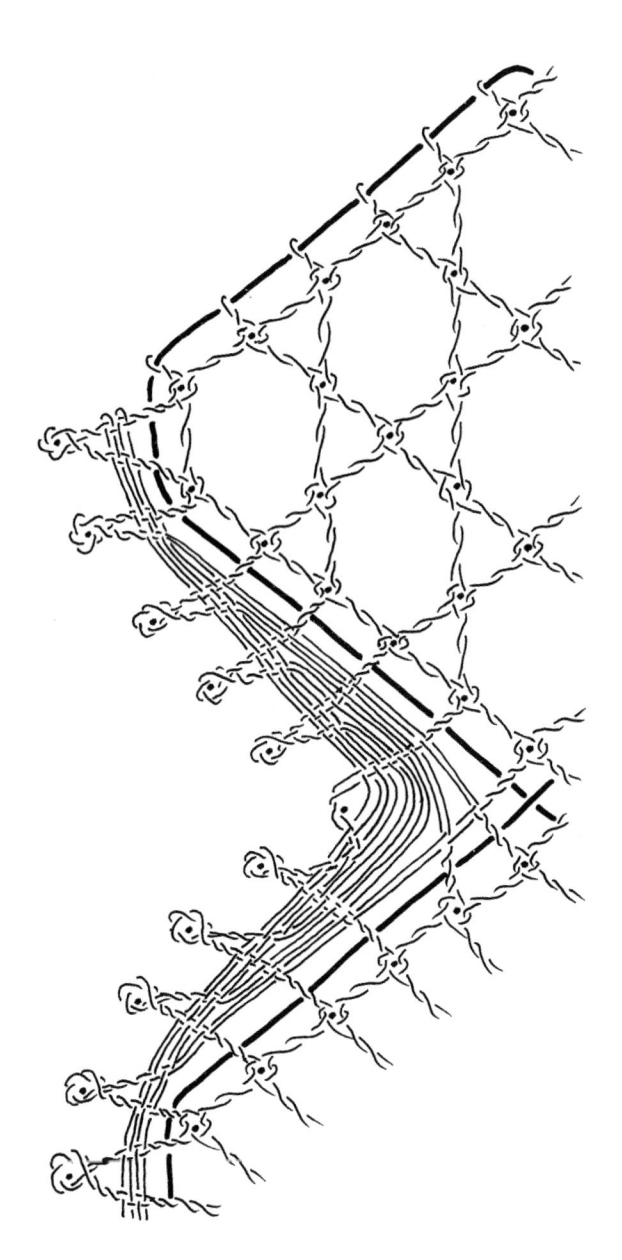

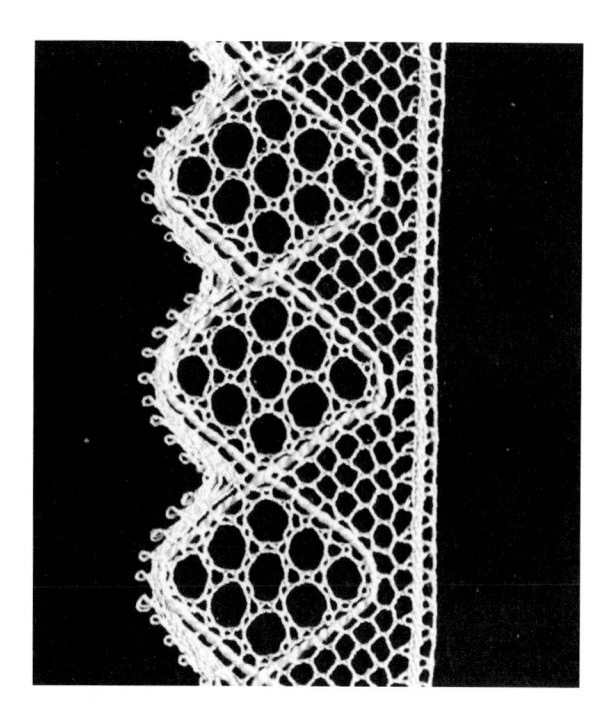

Figure 182 (left) thread diagram

Figure 183 (above) lace

a stacking through two pairs
b two twists around the valley pin
c working out of the valley - 2nd passive pair to make 1st picot
d no mayflowers

4 Managing large numbers of bobbins
Better results are achieved when there is plenty of room to work, and bobbins can be shifted from side to side to get the best possible tension. With relatively small numbers of bobbins this is achieved by using a cover cloth, across the pillow, pricking and lace behind the pins in use, and placing the bobbins, not currently being used on this cover cloth, as far round to the back as possible. When larger numbers of bobbins are needed, than can be comfortably accommodated on the pillow, they need to be stacked out of the way.

Chapter 6

4a Using stitch pins
Bobbins not currently in use can be threaded on stitch pins and heaped at the back of the pillow (figure 184)

Figure 184 Stacking bobbins on stitch pins

4b Layering
Push the bobbins not currently in use back out of the way and pin a cover cloth tightly across them (figure 185). Other bobbins not currently in use can be moved out of the way onto this area. When using larger numbers of bobbins several layers can be made.

Figure 185 Stacking bobbins by layering

Chapter 7

PROJECTS 5 & 6 MIRROR MOTIFS (Plates 2 & 6)

Project 5 **Mirror Motif** (Hexagon)
Project 6 **Mirror Motif** (Pentagon)

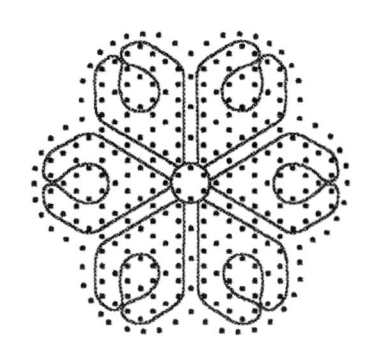

Figure 186 (left) Handbag mirror

Figure 187 (above) Pattern draft

Figure 188 (below) Motif

New Techniques
  starting a hexagonal/circular motif
  working a hexagonal motif
  picots in shallow valleys
  modified honeycomb stitch
  mounting lace on a backing

Materials required
  pricking (figure 187)[1]
  14 pairs Egyptian cotton no. 60
  1 pair perle thread, no 8
  handbag mirror kit

End Notes
  1 drafting the pattern
  2 pentagons
  3 Adapting an edging to produce a hexagon or pentagon
  4 dressing a pillow for a hexagonal/pentagonal/circular motif
  5 moving cover cloths and pushing down pins
  6 modified honeycomb stitch (alternative version)

Chapter 7

Working a hexagonal motif[4&5]
A hexagonal motif is drafted on a grid with a 60° angle and consists of six sections, each of which could be part of a straight edging. The sections meet along a line of ground, in this case honeycomb ground. It is important to identify the sections and the diagonals where they meet as the working cloth, or worker, should be placed parallel to the horizontal line through the centre of the section (figure 189). This is your 'horizon' when working the section and all continuous and point ground rows should work towards it.

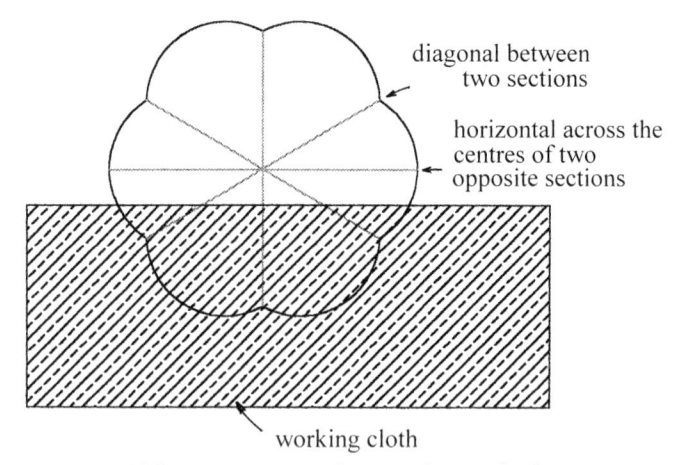

Figure 189 Positioning the working cloth

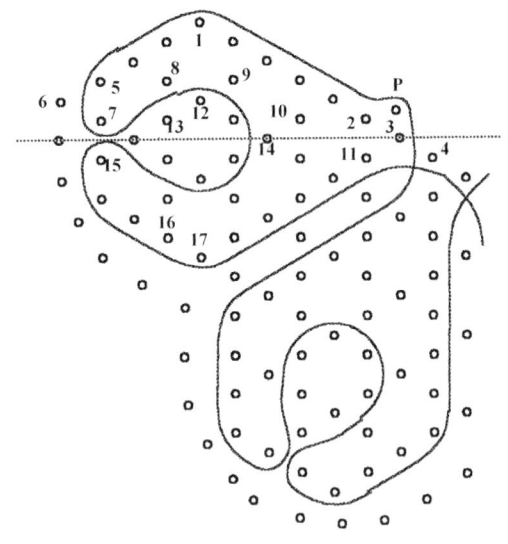

Figure 190 Setting in

Setting in
1. Start with two pairs crossing the gimps and make a honeycomb stitch at pin 1 (figure 190). Work to the right adding a pair, at each honeycomb stitch, down the row to pin 2. Make an extra hole for pin P, to hold the gimp in such a way that, when the motif has been completed, the gimps will join at the point between the two honeycomb stitches of the final gap row. The join occurs just below the centre in figure 188. Add the last pair within the gimp, pin 3.
2. Pass the gimp through the last pair of the honeycomb and make a honeycomb stitch with a new pair at pin 4. This is the last pinhole of the first row on the diagonal between the sections, and is part of the central ring. Pass the gimp through the nearest pair, from this stitch, and twist the pair.
3. Return to the unused pair from pin 1 and work, towards the left, down the row, adding a pair at each stitch, as far as pin 5.
4. Pass the gimp through the left pair from pin 5 and twist the pair. Cloth stitch this pair through two new pairs, the headside passives, make a picot, pin 6, and return it through the passives and the gimp and make a honeycomb stitch, pin 7, with the remaining pair from pin 5. This is part of a gap row. With the next two pairs on the right make the other honeycomb stitch of the gap row, pin 8.
5. Make the three stitches of the gap row along the other diagonal pins 9-11.
6. Pass the gimp through pairs 3-8.
7. The area within the gimp is a cloth stitch diamond, with three pins along each side like a Mayflower. Start at pin 12 with the pairs from pins 8 & 9 and, work the first row towards the left. Work the diamond as far as pin 13). Cloth stitch across the row, but now the workers travel across the gimp to make a modified honeycomb stitch in the ground, pin 14 (figure 191), and return across the gimp to finish the cloth stitch area. There are no twists between the workers and the gimp on the cloth stitch side of the gimp as they pass out and return.

74

Modified Honeycomb stitch[6]

8 For the same reason that we modify the ground adjacent to the footside by using catch-pins, here we modify the honeycomb stitch to prevent the increased tension, required to firm up cloth stitch, from causing threads to be pulled out of position (figure 191). This version is worked as -

   cloth stitch, twist twice, pin, half stitch, twist.

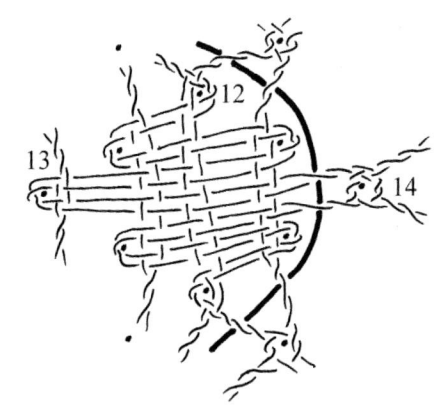

Figure 191 (right) Modified honeycomb stitch

The cloth stitch results in both cloth stitch workers passing around pin 14. The following two twists imitate the two twist of the honeycomb stitch. After the pin is set up cover it with the normal second half of a honeycomb stitch

Continue the section

9 Complete the cloth stitch area, twist the pairs, pass the gimp through all the pairs from the diamond and twist the pairs again.
10 The other pair from pin 7 (figure 190) works out to make a picot and returns past the gimp to make the first of the gap row stitches, pin 15, with the first pair from the diamond. Work the other gap row stitch on this side and the two stitches of the gap row on the other side of the diamond.
11 With a pair from pin 15 make another picot and work the continuous row to pin 16. Starting with a pair from pin 11, work the continuous row to pin 17.
12 Pass the headside gimp through the pairs from the honeycomb until it meets the other gimp, near the centre, and cross them.
13 Work the remaining three honeycomb stitches of the gap row along the diagonal between the sections, and pass the nearest gimp through the pairs from these stitches..
14 Work into and out of the valley moving the working cloth to its next position parallel to the horizontal line through the centre of the next section (See End Notes). Since the valleys are very shallow, picots can be used for the valley pins.

The Next Section[5]

Use the innermost headside passives from the previous section and a pair from the outermost honeycomb stitch to start the continuous rows of honeycomb. The last pair from this row crosses the gimp to work the last stitch, of the row, which is on the diagonal between this, and the next, sections. Continue as for the previous section.

Continue round the motif completing each section and moving the cover cloths before starting the following section (see End Notes 4).

When the end meets the start, sew the ends through and knot leaving at least 15 cms (6 ins) thread. Do not cut these ends off, as they will be needed when mounting

Chapter 7

Mounting a motif in a mirror
1 Cut out a piece of felt, or other suitable fabric, using the template supplied with the mirror.
2 Place the motif, with the knots against the fabric, in the centre of the circle of fabric. Pin, and then tack, one half of the motif to the fabric, leaving the line of knots just free along the edge of the tacking.
3 Starting from the centre, thread both threads from a knot through the eye of a needle and pass through the fabric immediately behind the knot. Leave the ends loose at the back. Repeat for the threads from the next knot. Take the two pairs of threads, now at the back, and tie a reef knot. Firm up the first half of the knot so that the knot in the lace on the other side of the fabric is pulled partway into the fabric. Do not over tension as this will distort the lace. Repeat for the remaining pairs and trim the ends.
4 Using a piece of the lace thread make several small stitches around the motif to keep it in place.
5 Assemble the mirror according to the manufacturer's instructions.

PROJECT 6 MIRROR MOTIF (pentagon[2])

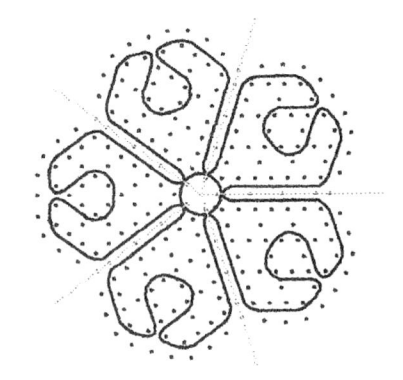

Figure 192 Handbag mirror motif

Figure 193 (above) Pattern draft

Figure 194 (below) Motif

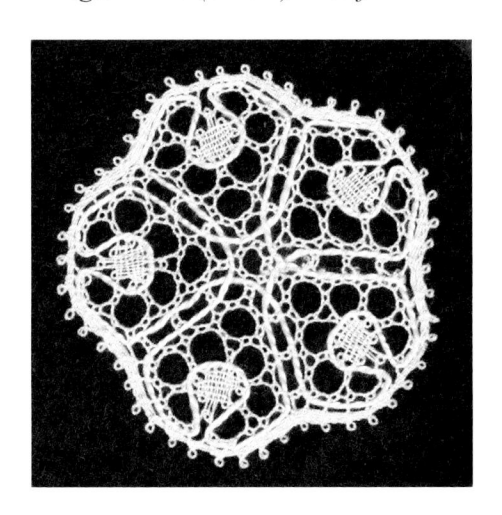

Materials required
   pricking (figure 193)[1,2&3]
   14 pairs Egyptian cotton no. 60
   1 pair perle thread, no 8
   mirror kit

Follow the instructions for the hexagonal motif above, the only differences between this and the hexagonal motif are that there are only five sections and the centre honeycomb ring has five pins, not six.

END NOTES

1a Drafting the pattern[2&3]

Use Grid no. 3 (60°, 40 pins per 10 cm vertically per section) for the hexagon or, Grid 4 (54°, 40 pins per 10 cm vertically per section) for the pentagon.

1 From a centre dot draw the six diagonals that divide the sections (figure 195).

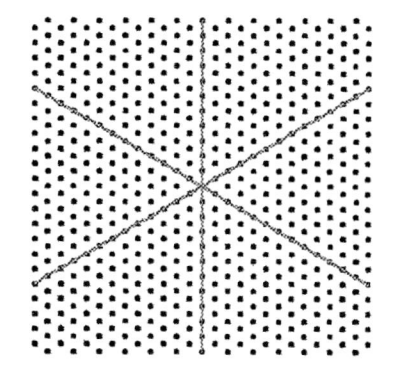

Figure 195 (right) Drawing the diagonals

2 Draw the gimps. Start with the centre honeycomb ring drawing a circle around the six dots around the centre point. From this circle draw a line each side of the diagonals. Then draw in the line at the headside, and lastly the line around the cloth stitch area (figure 196).

Figure 196 (left) Drawing the gimps

3 Remove alternate dots within the gimps for the honeycomb. The whole area is regular with alternate dots removed from alternate lines (figure 197)

Figure 197 (right) Dots removed for honeycomb

4 Trim along the headside gimps, removing unwanted dots, and stick onto white paper (figure 198).

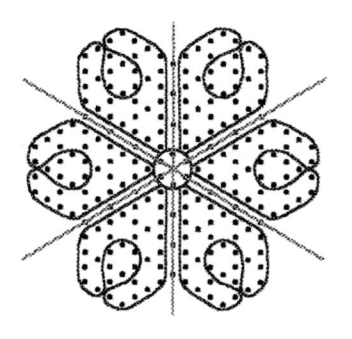

Figure 198 (left) Edges trimmed

Chapter 7

5 Draw the line of the headside around three heads, i.e. the head you are working on and the one either side, so that you can see the relationship between the one you are working on and its neighbours. The heads either side have an effect on the spacing of the dots (figure 199),

Figure 199 (right) Drawing the headside line

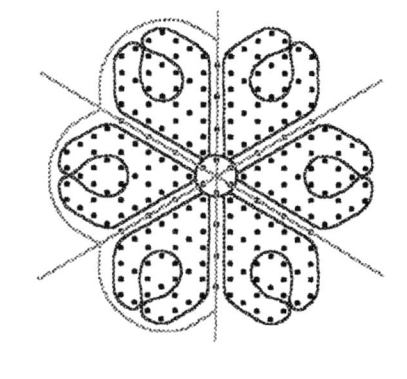

6 Draw the dots along the headside line of one head, spacing them evenly (figure 200).

Figure 200 (left) The headside dots around one head

7 Make a transparent template of the headside dots and prick the adjacent two heads (figure 201), adjusting the dots in the valleys if necessary.

Figure 201 (right) The headside dots around three heads with the dots adjusted in the valleys

8 Use the transparent template and prick the headside dots around the remaining heads. The diagonals may be left in or removed (figure 187).

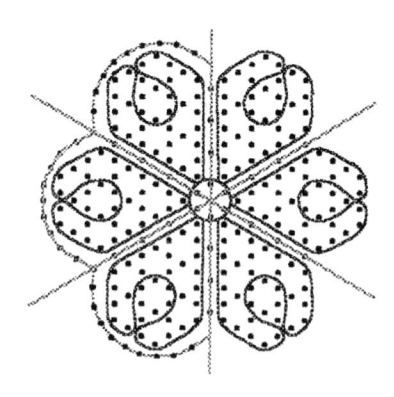

2 Pentagons[3]
When a circle is divided into five sections each section has an equivalent angle to the footside of 54°. Thus we can make pentagonal motifs. To plot this motif use the pentagonal grid, Grid no 4, and plot each section as for the hexagonal motif.

3 Adapting an edging to produce a hexagons or pentagon
Of all the design techniques, this is the easiest. Using two plain rectangular mirrors, place them on an edging so that they lie along the two diagonals of the ground. If the angle to the footside is 60° you will see a hexagon (figure 202); if it is 54° you will see a pentagon (figure 204). (If the angle is neither of these there will still be a recognisable motif that can be interpreted as one of these). Sometimes it is easier to draft the edging before translating it to a motif (figures 203 & 205). The mirrors are easier to handle if transparent sticky tape is used to hinge them together.

Chapter 7

Figure 202 Using mirrors to see a hexagon

Figure 203 The positions of the mirrors on the pattern draft

Figure 204 Using mirrors to see a pentagon

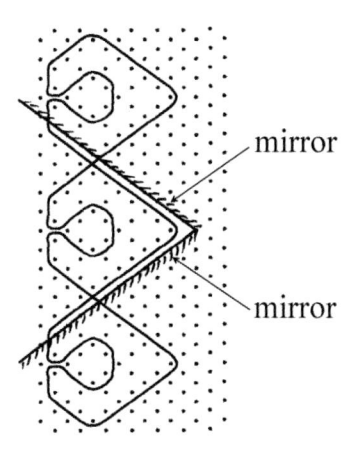

Figure 205 The positions of the mirrors on the pattern draft

4 Dressing a pillow for a hexagonal/pentagonal motif
The cover cloth is always placed parallel to the horizontal line through the centre of the section currently being made. This provides the 'horizon' to which you work, i.e. continuous rows can only be worked diagonally downwards towards the edge of the cover cloth; never backwards away from it. The row of honeycomb stitches along the diagonal can belong to either section.

5 Moving cover cloths and pushing down pins
After completing a section move the cover cloths to provide the 'horizon' for the next section. After passing the halfway line the pins from the first section become a nuisance and they can be pushed right into the pillow so that the heads meet the card. There are specialist tools that can be used to push pins down, sometimes called 'push me pull yous' or use the square end of an ordinary wooden pencil. Place a cover cloth across the heads of the pins, to stop the threads from catching on them (figure 206), and replace the working cloth in its correct position (figure 207). Push down more pins and adjust the cover cloth after each section has been completed.

Chapter 7

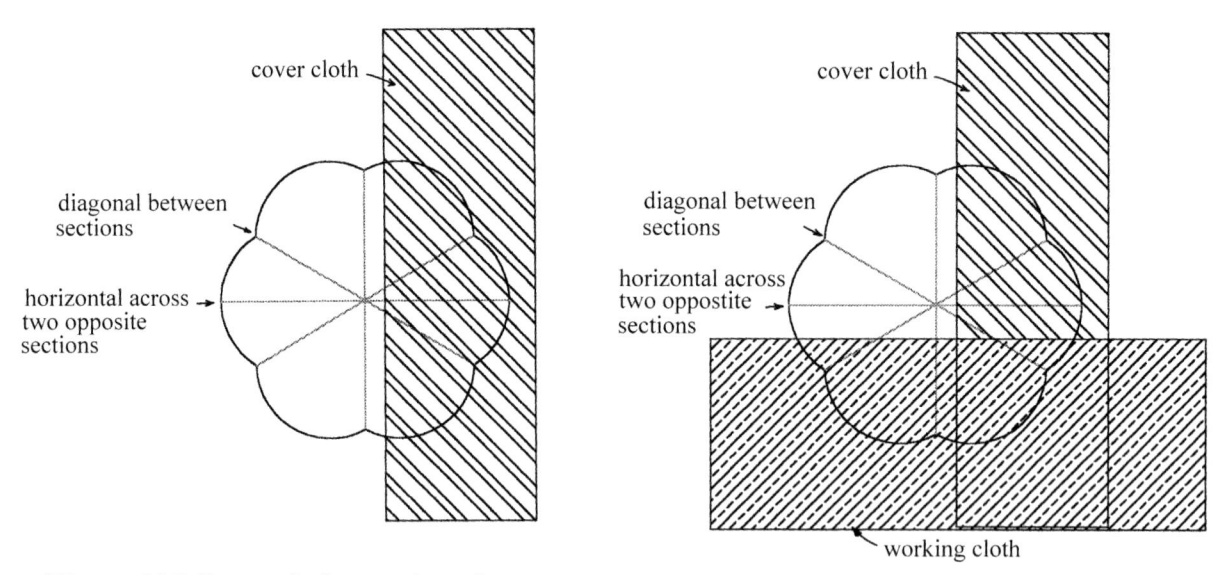

Figure 206 Cover cloth covering pins

Figure 207 Working cloth

6 Modified Honeycomb Stitch (alternative version)
Different parts of the East Midlands lacemaking area developed slightly different techniques, and sometimes local traditions link certain techniques with particular areas. The modified honeycomb stitch described above is believed to be of North Bucks origin. This alternative form is believed to be of South Bucks origin. The two are very similar and have very similar results, the only difference being that the pin is covered using a cloth stitch and two twists (figure 208), instead of a half stitch and twist (figure 191).

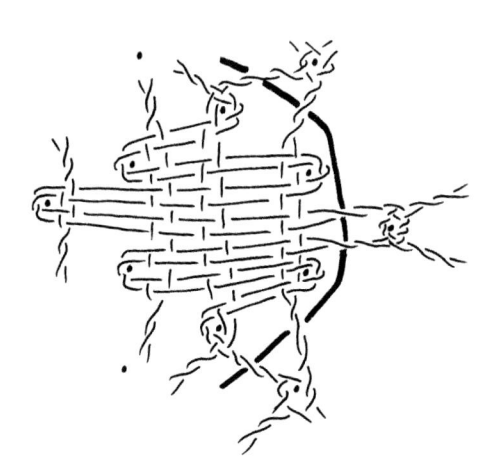

Figure 208 Modified honeycomb stitch, South Bucks version

80

Chapter 8
PROJECT 7   HANDKERCHIEF JABOT (Plate 6)

Figure 209 Handkerchief folded as a jabot

New Techniques
starting at a corner
corner changing direction along the diagonal at 45° to the footside
cornering the footside
cornering a straight headside
cloth stitch trail
gimp fingers within ground
folding a square into a jabot
seven-pin honeycomb ring

Materials
  pricking (figure 210)[1]
  25 pairs bobbins Egyptian cotton no. 60
  1 pair + one single gimp, perle no. 8
    + extra pair gimps for corner
  20 cm (8 in) square fine linen or cotton fabric
  ballpoint needle

End Notes
  1 drafting the pattern
  2 cornering a Geometrical Bucks point
    pattern
  3 schematic diagrams
  4 cloth stitch trail
  5 block & 'U' shaped pillows

Chapter 8

Figure 210 Pattern draft

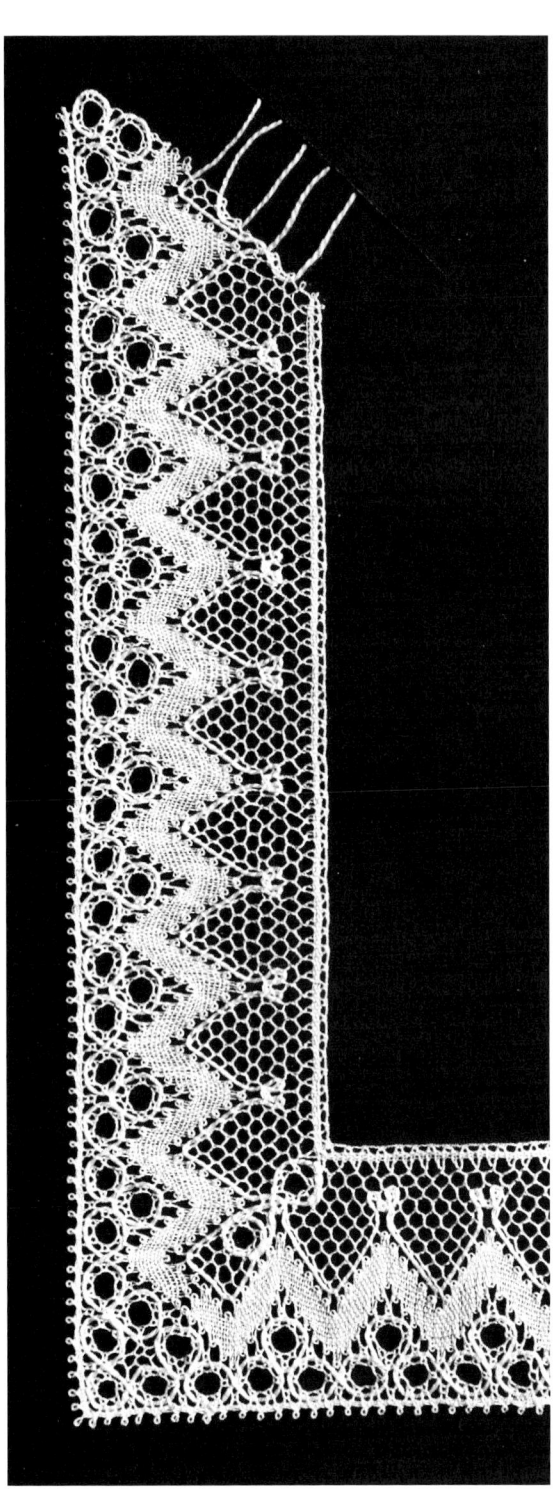

Figure 211 Lace edging

82

Chapter 8

Setting in[4]

1 Start along the diagonal through the corner with the triangle of three honeycomb rings, A, B & C. Start at pin 1 and add pairs as required until the picot, pin 2, has been made. Return the picot pair across the gimp to make the next honeycomb stitch, in ring A. Continue the other side of the ring making a point ground stitch at pin 3. (For the majority of repeats this pin will be a honeycomb stitch but, in this design, the corner has point ground stitches.) Complete the ring and cross the gimps (figure 212)

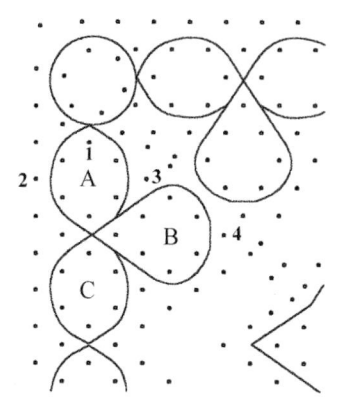

Figure 212 (right) Setting in the first honeycomb ring

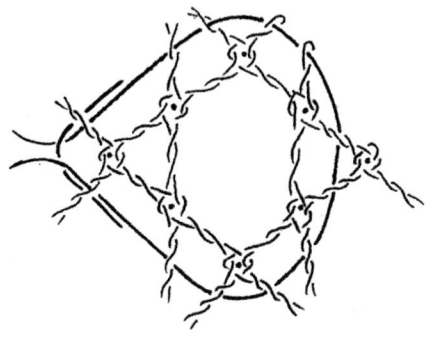

2 Continue adding pairs as required and make the second ring, B. This ring is a seven-pin honeycomb ring, the gimp enclosing seven honeycomb stitches (figure 212). The single pinhole at the side of the seven-pin ring, pin 4, is a honeycomb stitch (figure 213).

3 Make the third honeycomb ring to complete the triangle.

Figure 213 (left) Seven-pin honeycomb ring

4 Start the cloth stitch trail at its top point, pin 5. Using a pair from the single honeycomb stitch and a new pair and work the first row towards the left. Continue working the trail adding two new pairs, one at the end of the next row worked towards the right and one at the widest point of the trail, pin 6. The pairs added into the trail will need supporting. Then work the trail to its first corner, pin 7 (figure 214).

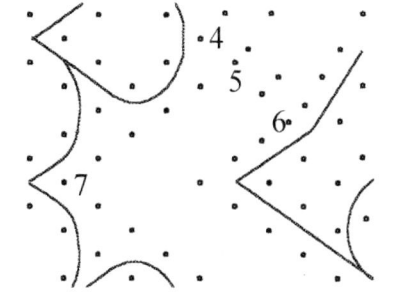

Figure 214 (right) Setting in the trail

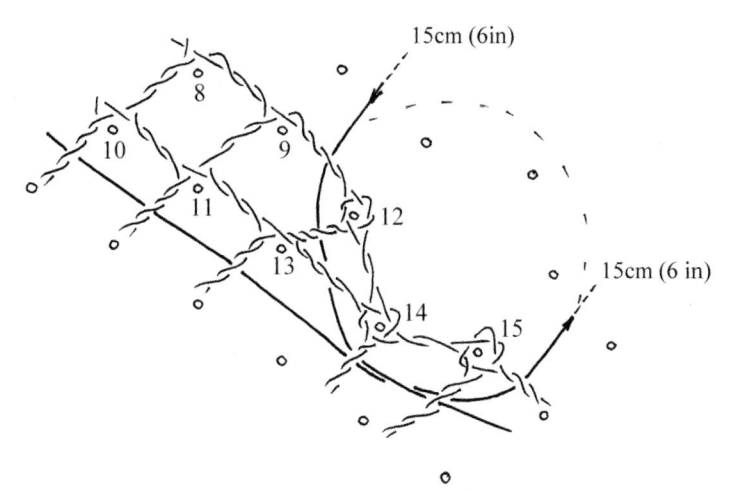

Figure 215 Setting in the point ground and half a honeycomb ring

5 Add a single gimp leaving about 15 cms (6 ins) above the start to allow for finishing off when the lace has been completed (figure 215), and leave this amount when starting or leaving out other gimps along the starting line. Pass the gimp through the two pairs left out from the trail.

6 Add pairs and work two point ground stitches, pins 8 & 9 down the diagonal towards the inner corner and work the two stitches that can be made with the other pair from the trail, pins 10 & 11 (figure 215).

83

Chapter 8

7   Introduce a new gimp and work the three honeycomb stitches of the half-ring, adding a pair at pins 12 & 15. The position of pin 13, outside the ring, is distorted to accommodate the 45° angle of the corner. Cross the gimps, when they meet, double the right one up and leave it out.

8   Add a pair and make the next point ground stitch along the starting line, pin 16 (figure 216).

9   Pass the gimp through and work the trail as far as its next corner, pin 17. Work the next triangle of honeycomb rings at the headside, the single stitches between the rings and the trail are honeycomb stitches, and work the trail until it changes direction.

10 Along the corner, pass the gimp through the remaining pair from the single point ground stitch, pin 16, add a pair across this gimp and make a honeycomb stitch, pin 18.

11 Introduce another single gimp across the current gimp and pass it through the two honeycomb pairs from pin 18 and the pairs left out from the trail. Work a row of point ground along the trail.

12 Add pairs as required, and work three honeycomb stitches for the next half-ring, along the corner, as before. Pass the gimp through the ring pairs and throw the gimp out. Work as many rows of point ground towards the trail as possible.

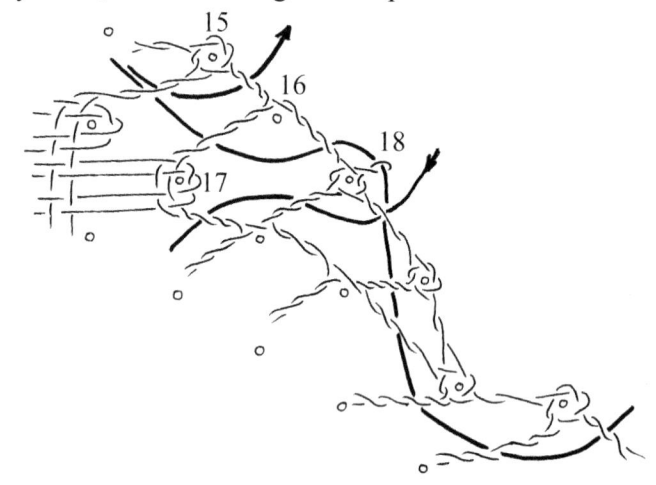

Figure 216 Setting in the finger

13 Work a point ground stitch with the last pair from the ring and a new pair (this pair will need supporting) as a catch-pin stitch, pin 19, (figure 217) and work a row of ground. Cloth stitch through two new pairs, the footside passives, and twist the workers. Cloth stitch through the last new pair, the edge pair, set up a pin, pin 20. Return the worker through the footside passives to make the next catch-pin stitch. Support the last three new pairs on a pin.

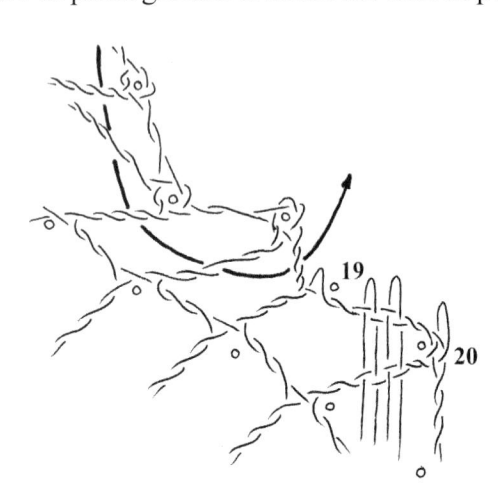

Figure 217 (left) Setting in the footside

Continue making point ground, trail and honeycomb rings until the gimps approach the fingers extending into the point ground. Work the trail as far as possible below the fingers. Work point ground from the footside until the gimp of the top finger is reached; then work the footside and catch-pin stitch of the next row.

Gimp fingers in ground

1 Pass the gimp through the pairs and make a honeycomb stitch in the top finger, pin 1, (figure 218).
2 Pass the gimp back through these pairs and one pair from the ground so that the pairs bridge the gimps, i.e. there are no twists between the two gimps where they touch. Make a honeycomb stitch, pin 2.
3 Make a point ground stitch with the other pair from the stitch in the top finger, pin 1, and the point ground pair on the right, pin 3.
4 Pass the gimp back through the two honeycomb pairs and a point ground pair at pin 3. Make the honeycomb stitch in the lower finger, pin 4.
5 Pass the gimp through the finger pairs and the pair from pin 2, bridging the gimps across this pair, and down through the trail pairs.
6 The first point ground stitch below the fingers is made with the pair from the point of the trail and a pair from the honeycomb stitch between the fingers, pin 2.

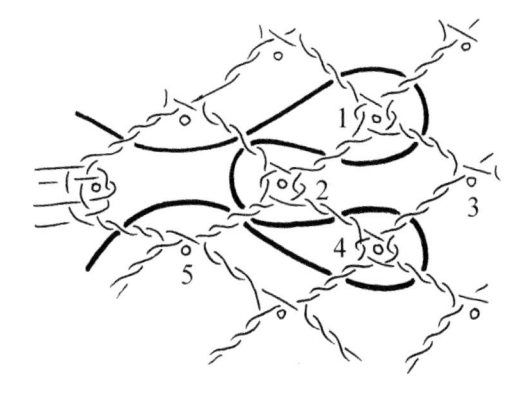

Figure 218 Fingers

Continue making the edging until there are 11 pairs of fingers.

Working into the corner [2,3&4]

1 Work the footside up to, and including, the pinhole immediately before the one on the diagonal through the corner, pin 1, and make the catch-pin stitch. Work rows of point ground from the footside towards the trail, except for the row from this last catch-pin stitch (figure 219).
2 Introduce a pair of gimps, for the inner ring, A, and, starting with this catch-pin pair, work three honeycomb stitches, with a catch-pin outside the gimp, and cross the gimps. One pair will pass out of the ring across the crossed gimps, and the other two pairs will cross the diagonal through the corner and will not be used until the corner has been turned.
3 Make the honeycomb stitch in the single finger, pin 2, pass the gimp through the pairs, work the single point ground stitch before the next ring, pin 3. One pair from the finger and a pair from the point ground stitch will cross the diagonal.

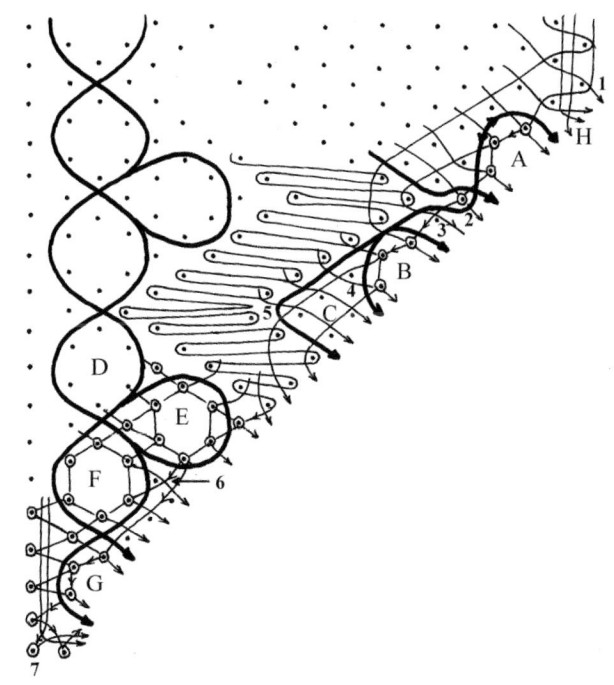

Figure 219 Working into the corner

    4 Introduce another pair of gimps for the honeycomb ring between the trails, B, and pass the new gimp towards the left through the left pair from pin 3, across the other gimp, and down through the rest of the pairs left out from the trail. Work three honeycomb stitches of ring B,

starting with the left pair that has crossed the gimp from the point ground stitch and pass the gimp through the last pair. Make a catch-pin stitch outside the ring, pin 4. Two pairs from honeycomb stitches will cross the diagonal the other will cross the gimp.

5 Make four point ground stitches between the ring and the trail, area C, and pass the trail gimp through. Two pairs and the gimp will cross the diagonal.

6 If the last section of the trail is worked normally, due to the design of the corner, it cannot be completed successfully. However, by making a back stitch, to change the alignment of the worker, the trail can be completed successfully.

6 Using a back stitch to change the alignment of the trail workers

7 Work the trail as far as the inside pin, pin 5 and twist the workers <u>once</u>. Return to the other side of the trail and back to the inner edge. Remove the corner pin, pin 5, and pin under the worker in the same pinhole, ignoring the previous loop. This loop will be absorbed into the trail. Do not firm up the workers too strongly, or you may pull this loop back too far

8 Complete the trail as for working the lower half of a diamond (not forgetting to cover the last pin). Work the triangle of three rings, D, E & F (at this point the stitch between the last two rings, pin 6, is a catch-pin stitch, not honeycomb). Work the next two picots and honeycomb stitch at the headside, returning the picot pair through the headside passives.

9 Work the three point ground stitches adjacent to ring F, starting with the remaining pair from the second of the triangle of rings, E, and the pair from the catch-pin stitch at the side of the third of the triangle of three rings, F. This seems a strange arrangement but it is necessary in order to negotiate the corner.

10 Work three honeycomb stitches of the ring at the outer point of the corner, G. After working the third honeycomb stitch the pair leaves the ring to make the picot, but only returns through the headside passives. The second pair of passives becomes the picot pair, and works out to make the picot at the point of the corner, pin 7.

11 At the footside, cloth stitch the remaining catch-pin pair through both the footside passive pairs, at H, and cloth stitch with the two original passive pairs now pairs 3 & 4, and leave them.

The first half of the corner is now complete. Turn the pillow through 90°, or lift the lace and replace it so that the next section of the pricking lies towards you. Work out of the corner starting from the headside.

Working out of the corner

12 Work the picot pair through the passives, and take the second passives pair out to make the first picot on this side of the diagonal, pin 8, (figure 220) and return across the gimp.

13 Complete the corner ring G, and use the right pair from the last pin to start the line of three point ground stitches along the diagonal to pin 9.

14 Work the triangle of rings. Start the second ring, K, with the remaining pair from the catch-pin stitch at the side of the first ring, J, and the remaining pair from the last point ground stitch, pin 9.

15 Start the trail, working the first row towards the headside, and continue as far as its first corner.

16 Below the trail and gimp, work two rows of point ground stitches.

17 Complete ring B, working a catch-pin stitch at the side, and cross the gimps so that the one following the trail doubles up around the ring and is thrown out, while the one it doubles with

doubles back along the trail gimp to be thrown out. The gimp from the left side of the ring becomes the new gimp following the trail.

18 Work the point ground stitch next to the diagonal, pin 10.
19 Work the trail as far as its next corner, and the next triangle of rings at the headside.
20 Work the single honeycomb stitch in the finger, pin 11, and cross the gimp from ring A with the gimp along the trail.
21 Starting with the first pair left out from the trail, with the pair from the finger, work the row of point ground below the trail and gimp.
22 Complete ring A (the stitch at the side of the ring can be pinned as a catch-pin Stitch mine looked better like this) and double up and throw out both gimps. Work the next three rows of point ground.
23 With the remaining pair from ring A, and the pair to its right, make a catch-pin stitch and work the next row of ground.

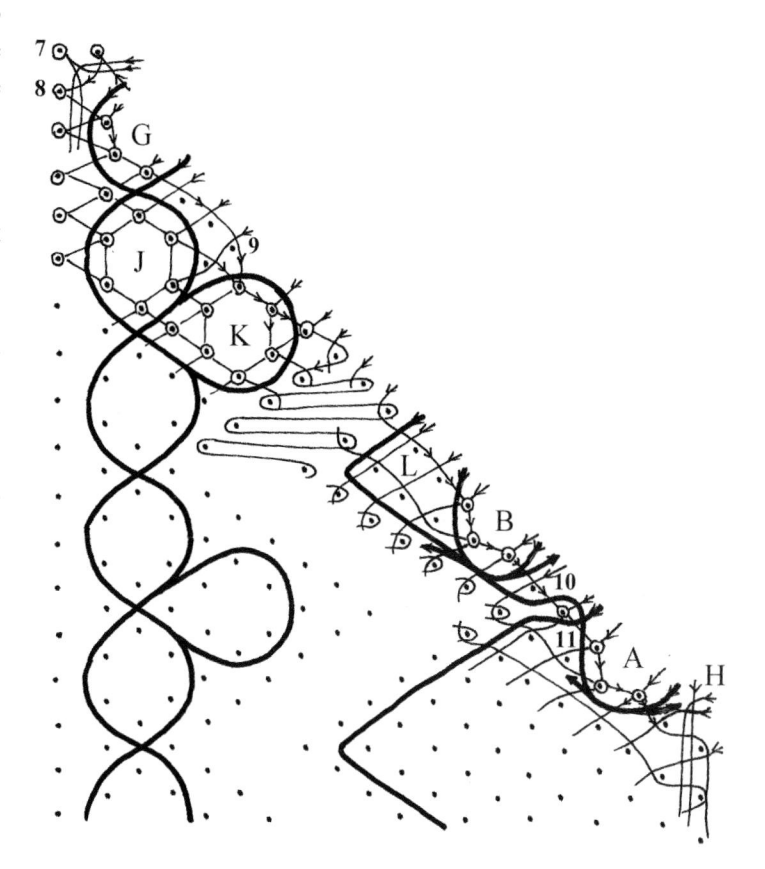

Figure 220 Working out of the corner

There is only a short space between the footpins on either side of the corner and twists may be taken off the edge pair to allow the stitches to lie comfortably. (Mine looked best when there were no twists on the edge pair).

The corner is now complete. Continue around the square, joining the end to the start. If pins have been removed to allow the pattern to be moved, 2.5cm (1in) of the start of the lace should be repinned in position, so that the process of joining does not distort the lace. Sew the free ends of the gimps, left at the start, along the current gimps to cast them off. When all pairs have been sewn through and knotted remove the pins, darn away the ends and trim off the surplus thread.

Check that the fabric has not been distorted, i.e. that the threads lie at right angles. If not, pull the fabric to correct it and press. Mount the lace to the fabric using four-sided stitch.

Chapter 8

Folding the jabot

If you experience any problems folding the jabot, practice using the paper pattern, using paper clips to hold the folds in position. Once the paper jabot works, there should be no problems folding the fabric. Using the pattern of the folds (figure 221) -

1 With wrong sides together fold along A-A and tack.
2 With wrong sides together fold along each B-B1 and B-B2 and tack.
3 With right sides together fold along each B-C1 and B-C2 and tack.
4 Tuck in the folds B-C1 until the ends, C1, of the folds meet, adjust folds if necessary and press into position.
5 Tuck in the folds B-C2 allowing the ends, C2, of the folds to overlap, adjust folds if necessary and press into position.
6 Use a brooch to attach the jabot in position.

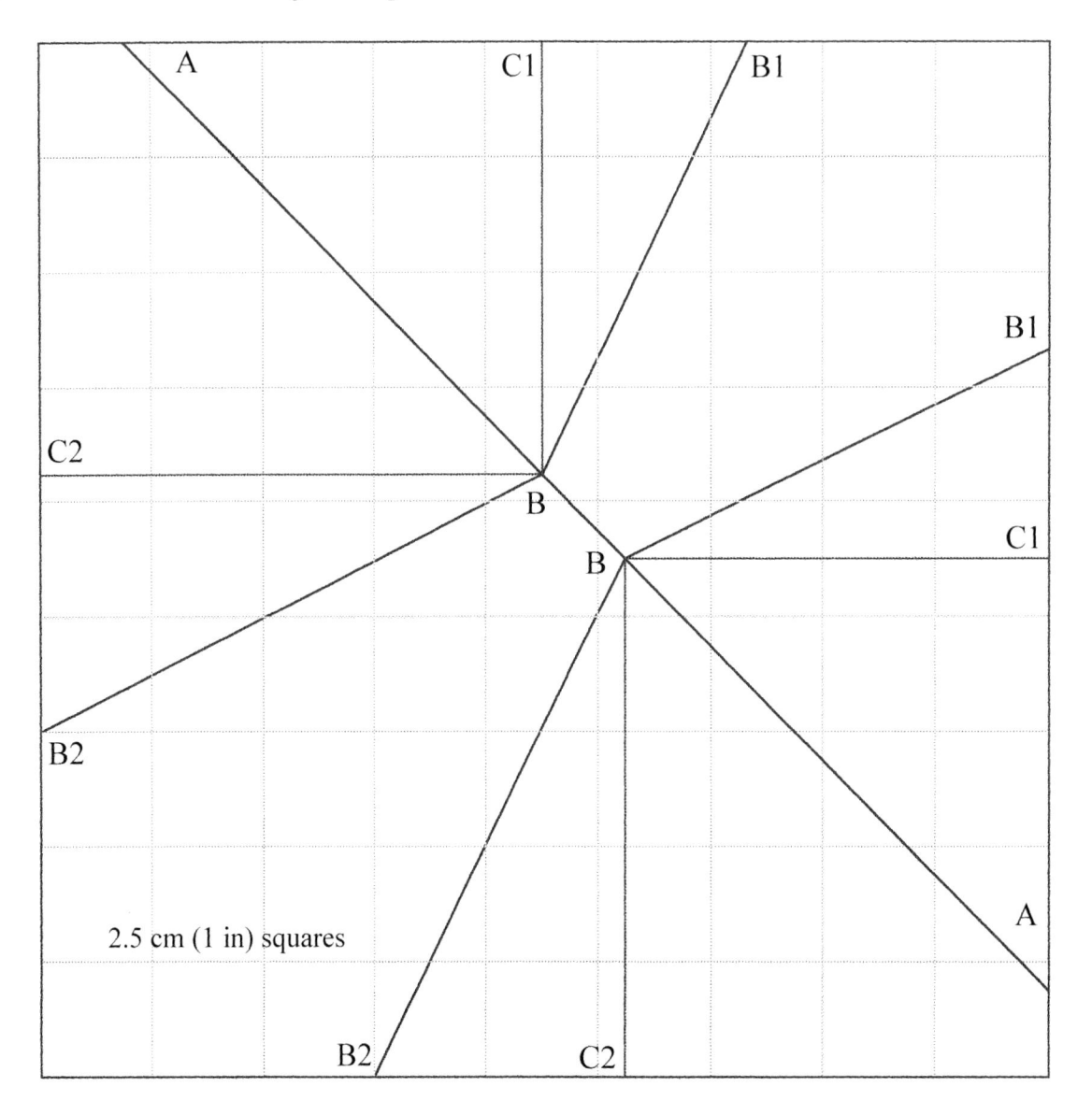

Figure 221 Folding the jabot.

Chapter 8

END NOTES

1 Drafting the pattern
1 Using Grid no. 1 (56°, 40 pins per 10 cm along the footside) Draw in the gimps (figure 222).

Figure 222 (right) Draw the gimps

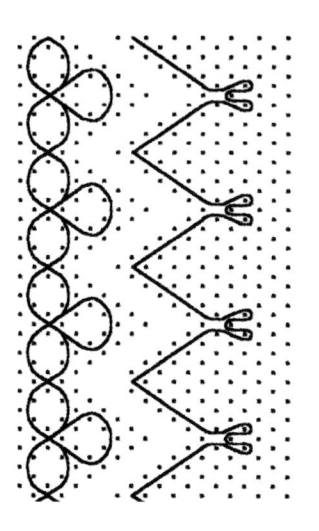

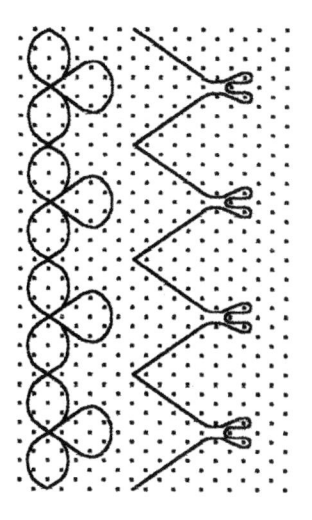

2 Remove the dots from centres of the honeycomb rings and the centre line of the trail (figure 223).

Figure 223 (left) Dots removed

The draft is now ready for the headpins and footpins and catch-pin row to be adjusted (figure 210), but if the edging is to have a corner, this is designed and drafted before the foot and headpins are adjusted, as the footpins and catch-pin row are not exactly mirrored across the diagonal through the corner.

1a Drafting the corner
Draw the line, at 45° to footside, for the diagonal through the corner, and cut the pattern draft along this line (figure 224).

Figure 224 (right) Pattern draft cut along the diagonal

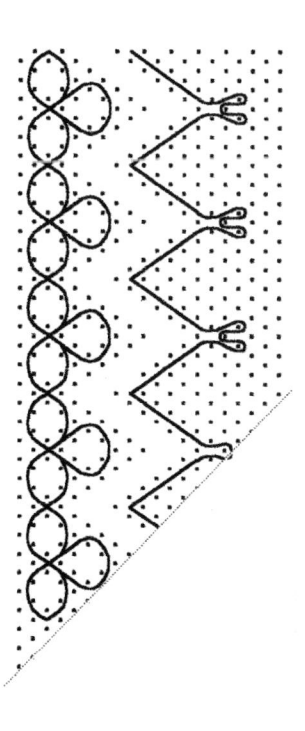

89

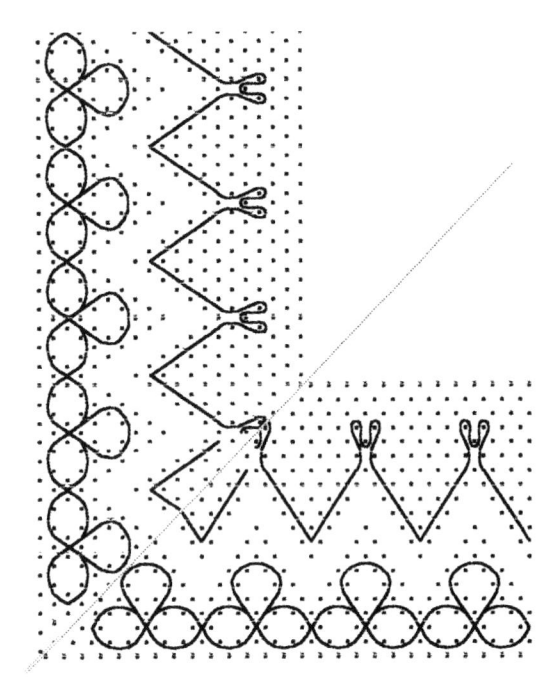

Chapter 8

3 Place the cut section at 45° on another section of pattern draft so that the pattern mirrors across the join. Remove the fingers that overlap, and the partial rings at the outer point (figure 225).

Figure 225 (left) Draft placed on another section at 45°

4 Draw three honeycomb rings along the diagonal, and redraw the fingers. There is now only one finger each side (figure 226).

Figure 226 (right) Draw the honeycomb rings and gimp fingers

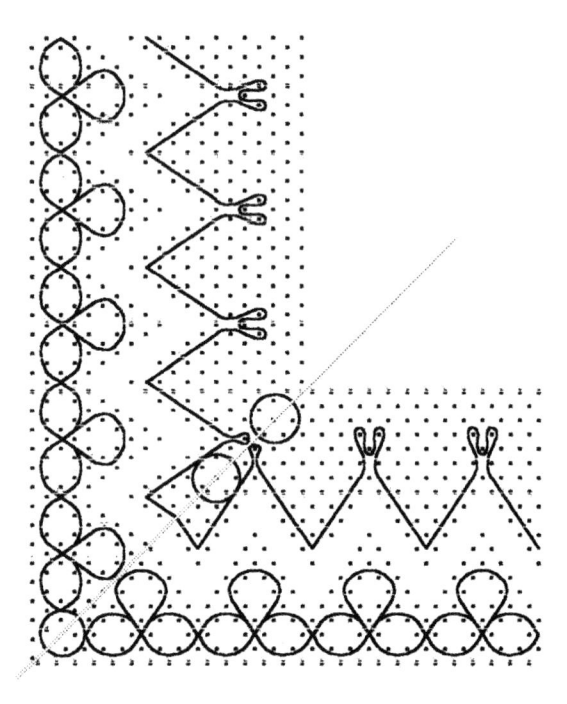

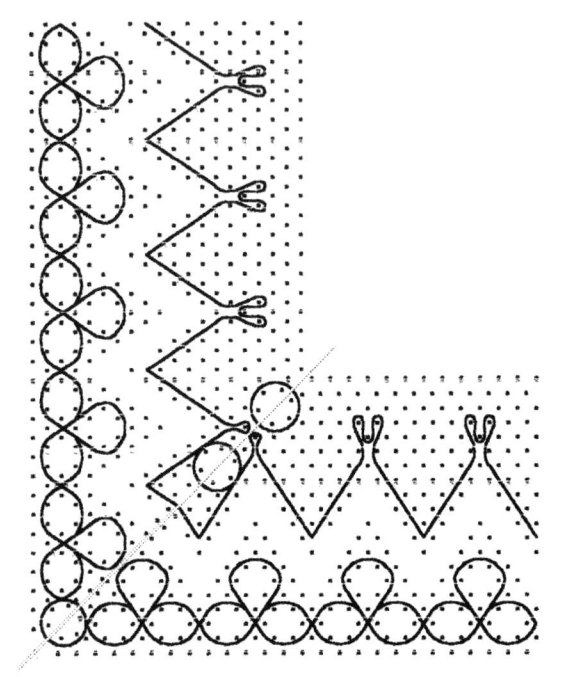

5 Remove the centre dots from the honeycomb rings along the diagonal. Adjust the dots within the rings, add another two, making six, in the ring at the outer point. On both sides adjust the single point ground dot between the finger and centre ring. Adjust the dots along the inner side of the trail and add a pinhole at the end of each trail, to make one finish and the other start, as a diamond (figure 227).

6 The pins in the point ground area and the two single point ground pins need adjusting because the stitches lie behind the pins and, if the pins are not adjusted, the stitches appear to have been off-set when the lace is made.

7 Complete the draft by adjusting the head pins, footpins and catch-pins (figure 210).

Figure 227 Final adjustments made to some pinholes along the diagonal through the corner

2 Cornering a Geometrical Bucks point pattern

When the grid is mirrored across a line drawn at 45° to the footside, the rows fall away from the diagonal line and new rows appear at intervals to fill the vacancy (figure 228). To work these part rows, a honeycomb ring is usually placed across the corner around the pinholes where the row starts. This allows two pairs, that would otherwise cross the diagonal, to work together at the pin that starts the row (figure 229).

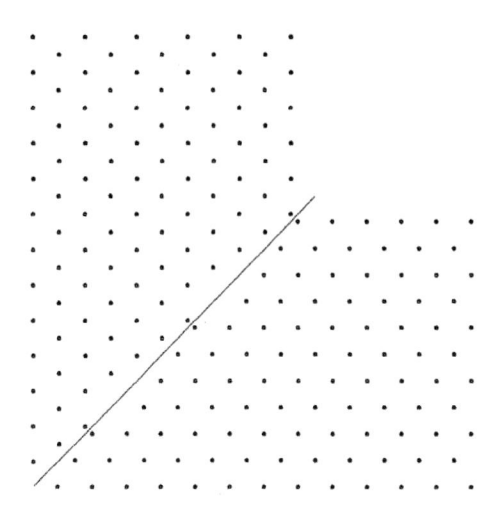

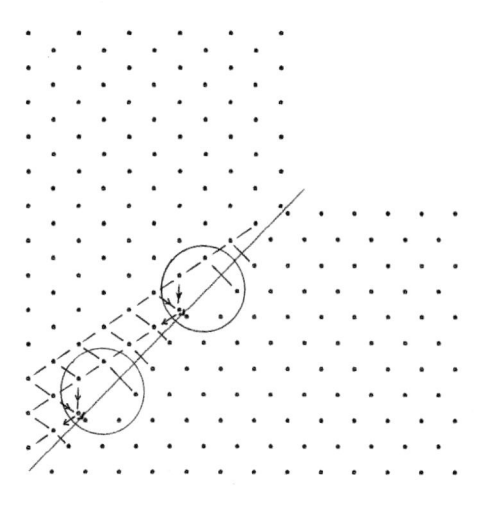

Figure 228 Grid mirrored across the corner

Figure 229 Starting new rows through a corner

Some pinholes of the rings may require adjusting to make them more evenly spaced. The new rows appearing through the corner can be seen in figure 225 and the following figures show how some pinholes have been adjusted.

3 Schematic diagrams

When diagrams have to show large areas it becomes impractical to show the path of every thread and the position of every twist. Also, having reached this stage the lacemaker should know the basic rules and not need so many details. For the more complicated diagrams, such as those for getting into and getting out of the corner (figures 219 & 220), a simplified version is used; in which single lines are used to represent pairs.

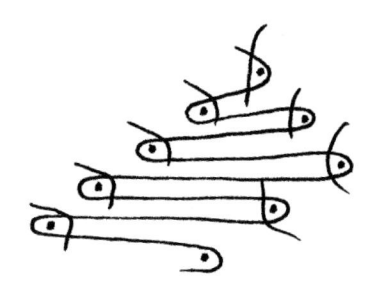

3a Cloth stitch and half stitch

Each worker and passive pair is represented by a single line. This creates an anomaly where half stitch is concerned, since some of the threads do not follow the paths of these lines; the lines only indicate the order of work, and the same diagram is true for both half stitch and cloth stitch rows. Also the diagram gives no indication as to which stitch should be worked (figure 230).

Figure 230 (left) Schematic diagram for starting both cloth stitch and half stitch trails

Chapter 8

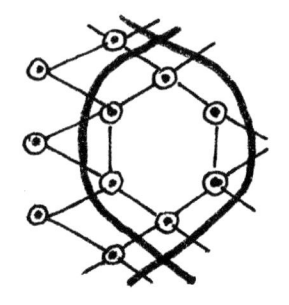

3b Honeycomb stitch & picots

Honeycomb stitch and picots are often represented by circles each surrounding the dot (figure 231). The headside passives are sometimes omitted, the lacemaker being expected to add the standard number.

Figure 231 (left) Honeycomb ring, two honeycomb stitches within the headside and three picots on the left hand side. The headside passives have been omitted.

3c Point ground and footside

Point ground can be represented by lines crossing above a dot, and the catch-pin stitch by the crossing of two lines occurring to the side of a dot. Footside passives are shown as two parallel lines, and they may be omitted. The edge pair is shown as a line outside the dots. The stitch about the pin occurs where a diagonal line meets the footside line above a dot, and returns into the work below it (figure 232).

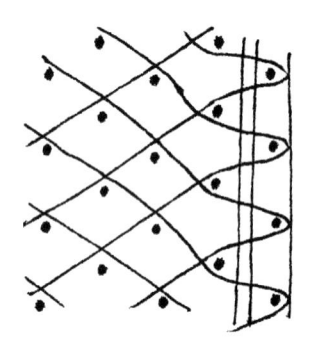

Figure 232 (right) Point ground and footside

4 Cloth and half stitch trails

Trails are bands of either cloth, or half stitch, that are worked diagonally towards the right or to the left. They may change direction from right to left, or vice versa, and trails may divide and/or combine; sometimes they look as though they cross (see Chapter 13, Project 20). For any trail, alternate rows are worked between two pins that are on the same horizontal line across the pricking, while the other rows drop from one horizontal to the next. In this pattern (figure 233) pairs a and b lie on a horizontal line, then from b the line drops down to c, the next horizontal row (c to d). A ruler placed through the pinholes a & b, b & c and c & d shows this clearly.) This results alternate rows having a different numbers of pairs. For this pattern the trails that travel diagonally towards the right, A and C, have five pairs in the horizontal rows (a to b), but six in the rows where the worker moves down to the next horizontal row (b to c). All the horizontal rows are the same length and have the same number of pairs, (in this pattern there are five pairs), but in the diagonal trails, A and C, the rows dipping down, (b to c), are longer than the horizontal rows. Therefore each of these rows

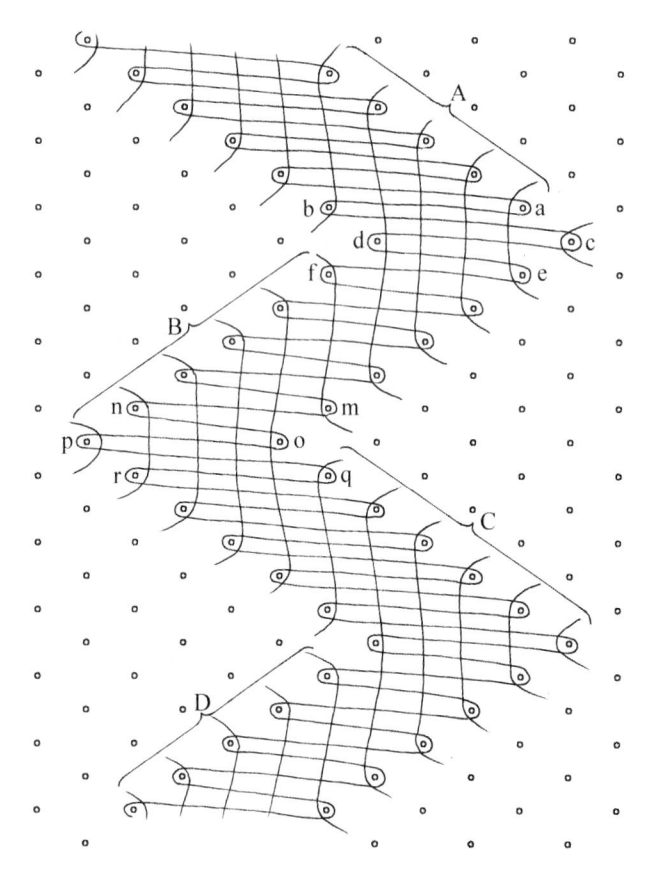

Figure 233 Trails

has one more pair. In the diagonal trails, B and D, the rows dipping down, (n to o), are shorter than the horizontal rows and therefore they have one less pair. So, when we look at the diagonals travelling towards the left, B and D, we count five pairs in the horizontal rows (m to n) but only four pairs in rows that drop down to the next horizontal (n to o). When a worker reaches an inner corner, where a trail changes direction, no pair is added, nor is one left out; similarly at an outer corner a pair is added while one is also left out. Providing the trails contain sufficient pairs, the variation in the number of pairs per row is not apparent. However, particularly if the thread is comparatively fine for the pattern, the trails with fewer pairs may look starved (look too open and need more pairs). In this situation an extra pair may be added and remain in the trail from start to finish.

Trails can be difficult to corner successfully and are better 'broken across' the corner, as in this pattern. Then the end of the current corner can be completed as for working the lower half of a diamond. Similarly, after turning the corner, the new trail can be started as for working the top half of a diamond. Very narrow trails, those worked between adjacent holes of the grid, may continue across the corner. For cloth stitch trails, back stitches can be used to accommodate the difference in the number of pins along the inside edge compared with the outside edge. For narrow half stitch trails alternate rows, that dip between horizontal rows, can all be worked so that they have one less pair than the horizontal rows. These trails corner successfully, but do not thicken the trail by adding another pair.

5a Using block pillow & 'U' shaped pillows
When making a square edging on mushroom pillow, the pricking and lace will probably have to be lifted and replaced at least three times to negotiate the corners; more if the sides are too long for the pillow. To make life easier, special pillows have been designed that allow the pricking to be turned through 90°. These are the traditional block pillow and the more recently invented 'U' shaped pillow.

5b Block Pillow
A rectangular pillow with a shallow channel down the centre containing three, square blocks and sloping, padded sides (figure 234). Traditionally the blocks were felt pads, now high-density polystyrene is used This pillow evolved on the Continent where unspangled bobbins are used, and the very flat section across the blocks is not helpful when using spangled bobbins, as it reduces tension on the bobbin threads and hitches are likely to 'pop off'.

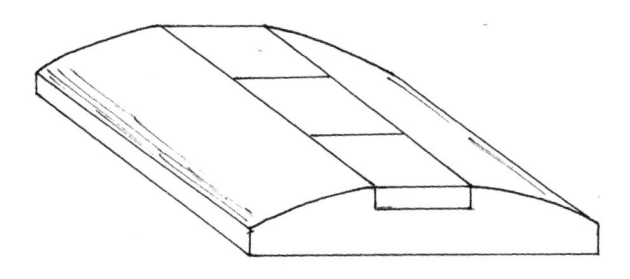

Figure 234 Block pillow

Chapter 8

5c 'U' shaped pillow
A 'U' shaped pillow is a cross between a mushroom pillow and a block pillow. The back section has a straight channel, like the traditional block pillow but usually containing only two blocks; the sides are padded. The curved, padded front, of the 'U' shaped pillow, copies the shape of a mushroom pillow, allowing the bobbins to lie more comfortably. Tension is better and hitches are more likely to stay in place when a pillow is curved down at the sides and front. (figure 235)

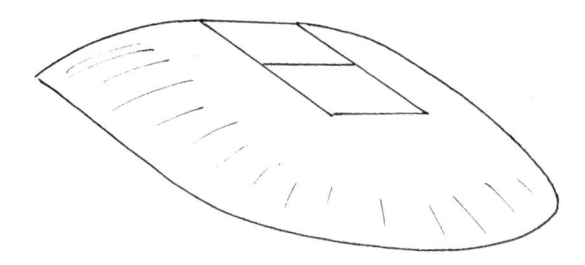

Figure 235 'U' shaped pillow

5d Using a block or 'U' shaped pillow for making a long edging or insertion
Place the pricking centrally on the blocks and start working. When you approach the front of the blocks on a 'U' shaped pillow, or as close to the front as is comfortable on a block pillow, remove the block at the back, slide the other block(s) backwards, and insert the free block at the front. Continue moving the blocks like 'stepping stones' as required.

5e Using a block or 'U' shaped pillow for making an edging or insertion with corners
Place the pricking centrally on a block checking the position of the corner. The corner should be in such a position on a block that, when the block is turned through 90°, the following section will be in the centre. Work the lace until you have worked into the corner and are about to work out of it. At this point lift the block, rotate it through 90° and replace it; the block may be moved back at the same time. Continue working, but be aware how the following corner relates to the blocks. Since edgings are all different lengths, it is unlikely that the next corner will be in the correct position so that, after turning a block at a corner, the following corner will be in correct position on a block. In this situation, use a half or one third block, when working along the side, to adjust the position of the square block on which the corner will be made.

5f Making best use of a block or 'U' shaped pillow
Pillows are expensive; the blocks are not. At any time, you can secure the bobbins by using stitch holders or making a tight bag around them with a cover cloth. The block together with the pricking, bobbins and lace can be removed from the pillow and stored in a box, while a spare block can be placed in the vacant space, and the pillow is ready for re-use.

CHAPTER 9

PROJECTS 8-11 CIRCULAR EDGINGS (Plates 1,7 & 8)

Project 8 Circular edging mounted to fabric
Project 9 Large UFO candleholder with coloured gimps and matching footside passives
Project 10 Large UFO candleholder with beads replacing pin chain and tallies
Project 11 Small UFO candleholder with coloured beads replacing pin chain and tallies

PROJECT 8
CIRCULAR EDGING
(mounted to fabric)

New Techniques
working a circle
cucumber foot
pin chain
coloured gimp
adding beads

Materials required
pricking (figure 238)
Egyptian cotton no 60
gimp, perle no 8
13cm x 13cm (5ins x 5ins) lawn
sharps needle no 10

End Notes
1 drafting a circular pattern
2 cucumber foot
3 making tallies left handed
4 gate tally
5 honeycomb stems
6 pin chain
7 coloured lace
8 using coloured gimps
9 adding beads

Figure 236 (above) Mounted edging

Figure 237 (left) Circular edging

Chapter 9

Figure 238 Pattern draft, the arrow is a reference point when counting pattern repeats

Choosing a starting line for the footside
Although other starting points are equally valid, in order to use the following instructions choose a starting point where a diagonal line drawn down from a pin above a tally, indicated by a dot, travels to the top pin of three vertical pins that lie between the gimps down the side of a motif (figure 239). This only works for every third motif.

Figure 239 (right) Choosing a starting line

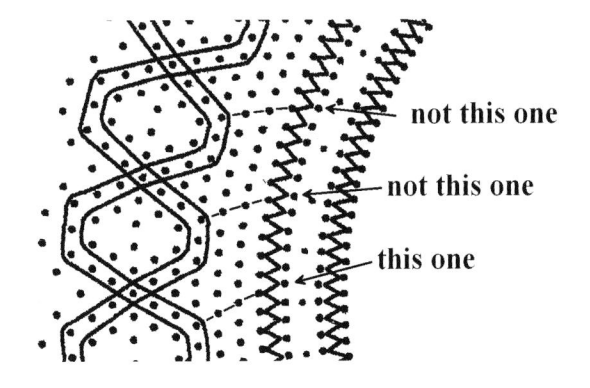

96

Chapter 9

Setting in the cucumber foot[2]

1 Start the outer section of the cucumber foot[1&5] with a whole stitch about the pin at pin 1 (figure 240).
2 Twist the workers as required, but the edge pair only once. The inner edge of a circular edging has the pins spaced much closer than the outer edge and, in this case, there is only sufficient room for one twist on the edge pair. Work through two pairs of passives to pin 2, at the inner edge of the outer passives, and twist the workers three times. Cloth stitch back through the passives, make up the edge at pin 3 and return through the passives to pin 4, twist the workers three times and leave them.
3 Place the workers for the inner passives of the cucumber foot on pin 5. Cloth stitch through two pairs of passives and set up the catch pin, pin 6. Work the catch-pin stitch and the next two point ground stitches setting up pins 7 & 8.
4 Return the catch-pin pair from pin 6 through the passives to pin 9, twist the workers three times and leave them.

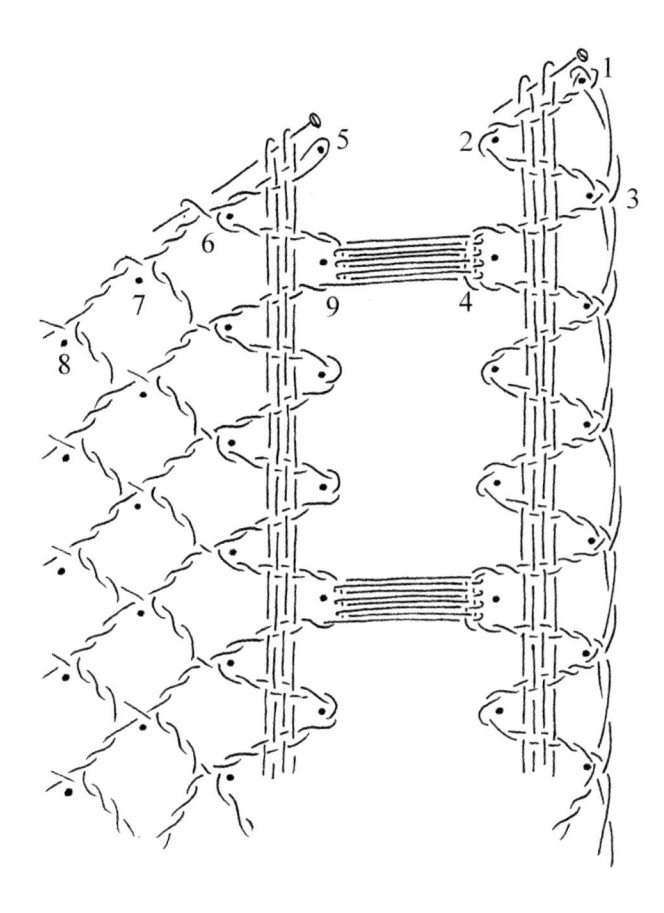

Figure 240 The cucumber foot

Tally[3&4]

The following method for making tallies is only one of the many I have experienced. However, although it is not the fastest, it is the one I have found to be the most successful.

A tally is made with one pair from each of the pins on either side of a large dot, the indicator for a tally. Using two pairs, one from pin 4 and one from pin 9, adjust the threads so that they are the same length.

1 Start the tally using bobbin no 2 (unless it has a knot that will be in the way, in which case use bobbin no. 3), as the weaver and weave it back and forth as follows -
2 Pass the weaver over bobbin 3 and under 4.
3 Hold the two outer passive bobbins in place placing the thumb and third finger of the other hand on them to hold the tension, and gently adjust the width of the tally (figure 241).
4 *Pass the weaver back under the centre passive and, holding the worker to the other side, again adjust the width of the tally. Pass the weaver under passive 1, over 2 and under 3 and. adjust the width of the tally**.
5 Repeat *-** several more times until the tally is a suitable shape, finishing with the weaver on the left, the side from which it started.
6 Twist the pairs until they each have three twists (figure 242).

Chapter 9

Be very careful how you handle the weaver as the slightest unguarded twitch can destroy the tally. Make a note of the number of passes you make, (preferably on the pricking), and make all the tallies in one piece of work the same size, unless there is a specific reason for varying them.

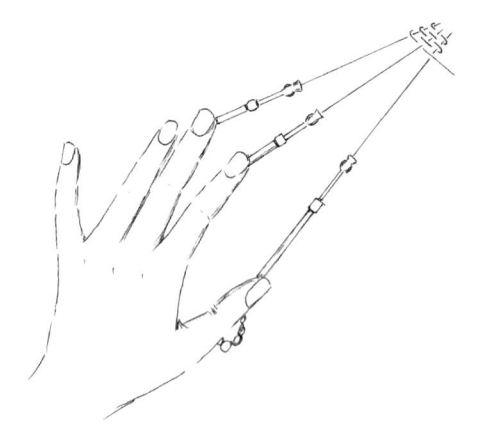

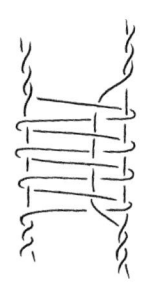

Figure 241 (left) Tensioning a tally

Figure 242 (above) Ladder tally

Continue the cucumber foot
5 Leaving the thread slack, pin the weaver out of the way with the spangle pointing away from you. Now begin to stabilize the tally by working <u>the other pair</u>, the right pair, as far as you can.
6 With the passive pair from the tally *work out through the passives and make up the edge (figure 240). Return through the passives and twist three times around the pin at the inner edge*. Work *to* twice more.
7 Only now should the left pair from the tally, the pair containing the weaver be worked carefully towards the left through the two pairs of passives, set up the catch-pin and make the catch-pin stitch. Keep a note of the weaver and tension this thread last.
8 Work the next point ground stitch using a pair from pin 8 and pin the tally worker safely out of the way after using it. A tally is usually safe after it has worked three stitches, depending on the tension being used.
9 Work the footside workers across the inner passives and twist three times around the pin. Work back through the passives and make a catch-pin stitch.

In this pattern the cucumber foot has two pins each side, between the tallies, where the worker make three twists around the pin, i.e. a tally is made at every third pin.

Setting in the honeycomb motif[5&6]
1 Set in at the top pinhole, pin 10, across two gimps (figure 243).
2 Cross the gimps as shown and work down each honeycomb stem[2] to pins 11 & 12, and pass the gimps through. (A honeycomb stem is a line of honeycomb stitches bounded on both sides by a gimp.)
3 Work the first five honeycomb stitches of the area within the honeycomb stems, from pin 13 to pin 14, and taking the other pair from pin 13 to pin 15.

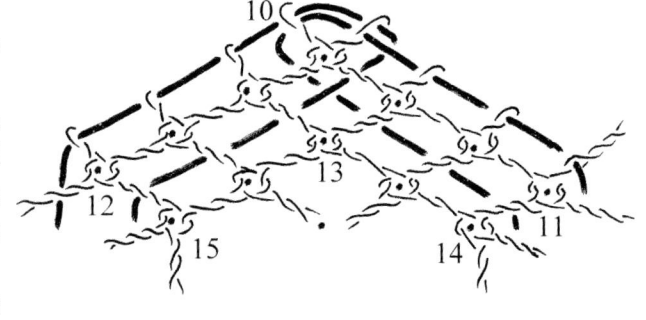

Figure 243 Setting in the honeycomb motif

Chapter 9

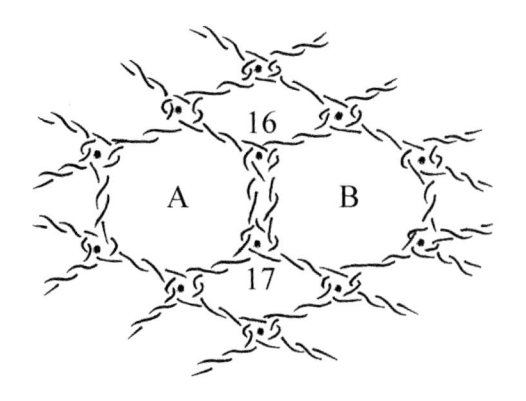

Figure 244 Pin chain

Pin chain[1&6]

Honeycomb filling has alternate pinholes along the diagonals omitted, causing the diagonal lines of holes typical of the ground. This honeycomb area has two pinholes omitted side-by-side resulting in two honeycomb holes, A & B (figure 244), side-by-side. Thus two honeycomb stitches, at pins 16 & 17, occur one above the other making a pin chain[6]. To make a pin chain from pin 16 to pin 17, make a honeycomb stitch, pin 16, then with the same two pairs make another complete honeycomb stitch using pin 17; i.e. after setting up pin 16 cover it with the second half of the first stitch. Then, with the same two pairs work the first half of the second honeycomb stitch, set up pin 17 and cover with the second half of the stitch.

Mounting the lace

1 Cut a circular template, from thick paper or thin card, that fits just inside the circle of lace.
2 Tack the template to the right side of the fabric.
3 Place the lace in position around the template and tack in place (figure 245). The template may now be removed.
4 Stitch the lace to the fabric by cording or four-sided stitch.

Figure 245 (right) Lace tacked around a template

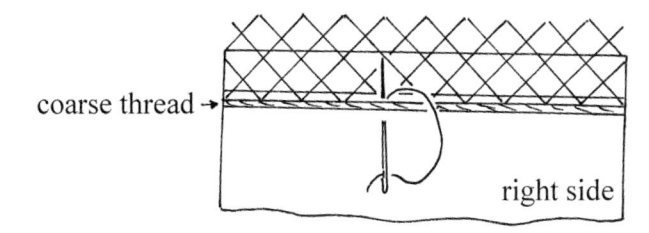

Figure 246 Couching the coarse thread

Attaching lace by cording

1 Work a foundation row to attach the lace firmly in position.
2 Lay a coarse thread of the same colour as the stitching along the footside, a gimp thread is suitable, (figure 246).

99

Chapter 9

3 Couch down the coarse thread, taking up a generous amount of fabric for each stitch (about twice the width of the coarse thread), and pull each stitch up tightly. Make one stitch through the hole where the footside was pinned and two stitches across the footside pair between two edge stitches.
4 Fold the excess fabric to the wrong side, away from the lace, and oversew the edge as before. The final effect should be of all the stitches touching side-by-side; adjust the stitching if necessary.
5 Trim away excess fabric.

PROJECT 9 LARGE UFO CANDLEHOLDER
(with coloured gimps and matching footside passives)

Materials required
pricking (figure 238)[1]
Finca cotton no. 60, neutral colour
coloured perle thread[8], no 12
Finca cotton no. 60, colour to match perle thread[8]
(The resulting colour of the passives is modified by the workers passing through them. It may be useful to make a sample and adjust the colour if necessary)
large UFO candleholder & candle

Figure 247 Candleholder with coloured gimps and matching footside passives, the lace lying against the base of the holder

Figure 248 Candleholder with lace pressed upwards in the base.

Chapter 9

Figure 249 Lace circle with coloured gimps and matching footside passives, see colour Plate 1

Setting in[2,3,4,5,6,7&8]

Coloured gimps are used in pairs, each being half the thickness of the single gimp that the pair replaces. The pairs of lace threads pass between the the gimp pair, instead of the gimp thread passing between the two threads of the lace pair. Lace pairs cannot be started across the gimp

101

Chapter 9

pairs, since the pairs would slide out. In this situation it is best to start along the first diagonal row of honeycomb ground each side within the gimps.

1 Using bobbins wound with neutral coloured thread, start by working a honeycomb stitch at pin 1 and, working towards the left, add pairs for the honeycomb stitches at pins 2 & 3 (figure 250).
2 Tie two gimps, A & B, behind the starting point, allowing 15cms (6ins) for joining, and place them to the left of pin 3. Lift the left gimp, Pass the left pair from pin 3 between the gimps, replace the gimp to the right of the pair (figure 251) and twist the gimps (figure 252). Add a pair and work the honeycomb stitch, pin 4, between the gimp lines. Add two more gimps, C & D, and pass the left pair from pin 4 between them and twist the gimps. Add two pairs of headside passives and work the picot, pin 5.

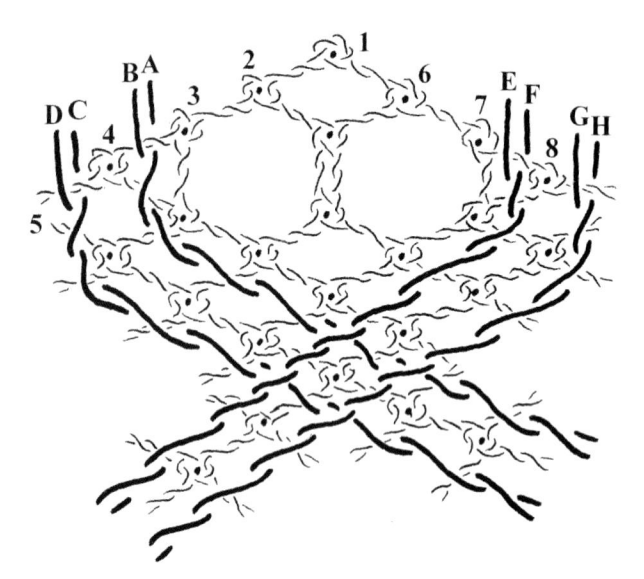

Figure 250 Setting in

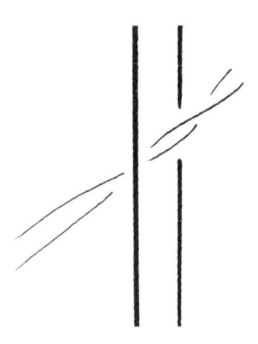

Figure 251 Pair passed to the left between gimp pair    *Figure 252 Gimps twisted*

3 Return the picot pair though the passives. Lift the left gimp and pass the pair between the gimps from left to right. Replace the gimp to the left of the pair (figure 253). Twist the gimps (figure 254).

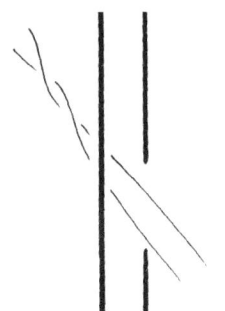

Figure 253 Pair passed to the right between gimp pair    *Figure 254 Gimps twisted*

Chapter 9

4 Return to the remaining pair from pin 1 (figure 250), and add a new pair at the next two honeycomb stitches along the diagonal, pins 6 & 7. Add two more gimps, E & F. Pass the pair between the gimps and twist the gimps. Add a pair, make the honeycomb stitch between the gimps, pin 8, add two more gimps, G & H, and pass the pair between them. Coloured gimps are always twisted after a pair has been passed between them.

Crossing coloured gimps[7&8]
When coloured gimps cross, the left gimp of one pair is lifted and the other pair of gimps passed through as passing through a lace pair. The gimps, that have had another pair of gimps passed through them, are twisted.

Continue until all pinholes have been used, then pass the pairs through the gimps. Join the lace pairs end to start and secure with a reef knot. Cut off all bobbins, leaving a sewing length and remove from the pillow. Sew away the lace pairs carefully as the colour contrasts with the gimp. Sew away the gimps using a sharp needle and sew each cut gimp through a line of twisted gimps. Trim the ends.

When an edging is placed in position in an UFO candleholder it may buckle; if so gently ease it flat. The problem may be that the edging is very slightly large, in which case, ease the edging outwards so that the picots are bent upwards at the outer curve of the glass, and at the same time ease the gimp motifs towards each other.

PROJECT 10 LARGE UFO CANDLEHOLDER
(with beads replacing the pin chain and tallies.)

Materials required
pricking (figure 256)[1]
Egyptian cotton no. 60
perle thread no 8
36 beads 3mm dia.
60 beads 2mm dia.
needle threader[9] or Lazy Susan[9]
large UFO candleholder, glass & spray of silk flowers

New Technique
adding beads[9]

Figure 255 (right) Large UFO Candleholder with beads replacing the pin chain and the tallies in the cucumber foot

Chapter 9

Figure 256 Pattern draft

Setting in[2&9]

Set in at the pinhole where the honeycomb stems[5] appear to cross. (figure 257), and work down each honeycomb stem. Work the first five honeycomb stitches of the area within the honeycomb stems and add a bead onto pairs A & B.

Figure 257 (right) Setting in

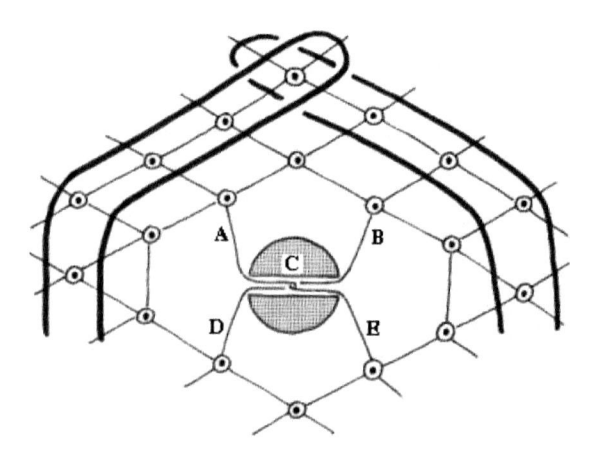

.

104

Chapter 9

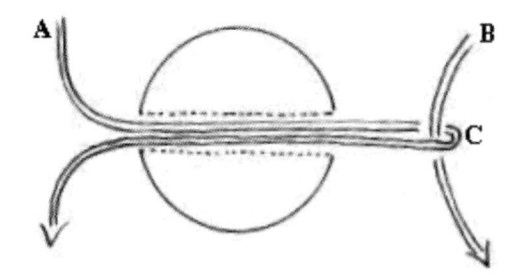

Adding beads[9]

1 Use a crochet hook, or if the hole is too small a lazy Susan[9] or needle threader[9], and pull a loop, C, of both threads of pair A, through the bead.
2 Pass both threads of pair B through loop C (figure 258) and firm up so that the linking of the two pairs occurs within the bead. Twist each pair twice.

Figure 258 (left) Adding a bead

A bead replaces both pins of each honeycomb chain and pairs A & B work the lower honeycomb stitches, D & E of their respective sides. The small beads replacing the tallies in the cucumber foot are added using the same method.

Figure 259 (right) Circle of lace with beads replacing the pin chain and the tallies in the cucumber foot

PROJECT 11 SMALL UFO CANDLEHOLDER
(with beads replacing the pin chain and tallies.)

Materials required
pricking (figure 248)[1]
Egyptian cotton no 100/2
gimp, 2 strands Anchor stranded embroidery thread
36 beads 2mm dia.
60 beads 0.5mm dia
needle threader[9] or Lazy Susan[9]
small UFO candleholder and candle

Chapter 9

Figure 260 Lace with beads replacing the pin chain and tallies in the cucumber foot

Figure 261 Lace with beads replacing the pin chain and tallies in the cucumber foot

Figure 262 (left) Pattern draft

END NOTES

1a Drafting the cucumber foot[5&6]

1 Using Grid no 1 and counting from the footside, remove the third vertical row of dots (figure 263)[2]. Continue counting from the footside.
2 Move rows 4 & 5 as for a normal footside (figure 264).
3 Move the dots of row 2 level with and slightly closer to those of row 4 (figure 265), and those of the edge upwards level with those of row 5.
4 Add a circular dot indicator between every third pair of dots in the gap between rows 2 & 4 (figure 266).

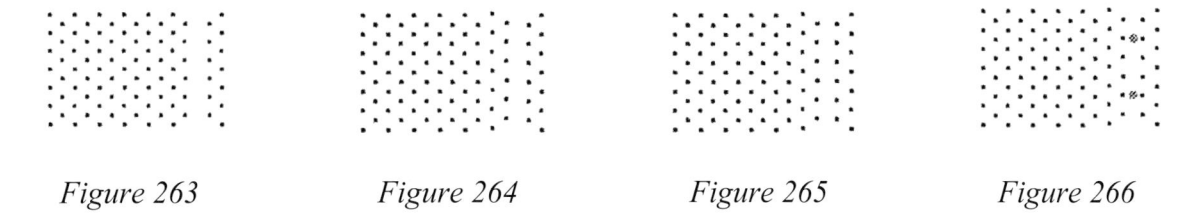

Figure 263   *Figure 264*   *Figure 265*   *Figure 266*

1b Drafting a circular pattern

Essentially there is no difference between plotting an edging on a circular grid from plotting one on a straight grid; it just looks odd at first. This design has a cucumber foot and, because the curvature causes the dots along the inner to close up it is not necessary to off-set the footside.

1c Drafting the pattern for the UFO candleholder

1 Using grid no 5 (for Projects 8 to 10) or Grid no 6 (for Project 11), remove the third row of dots from the footside, move the second and fourth rows slightly closer together and add the indicators for the tallies of the cucumber foot[5] (figure 267).
2 Draw the gimps (figure 268).
3 Remove two pinholes, side-by-side, from the area within the gimps, for the honeycomb and pin chain[6] (figure 269).

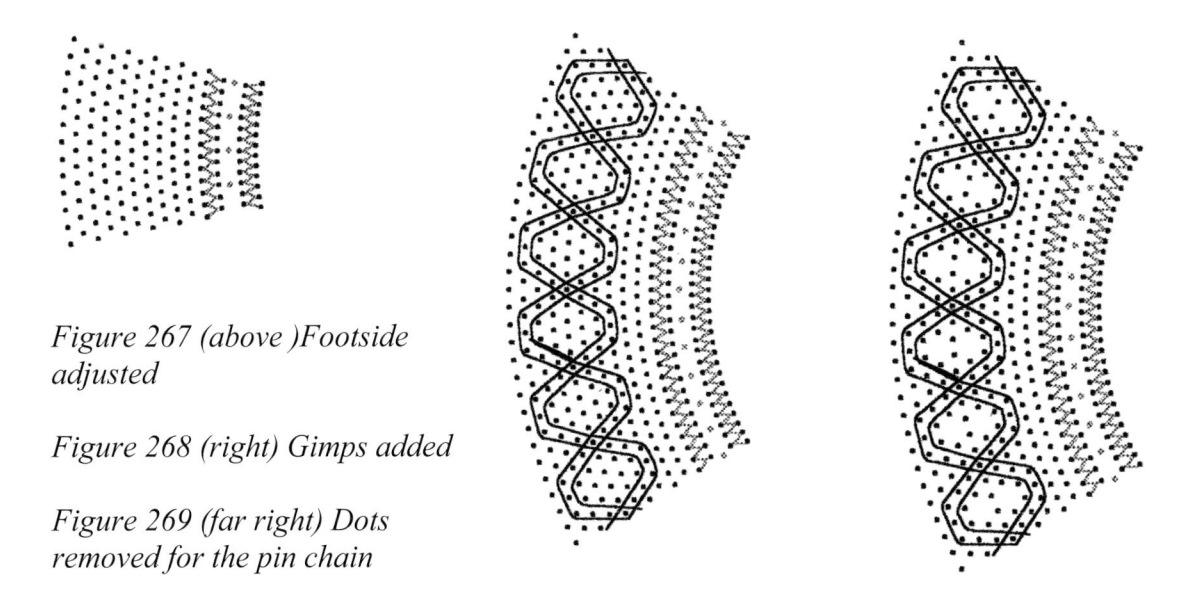

Figure 267 (above) Footside adjusted

Figure 268 (right) Gimps added

Figure 269 (far right) Dots removed for the pin chain

Chapter 9

4 Remove the pinholes outside the gimps (figure 270).
5 Draw the curve for the headside around three heads, add the picot line and the dots for the picots (figure 271). Repeat these as required and remove the construction line.
6 For the circular edging with beads replace the two dots in the centre of the honeycomb area with a large dot, the indicator for a bead[9] (figure 272).

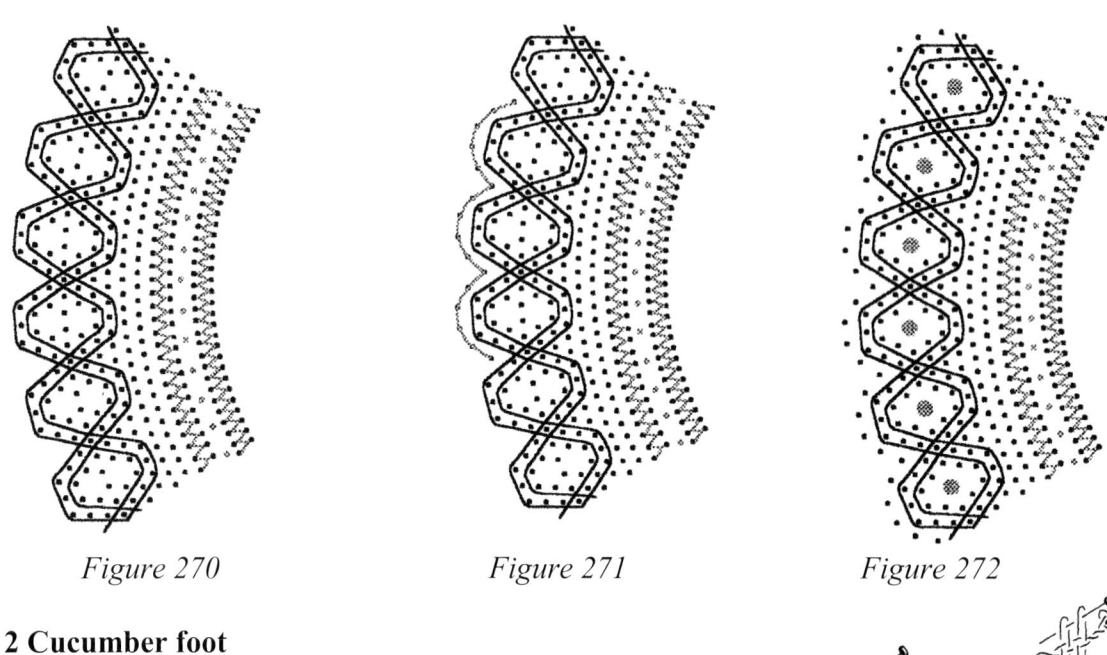

Figure 270   *Figure 271*   *Figure 272*

2 Cucumber foot
The standard cucumber foot has the standard number of twists on the edge pair and workers and a wide, usually ladder tally, between every third pair of pinholes down the gap between the two sets of two passives (figure 273). There may be two or three twists around the pins between the tallies and there may be only one pin between tallies.

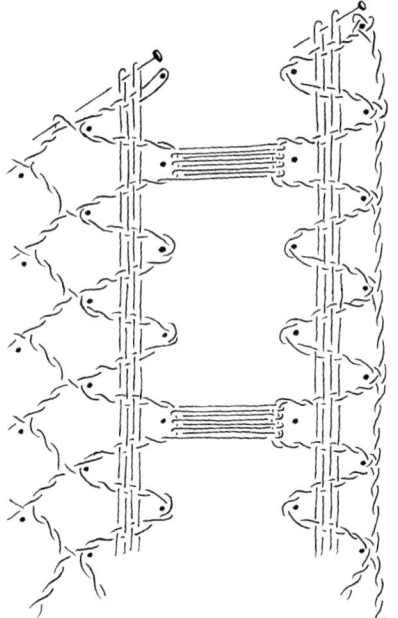

Figure 273 (right) Cucumber foot

3 Making tallies left handed
It is usually accepted that bobbin no. 2, of the two pairs making a tally, is the weaver. However, I was not completely satisfied with my tallies as the top thread had a tendency to separate from the rest. When, because there was a knot on thread no. 2, I had to make a tally with bobbin no. 3 as the weaver, the result was much improved. I now prefer to use bobbin no. 3 as the weaver. I believe my tensioning caused the difference; I am left-handed.

Chapter 9

4 Gate tally
When the tally is complete the weaver may be left as part of the other pair, i.e. not as part of the pair on the side from which it started, in which case the tally is called a 'gate' (figure 274), as the central passive thread looks like the cross bar of a five-barred gate; whereas in the 'ladder' form the centre passive ends up on the same side from which it came. Both forms were well represented in the antique lace I studied. Many pieces had mainly one type; many the other, and a fair number had both types. Some situations may dictate which thread should be the weaver, and some dictate where it should finish. There appears to be no hard and fast rule.

Figure 274 (left) Gate tally

5 Honeycomb stems
When the stem travels diagonally, one pair travels down the diagonal between the gimps, while the other pair for each stitch enters from one side and leaves from the other (figure 275) When the stem travels vertically, the two pairs for each stitch enter the stem one from each side, make a stitch and leave one to each side (figure 276).

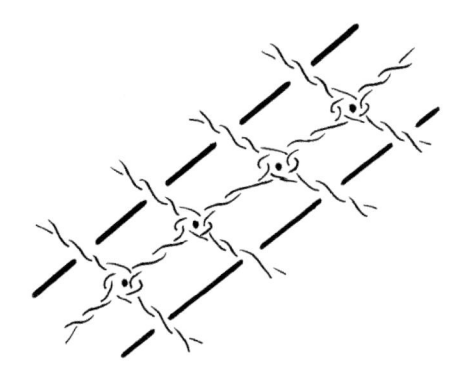

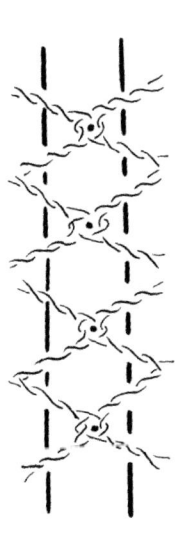

Figure 275 (above) Diagonal honeycomb stem

Figure 276 (right) Vertical honeycomb stem

When the stem travels horizontally the two pairs for each stitch enter the stem from above the pinhole, make the stitch and leave below (figure 277).

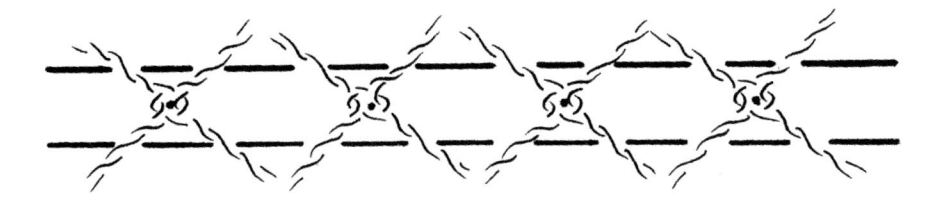

Figure 277 Horizontal honeycomb stem

Chapter 9

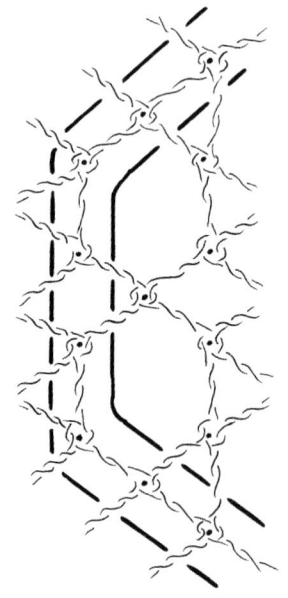

If stems cut through a set of six pins that make a unit of honeycomb ground, then the pairs will be used as if completing the unit of six stitches (figure 278).

Figure 278 (left) Honeycomb stems cutting through units of honeycomb ground

6 Pin chain
The pin chain described above (figure 244), was traditionally made in the North Buckinghamshire & Northamptonshire area. The South Buckinghamshire lacemakers used a slightly different version working a complete honeycomb stitch using pin 1, then setting up pin 2 between the pairs and working the second half of the stitch (figure 279). There is only a single half honeycomb stitch between the pairs.

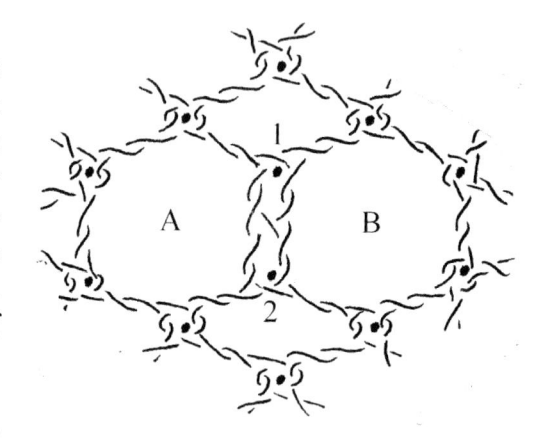

Figure 279 (right) Pin chain, South Bucks version

7 Coloured lace[8]
From the earliest times lace was made in white, off-white, a natural ecru, in metallic thread and later black. There has been some coloured lace made over the centuries, but it was generally as a momentary fashion statement or in peasant lace. Thus lace has developed in monochrome and introducing colour must be approached with care. Our elaborate fillings are our 'colour'.

The artists sketching and pen and ink is not usually coloured, and if it is, it is a delicate colour wash. The delicate but busy lines of the sketching and pen and ink are either overpowered by the colour or the addition of colour causes too much confusion. The same happens when introducing colour, or beads etc. into lace.

These coloured pieces have the colour limited to the gimps, the footside passives and/or beads. The design is deliberately kept very simple, thus avoiding visual confusion. Look at coloured lace with a critical eye. There are some very beautiful coloured pieces being made, many that are indifferent and some that are ugly.

Starting gimps that work in two directions

1 The first pair of gimps is introduced at A (figure 291).
2 The left gimp passes towards the left through two pairs to the left to B. The right gimp passes towards the right through two pairs to C.
3 The four honeycomb stitches of the top four-pin honeycomb ring are made.
4 The left gimp passes towards the right through two pairs to D. The right gimp passes towards the left through two pairs to D. These two gimps do **NOT** cross.

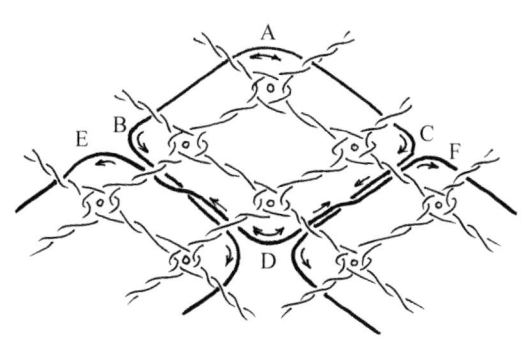

Figure 291 Gimp path around the first ring

5 Place a new gimp pair on a temporary pin at any pinhole just below the four honeycomb stitches of the top ring, so that they lie between the original gimps.
6 Pass the left gimp, of this new pair, towards the left across an original gimp and through two pairs from the honeycomb stitches to E, and then through two more pairs.
7 Pass the right gimp of the new pair towards the right, crossing over an original gimp, through two pairs from the honeycomb stitches to F, and then through two more pairs. The actual position of the gimp crossings may move and settle anywhere between the pairs that bridge the doubled gimps (figure 291).
8 Work the four honeycomb stitches for the rings on each side. The gimps follow the black lines on the pricking following a figure '8' formation and crossing right over left when they meet.

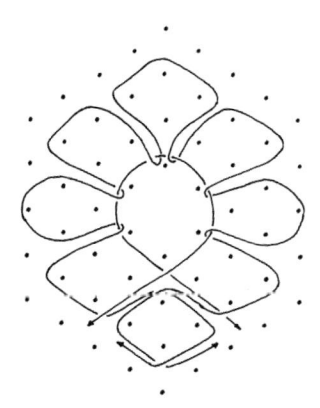

Gimps around the large motif

Two pairs of gimps are needed for this motif. One pair supplying a gimp for each side of the outer ring of gimp and one pair to surround the centre six-pin honeycomb ring (figure 292). Each time a four-pin block has been completed, the outer gimp passes through to the inner ring, passes right around the inner gimp and returns. The pairs are not twisted between the gimp passing to the centre and returning to the outer position. When the centre ring has been completed the centre gimps cross, pass through to the outer edge through two pairs, and are thrown back to be trimmed off later.

Figure 292 (left) Gimp path around the large motif

Casting off along a diagonal line of picots[6]

When the four-pin honeycomb edge is complete, double up the gimps and throw them back to be cut off later. The pairs each side are stacked as for working into a valley but some threads are removed so that they do not accumulate. In this pattern pairs are stacked as the second pair of passives after working the corner picot (figure 293). After the third picot has been made, and the pair stacked, the second and third threads, from the gimp, are thrown back to be trimmed off

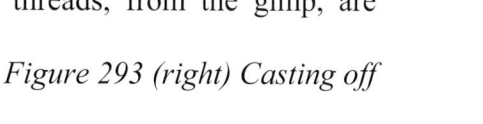

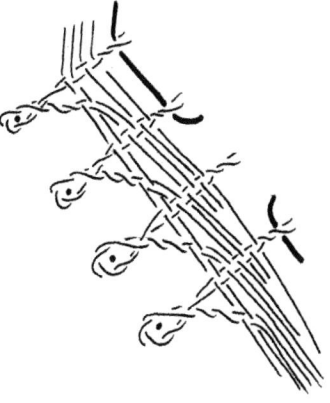

Figure 293 (right) Casting off

later This happens with every subsequent pair entering the headside. Work the other side similarly until all pairs have been worked. Only the last picot pin, the one at the point, remains unused.

Tying off at the point[9]
1 Remove most of the pins, leaving only those in the picots along the diagonals approaching the end point and those in the last three of the four-pin honeycomb rings, and trim the gimps and the pairs thrown back. Except for the pins either side of the join push all remaining pins right down to the pricking.
2 Use the innermost passives from the left section of headside, cloth stitch out through the other passives, make a picot and return through three passive pairs belonging to the other side.
3 At this point turn the pillow through 180° so that the lace is upside down. (Now use figure 294).
4 Keeping them in order, bring the bobbins through the gap between the picot pin at the point and the pin now on its left. The edge passives will be the outside, close to the pins, and the pair that made the picot in the centre.
5 Working in order from the outer edge take one thread from each side and tie a reef knot, the last two knots being made with the threads from the picot pair and the last pair now on the left. Do not trim off these pairs.

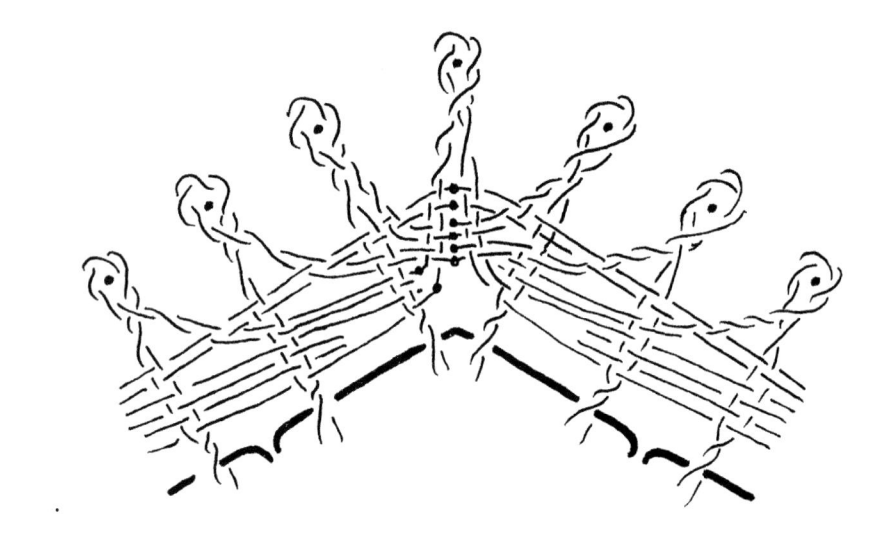

Figure 294 Tying off at the point after turning the pillow through 180°

Making up the porcelain pot lid
1 Using the template supplied with the kit, cut a piece of fabric to fit the lid and mount the lace as for the handbag mirror motif.
2 Make up the lid according to the manufacturer's instructions.

Chapter 10

PROJECT 13 BRUSH BACK INSERT

Figure 295 Brush with lace insert

Materials required
pricking (figure 296)[1&2]
Egyptian cotton no. 100/2
perle thread, no 8 for gimp
brush kit

New Technique
gimps around four cloth stitch diamonds

*Figure 296 (right)
Pattern draft*

*Figure 297 (far right)
Lace insert*

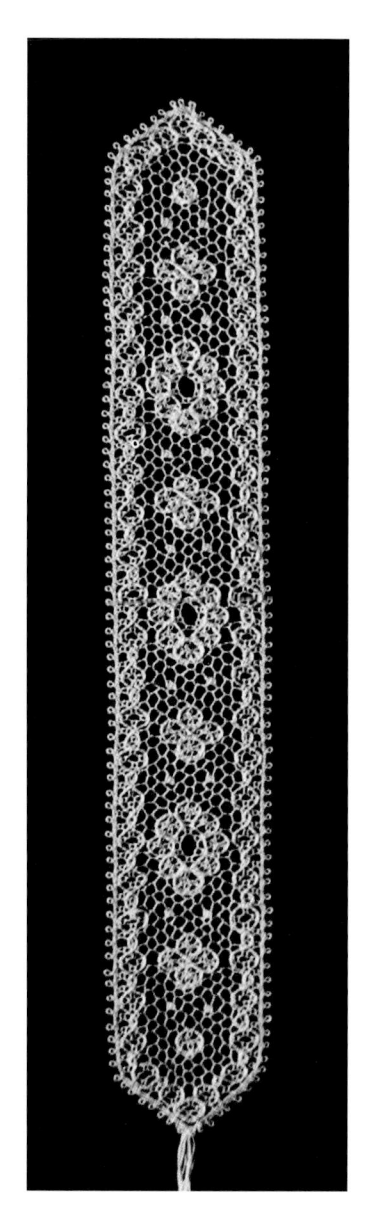

117

Chapter 10

Making the insert
1 Set in as for the small motif; note that the arrangement of four-pin honeycomb rings and single pin rings around the edge is different from the small motif (Project 12), and start working the ground.
2 Introduce a gimp, work the four-pin bud in cloth stitch and cast off the gimps by doubling up.
3 Work as far as possible before making the tallies, i.e. as far as possible along the row past pin 1 towards A, and the row past pin 2 towards pin B. The the short row to pins 3 and pins 4 & 5 (figure 298)

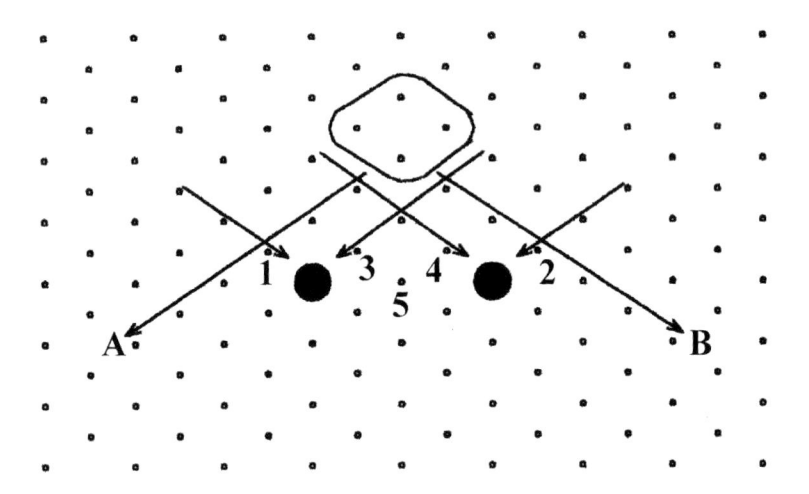

Figure 298 Preparation for tallies

4 Using a pair from pin 1 and another from pin 3 make a gate tally, leaving the weaver on the right..
5 Leaving the thread slack, pin the weaver out of the way with the spangle pointing away from you. Now begin to stabilize the tally by working the other pair, the left pair, as far as you can towards the left.
6 Using pairs from pins 2 & 4 make the right hand tally, another gate tally, leaving the weaver on the right and pinning it out of the way. With the pair without the weaver work one ground stitch towards the left.
7 Only now should the right pair from the left tally, the pair containing the weaver be worked carefully towards the right through two pairs, a ground pair and the left pair (without the weaver) from the right tally. Keep a note of the weaver. Tension this thread last, and pin it securely out of the way. Work the next two rows towards the left.
8 Work the right pair from the right tally (containing the weaver) carefully towards the right as far as possible, keeping a note of the weaver and tensioning this thread last. After three stitches have been worked the tally should be reasonably stable.
9 Start working the next row of ground stitch towards the right using the weaver from the left hand tally and this should be handled with care for the first few stitches.

Continue working until you reach the motif with four cloth stitch diamonds.

Gimps around the four cloth stitch diamonds.

1. Introduce a pair of gimps at A (figure 299), passing the left gimp through two pairs to B and the right gimp through two pairs to C. Work the top diamond.
2. Pass each gimp back through two pairs from the diamond until they meet in the centre. Cross the gimps and pass the gimp, now on the right, through two pairs towards the right (the gimps should lie parallel, i.e. no twists between them), to D and through two more pairs to E. The point where the gimps cross tends to move to some point between C and D. Work the right diamond.
3. Pass the right gimp through the two pairs from the right diamond to F, and then the other two pairs to the centre. Cross the gimps.
4. Continue passing the same gimp through two pairs to G and another two pairs to H, for the left diamond. Work the left diamond.
5. Pass the left gimp through the four pairs from the left diamond.
6. Cross the gimps when they meet.
7. Pass the gimp now on the right, towards the right through two pairs to I, and the gimp now on the left through two pairs to J.
8. Work the lower diamond.
9. Pass both gimps back through two pairs until they meet at the base of the motif, K,
10. Cross the gimps, Double each gimp back through two pairs, the one now on the left back to J and the one now on the right to I.
11. Throw the gimp bobbins back over the pins and leave until they are required for the next motif.
12. When gimps are needed for the next bud cut off those thrown back leaving 15cm (6 ins) of thread and reuse them[9&10]. Trim the ends off later.

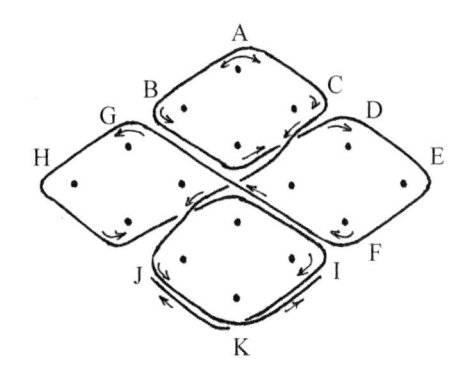

Figure 299 Gimps around the four diamonds

Continue making the insert and cast off as for the small motif.

Making up the brush[8]
Mount the lace as for the small motif, securing the lace in place with a few small stitches along the footside passives, and make up the brush according to the manufacturer's instructions.

This design also fits into the 15cm (6in) ruler

PROJECT 14 RULER INSERT *Figure 300 Ruler with lace insert*

Chapter 10

Materials required
pricking (figure 302)[1&2]
Egyptian cotton no. 100/2
perle thread, no 8 for gimp
30cm (12in) ruler kit

New Technique
neatening a point where both sides will be visible

Figure 301 Right side of insert showing neatened point

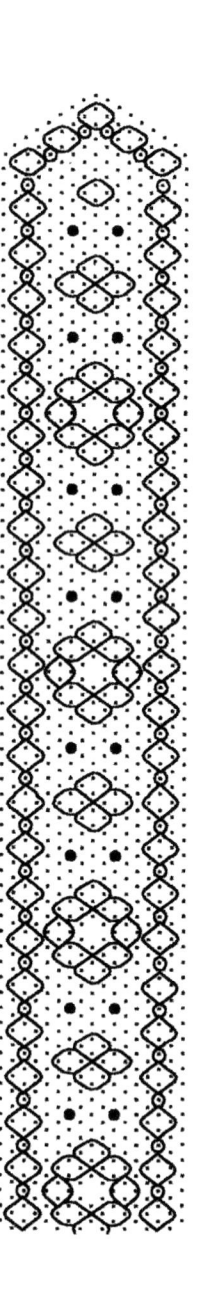

Pattern Draft
Make two copies of the pattern draft (figure 302) and join them A-A to make a length 19.5cm (11½ ins) long or adjust according to the length of the ruler. <u>Note:</u> Check the arrangement of four-pin and single stitch honeycomb rings at the points. This arrangement is dictated by the number of rings down the sides.

Making the insert
This lace insert is made using the techniques described above and is finished by neatening the end since both sides of the lace insert will be visible.

Figure 302 (right) Pattern draft

Neatening at a point when both sides will be visible

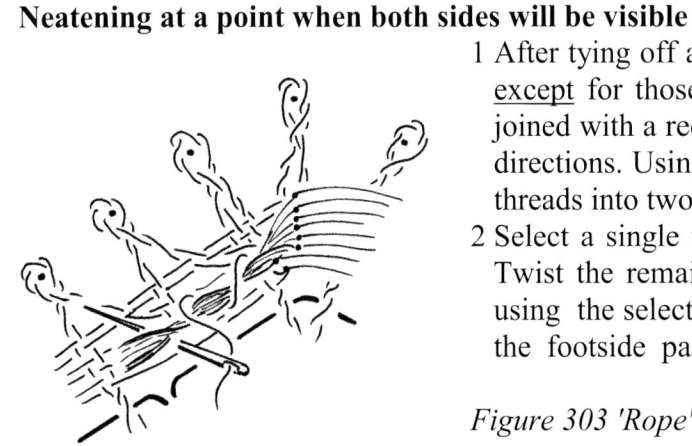

1 After tying off at the point trim all threads close to the work <u>except</u> for those that were knotted. When two threads are joined with a reef knot the threads leave the knot in different directions. Using this natural 'parting' separate the remaining threads into two groups.
2 Select a single thread, usually the longest, from one group. Twist the remaining threads of that group into a rope and, using the selected thread, whip the 'rope' along the gimp or the footside passives (figure 303). Only three or four small

Figure 303 'Rope' sewn to the back of the footside passives

120

Chapter 10

stitches are needed, then fasten off the thread securely.
3 Repeat for the other group of threads.
4 Trim all remaining threads close to the work (figure 304).
5 Make up the ruler according to the manufacturers instructions.

Figure 304 Back of insert showing neatened point

END NOTES

1 Drafting the patterns.

Adjusting size
Note: The brush back pattern is worked on a different grid from the others, the grid having been reduced slightly so that the pattern fits comfortably into the space available.

Sometimes patterns will not quite fit the available space and small increases or decreases in size can make all the difference to the final effect (use a photocopier), often without requiring a change in thread size. The brush back grid is slightly smaller than the grid used for the other projects in this chapter, but the difference is so slight that the same thread is be used.

1a Drafting the small motif pattern
1 Using Grid no. 2 (56°, 50 pins per 10 cm along the footside) draw the gimps (figure 305).
2 Remove the centre dot from the honeycomb ring in the large motif and trim, allowing one row of pins surrounding the gimps for the picots (figure 306)
3 Adjust the dots for the picots (figure 287).

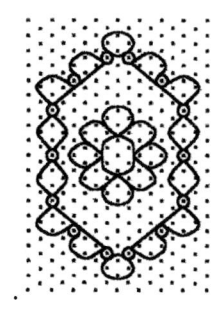

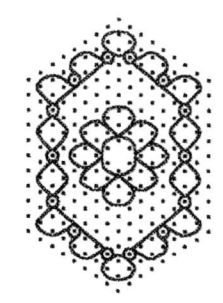

Figure 305 Gimps drawn   *Figure 306 Centre dot removed and edges trimmed*

121

Chapter 10

1b Drafting the brush insert pattern
1 Using Grid no. 6 (56°, 50 pins per 10 cm along the footside) draw the gimps (figure 307).
Note There are three four-pin honeycomb rings together at the points.
2 Remove the centre dot from the honeycomb rings in the three large motifs; draw the large dots, the tally indicators (these are not pricked), and trim allowing one row of pins, surrounding the gimps, for the picots. (Note how the two tallies 'fill' the space between the motifs.)
3 Adjust the dots for the picots (figure 296).

Figure 307 (right)Brush insert, gimps drawn, edges trimmed, dot removed from honeycomb ring and, tally indicators added

1c Drafting the ruler insert pattern
1 On Using Grid no. 2 (56°, 50 pins per 10 cm along the footside) draw the gimps (figure 308). <u>Note:</u> this pattern draft has the same arrangement of four-pin and single stitch honeycomb rings at the points of the small motif.
2 Remove the centre dot from the honeycomb rings in the three large motifs, draw the large dots and the tally indicators and trim allowing one row or pins surrounding the gimps for the picots.
3 Adjust the dots for the picots (figure 302).

Figure 308 (far right) Ruler, gimps drawn, dot removed from honeycomb ring and tally indicators added

2a Calculating the number of pairs required when there is a footside on one side and a headside on the other
On the pattern draft (e.g. figure 309) or pricking, select a diagonal line across the pattern at one of the widest parts. If a pattern draft is used draw a line through the dots. If a pricking is used a transparent ruler can be used to identify the line. Working from the footside allow:

A	two pairs for the footpin (edge pair and footside workers).
B	two pairs for the gap between the footpin and the catch-pin (footside passives).
C	one pair per ground pin, including the catch-pin.
D	one pair for per pin along the side of a cloth stitch area.
E	one pair per pin along the line within the cloth stitch area where a dot was removed. when the pattern was drafted.
F	one pair per pin for each honeycomb stitch (continuous or gap row).
G	one pin per gap along a gap row of honeycomb.
H	two pairs for the gap between the headpin and the first pin within the headside.

Chapter 10

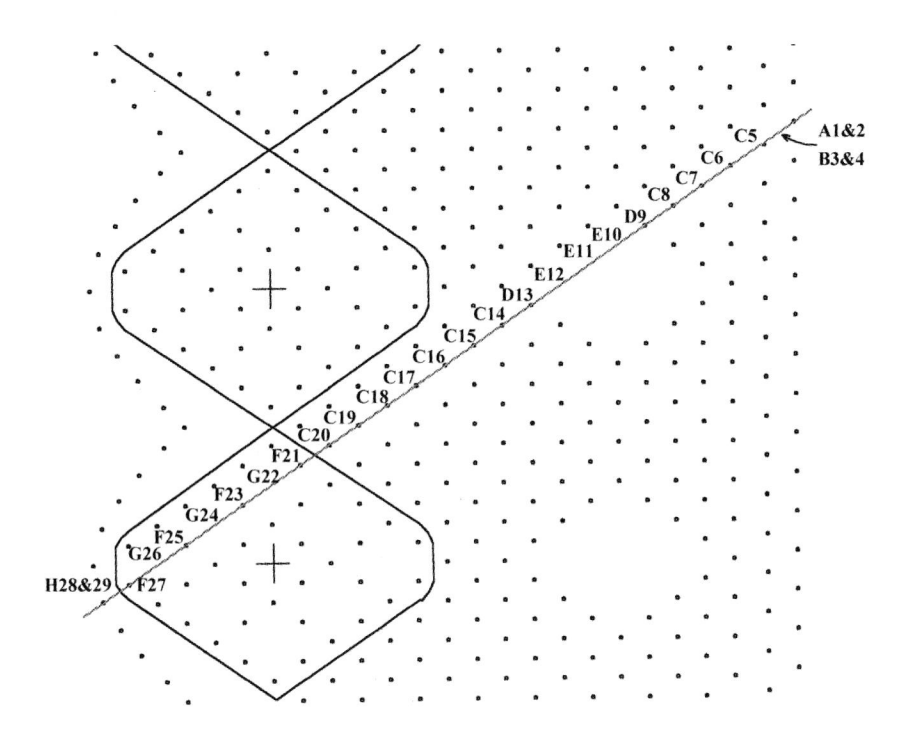

Figure 309 Counting pairs from the footside 29 pairs will be needed to make this lace

In practice it is not necessary to count the number of pairs required. Most lacemakers wind some bobbins then start setting in; more bobbins being wound as required. The same is true for the gimps. Even if you have counted the number of pairs you will need, it is wise to keep some extra bobbins and thread available just in case!

2b Calculating the number of pairs required when there is a headside on both sides

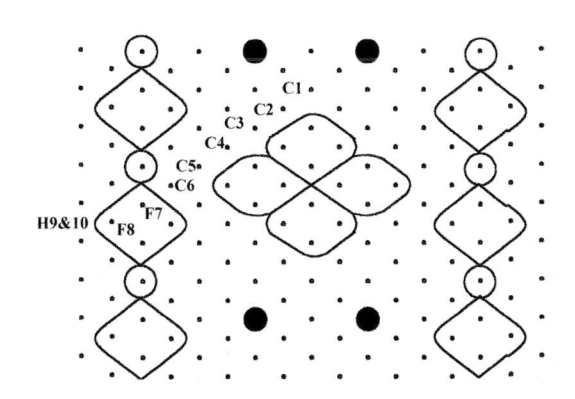

Figure 310 Counting pairs from the centre of the headside. 29 pairs will be needed to make this lace

On the pattern draft, or pricking, select a diagonal line across the pattern from a centre dot to one side at one of the widest parts and from the same centre dot along the diagonal to the other side. Starting from the centre dot, C1 (figure 310), count the pairs towards one edge as for figure 309, and since both sides are the same double the number. (The centre pin, C1, is counted for both sides.) If the sides are different, count each separately, and then add together. For this pattern 10 pairs will be required each side making a total of 20. A pair of gimps will be required each side and a pair for the small cloth stitch diamond and the set of four cloth stitch diamonds. For the brush insert and ruler an extra pair will be required for the larger motifs, making four pairs in total.

123

Chapter 10

2c Calculating the number of pairs required when there is a footside on both sides

On the pattern draft or pricking select a diagonal line across the pattern from a footside dot to one side at one side to a centre dot, and from the same dot to the other footside. For this pattern the easiest line would be one through only ground, but to illustrate how to count through the motif a more difficult route has been chosen. Starting from the footside dot (figure 311) count the pairs required as far as the centre dot and, since both sides are the same, double the number. (The centre pin, D12, is counted for both sides.) If the sides are different, count each separately and add together.

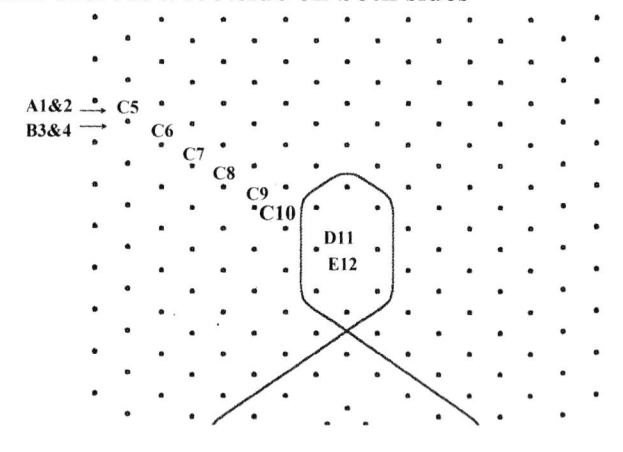

Figure 311 Counting pairs from the footside to the centre. 24 pairs will be needed

3 Traditional method for adding pairs along a diagonal row of picots

This is the traditional method for adding pairs. However, it causes the picots to sit at different angles and they group into pairs, looking like a row of bunnies' ears poking up from behind the gimp (figure 313). The former method may not be traditional but gives better results.

1. Set in at the point with three false picots (figure 312).
2. Introduce the gimp and make the top honeycomb stitch of the four-pin honeycomb ring.
3. Make a false picot at the next picot position, pin 4, and work pair 2 across the passives and gimp to work the next honeycomb stitch of the ring.
4. Cloth stitch the other pair from the false picot at pin 4 through the two pairs of passives. Take the second of those passive pairs to work the next picot, return through the passives and gimp to enter the motif. Repeat these steps 3 and 4 as required.

Figure 312 (upper right) Traditional method for adding pairs along a diagonal row of picots

Figure 313 (lower right) Traditional method for adding pairs along a diagonal row of picots

4 Adding a single pair at a picot (traditional method)

If only one more pair is required slip this pair on the picot pair immediately before the picot is made (figure 314).

Figure 314 (right) Slipping a new pair onto the picot pair

Make the picot and return it through all the passive pairs (figure 315).

Figure 315 (left) Single pair added at a picot

If this is the last pair required along a diagonal line of picots, the inner of the three pairs of passives works out to make the next picot.

5 Picots on the right side

Picots on the right hand edge made with five twists, as for the left hand edge, frequently split. When the twists are examined it become apparent that, when making a left hand picot, the process produces another twist resulting in a total of six twists. When a right hand picot is made the process undoes one of the twists resulting in a total of four twists. The reason for split picots is now apparent. Making an additional two twists on the picot pair on the right side, i.e. making seven twists before the picot is made, will give a final total of six twists after the picot is made and should result in better picots (figure 316). This may not be traditional but it gives good results.

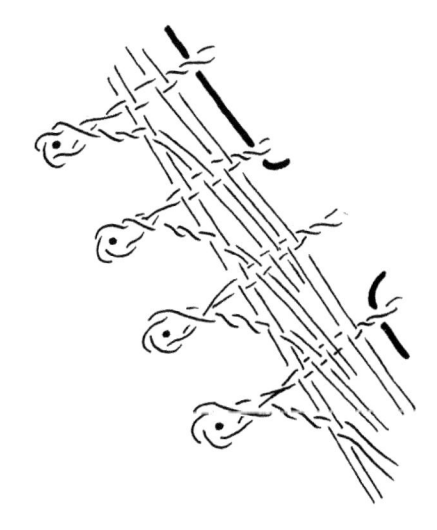

Figure 316 Right side picot

Figure 317 Casting off along a diagonal line of picots

6a Alternative method for casting off along a diagonal line of picots

After stacking the third pair, throw back the second pair from the gimp (figure 317). This method has the disadvantage that both threads being thrown out come from the same picot. When the second and third threads from the picot are thrown out one of them has been in the stack longer (figure 293).

6b Another method for casting along a diagonal line of picots
Although not a traditional English technique this method results in a stronger finish and tends to separate the footside passives from the gimp. Work the picot pairs through all the passives and leave, and then throw back the second and third threads (figure 318) or the second and fourth threads (not illustrated).

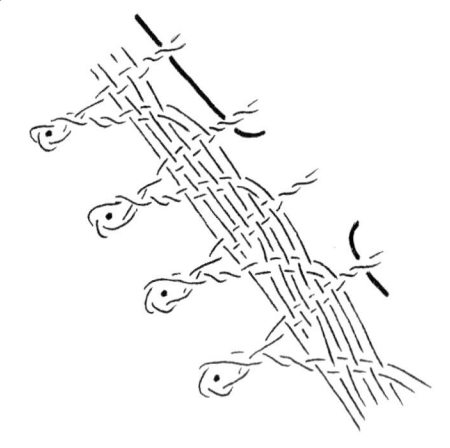

Figure 318 (right) Casting off along a diagonal line of picots

8 Reef knot with extra turn
Sometime problems are encountered with the first half of a reef knot slipping before the second half can be firmed up. To minimize this slipping pass the right thread twice round the left thread when making the first half of the stitch (figure 319). This is less likely to slip while the normal second half, left over right, is made and firmed up (figure 320), although it adds a little to the bulk of the knot.

Figure 319 Reef knot with extra turn -1st half 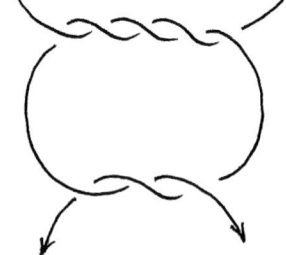   *Figure 320 Reef knot with extra turn - 2nd half*

8 Right or wrong side
The side uppermost when Bucks point is made, is considered to be the right side, because when lace is freshly made the gimps stand proud on this side and make it more interesting than the side that was pressed against the pricking and is, therefore, much flatter. However, when the lace is finished at a point the knots show more on the upper side than the underside there is a good case for turning the lace over.

9 Bowing off
Originally a Honiton Lace technique, this is a useful method for cutting off pairs of bobbins in such a way that they remain knotted together for reusing. Use a loose bladed, preferably blunt, pair of scissors.
1 Lay the blades of the scissors flat on the pair of threads and wind the blades round the threads. (figure 321).
2 Open the blades and close them over the threads without cutting them (figure 322).
3 Draw the gripped threads through the loop around the blades (figure 323).
4 Cut the threads.
5 Separate the bobbins to tighten the knot

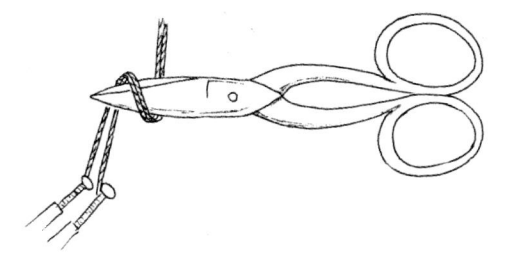

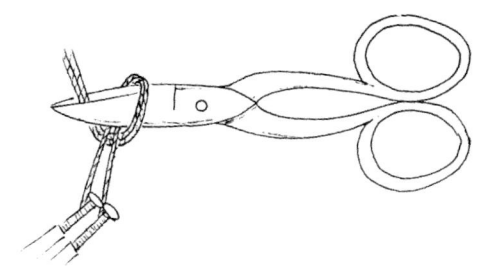

Figure 321 Wind the thread around the blades *Figure 322 Grip the threads*

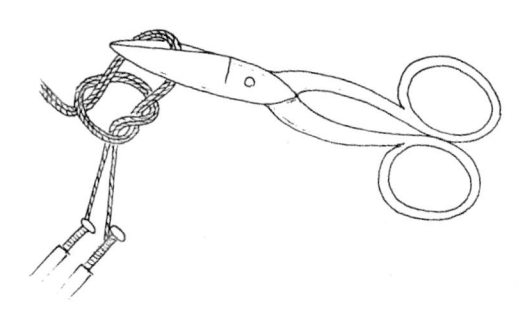

Figure 323 Pull the threads though the loop

10 Winding on

When reusing bobbins that have been bowed off, or joined by knotting, wind some thread from one bobbin onto the other and replace the hitches. The bobbins can now be reused to start a piece of lace without knots along the starting line. When knots are encountered replace a thread in the usual way.

Warning! Do not wind on the same amount for each pair, otherwise half the bobbins will need replacing at the same time!

Chapter 11

PROJECTS 15-18 WEDDING GIFTS (Plate 4)

Project 15 Garter
Project 16 Ring Pillow
Project 17 Photograph Trim
Project 18 Handkerchief

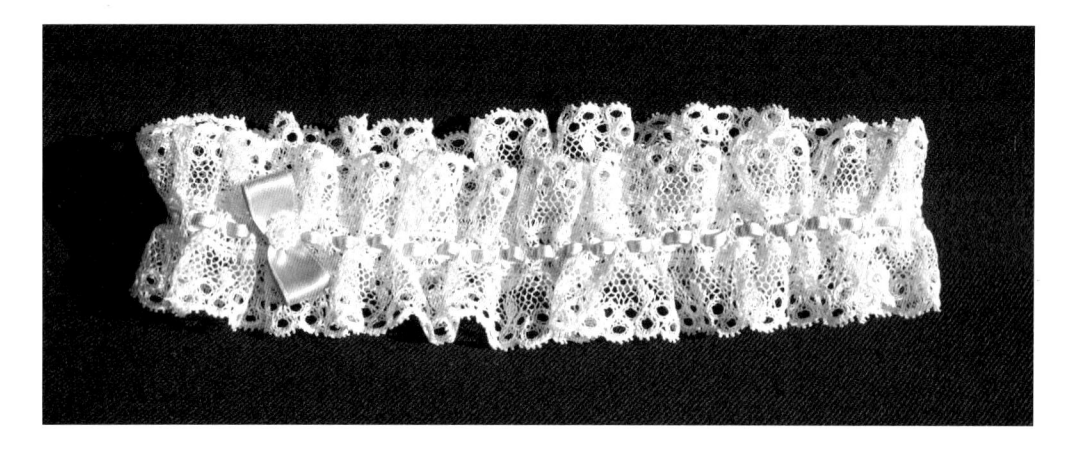

Figure 324 Wedding Garter

New Techniques for Projects 15, 16, 17 & 18
   footside on the left
   irregular valley
   fingers in point ground
   footside with half stitch about the pin
   using a French pillow
   attaching gathered lace
   gathering lace around a corner
   side reverse
   reusing a pin when turning a corner at the footside
   joining lace by oversewing
   neatening fabric with minimum bulk
   attaching a lace overlay to a neatened edge

Materials for Project 15 Garter
   pattern drafts (figures 325 & 330)[1]
   Egyptian cotton no. 60
   gimp, perle no 8
   1m of 4mm elastic
   1m of 3.5 mm blue ribbon
   10 cms of 15 mm blue ribbon for bow
   pearl trim

End Notes
1 drafting the pattern, designing the corner, designing the side reverse
2 Estimating extra pairs required in the headside when not starting at the widest point
3 using a French pillow
4 half stitch about the pin

Chapter 11

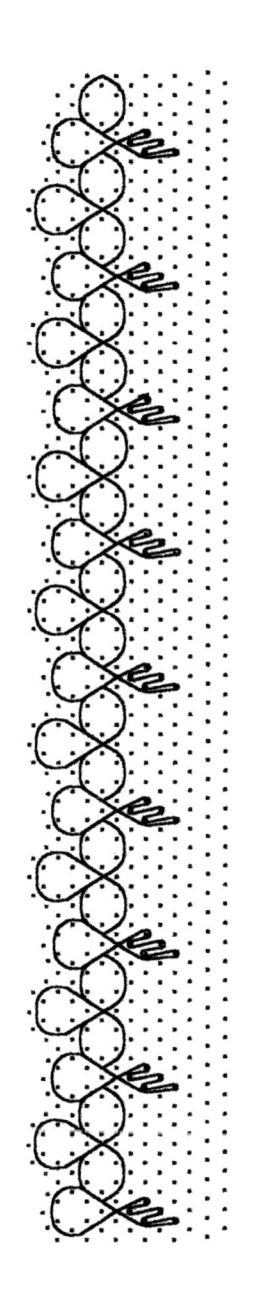

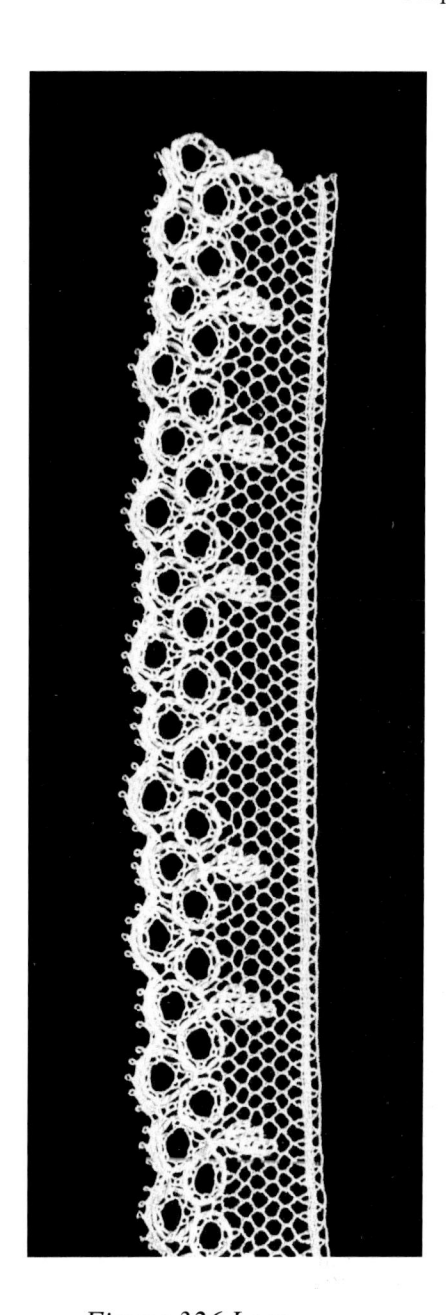

Figure 325 Pattern draft   *Figure 326 Lace*

Estimating the lengths of lace required for the garter
Garters come in various sizes and the distance around the leg should be checked. My garter consists of an insertion having 94 pattern repeats, between two edgings each having 60 repeats.

In this and subsequent chapters it is assumed that, unless otherwise stated, in, that pairs will be added as required when setting in, and that no twists will be made where two gimps lie adjacent to each other.

129

Chapter 11

Setting in the edging[2,3&4]

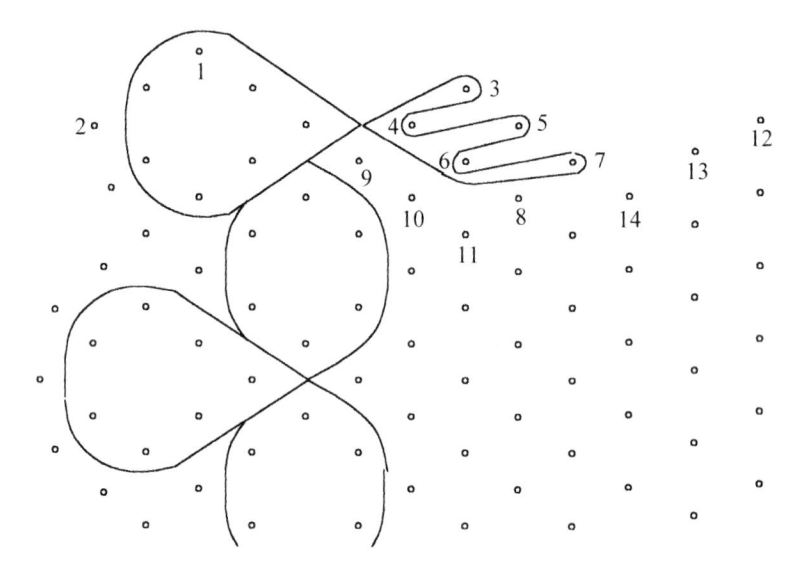

Figure 327 Setting in

1 Start at the top of an indented ring, pin 1, (figure 327) and work the pins either side. Add three pairs[2] of headside passives when starting the headside at the centre picot, pin 2, and complete the ring.
2 Pass the gimp, nearest the headside, under the completed ring and up the other side to cross the other gimp.
3 Work the fingers in the ground, according to the indicator line on the pricking, making point ground stitches in the loops, pins 3-7. The pairs work normally as for point ground, the gimps just pass through.
4 Work the point ground stitch below the fingers, pin 8. Both gimps now travel to the top of the next six-pin ring. Make the point ground stitch, pin 9, work the other two point ground stitches down the side of the fingers, pins 9-11, and cross the gimps.
5 Start the footside, pin 12, (figure 328) at the top of the diagonal that passes immediately below the fingers, with the stitch at pin 14 joining the sections.
6 All the pairs are now in use.

Half stitch at the footside[4]

For the edgings and insertion, for this item, a half stitch should be used for the stitch about the pin[4] instead of the usual cloth stitch. The half stitch at the edge reduces the bulk where two footsides are joined, (see pin 15 figure 328).

Figure 328 (right) Setting in the footside and the first catch-pin stitch having a half stitch about the pin

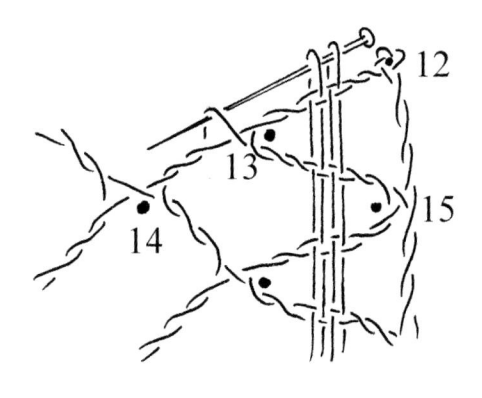

130

Chapter 11

The headside

There are many ways in which this headside can be worked. This is the one that gives me the best finish, but there are others that may suit other lacemakers.

1 Ring A has been set in with a picot, pin 1, (figure 329) at the side.
2 Using a pair from the ring work the next picot, pin 2, and return the picot pair through one pair of passives.
3 Work ring B, making the honeycomb stitch at the side, pin 3, with the innermost pair of passives. (Twist the passives twice before making the stitch.) Complete ring B.
4 Work the valley pin, pin 4, using the remaining pair from ring A, and return it through one pair.
5 Work the remaining pair from pin 3 out to make the next picot, pin 5, and return it through three pairs of passives.
6 Start ring C with the picot pair from pin 5 and the fourth pair of passives.
7 Work the second pair of passives out to make the next picot, pin 6, and return it to the ring to make a honeycomb stitch. From this stitch a pair works out to make the next picot, pin 7. Complete ring C.
8 Work the next pair from, ring C, out to make the next picot, pin 8, and return it through one pair. Repeat this with the next pair from ring C, pin 9.
9 Work ring D, using the remaining pair from ring C to make the honeycomb stitch, pin 10, at the side of the ring.

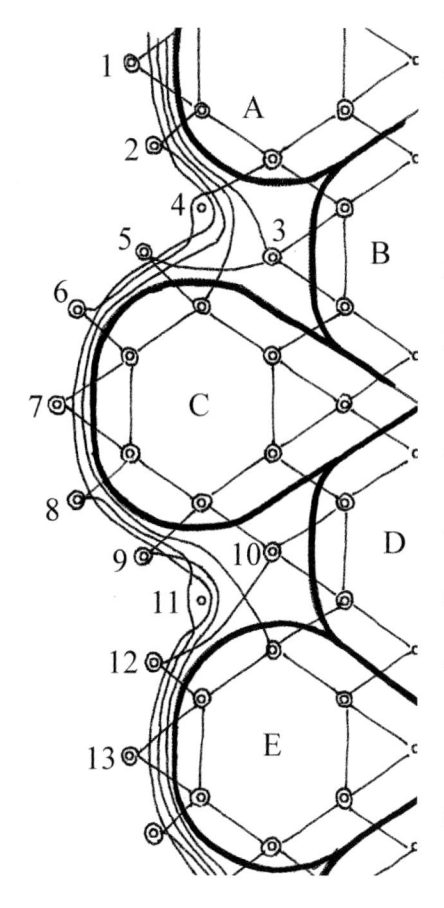

Figure 329 The headside

10 Work the valley pin, pin 11, with the third pair of passives and return it through one pair of passives.
11 Work the remaining pair from pin 10 out to make the next picot, pin 12 and return it through the passives and gimp.
12 Start ring E using the innermost passive pair and a pair from ring D and use the pair from the picot, pin 12, for the next stitch near the headside.
13 The next picot, pin 13, is in the same position as the first picot, pin 1.

Continue the edging

Continue for 60 pattern repeats and join the end to the start. Remove all the pins, darn the ends away, and trim all ends off closely. Make another to match.

Making the insertion

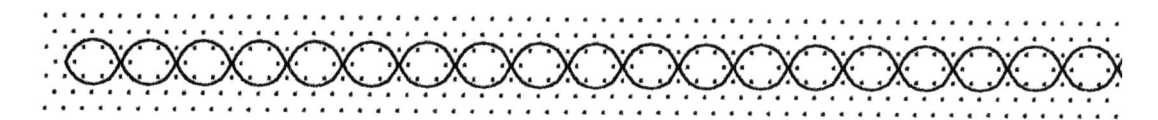

Figure 330 Pattern draft for the insertion

131

Chapter 11

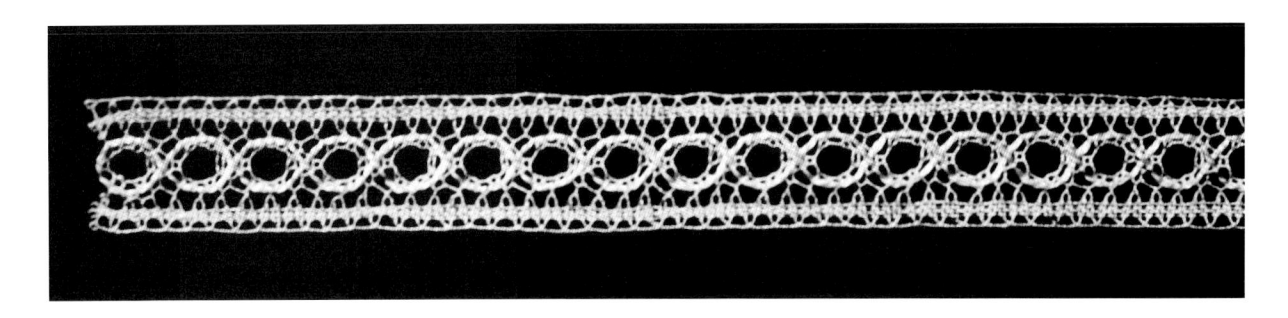

Figure 331 Insertion

Setting in
Make a pricking of the pattern draft (figure 330), dress the pillow, and wind the bobbins, and one pair of gimps, in couples.

Setting in the right footside
Starting at pin 1 (figure 332) set in as far as pin 4 as for making the edging, again using a half stitch about the pin. The catch-pin stitch at pin 4 cannot be made until after the honeycomb stitch at pin 6 has been made.

Setting in the honeycomb ring
1 Place two pairs of bobbins and a pair of gimps on separate temporary pins to the left of the work, with the gimps between the two pairs. Pass each gimp through the adjacent pair, twist the pairs and work a honeycomb stitch, pin 5.
2 Pass the right gimp through the pair from catch-pin stitch, pin 2, and work a honeycomb stitch, pin 6. Pass the gimp through the nearest pair from the honeycomb stitch and work the catch-pin stitch at pin 4. Let down the passives and catch-pin pair onto a support pin. Pass the gimp back through the nearest pair from this stitch and work a honeycomb stitch, pin 7.

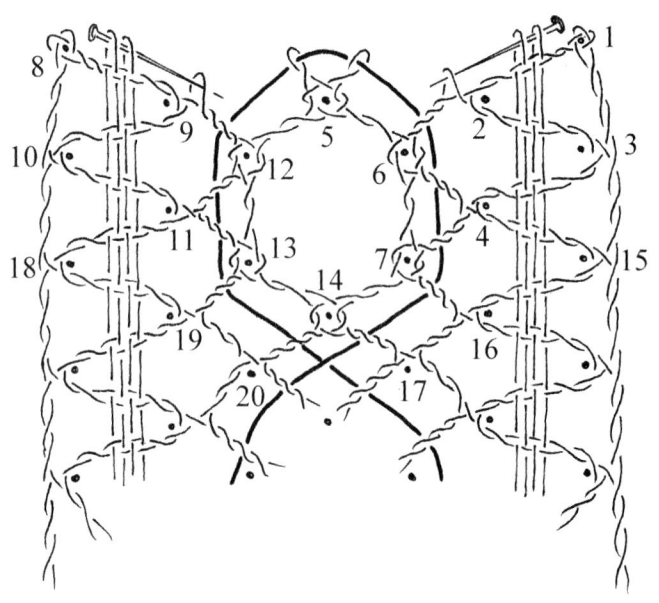

Figure 332 Setting in the gimp and honeycomb stitch

Setting in the left footside
1 Starting at pin 8, set in with a whole stitch round the pin. Cloth stitch through two pairs of passives, set up the catch-pin, pin 9, work the catch–pin stitch and let down the passives and catch-pin pair onto a support pin.
2 Work the footside, pin 10, making a half stitch about the pin as at the other side, and set up the catch-pin, pin 11. The catch-pin stitch at pin 11 cannot be made until after the honeycomb stitch at pin 12 has been made

132

Continue the honeycomb ring
3 Pass the left gimp through the pair from catch-pin stitch, pin 9, and work a honeycomb stitch, pin 12. Pass the gimp through the nearest pair from the honeycomb stitch and work the catch-pin stitch with the pair at pin 11. Pass the gimp through the nearest pair from this stitch and work a honeycomb stitch, pin 13.
4 Work the last honeycomb stitch of the ring, pin 14, pass the gimps through the pairs and cross the gimps.
5 Starting from the right footside work the footside, pin 15, the catch-pin stitch, pin 16, and a point ground stitch, pin 17.
6 Starting from the left footside work the footside, pin 18, catch-pin stitch, pin 19 and a point ground stitch, pin 20.
Continue until 92 pattern repeats have been made.

Joining the insertion
1 When the lace is approaching the required length repin the start of the work back on the pricking.
2 Complete the last honeycomb ring and thread one gimp through the start of the gimp and double up along one side of the ring so that two pairs cross the doubled gimps and throw both gimps back.
3 Make the remaining catch-pin and ground stitches working a pair from the last catch-pin stitch back to the footside.
4 Join a pair from the point ground stitch to the start of the pair that worked the first honeycomb stitch by sewing one thread through the loop over the gimp and tying it to its partner. Repeat on the other side by joining the pair from the point ground stitch to the remaining loop from the support pin by sewing one thread of the point ground stitch through the loop and tying it to its partner with a reef knot (figure 333).
5 Join the footsides passives.
6 Join the footside workers and edge pair to the whole stitch around the pin at the edge.
7 Remove all the pins and sew all the ends away. Trim all ends off closely.

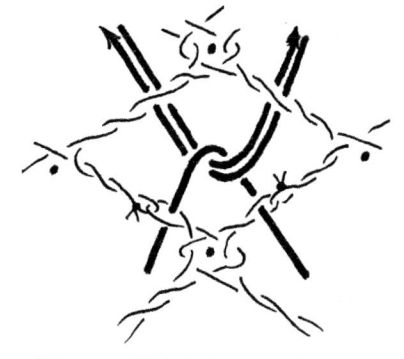

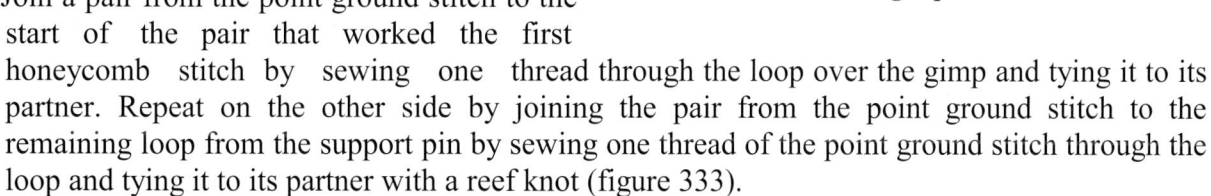

Figure 333 Joining gimps and joining point ground to honeycomb across the gimp

Joining the edgings to the insertion
1 Using a ballpoint needle, introduce a gathering thread along the edging by oversewing through the footside pinholes of the lace.
2 Gather the edging to fit the insertion and oversew the two together, using footpin holes whenever possible.
3 Repeat, attaching the other edging to the other side of the insertion.
4 Sew the one end of the narrow ribbon and elastic together and thread them through the honeycomb holes of the insertion.
5 Cut the ribbon a little shorter than the insertion, to prevent the lace from being stretched out of shape. Check that the wearer's foot passes through easily, and join to its start.
6 Adjust the elastic to make a snug fit around the leg, and stitch the ends together.

Chapter 11

Making the bow
1 Cut a 10cm (4in) length of 15mm wide ribbon.
2 Overlap the ends and, using double thread, make a line of small running stitches through the centre of the overlap (figure 334).

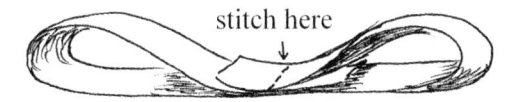

Figure 334 (left) Stitching the bow

3 Gather the stitches tightly. Fasten off, but do not cut off. Use the same double thread to bind several times tightly round the ribbon over the gathered stitches. Fasten off the thread but leave the end.
4 Using the remaining thread, to stitch on a pearl trim or piece of narrow ribbon to cover the binding thread, and to attach the bow to the garter.

Ensure a comfortable fit, while making sure the garter will not slip. For extra security, two small safety pins can be used to attach the garter to tights or stockings

PROJECT 16 RING PILLOW
Materials
   pattern draft figure 325
   pattern draft figure 330
   Egyptian cotton no. 60
   10 cm (4 ins) X 19 cm (7½ ins) fabric
   sewing thread to match fabric
   stuffing
   gimp, perle no 8
   0.5 m (½ yd) 3.5 mm blue ribbon
   0.75 m (¾ yd) 3.5 mm blue ribbon for bows, or purchase ready-made bows to match
   0.25 m (¼ yd) 6 mm white ribbon for bow to hold rings

Figure 335 Ring pillow

For the ring pillow[4]
Make one edging with 36 pattern repeats, (pattern draft figure 325), with a half stitch about the pin along the footside[4]. Join the edging end to start.

Make one insertion with 44 pattern repeats, (pattern draft figure 330), with a half stitch about the pin along one foot side and a cloth stitch about the pin along the other foot side. Join end to start.

Making up the pillow

1. Fold the fabric in half, right sides together, and stitch round three and a half sides (0.5 (¼ in) cm seam allowance). Turn through, stuff and close the opening.
2. Starting from the join of the insertion, mark each 11 pattern repeats along the edge with a half stitch about the pin with a pin or coloured thread. Pin the insertion on the cushion with the marked points at the corners and fold over the corners to make them lie flat. Sew both the outer and inner edges of the corners to the cushion to stabilize them while the edging is being attached; stitching all the way across would prevent the ribbon being passed through. (The insertion will not reach the edges of the cushion; the small portion of the cushion behind the lace stops it drooping.)
3. Introduce a gathering thread along the edging by oversewing through the footside pinholes. Pull up the first three pattern repeats as closely as possible *and arrange evenly around one corner of the insertion; the gathered section will not make an exact right angle around the corner but a small curve..
4. Gently gather the next six pattern repeats to fit between the attached corner and the next corner, then oversew this section of the edging to the insertion.
5. Pull up the next three pattern repeats as closely as possible* and repeat *to* three times.
6. Introduce the narrow ribbon through the rings of the insertion and sew its corners in place.
7. Make four small bows and sew in place at the corners.
8. Sew the centre of the white ribbon to the centre of the cushion, thread one ring on each end and make a bow to secure them in place.

PROJECT 17
PHOTOGRAPH TRIM

Materials
pattern draft figure 337
pattern draft figure 338
Egyptian cotton no. 60
gimp, perle no 8
ballpoint needle
photograph frame with glass both sides

*Figure 336 (left)
Wedding photograph trim*

Chapter 11

Figure 337 Pattern draft (edging) This draft has one less row of pins in ground than the pattern draft for the garter (figure 325)

Side reverse
This edging has a one way pattern, i.e. parts of the pattern, namely the fingers, change direction when the pattern is turned at the corner and, if no change was made, another corner would have to be designed with the fingers facing the other way, and the square would have to be made with these two different corners. To avoid this problem the pattern is reversed, usually half way along each side. The change in the design at this point is known as a side reverse and occurs between the centre two sets of fingers in the ground, figures 337 & 339.

Making the edging
Make one edging piece pattern draft figure 337, with a half stitch about the pin[4 at] the footside, starting with the fingers immediately below a corner as for the garter but, since there is one less row of pins between the footside and the fingers, there will be one less pair.

Chapter 11

Working fingers after the side reverse
Half way down the side there is a side reverse and the remaining fingers are drawn the 'other way up' and worked accordingly.

Figure 338 Pattern draft (insertion)

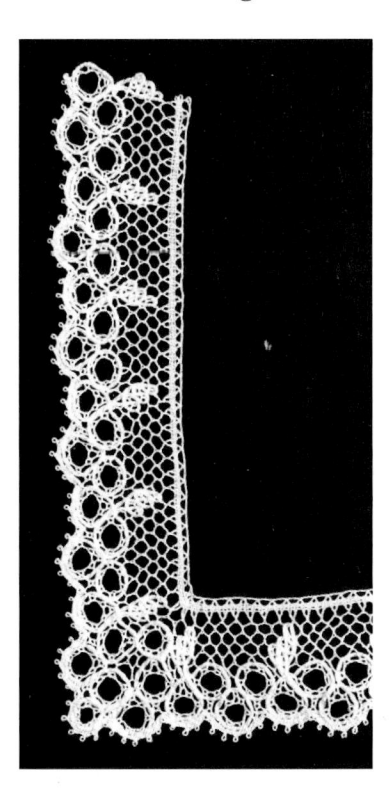

Figure 339 Lace edging 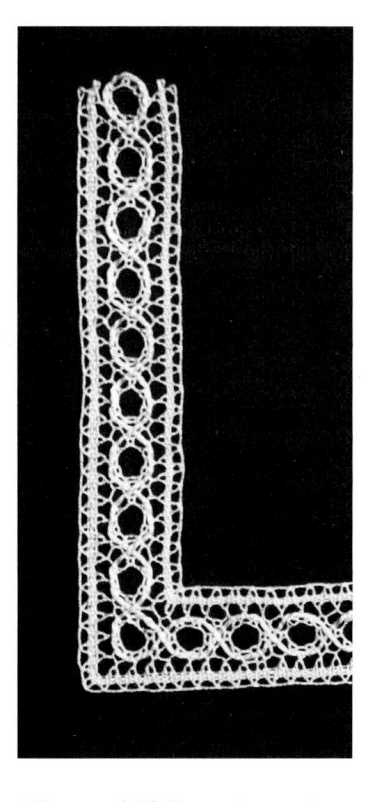   *Figure 340 Lace insertion*

137

Chapter 11

Working a corner with a single pin at the footside

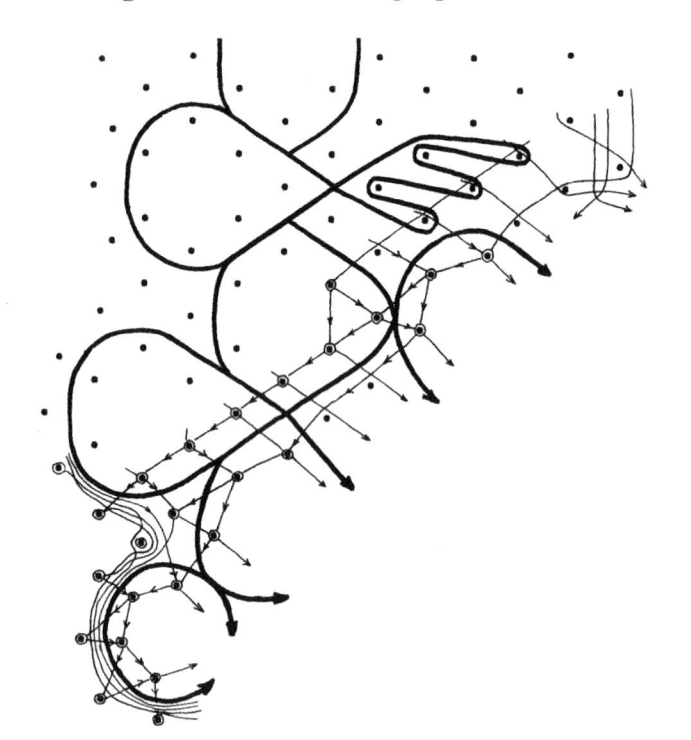

This corner was designed the same way as the corner for the Handkerchief/Jabot, (Chapter 8, Project 7) and worked along similar lines. However, since the two corner pinholes were too close to work satisfactorily, they were erased and replaced by a single pinhole in the corner.

Work as far as the diagonal through the corner, making a cloth stitch about the pin at corner pin of the footside (figure 341). Now turn the pillow through 90° and rearrange the cover cloths ready to work the next side.

Figure 341 (left) Working into the corner

After turning the pillow, always start working from the outer edge. It is easier to work in sections travelling from the diagonal towards the outer edge, i.e. finish the corner ring (figure 342). Complete the next ring that crosses the diagonal and work the seven-pin ring at the headside. Work the two point ground stitches by the diagonal and the adjacent seven-pin ring. Finish the last ring across the diagonal, the two point ground stitches towards the left and the next seven-pin ring. Work the point ground stitch next to the diagonal and the catch-pin stitch. The next pin appears to be the corner pin at the footside and that has already been used. Remove any twists on the edge pair, remove the corner pin, make up the footside and replace the pin in the pinhole as if it had not been previously used, i.e. do not try to replace it in the previous loop (figure 343). Firm up carefully. This stitch about the pin may be either a cloth stitch or a half stitch

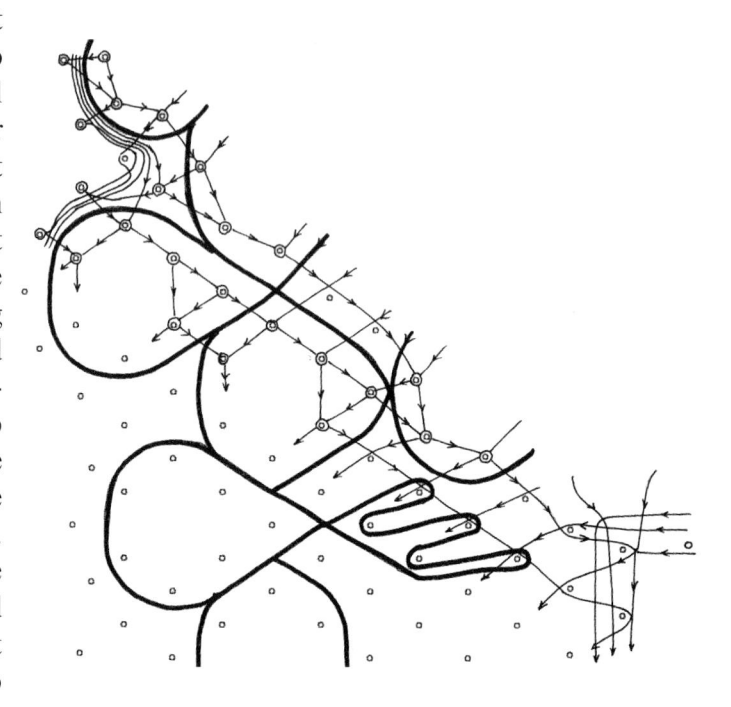

Figure 342 Reusing the corner pin

Chapter 11

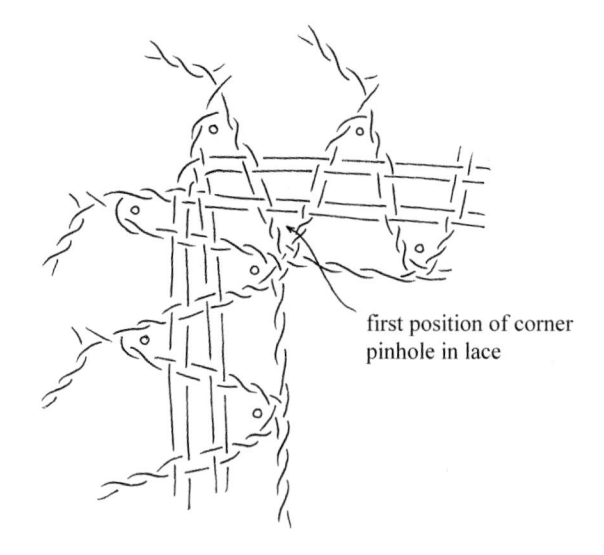

Figure 343 (left) Working out of the corner, reusing the corner pin

first position of corner pinhole in lace

Continue around the remainder of the square and join end to start darning the ends away carefully (both sides of the lace will be on show).

Making the insertion

Make one insertion piece using pricking figure 338, reusing the corner hole at the footside as for the edging (figures 343-344) and working the outer point of the corner as Figure 344. Continue around the remainder of the square and join end to start darning the ends away carefully (both sides of the lace will be on show).

Figure 344 (right) Insertion corner

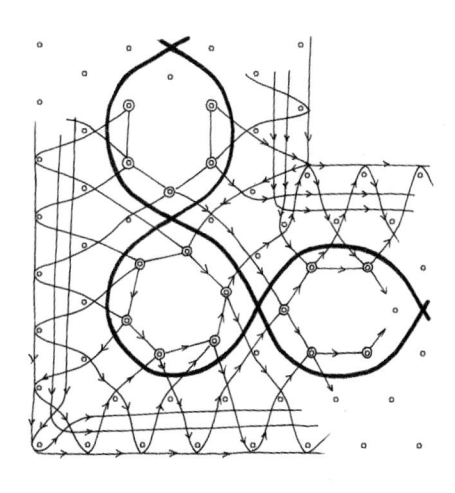

Making up the wedding photograph frame

Join the edging and insertion by oversewing through the footside holes. The two do not match exactly, due to the different numbers of pins per pattern repeat of the edging and insertion, so some adjustment will have to be made. Take great care, as both sides of the lace will be seen.

PROJECT 18
HANDKERCHIEF
Materials
    prickings (figures 346, 348 & 350)
    Egyptian cotton no. 60
    gimp, perle no 8
    20 cm (8 in) square fine linen or cotton fabric
    ballpoint needle

Figure 345 (left) Wedding handkerchief

139

Chapter 11

Figure 346 Pattern draft for corner

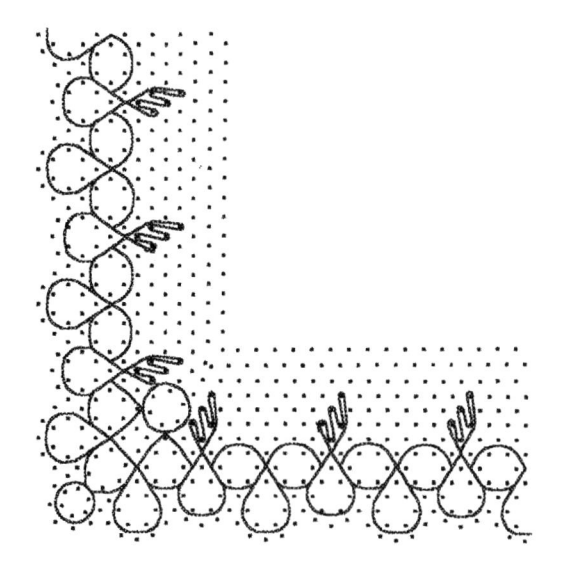

Figure 347 Lace edging with corner

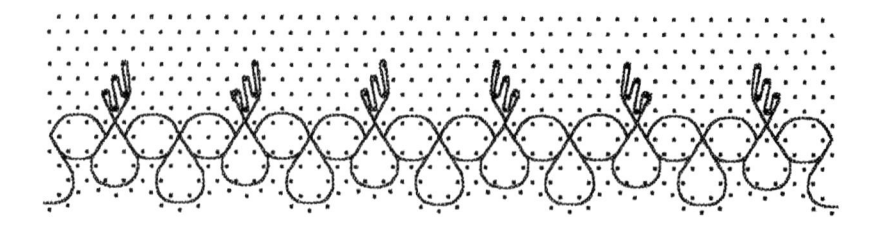

Figure 348 Pattern draft for side reverse

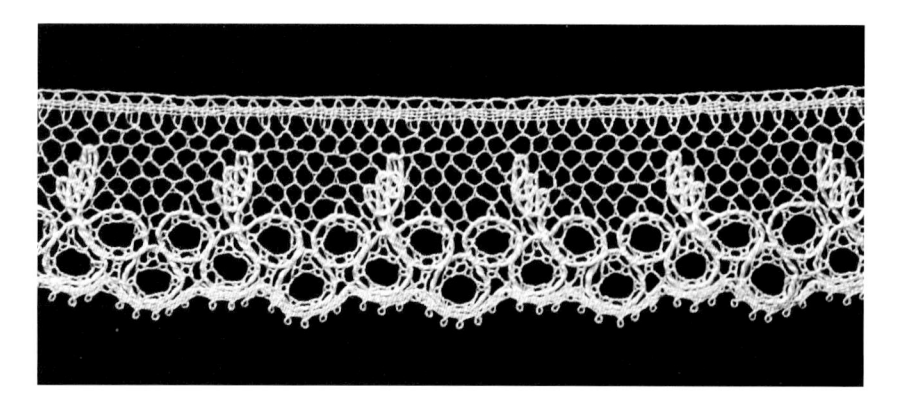

Figure 349 Lace edging with side reverse

For the edging
Make prickings for the edging using the pattern drafts for the corner and side reverse (figures 346 & 348), and for a 20 cm (8 in) handkerchief, including lace, dovetail them so that there are five sets of fingers, including the one at the corner, either side of the side reverse. Increase or decrease the number of pattern repeats if a different size is required.

Set up as for the garter and make a square edging with a half stitch about the pin[4] at the footside and reusing the corner pinhole at the footside as for the photograph trim. Join end to start.

Chapter 11

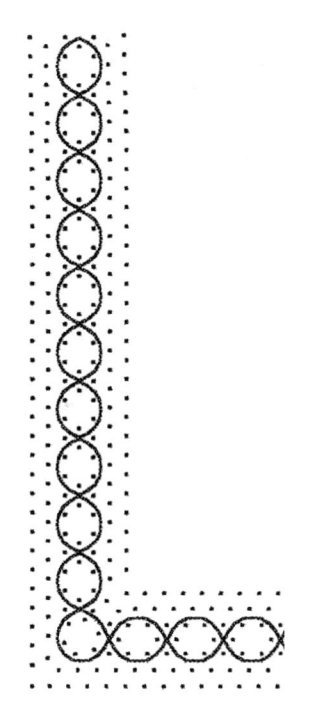

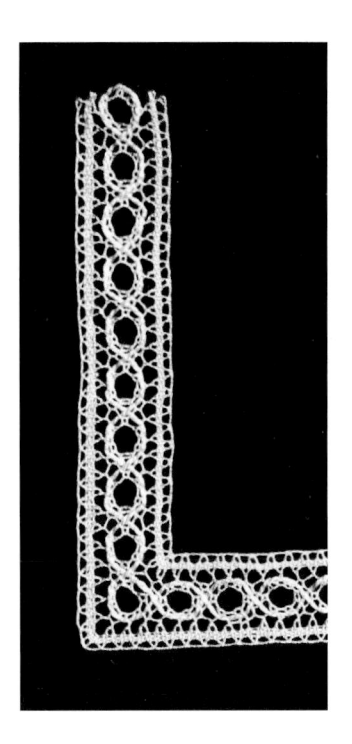

Figure 350 Insertion pattern draft *Figure 351 Lace Insertion, corner*

For the insertion
Make two prickings for the insertion from the pattern draft (figure 350), and dovetail them so that there will be 20 honeycomb rings, including corners, per side or adjust to fit within the edging if the edging was adjusted. Set up as for the garter and make a square insertion with a half stitch about the pin on both sides, and reusing the corner pinhole at the footside as for the photograph trim. Join end to start.

Attaching the edging to the fabric with the minimum of bulk when there will be an overlay applied next to it
1 Check that the fabric has not been distorted, i.e. that the threads lie at right angles. If necessary, pull the fabric to correct it and press.
2 Place the lace edging on the fabric, right side of lace to wrong side of fabric, and withdraw one fabric thread just inside the footside along each side. (About 2-3 threads inside)
3 Turn the lace over so that there are wrong sides together and offer one side up to the line of withdrawn thread, with headside facing away from the edge of the fabric. Pin, and then tack, in place (figure 352). The lace may need easing in slightly. The lace will 'stand out' at the corners.
4 Hemstitch the lace to the fabric along the footside

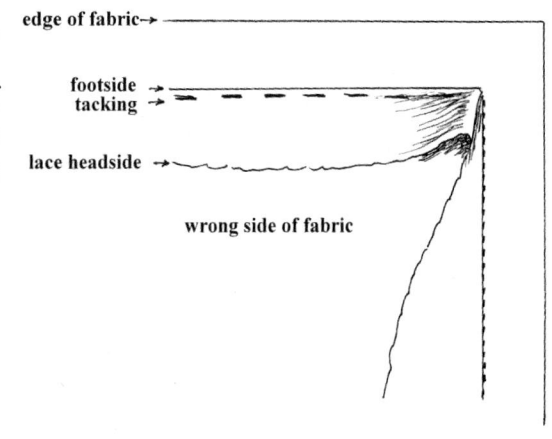

Figure 352 Edging tacked in place

141

Chapter 11

Hemstitching

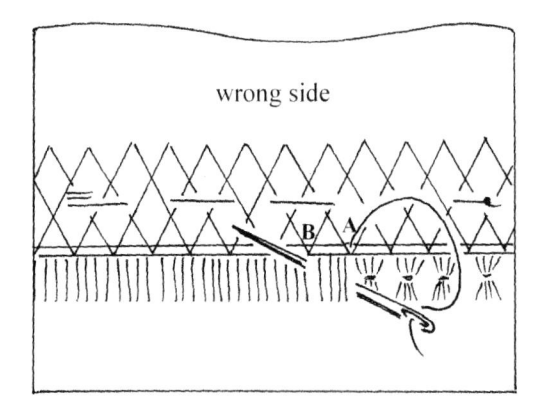

1 Using a ballpoint needle[6] fasten on the thread at A, a footside hole. *Pass the needle between the threads below A and bring out between the loose threads below the next footside hole, B. (figure 353).

Figure 353 (left) Hemstitching, 1ˢᵗ stitch

2 Insert the needle between the loose threads below A and bring out through the footside hole B (figure 354). Pull up tightly to bunch the loose threads, leaving holes on either side of the bunch*.
3 Repeat the process *to* at each pinhole of the footside.

Figure 354 (right) Hemstitching, 2ⁿᵈ stitch

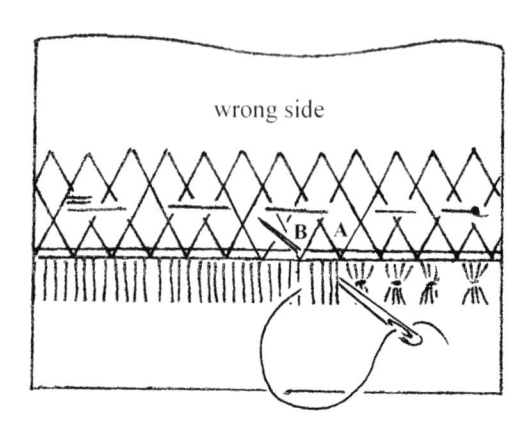

4 Remove the tacking and repeat steps 1-4 for each side in turn

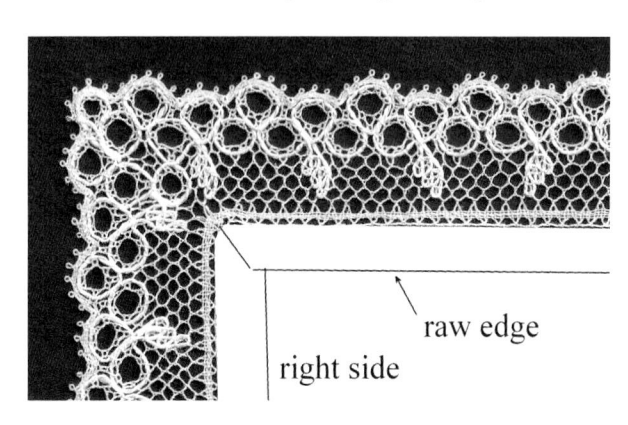

5 Turn back the free edge of the fabric, close to the seam, and flatten out the lace around the edge of the fabric. Turn the excess fabric onto the right side of the fabric centre, press along the seam and trim the 2mm ($\frac{1}{8}$ in) from the seam (figure 355); the raw edge is lying on the right side. Fold the raw edge neatly at the corners and tack in place.

Figure 355 (left) Fabric trimmed

6 Place the insertion onto the right side of the fabric, within the edging, hiding and protecting the raw edges. Oversew the insertion to the edging and fabric through the footside holes of both pieces of lace, easing in as necessary since the numbers of pinholes of the pattern repeats of the edging and insertion do not match exactly.
7 Tack the inner edges of the insertion in place and withdraw a thread along each side, taking care not to withdraw threads beyond the points where two sides meet. Attach the inner edge of the lace to the fabric by hemstitching (figures 353 & 354).

Chapter 11

*Figure 356 (left)
Finished corner at the
join (right side)*

*Figure 357 (right)
Finished corner at the
join (wrong side)*

END NOTES
1a Drafting the pattern
1 Using Grid no. 1 (56°, 40 pins per 10 cm along the footside) draw the gimps (figure 358). The pattern draft for the ring pillow has one less row of ground, see figure 337.

Figure 358 (right) Gimps drawn in

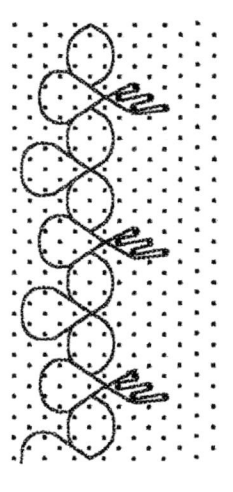

Chapter 11

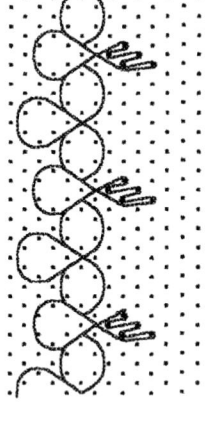

2 Remove dots from centres of the honeycomb rings (figure 359).

Figure 359 (left) Dots within honeycomb rings removed

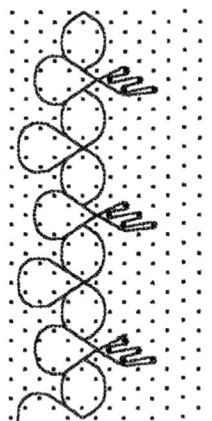

3 Remove unwanted dots from the headside and adjust the positions of the remaining dots, i.e. move them out slightly (figure 360).

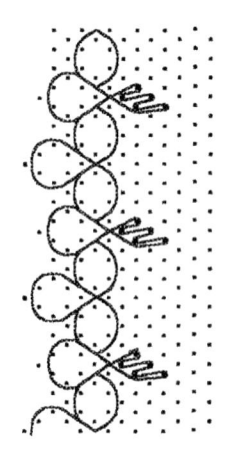

Figure 360 (right) Unwanted pinholes removed from headside

4 Draw curves joining the headside dots (figure 361)

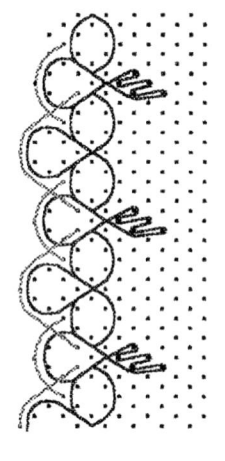

Figure 361 (left) Curves for headside drawn

5 Draw the dots for the headpins for one pattern repeat, make a transparent template and repeat for the adjacent pattern repeats and adjust the dots where they meet if necessary (figure 362)
6 Adjust the foot and head pins (figure 325, 337 & 346)

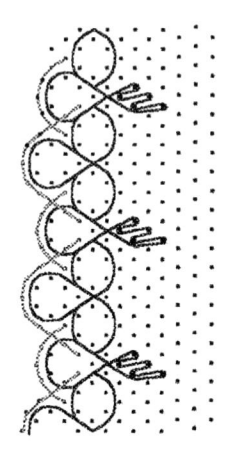

Figure 362 Dots for picots put in along the headside curves

Chapter 11

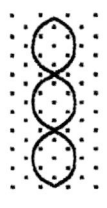

1 Using Grid no. 1 (56°, 40 pins per 10 cm along the footside) Draw the gimps (figure 363).
2 Remove the dots within the honeycomb rings.
3 Adjust the foot and head pins (figures 330, 338 & 350)

Figure 363 Plotting the insertion

1b Drafting the insertion

1c Designing a corner for an edging

1 Hold a mirror at 45° to the footside and, without changing the angle to the footside, move it along the lace. Hopefully, the mirror will show a possible corner (figure 364).

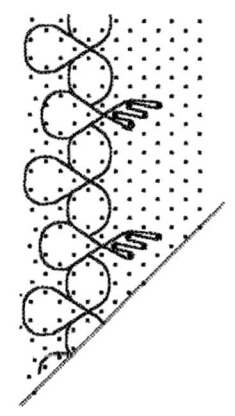

Figure 364 (right) Using a mirror to design the corner

2 Using the mirror, check the position of the diagonal through the corner and cut the pattern draft along this line (figure 365).

Figure 365 (left) Pattern draft cut along the diagonal

3 Plot a length of pattern with the fingers mirror imaged, (use a mirror imaged photocopy or turn over a transparent photocopy), and place the cut section onto it, with the footsides at 90°, so that the pattern mirrors across the join. Secure them together with transparent sticky tape. Remove the fingers that overlap (figure 366).

Figure 366 (right) Draft placed at 90° on another section

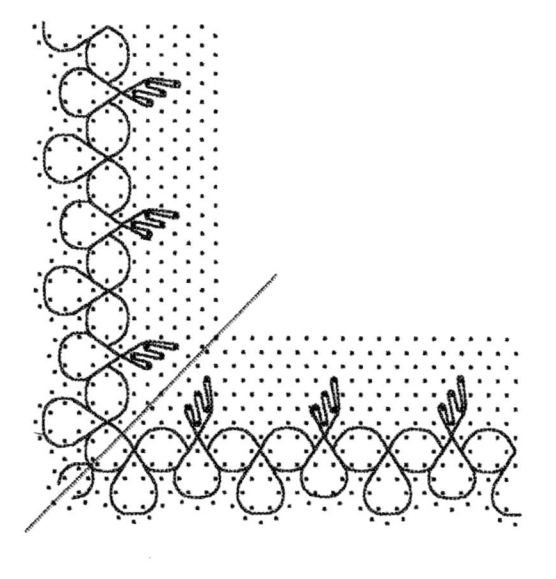

145

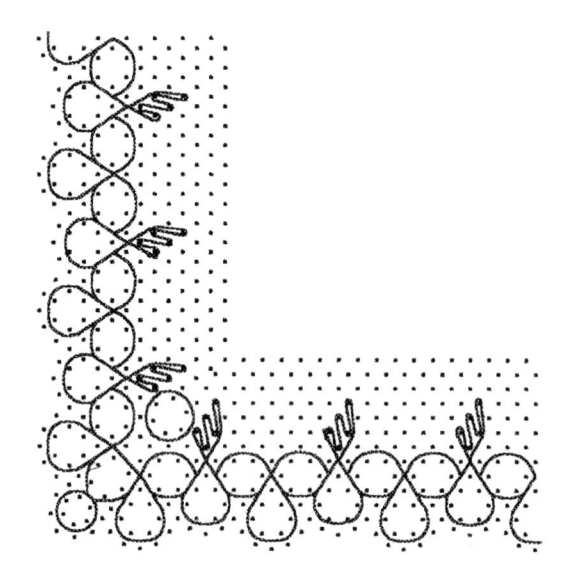

Chapter 11

4 Redraw the honeycomb ring on the diagonal, redraw the incomplete ring at the outer corner and draw a new ring between the fingers realigning dots as required (figure 367).

5 Redraw the honeycomb rings either side of the new ring and make them seven-pin rings touching the new ring, and make final adjustments to point ground through the corner (figure 368).

Figure 367 (above) Draw the honeycomb rings

6 Complete the draft by adjusting the footpins, catch-pins and head pins (figures 337 & 346, Note: figure 337 has one less row of ground).

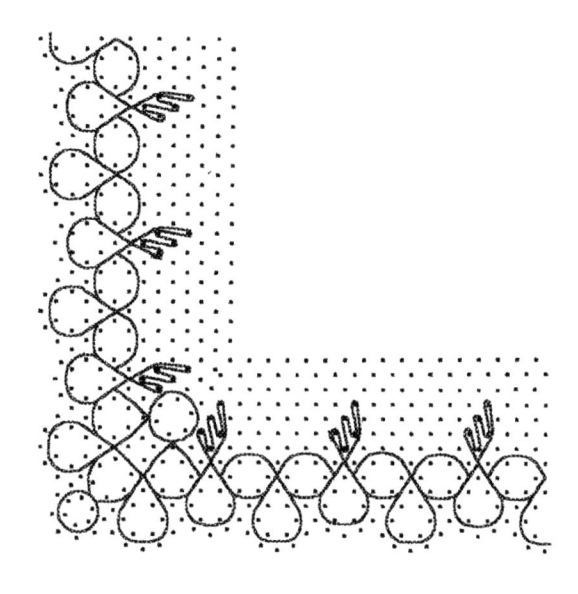

Figure 368 (right) Six-pin rings changed to seven-pin rings and final adjustments made to the point ground through the corner

For the photograph frame trim remove the inner row of dots before adjusting the footpins, catch-pins and head pins. Remove the dots now at the corner of the footside and replace them with a single dot in line with both footsides.

1c Designing a corner for an insertion
1 Using a mirror, find the position for the diagonal through the corner and cut the pattern draft along this line (figure 369)

Figure 369 (right) Pattern draft cut along the diagonal

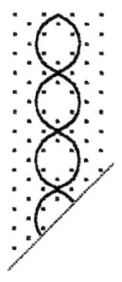

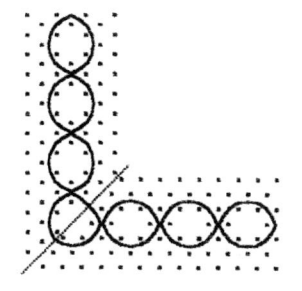

2 Place the cut section at 90° on another section of pattern draft so that the pattern mirrors across the join and secure together (figure 370).
3 Adjust dots as necessary, including head and footpins (figures 338 & 350).

Figure 370 (left) Draft placed at 90° on another section

1d Designing a side reverse

1 Hold a mirror at 90° to the footside of the edging (lace, pricking or pattern draft) approximately where the side repeat is required and, keeping it at right angles to the footside, and slide it back and forth while looking for a suitable position (figure 371). This one has an obvious position i.e. half way between two sets of fingers.

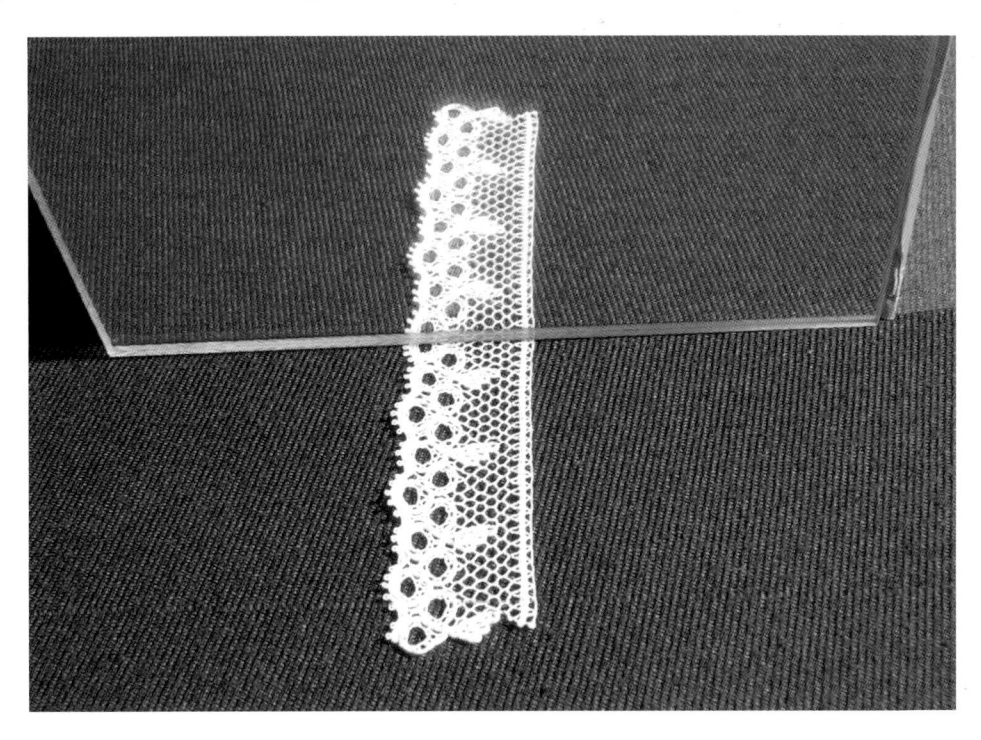

Figure 371 Using a mirror to design the side reverse

2 Plot a length of pattern with the fingers mirror imaged, for this pattern only the gimps need to be drawn 'the other way up', (or use a mirror imaged photocopy or turn over a transparent photocopy). Using the mirror, check the position of the diagonal through the corner and cut the original pattern draft along this line (figure 372).

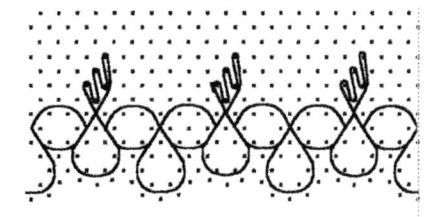

Figure 372 (left) Draft cut across the 'side reverse' line

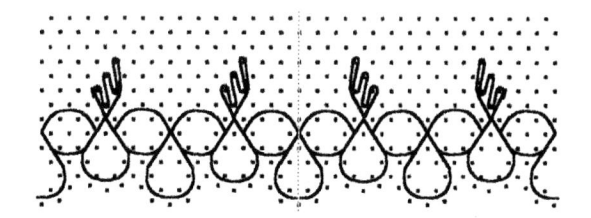

Chapter 11

Figure 373 Two sections joined together

3 Place the cut section on the reversed section of pattern draft so that the pattern 'mirrors' across the join and the pinholes match, (I find it more accurate to cut through the dots and match them), and secure together with transparent sticky tape (figure 373). Adjust the headpins, catch-pins and footpins. For the photograph frame trim remove the row of dots along the inner edge before adjusting the catch-pins and footpins (figures 325 & 348).

2 Estimating extra pairs required in the headside when not starting at the widest point

The protruding rings, C, have pins 3 and 4 on the vertical row, Y, that is one row further out than pins 1 and 2 of rings A on the vertical row X (figure 374). Therefore three pairs of passives are required when starting at ring A, so that one of the pairs can feed the honeycomb stitch at pin 3, leaving only two passives at the headside by pin 3 and 4.

Figure 374 (right) Starting with extra pairs in the headside

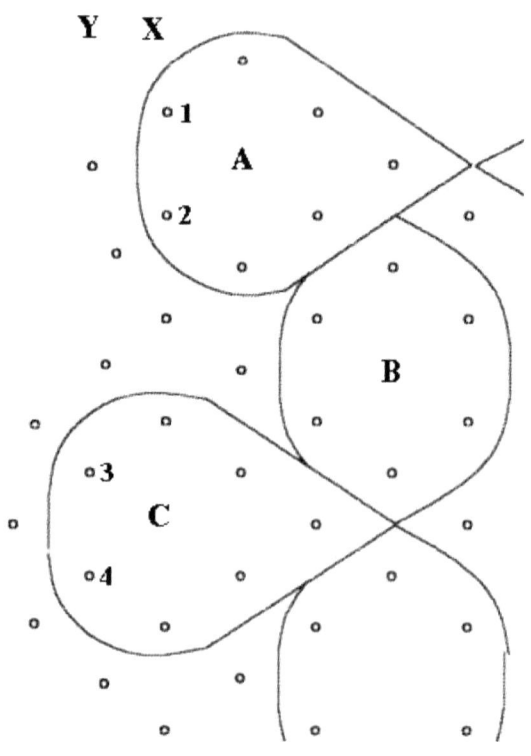

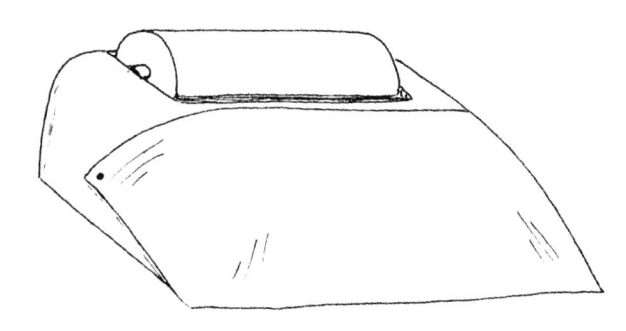

Figure 375 French pillow

3 The French pillow

When making a long edging on a mushroom pillow, the pricking and lace will be continually lifted and replaced. To make life easier for us a special pillow has been designed that allows the pricking to be used continuously. This is the traditional French or roller pillow (figure 375).

3a Using a French pillow

1. Make a pricking that will go around the roller and overlap by at least two repeats. Make a dovetail where pattern repeats overlap, keeping the pricking as short as possible, but even so the pricking may be too large for the roller.
2. If the pricking is too large wind a strip of thick fabric around the roller, adjusting the length of the packing until the ends of the pricking meet comfortably. Traditionally woollen blanket material was used, but any thick, loosely woven material that allows pins to pass through easily, or even thin polystyrene sheet (for behind wallpaper) is suitable. (This is the reason why there is a gap of about 1cm, ($^3/_8$ in) in front of, and behind, the roller.
3. Some rollers are a tight fit and remain in place while lace is made. If the roller does not stay in place use a wedge in the gap to stop it rotating.

4 Half stitch about the pin

Currently we make the footside with a cloth stitch for the stitch about the pin. However, in the 19th century, about one third of Bucks point edgings were made with a half stitch about the pin and various reasons have been put forward for this variation. In Chapter 3 the idea that it was to prevent lace from curving and that it made gathering easier were shown not to be true. The one time when using a half stitch is an advantage, is when two lengths of lace, each having a footside, are joined. When the footsides are made with a half stitch about the pin, the ridge where they are whipped together is less bulky than when cloth stitches are used about the pin (figure 376). Also the join is slightly more elastic.

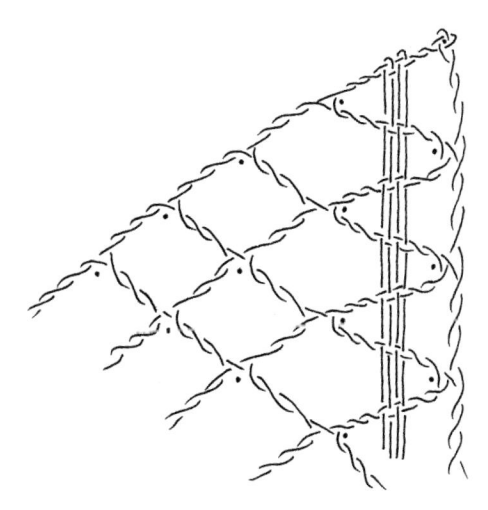

Figure 376 Footside with half stitches about the pin.

Chapter 12
PROJECT 19 BOOKMARK SAMPLER (Plate 7)

New Techniques
    various fillings
    adjusting filling to adjacent work
    finishing a bookmark with a tail

Materials
    pattern draft (figure 378) [1&2]
    Egyptian cotton no 100/2
    gimp perle 12
    bookmark sleeve
        3mm ($2^{1}/_{8}$ in) x 256mm (10 in)

End Notes
    1 drafting the pattern
    2 using fillings, names of fillings, drafting
        the fillings
    3 using fillings in designs
    4 finishing a bookmark by bunching pairs

Figure 377 (right) Bookmark

Chapter 12

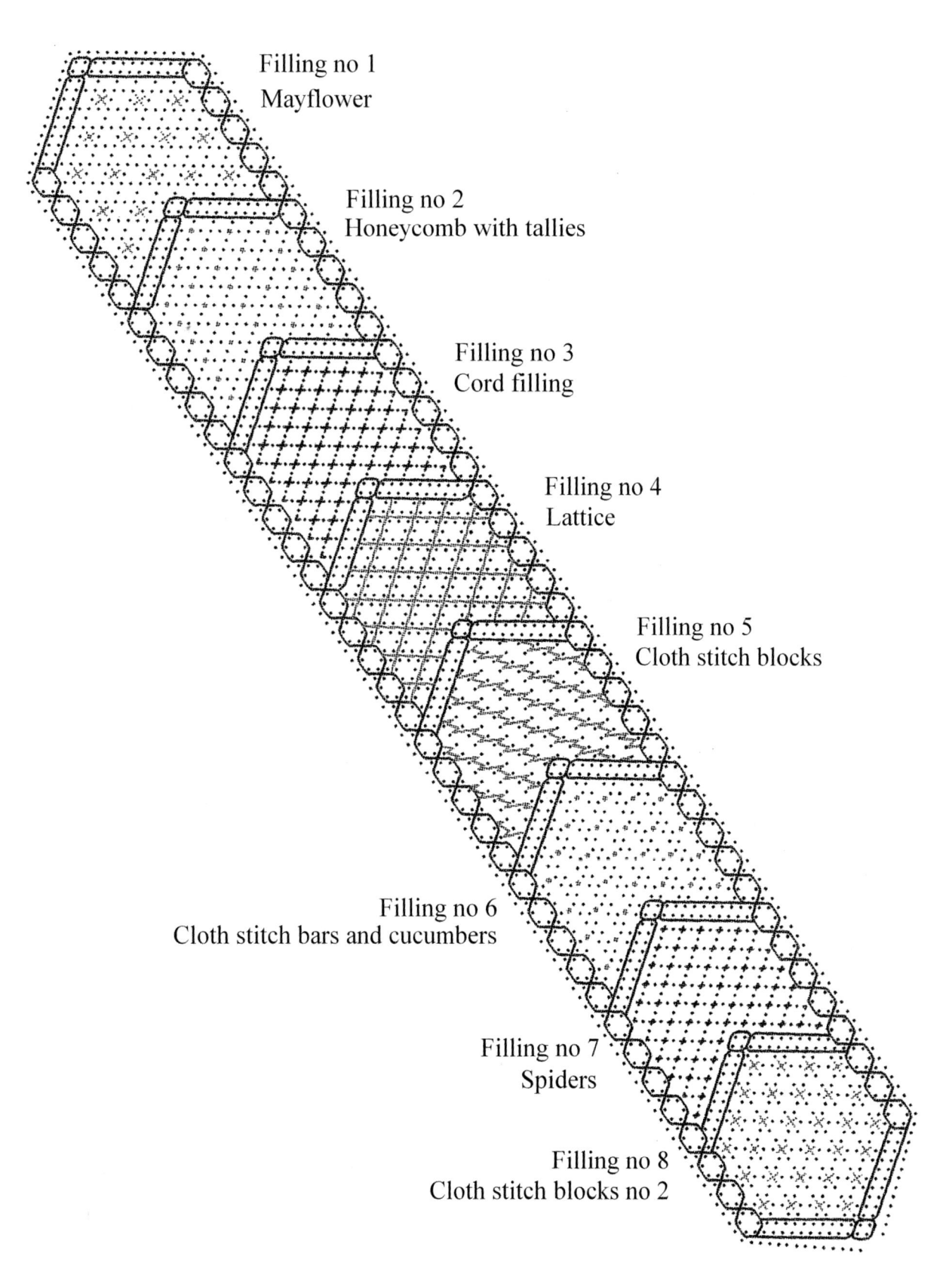

Filling no 1
Mayflower

Filling no 2
Honeycomb with tallies

Filling no 3
Cord filling

Filling no 4
Lattice

Filling no 5
Cloth stitch blocks

Filling no 6
Cloth stitch bars and cucumbers

Filling no 7
Spiders

Filling no 8
Cloth stitch blocks no 2

Figure 378 Pattern draft

Chapter 12

Making the bookmark
Starting at the top point, set in diagonally both ways with picots. Add the gimps and work a four-pin honeycomb ring at the point, add a new pair of gimps below the ring and cross the gimps both sides. The direction of the first row of the cloth stitch bars determines whether the cloth stitch has a denser or lighter texture.

For a denser bar
After setting up the top pin of the bar work the first row outwards, i.e. in the direction in which the bar extends (figures 379 & 380). When working across the full width of the bar the rows working outwards have four pairs of passives and the rows working inwards have three.

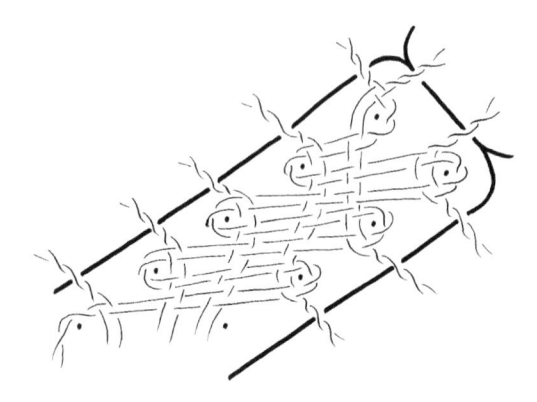

Figure 379 First row worked outwards

Figure 380 First row worked outwards

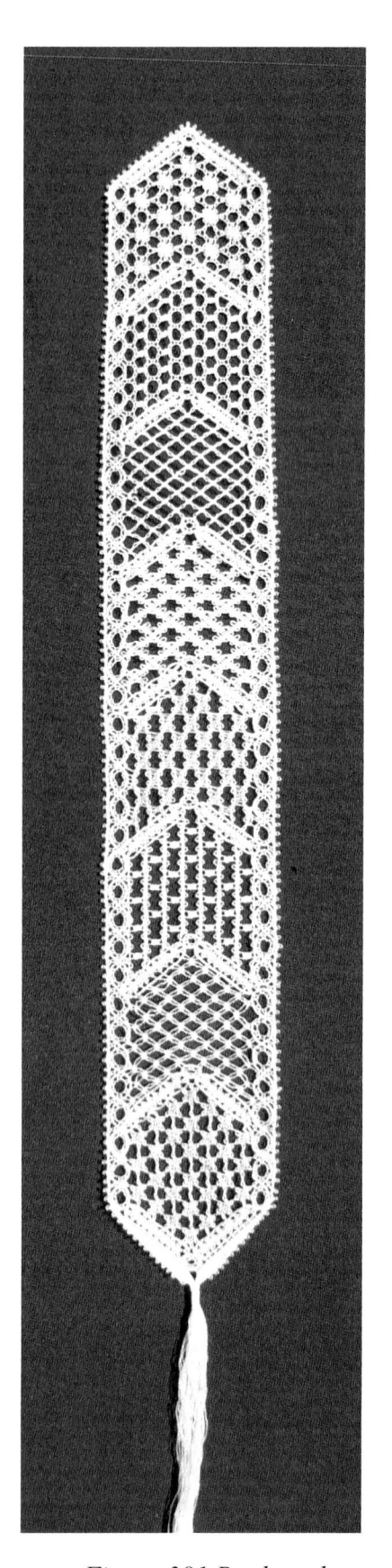

Figure 381 Bookmark

152

Chapter 12

For a lighter bar
After setting up the top pin of the bar work the first row inwards, i.e. away from the direction in which the bar extends (figures 382 & 383). When working across the full width of the bar, the rows working inwards have two pairs, the rows working outwards have three.

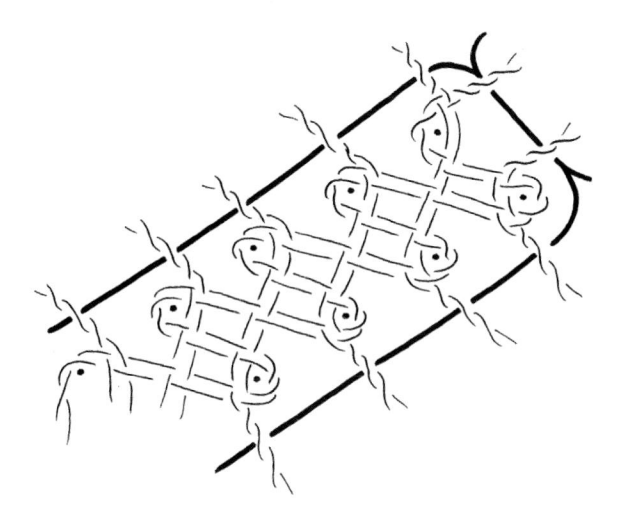

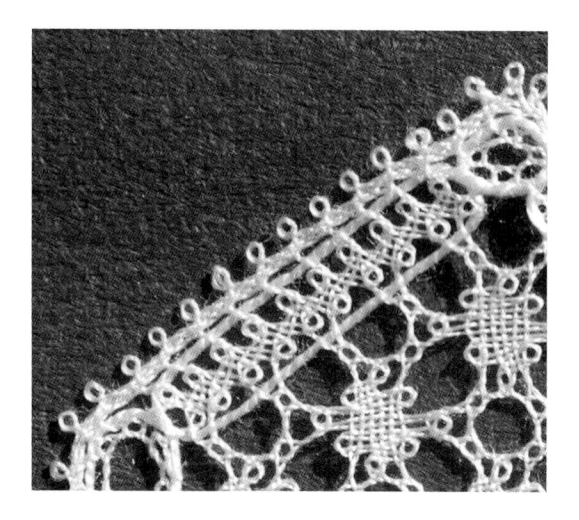

Figure 382 First row worked inwards

Figure 383 First row worked inwards

This difference occurs because when the first row is worked in the direction in which the bar extends more pairs are added before they are discarded, than when first row is worked away from the direction in which the bar extends. (Count the pairs added before one is discarded in figures 382 & 383).

Filling no. 1 Mayflower[2&3]
This filling is honeycomb filling with a regular pattern of cloth stitch diamonds each having three pins per side (figures 384 & 385). The traditional indicator for Mayflower filling is a cross, placed in the centre of each honeycomb ring that has been replaced by a cloth stitch diamond. The honeycomb stitches and cloth stitch diamonds are worked in the usual manner.

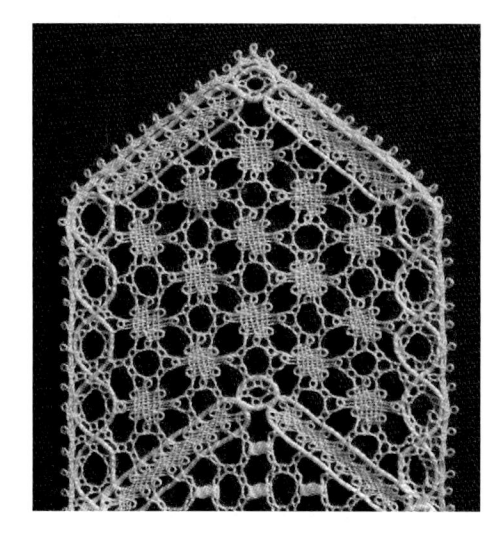

Figure 384 Mayflower filling

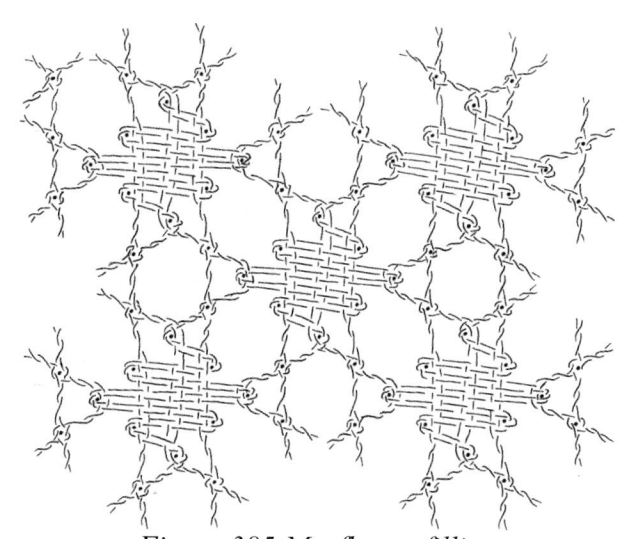

Figure 385 Mayflower filling

Chapter 12

Binding on a gimp (using the same pair for the next honeycomb stitch at the side of a ring)
When a honeycomb ring is adjacent to a filling, a gap in the filling may occur adjacent to the side of a honeycomb ring, so that the pair leaving the ring from the upper stitch on that side has nowhere to make a stitch before returning to make the lower stitch on that side. In this situation, after making the upper honeycomb stitch, pass the gimp through the pair, twist the pair, pass the gimp back through the pair, twist the pair and make the next honeycomb stitch on that side (figure 386). Any pinholes adjacent to the edges, that should be part of a Mayflower, are worked as normal honeycomb.

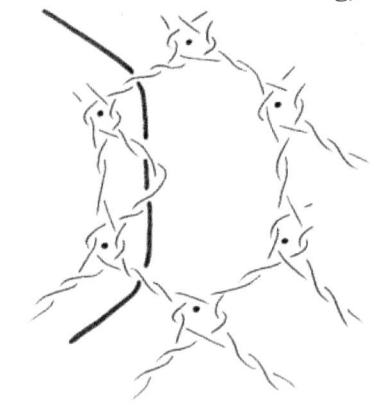

Figure 386 (right) Binding on the gimp

Managing the gimps
After completing the last honeycomb rings adjacent to the filling, introduce a new gimp, N, across the top of the four-pin honeycomb ring and work the ring (figure 387). Pass each of these gimps through two pairs until they meet but do not cross them. Now pass the outer gimp, from one side (in this case the right side), through the pairs leaving the filling on that side, across the gimps under the four-pin ring and down the other side. Work the bars. Pass each new gimp, from the four-pin honeycomb ring, outwards through the pairs of the bars to the outside of the next six-pin honeycomb ring. On one side there will be just two gimps for the next honeycomb ring, on the other, (in this case the left side) there will be four. The two spare gimps will double up with the two pairs of gimps working the next honeycomb ring After two or three pairs have crossed the doubled gimps, one may be left out.

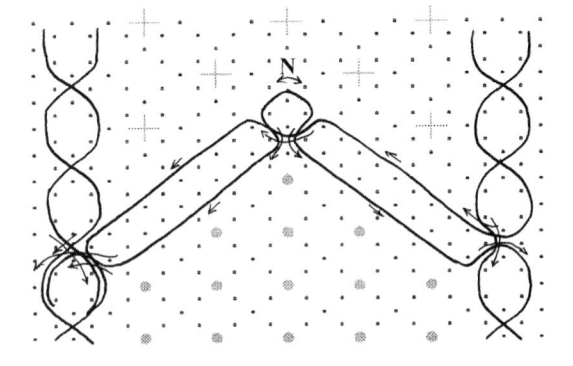

Figure 387 (right) Paths of the gimps for the bars

Filling no 2, Honeycomb with tallies
This is one of many fillings that have a regular pattern of tallies. In this case each tally replaces an alternate honeycomb stitch along a continuous rows of honeycomb ground (figure 388)& 389)

Figure 388 Honeycomb with tallies 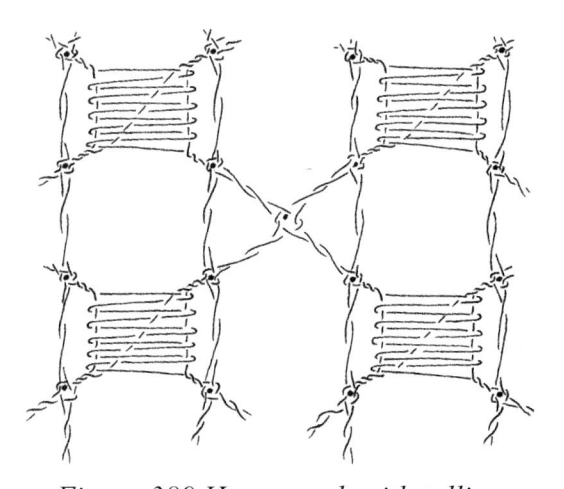   *Figure 389 Honeycomb with tallies*

154

Chapter 12

Filling no 3 Cord filling
In this filling, each alternate honeycomb stitch along the continuous rows of honeycomb ground is replaced by the pairs crossing each other in cloth stitch (figures 390 & 391), honeycomb stitches being worked between these crossings. Problems can occur where the filling meets the surrounding parts of the design, in this case down the sides. The crosses, closest to the sides, can be replaced with honeycomb stitches, making the working straightforward, or modified motifs can be worked.

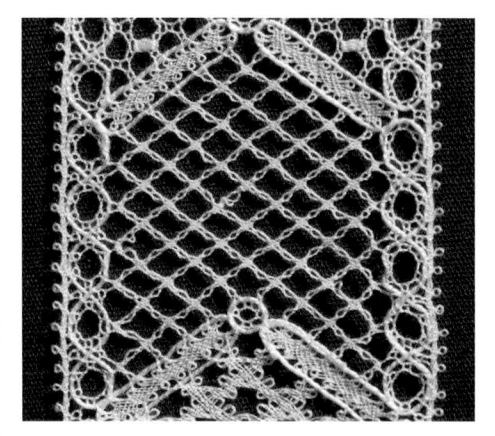

Figure 390 (right) Cord filling

Figure 391 Cord filling

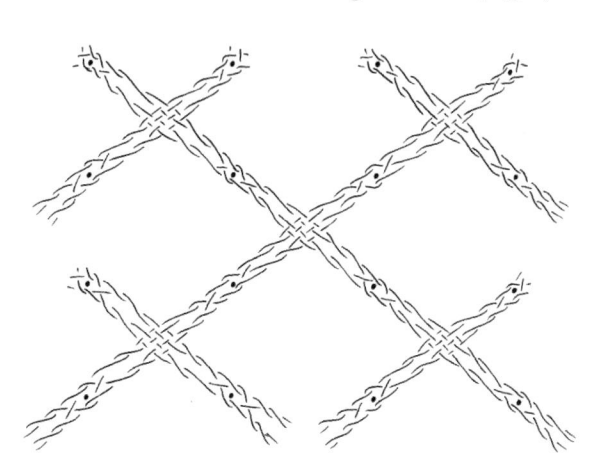

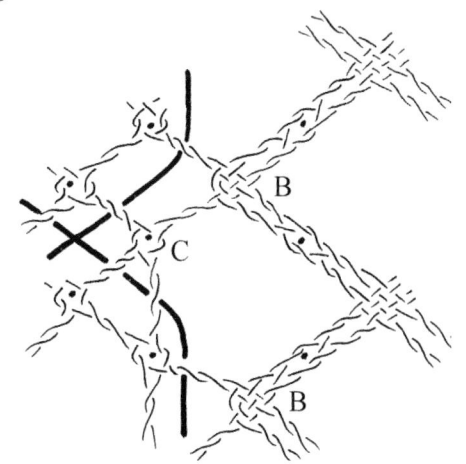

Figure 392 Modified motif

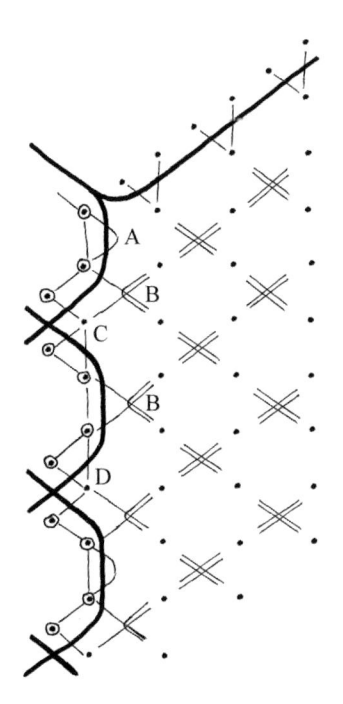

Using a modified motif
At A (figure 393), bind on the gimp, i.e. use the pair leaving the upper stitch for the lower stitch at that side. The pair leaving the second honeycomb stitch at this side of the ring works a modified motif, B, with two pairs approaching from the ground (figures 392 & 393). At B, the pair from the ring cloth stitches through the two ground pairs and the two ground pairs make a cloth stitch. Twist all three pairs twice; there is no pin. After working the modified motif two pairs travel into the ground to make the next motif, while the third pair makes a honeycomb stitch at C. The first pair leaving the next honeycomb ring makes a modified motif and a pair returns into the ring. The pair leaving the second honeycomb stitch at the side of the ring makes a honeycomb stitch, D, with the pair leaving the bottom honeycomb stitch of the ring; one pair enters the next ring, the other works a modified motif. Continue the filling using modifying motifs as required.

Figure 393 (left) Modified motifs

155

Chapter 12

Filling no 4, Lattice
This filling consists of crossing trails, each having one pair of workers and two pairs of passives (figure 394 & 395).

Figure 394 (right) Lattice filling

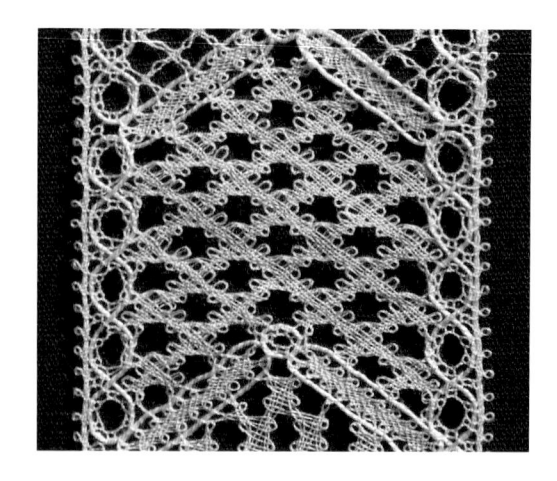

Taking the centre pair of the first three pairs, on one side, work the first row towards the centre (figure 395).

Figure 395 (left) Starting the filling

As the crossing is reached, work both trails towards the centre, make a cloth stitch and set up the top pin of the crossing pin, pin A, below the stitch. There are no twists. Work both pairs outwards though two pairs of passives, set up the side pins, pins B, and twist each worker pair twice. Cloth stitch the two passive pairs of the trails across each other. Set up a pin, pin C between the two sets of passive pairs. Cloth stitch the two worker pairs towards each other, work them together and then work each outwards through two pairs of passives (figure 396).

Figure 396 Lattice filling

156

Chapter 12

When one of the trails approaches the honeycomb rings, the last two pairs from the bar, pin 1, go into the ring. The nearest pair works the upper stitch at the side, pin 2. A pair from this stitch then crosses the other pair from pin 1 at the same time as it crosses the gimp, i.e. it bridges both. The pair from pin 1 then makes a stitch with the other pair from pin 2 at pin 3. The pairs leaving the ring from pins 2 and 3 become the passives, b and c, of the new trail. After the ring has been completed at pin 4, a pair, d, leaves to become the workers for the new trail, which immediately crosses the one approaching the rings (figure 397). There may be a better way, (working modified motifs at the edges of a filling is not an exact science), but I preferred ignoring pin X.

Figure 397 (right) Filling adjacent to honeycomb rings

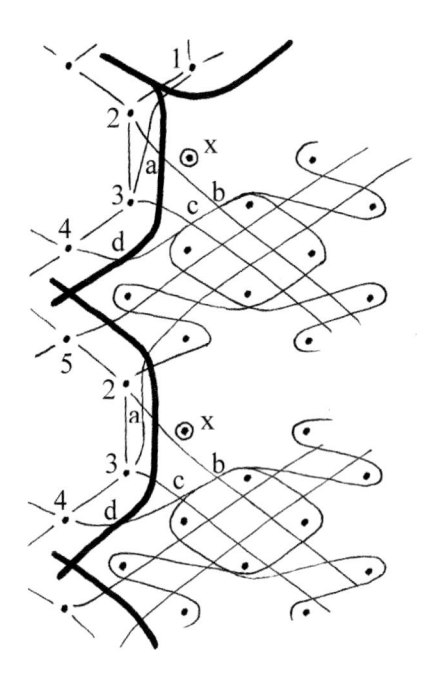

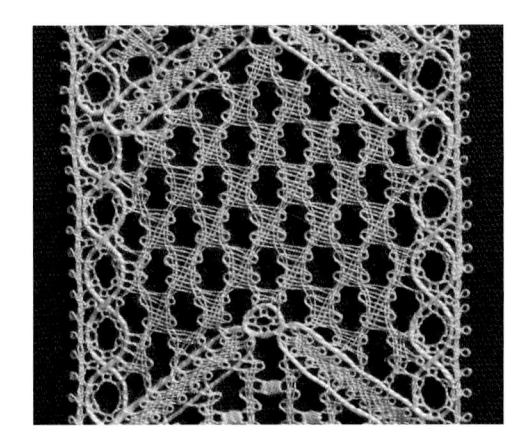

Filling no. 5, Cloth stitch blocks
This filling is a series of cloth stitch blocks with the workers making one more row of stitches below a block and passing immediately, on the diagonal, to the next block. The only twists are the two twists made by the workers when they pass around a pin (figures 398 & 399).

Figure 398 (left) Cloth stitch blocks

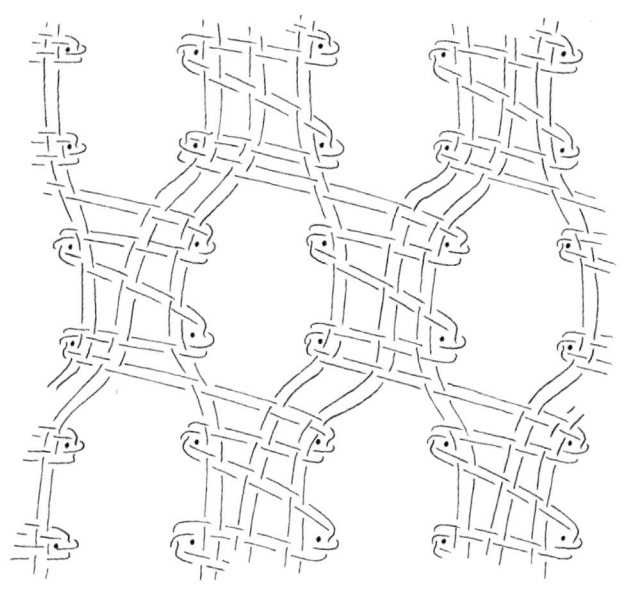

Figure 399 Cloth stitch blocks

Chapter 12

Modifying blocks where they meet adjacent motifs[3]

Because of the number of the dots in each design repeat they do not meet the boundary with at the gimp comfortably, and the treatment of the blocks here is, at best, fudge. Figure 400 indicates possible routes that can be used, but there are probably many more. The aim, each time, is to preserve the lines of the workers and passives and keep them travelling in the direction they would have taken if the boundary had not been reached. Look at my solutions and the way I have approached the different problems; then try to work the filling by looking at the pricking and the positions of the pairs and reason it out, rather than following the route map. Providing the lace looks good, and is structurally sound, your interpretation is as valid as mine.

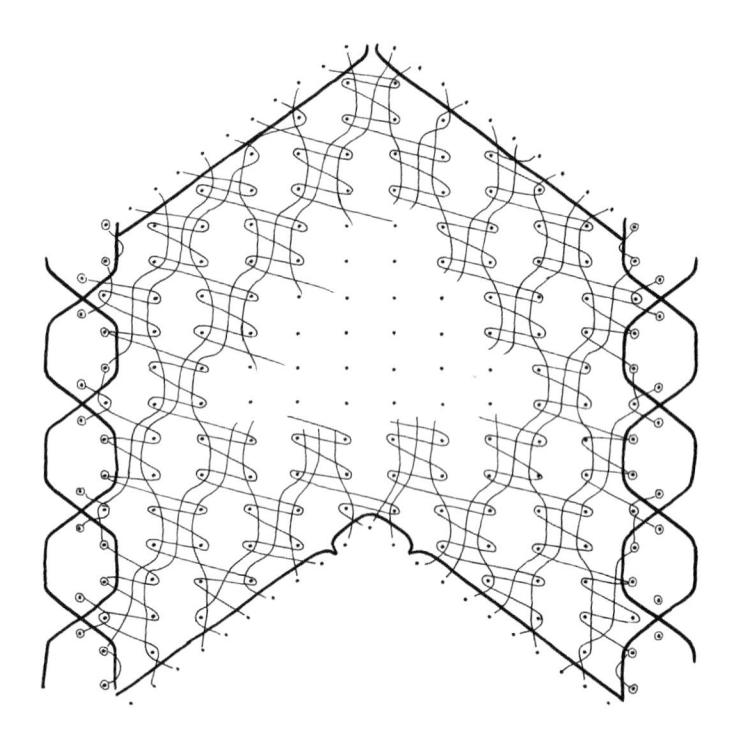

Figure 400 Modified blocks

Filling no. 6, Cloth stitch bars and cucumbers

This is another filling with a regular pattern of tallies, this time between cloth stitch bars (figures 401 & 402). The term cucumber is applied to tallies that are much wider than they are deep, especially those used adjacent to the footside in the cucumber foot.

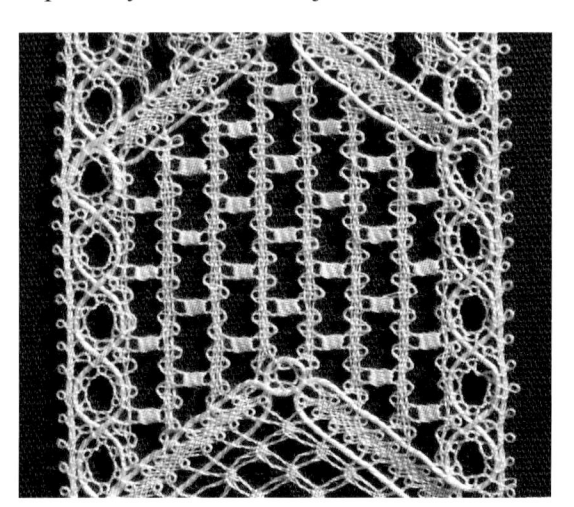

Figure 401 Cloth stitch bars & cucumbers

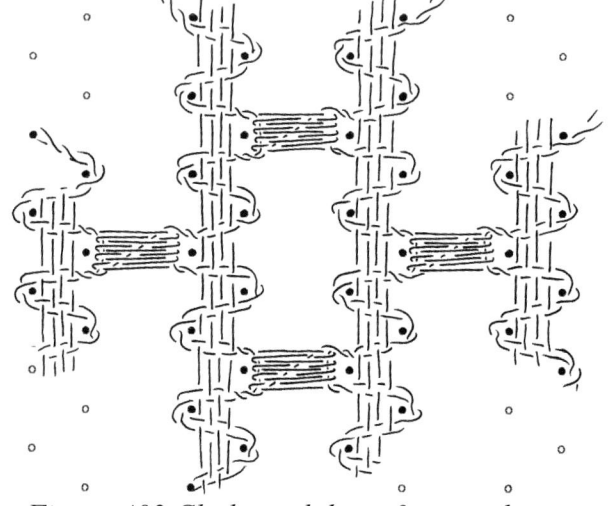

Figure 402 Cloth stitch bars & cucumbers

The bars adjacent to the honeycomb rings are modified in a fashion similar to the modification of the blocks for Filling no 5.

158

Chapter 12

Filling no 7, Spiders
Each spider motif is made using two pairs from each side, each having three twists. The spider consists of cloth stitches made in the following order
    two centre pairs. two left pairs, two right pairs,
    two centre pairs. two left pairs, two right pairs, two centre pairs
Pins are placed between each two pairs leaving the spider (figures 403 & 404).

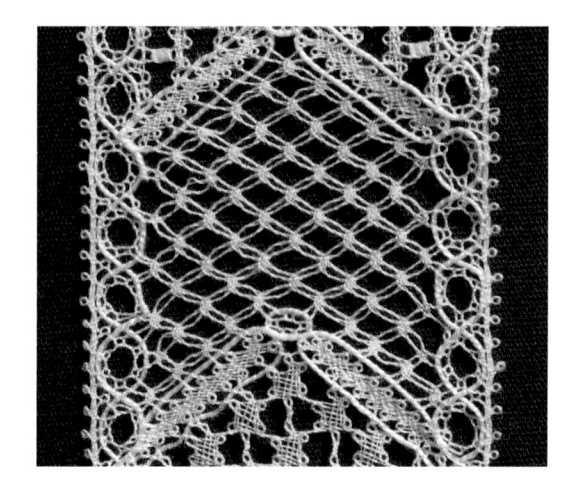

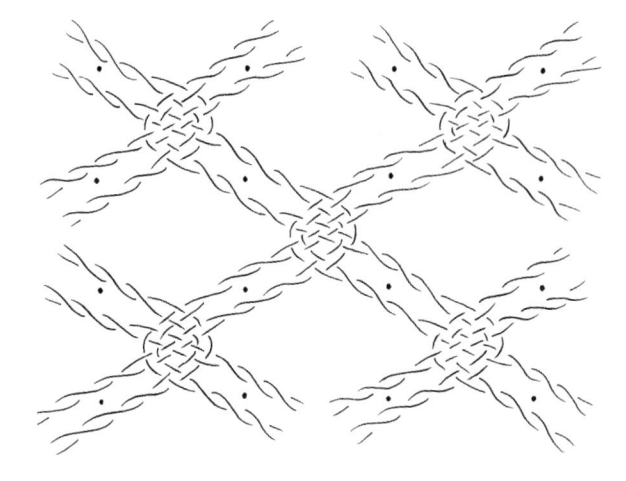

Figure 403 Spider filling

Figure 404 Spider filling

Modified spiders, made as for Cord filling, can be used adjacent to the edges where necessary. An extra gimp will be necessary when working the bars as worked here, since they occur in a different position relative to the rings on either side. Otherwise the design would be compromised.

Filling no. 8, Cloth stitch blocks no. 2
As the last pin of each hexagonal block is set up, both pairs are twisted twice and work cloth stitch, twist, cloth stitch twist twice before the pin immediately below, the top pin of the next hexagon, is set up (figures 405 & 406). This filling fits comfortably within its allotted area without any modification.

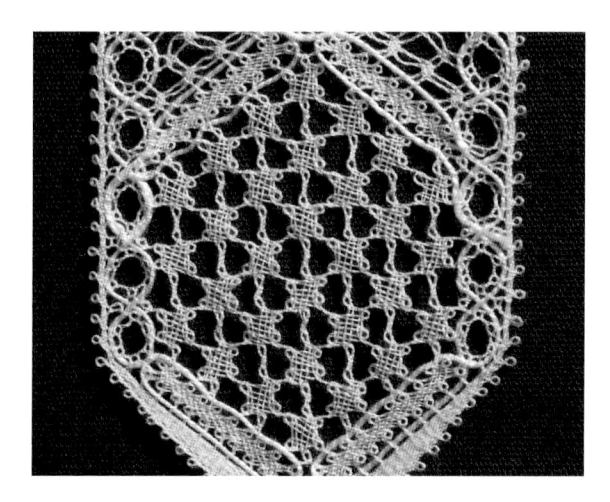

Figure 405 Cloth stitch blocks no. 2

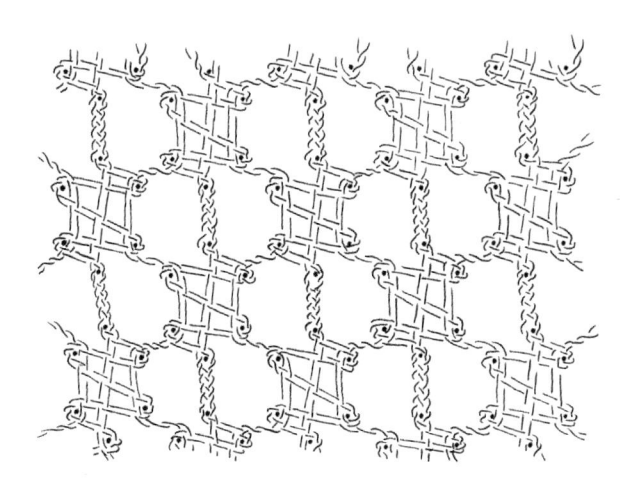

Figure 406 Cloth stitch blocks no. 2

Chapter 12

2b Names of fillings
Undoubtedly the fillings had names that may have been local or universal. The majority have been lost but some have been retained and I have indicated which these are. The others are names that have been recently applied to the fillings and are useful for reference.

2c Drafting Filling no. 1 Mayflower
Traditionally the term 'Mayflower' was used for the filling with a regular pattern of cloth stitch diamonds, each having four pins per side, within honeycomb filling. Unfortunately this filling does not work well in Geometrical Bucks patterns. Today the term is also used to denote a filling containing cloth stitch diamonds each having three pins per side, and also a single cloth stitch motif in honeycomb.

1. Remove alternate dots (ringed) from alternate lines, this works in all directions diagonally, vertically and horizontally to produce an area of honeycomb ground (figures 413 & 414).
2. The indicator usually used is a plus (+) sign so place one indicator in alternate spaces. Again this works in all directions diagonally, vertically and horizontally (figure 415).

Figure 413 (right) Alternate dots ringed

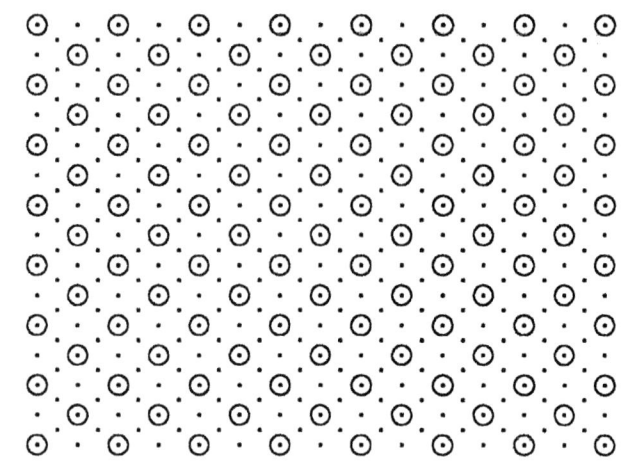

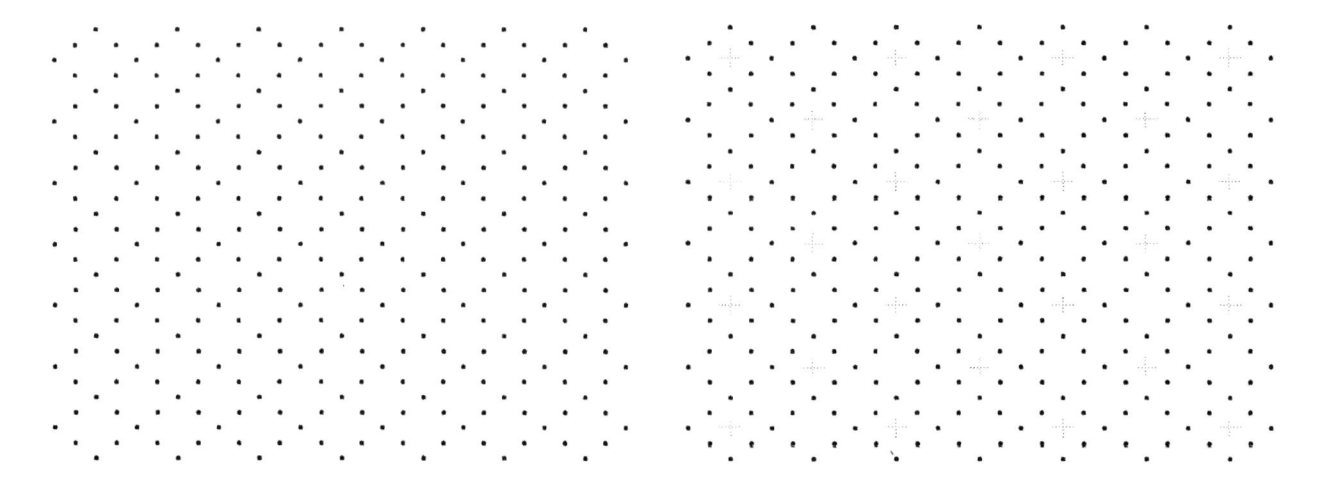

Figure 414 Alternate, (ringed) dots removed

Figure 415 Indicators placed in alternate spaces

162

Chapter 12

2d Drafting Filling no. 2 Honeycomb with tallies
This is one of the many fillings containing a regular pattern of tallies, this one in honeycomb ground. Prepare the filling by removing dots as for honeycomb ground (figure 414) starting with gap rows immediately below the gimps. Draw a large dot, the indicator for a tally, over each dot down the centre line of dots. From each of these indicators draw one over each dot horizontally (figure 416). The large dots are indicators for tallies, they are not pricked.

Figure 416 (right) Indicators drawn in

2e Drafting Filling no. 3 Cord filling
Some fillings do not have standard indicators, and they can be very confusing to work when there is only a pattern of dots. In these cases I invent my own (and usually write a description on the pricking as a reminder for next time). Your pricking is for your personal use; it is for you to make your own lace on and, you can draw and write any information you require to help you make the lace on it. Use a different colour for different gimps, or your own symbol as an indicator for a fillings etc. For this filling I place a cross where the pairs cross in cloth stitch; this is my own indicator, without it I get lost.

1 Start by removing dots, as for honeycomb ground, with gap rows immediately below the gimps (figure 414).
2 Place crosses over alternate dots along the continuous rows where the continuous rows cross (figure 417). Do not prick the centres of these crosses.

Figure 417 (right) Crosses drawn in

2f Drafting Filling no. 4, Lattice
Although not universally used, narrow trails can be indicated by a line passing between the two lines of dots that are the sides of the trail.
1 Starting in the gap between the first two pins of the bar draw diagonal lines, in both directions, across the filling. Leave two spaces (three dots) between subsequent lines (figure 418).
2 Remove the centre dot from each box formed by the diagonal lines (figure 419).

Chapter 12

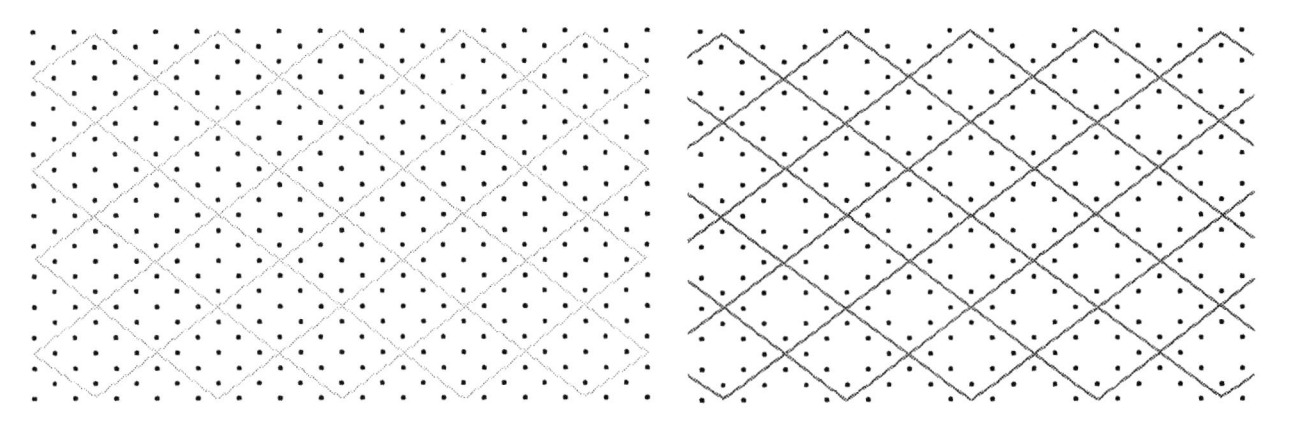

Figure 418 Indicating the trails

Figure 419 Unwanted dots removed

2g Drafting Filling no. 5, Spiders
1 Starting at the centre at the top draw crosses in alternate spaces in both directions (figure 420).
2 Place dots half way between the current dots both horizontally and vertically each side of the indicator (using a different colour makes it easier later on) (figure 421).
3 Remove all the original dots from the filling (figure 422).

Figure 420 (right) Indicators drawn in

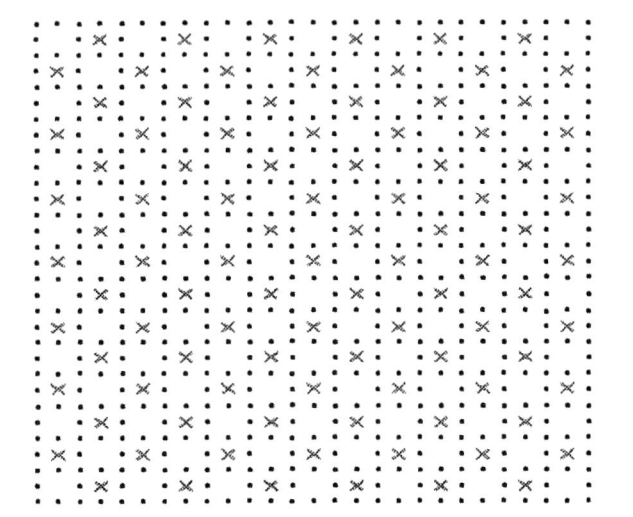

Figure 421   Extra dots added

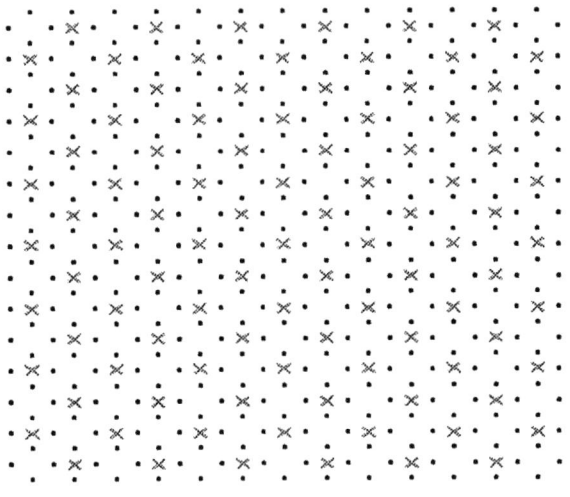

Figure 422 Original dots removed

Chapter 12

2h Drafting Filling no. 6, Cloth stitch blocks
Starting from the centre, remove alternate vertical lines of dots (figure 423). Draw the indicators, the lines indicating the paths of the workers (figure 424).

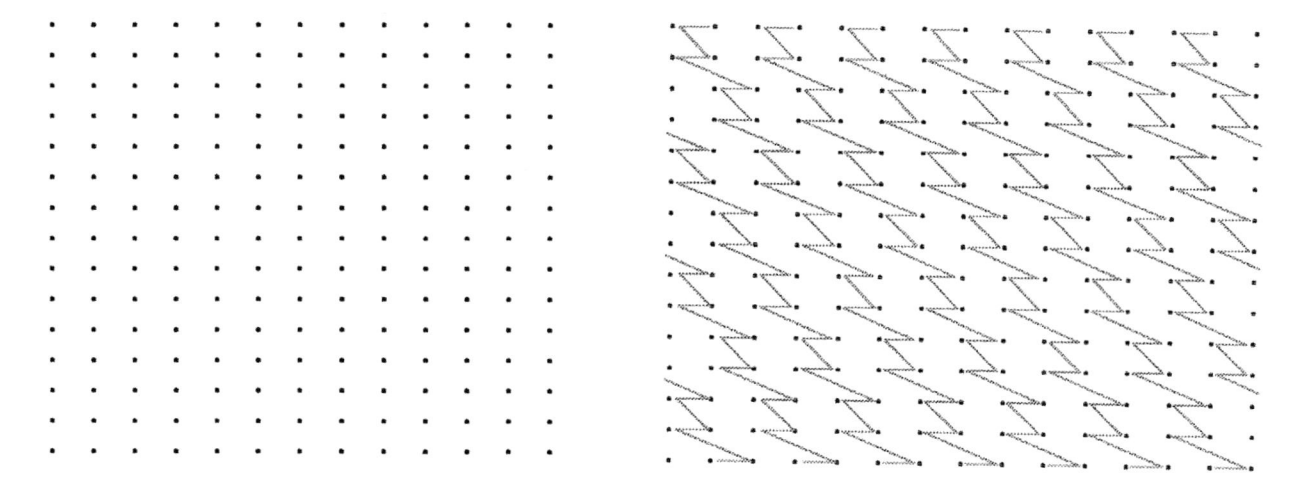

Figure 423 Vertical lines of dots removed   *Figure 424 Indicators drawn in*

2i Drafting Filling no. 7, Cloth stitch bars and cucumbers
Starting with the centre line remove every third vertical line of dots (figure 425). Place an indicator, for a tally, between every third pair of pinholes down the gaps, with those in adjacent gaps placed half way between the ones either side (figure 426). Do not prick the large, indicator dots.

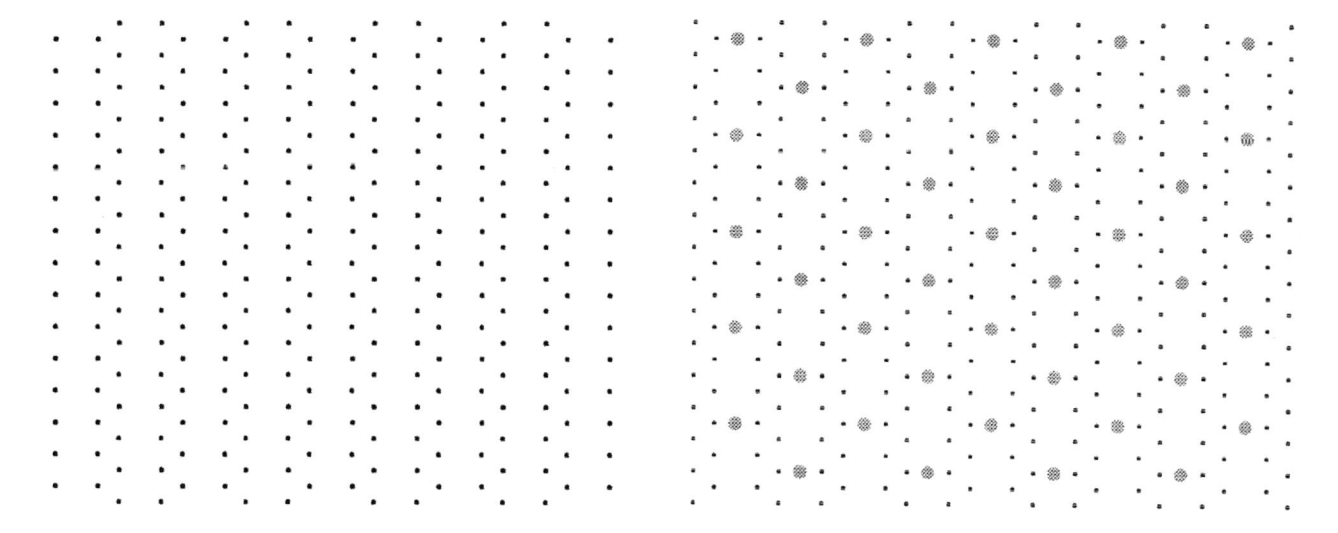

Figure 425 Vertical lines of dots removed   *Figure 426 Tallies indicated*

Chapter 12

2j Drafting Filling no. 8, Cloth stitch blocks no 2
1 Place a plus (+) sign on every third dot horizontally, vertically and diagonally starting with the third dot down the centre line (figure 427).
2 Remove all dots along the horizontal lines through the indicators (figure 428). Do not prick the plus signs.

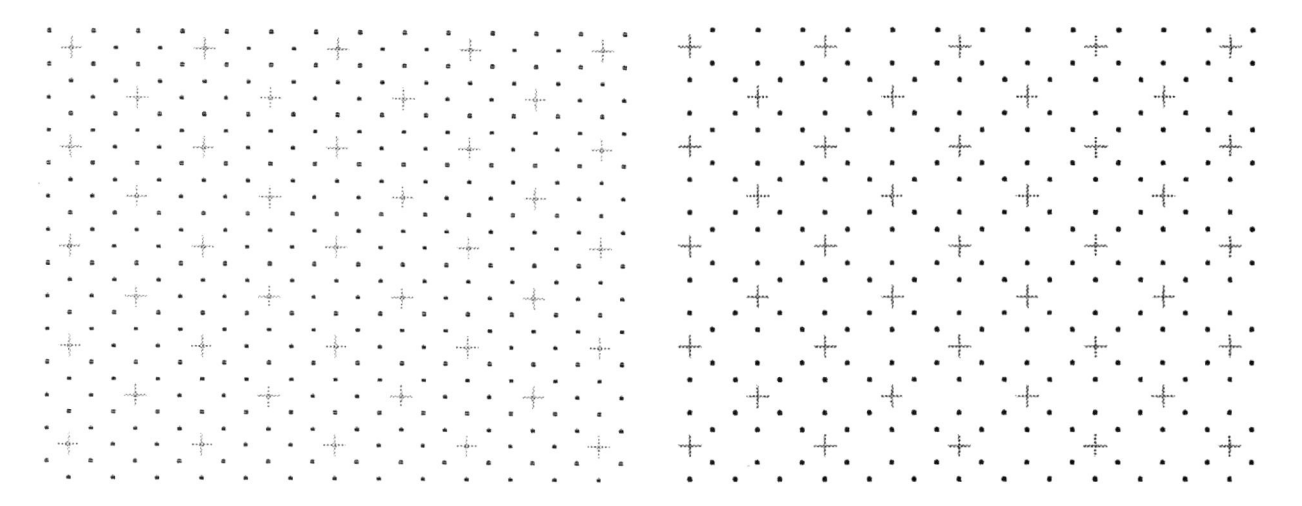

Figure 427 Indicators drawn   *Figure 428 Horizontal lines of dots removed*

3a Using fillings in designs
Fillings are used to add interest to designs. Apart from the standard honeycomb filling, and situations where only a single motif from a filling is used, the space for the filling should be large enough for sufficient repeats of the filling, so that the beauty and rhythm of their design can be appreciated. Using a filling with a large repeat in a small space causes confusion to the eye and makes the piece look cluttered.

The fillings used in this bookmark work in geometrical designs, but there are many that can only be used in floral Bucks. When selecting a filling for a geometrical Bucks design check that the pairs required from the surrounding work fit with the number that are available. There are many fillings that require less than the number geometrically available, a situation that can be accommodated for in floral but not in geometrical. The spider filling used in the bookmark is frequently used in floral with much wider spacing, but it also works successfully here. Also check the visual impact of the filling. When viewed from a distance they lead the eye in different ways.

Filling no. 1 The Mayflowers attract the eye, each acts as a focus.

Filling no. 2 The eye is taken down the parallel lines of tallies.

Filling no. 3 The eye is taken downwards and outwards by this filling, but this is also influenced by the cloth stitch bars surrounded by gimps because the filling is not particularly interesting and the eye tends to wander away from it

Filling no. 4 The eye is attracted to the spaces between the trails and is taken downwards and outwards by the filling, but this one is also influenced by the cloth stitch bars surrounded by gimps.

Filling no. 5 An interesting filling, the blocks and spaces are different in shape from other parts of the lace. However, this produces an optical illusion; an unusual angle appears. Start by looking at the top block and the eye follows down through the diagonal line of blocks in both directions (figure 429). The angle between the lines is easier to measure from a draft (figure 430) and is 69°, which is 34.5° to the footside; quite different from the 56° to the footside on which this filling was drafted. Optical results like these can have an unsettling effect on a design.

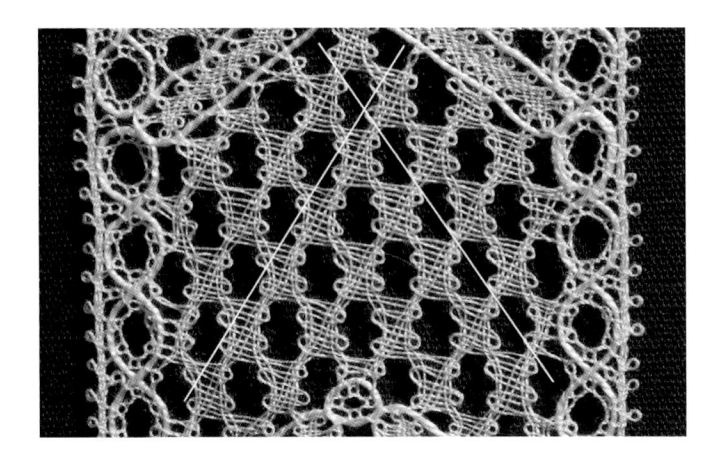

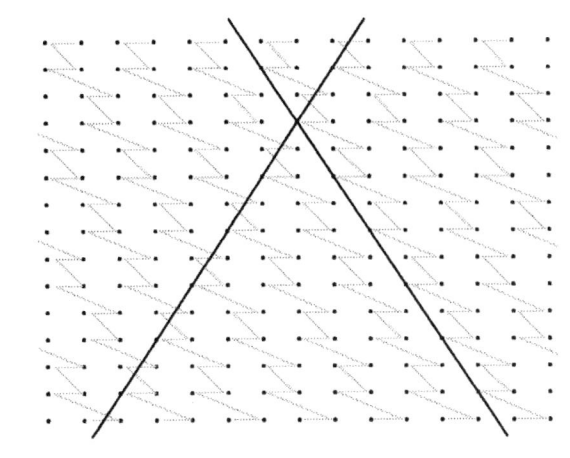

Figure 429 Optical illusion

Figure 430 Measuring the angle of the optical illusion

Filling no. 6 Similar to filling no 2 but the eye is led down by the vertical bars of cloth stitch not the tallies, in fact the tallies in this filling tend to arrest the movement of the eye rather than encourage it.

Filling no. 7. Although superficially similar to filling no 3 the eye does not move around as quickly, the spiders are more interesting than the plain crossings. This filling does not fit satisfactorily in the same space as the other fillings so an extra line of dots is required. This moves the cloth stitch bars which, in turn, change the number of rows for the next filling.

Filling no. 8 Superficially similar to filling no 1, the blocks of cloth stitch attract the eye but the diagonal and vertical lines in the design tend to move the eye around, so that it is led from one block to the next rather than jumping from one to the other as happens in filling no 1.

3b Fitting fillings into the spaces available
Since different fillings require different numbers of pairs per repeat, check that the selected filling fits into the allotted space with a minimum of problems where the filling meets the adjacent parts of the design. Some of the fillings in the bookmark would not fit in a space with one or two extra rows of pinholes vertically or horizontally. Some can be worked with modified motifs adjacent to the edges; some are more difficult to fit into restricted spaces. Sometimes surrounding areas can be adjusted to accommodate the filling. Sometimes a filling fits better if it is moved slightly.

Fillings nos. 1-6 all fit reasonably comfortably into the same space.

Filling no. 1, 3 & 8 have spare pinholes worked as honeycomb stitches.

Chapter 12

Filling nos. 3 & 7 have modified motifs where the space is half that of a complete motif.

Figure no. 4 has the correct number of pairs entering the filling but judgment has to be used when deciding how to start the trails. I have started them with the centre of the three pairs as the workers as I consider this gives me the best result but there are other possibilities. Although fillings should be pricked as an all over design right up to their edges and, in principle, all pinholes should be used, I occasionally omit pinholes if by using them the pattern is disrupted; I could not find a way of using pin X that kept the design working to my satisfaction. It is more important for the lace to look beautiful and be structurally, sound than to follow a principle rigidly.

Filling no 5 overlaps the edges of the space it occupies and the motifs are modified at these points. It is important that the angle at which the worker travels should be the same for each part of the motif, even if it means passing across the gimp into the honeycomb ring and back. (The pair is usually twisted before and after crossing the gimp). The workers may, or may not, be twisted adjacent to the gimp. It is your choice. Occasionally I have omitted using a pinhole as described for filling no 4.

Filling no 6 has cloth stitch workers of the bars adjacent to the honeycomb rings passing into the rings and returning into the blocks as for filling no 5.

Filling no. 8 fits comfortably into the allotted space, only possible because the bars were moved to accommodate the previous filling.

Honeycomb filling is the most popular because it is the most versatile and causes few problems when designing. Many fillings can be surrounded by honeycomb stitches to enable them to work comfortably within the allotted space.

4 Finishing a bookmark by bunching the passives

The technique of bunching pairs in the valley, instead of stacking them, is found in many pieces of antique lace.

1 Start as for working into a valley by taking a pair that has been left out across a gimp to make a picot and return through one pair. There are now three pairs of passives (figure 431).
2 Take the next pair left out across the gimp to make the next picot and cover the pin with a cloth stitch.
3 *Now, open the working pair and pass the other passive pairs (two this time) between the workers, twist the workers and leave them next to the gimp.

Figure 431 Bunching pairs

Chapter 12

4 Cloth stitch the next pair left out across the gimp with the innermost pair of passives (the previous pair of returning workers that were twisted and left next to the gimp).
5 Open the working pair and pass the other passive pairs, except for the outer edge pair, between the workers, twist the workers.
6 Cloth stitch the workers and outer edge pair of passives, make the next picot and cover the pin with a cloth stitch*.
Repeat *to* as required (figure 432).

Figure 432 Bunching pairs

This is considered by some to be a time saving technique at the expense of good practice, it does, however, have another advantage. When a valley is deep there will be a lot of pairs to stack. This will result in an obvious triangle of clothwork extending from the top of the diagonal to the end of the bookmark. While this may, in some cases, be used as a design feature, in others it will not add to the design and bunching the passives to form a narrower band of accumulated pairs may be preferred. This technique makes an excellent finish for a bookmark. The bookmark may also be finished without a tassel.

Chapter 13

PROJECT 20   FINGER PLATE (Plate 8)

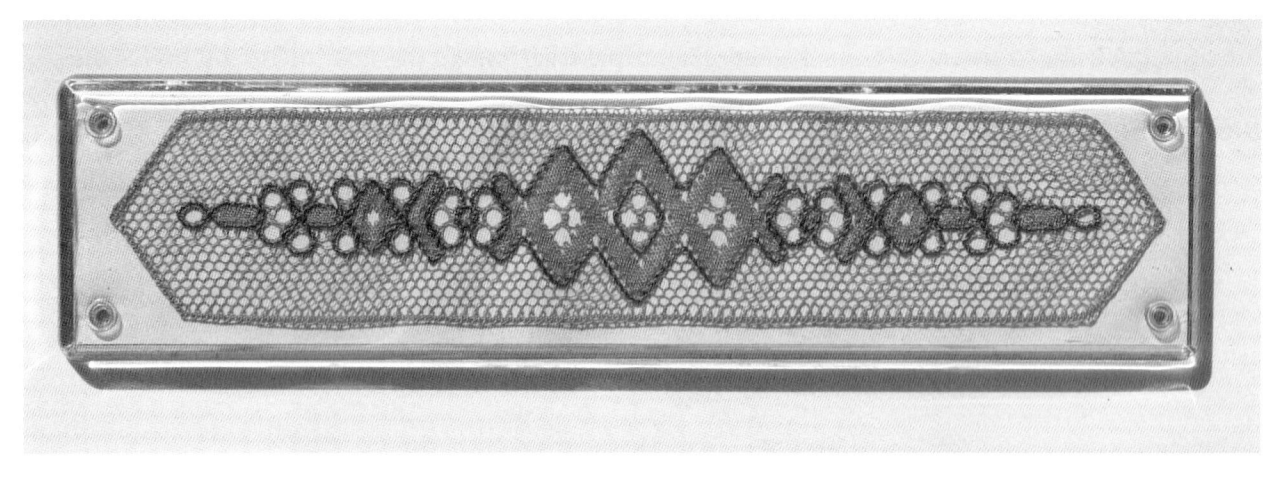

Figure 433 Fingerplate with lace insert

New Techniques
   setting in footside both ways from a point
   cloth stitch motifs with vertical sides
   eyelet
   trails combining, dividing and crossing
   binding on a coloured thread

Materials required
   pricking (figure 435)[1]
   Finca cotton no 50, coloured
   gimp no 8 perle to match or stranded embroidery thread to match or contrast[2]
   (use 2 strands per gimp when using contrasting coloured gimps doubled)[3]
   finger plate kit

End Notes
1 drafting the pattern
2 working with colour
3 binding on when using coloured gimps
4 catch pin by vertical gimp
5 dividing clothwork
6 combining clothwork
7 winkie pin
8 dividing for an eyelet in clothwork
9 clothwork dividing into narrow trails
10 narrow trails combining then dividing into wider trails
11 wider trails dividing & combining
12 casting off along a diagonal

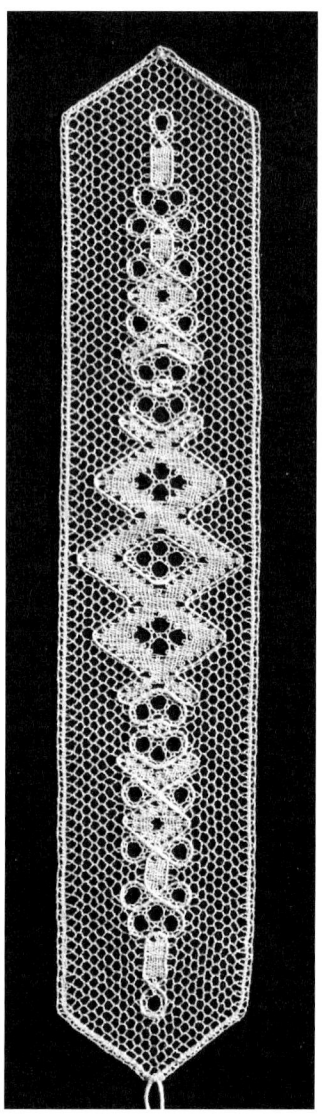

Figure 434 (right) Lace insert

Chapter 13

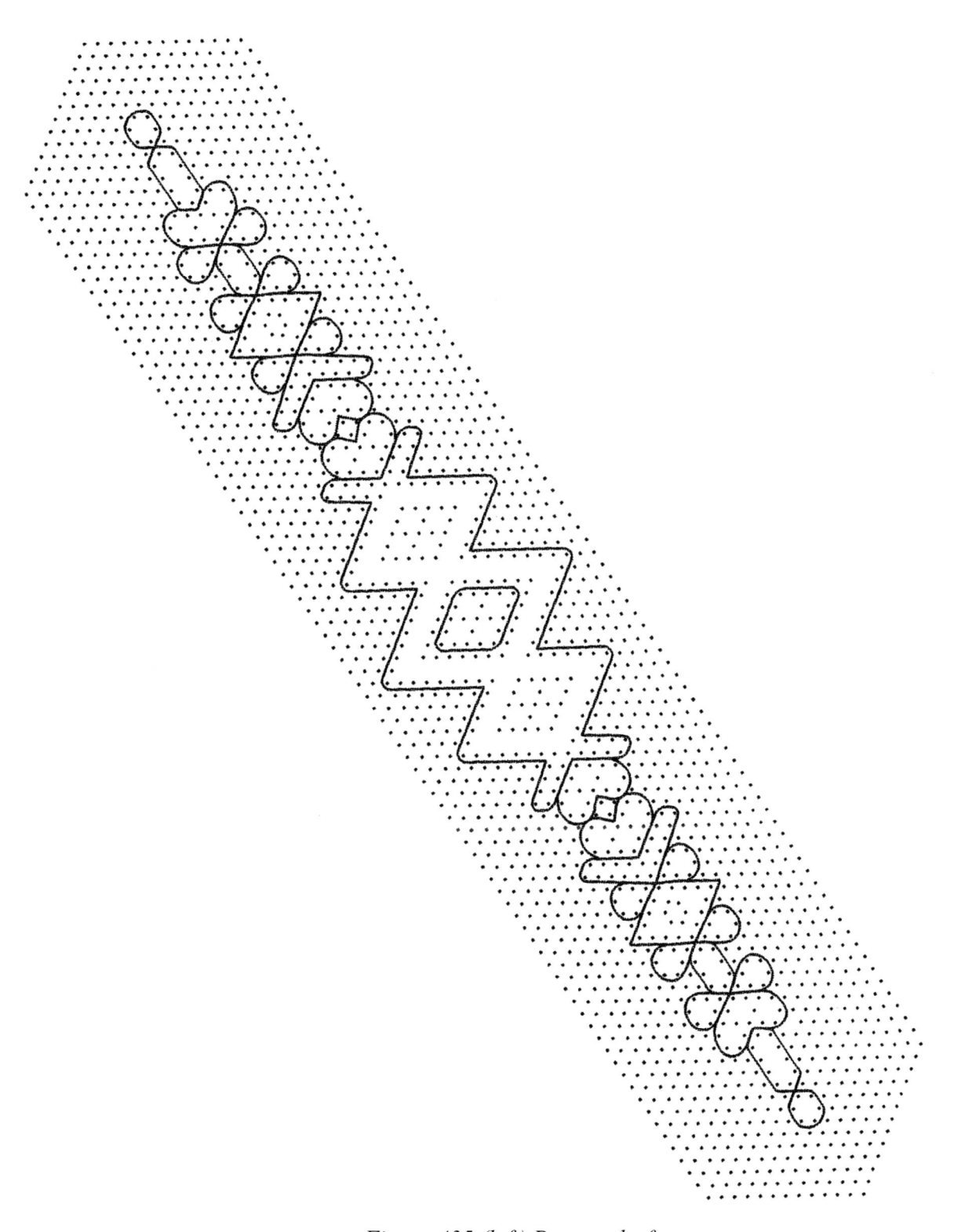

Figure 435 (left) Pattern draft

171

Chapter 13

Setting in footsides from a point

1. Place two temporary pins, side-by-side above A (figure 436) with two pairs straddled over each. Cloth stitch the two centre pairs (stitch a) twist them (as for between the edge pair and passives) and set up pin A between them. Twist the other pairs, the edge pairs, and remove the temporary pins.
2. Place a temporary pin above B with two pairs straddled over it. Cloth stitch the left pair from A through the right pair from B (stitch b) and set up pin B between them. Twist them (the left pair is the edge pair, the others will pass through the passives). Remove the temporary pin.
3. Place a temporary pin above C with two pairs straddled over it. Cloth stitch the right pair from A through the left pair from B (stitch c), set up pin C between them and twist them (the right pair is the edge pair, the other pairs will pass through the passives). Remove the temporary pin.
4. Cloth stitch the right pair from B through the left pair from A (stitch d) and the left pair from C through the right pair from A (stitch e).
5. Cloth stitch the two centre pairs (stitch f).
6. Cloth stitch each centre pair with the other adjacent pair (stitches g & h).
7. Cloth stitch the two centre pairs (stitch i).
8. There are now two passive pairs each side. Cloth stitch the non-edge pair from pin B through two passive pairs and twist (it is entering the ground). Cloth stitch the non-edge pair from pin C through two passive pairs (it is entering the ground).
9. Work a point ground stitch with the two centre pairs setting up the first pin ground pin, pin 1.
10. Place a temporary pin above D, with two pairs straddled over it. Cloth stitch the edge pair from B with the nearest pair from the temporary pin and set up pin D between them. Twist the pairs Cloth stitch the two inner pairs from D across the passives and twist. Make the next ground stitch at pin 2.
11. Place a temporary pin above E, with two pairs straddled over it. Cloth stitch the edge pair from C with the nearest pair from the temporary pin and set up pin E between them. Twist the pairs. Cloth stitch the two inner pairs from E across the passives and twist. Make the ground stitches at pin 3 & 4.
12. Slip a new pair onto the remaining pair entering the ground from pin D and lay it aside. Make the ground stitch, pin 5 and continue down the diagonal row of point ground.

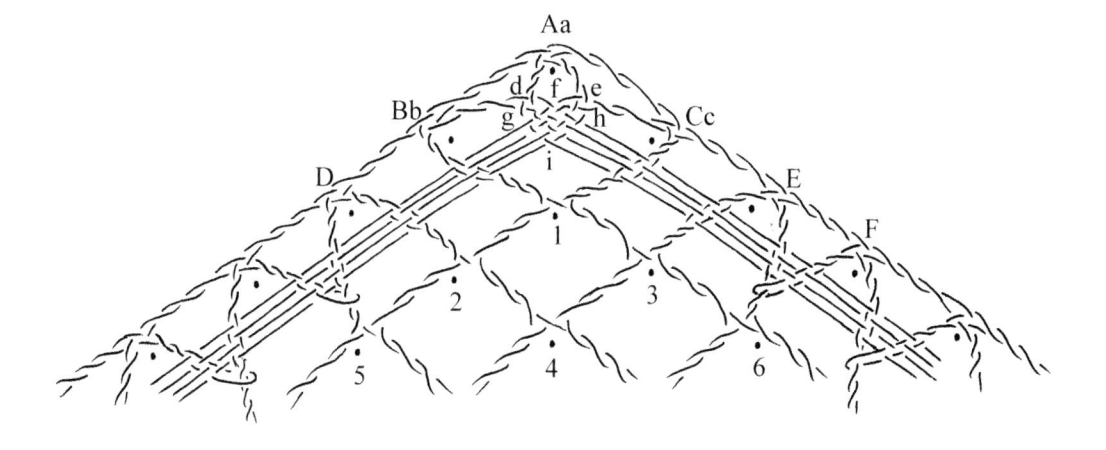

Figure 436 Setting in

13 Slip a new pair onto the remaining pair entering the ground from pin E and lay it aside. Make the ground stitch, pin 6 and continue down the diagonal row of point ground.
14 *Using the 'slipped on' pair, cloth stitch out through the passives, make up the edge and return through the passives. Twist the workers, entering the ground, three times and slip on a new pair. Work point ground down the diagonal*.
15 Repeat the sequence *to* down both sides as far as the third pins from the corners.

Negotiating the corner where the diagonal footside becomes the vertical footside
1 The last pair to be added along the diagonal is slipped on at A (figure 437), after setting up the third pin, pin 1, before the corner pin, and working back through the passives. This pair works through the footside passives to make up the edge at the next pin, pin 2.
2 The former edge pair returns through the passives and exchanges with the inner pair at B, the workers becoming the inner passives and the inner passives working out through the outer pair of passives to make up the edge at the corner pin, pin 3.
3 The pair returning through the passives from pin 3 makes a normal catch-pin stitch at pin 4. The vertical footside continues normally.

Figure 437 (right) Negotiating the corner

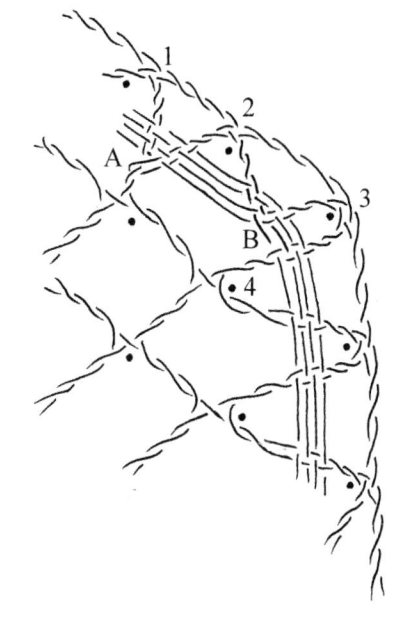

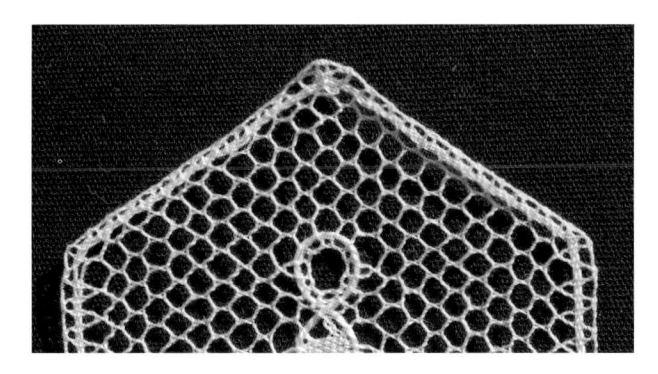

Figure 438 (left) Diagonal and vertical footsides

Continue working, adding a pair of gimps to surround the first honeycomb ring and cross the gimps. When working in colour, work the gimps accordingly.

Working the cloth stitch areas with vertical gimps[3&4]
1 After crossing the gimps at the end of the honeycomb ring work the first three pins of the cloth stitch lozenge as for working a diamond, pins 1-3 (figure 439).
2 After setting up pin 3 the worker cloth stitches through three passive pairs. Pass the gimp between the untwisted workers (keeping the weave going), twist the workers twice, set up a catch-pin, pin 4 (figure 440), under the workers and make a catch-pin stitch with the nearest ground pair. (In figure 440 the worker appears to be twisted before the gimp, but this is the result of the twist made after the gimp has been passed through.) Pass the gimp between the pair from the catch-pin stitch, the new workers, do not twist, and cloth stitch back across the passives.

Chapter 13

3 Take the workers past the gimp to make a catch-pin stitch, pin 5, and return them as when working pin 4. Work back across the passives.
4 Set up pin 6 under the workers and bind the gimp on, i.e. twist the workers twice, pass the gimp between the workers, twist the workers and pass the gimp back between the workers and twist the workers. Return across the passives and repeat at the other side, pin 7.

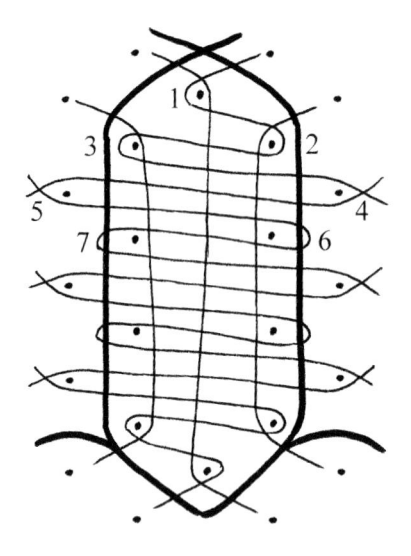

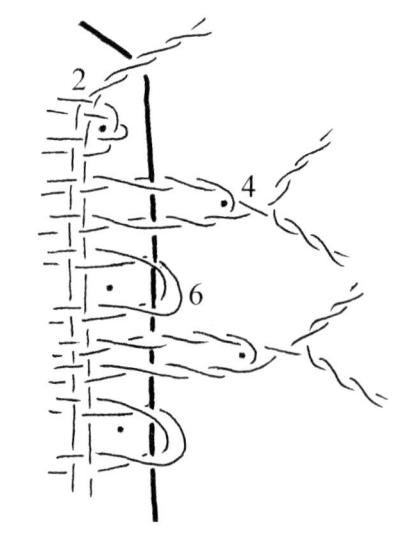

Figure 439 Cloth stitch lozenge   *Figure 440 Detail of catch-pins & binding on*

Continue working the lozenge, making a catch-pin stitch each side, then binding on the gimp each side and working another catch-pin stitch each side. The last three pins are worked as for finishing a diamond.

Cross the gimps, work the heart-shaped area of honeycomb, cross the gimps and work the seven-pin honeycomb rings, using the same gimp around both to prevent a hole in the centre. Work the next cloth stitch lozenge and two more seven-pin honeycomb rings.

Cloth stitch diamond with eyelet, [5,6,7&8]
1 After crossing the gimps start the diamond at the point, in the usual manner, with the workers starting in the same direction as the previous clothwork area. Add pairs as required until three pins have been set up each side; the top pin is counted for each side, pins 1-5 (figure 441). The cloth stitch area now divides to make the eyelet. The sides are worked separately, then combined and the diamond finishes at a point.
2 After setting up pin 5, cloth stitch through three pairs, half the passives plus one pair

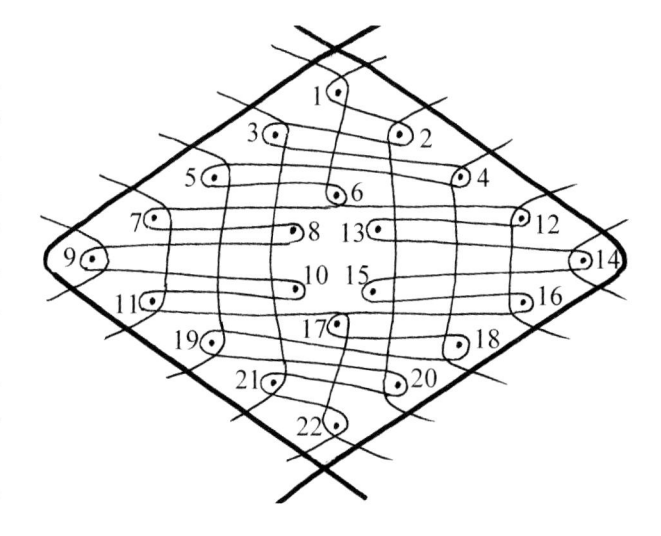

Figure 441 Cloth stitch diamond with eyelet

174

(the workers for the other side). Set up the top pin of the eyelet, pin 6, twist the workers and cloth stitch across the row, adding a pair at pin 7.
3 Twist the workers and return, leaving out the pair immediately before pin 6 (the workers for the other side). Twist the workers two or three times, set up the winkie pin, pin 8 (a winkie pin is one at which a pair is neither added nor left out). Return to the point at the other side, adding a pair at pin 9. Cloth stitch across to the next winkie pin, pin 10 and twist as before. Return to the outer edge, pin 11, leaving out a pair and back through the passives. The pin where the two sides combine, pin 17, cannot be set until the other side has been completed.
4 Using the remaining pair from pin 6, as workers, complete the second side, pins 12-16, as for the first side and return the workers through the passives after setting up pin 16.
5 Cloth stitch the workers, from the two sides, together and set up pin 17 between them. The half row immediately before the division was on the left side therefore the half row immediately after the sides have combined should be towards the right to balance the upper and lower sections. Using the left pair as workers, twist them, then work towards the right to pin 18. Leave the other pair of workers, untwisted, as passives.
6 Continue working until the diamond is complete.

Cross the gimps and work two seven-pin honeycomb rings.

Dividing clothwork into narrow trails[5&9]

1 After crossing the gimps start the clothwork as usual until three pins have been set up each side; the top pin is counted for each side, (pins 1-5, figure 442).
2 The cloth stitch area now divides. After setting up pin 5, cloth stitch through three pairs, half the passives plus one pair (the workers for the other trail). Set up the pin at the division, pin 6, twist the workers and cloth stitch back to pin 7.

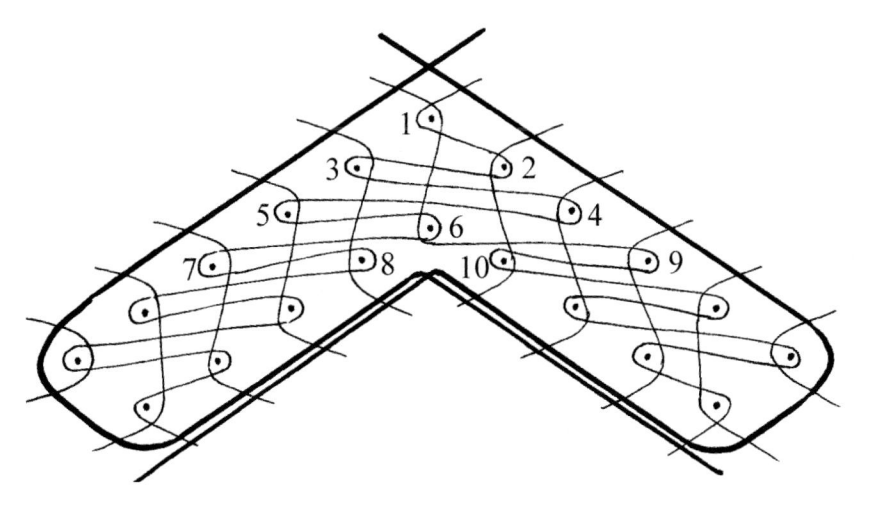

Figure 442 (left) Cloth stitch area dividing into two narrow trails

3 Return, leaving out the pair immediately before pin 6 (the workers for the other trail), and set up pin 8. Continue this trail and finish it as usual.
4 Using the pair left out at pin 6 as workers, work the right hand trail starting with pins 9 and 10 and finish it as usual.

Cross the gimps and make the heart-shaped areas of honeycomb with the four-pin cloth stitch diamond between them.

175

Chapter 13

Combining narrow trails [6&10]
Start each trail working so that it has the maximum number of pairs i.e. the left trail starts towards the right and the right trail towards the left. After working the third pin from the outer point the workers meet at the central pin, pin 1 (figure 443). Cloth stitch the worker pairs together, set up the pin,, pin 1, and cover with a cloth stitch. Continue the cloth stitch area by working towards the right, setting up pins 2 and 3. The other workers are left untwisted and become passives. (The workers could have equally been worked towards the left, but this direction is more in keeping with previous clothwork areas, and the following instructions rely on the right pair being used as workers at this stage).

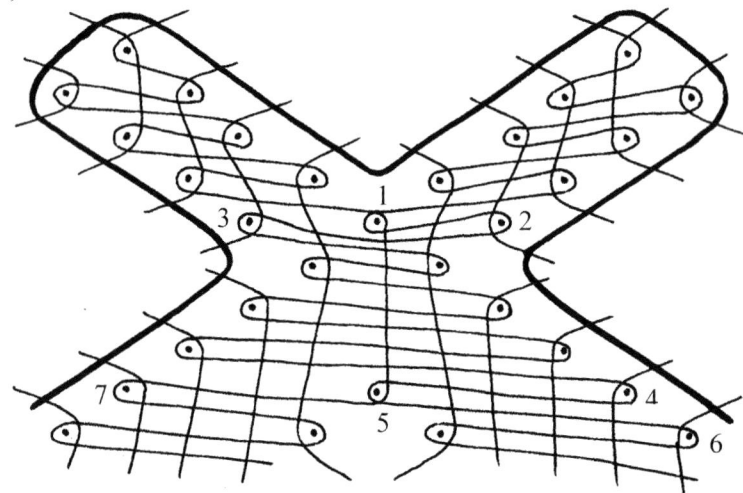

Figure 443 Narrow cloth stitch trails combined then divided into two wider trails

Dividing clothwork into wider trails [5,10&11]
Continue working rows of cloth stitch until the fourth pin, on the right, from the narrowest point (figure 443), pin 4, is set up.
1 Return back through five pairs, half the passives plus one pair, the workers for the other trail (The pair that will be entering the row at pin 7 must be counted as one of the passives), and set up the dividing pin, pin 5, under the workers.
2 Return to set up pin 6. Continue this trail, leaving out a pair at pin 5, the workers for the other trail, and work as far as the outer corner.
3 Using the pair left out at pin 5 as workers, work the left hand trail, starting with pin 7, as far as the outer corner.
Work the honeycomb centre; there is no gimp between the trails and the honeycomb.

Combining wider trails [6&11]
1. Work both trails until they meet at the centre pin, pin 1 (figure 444).
2. Cloth stitch the two worker pairs and set up pin 1.
3 When the trails divided for the honeycomb centre the half row occurred on the right. Therefore the worker should continue towards the left, to pin 2, to make a half row to balance the upper and lower parts.
Continue the clothwork until the area divides.

Chapter 13

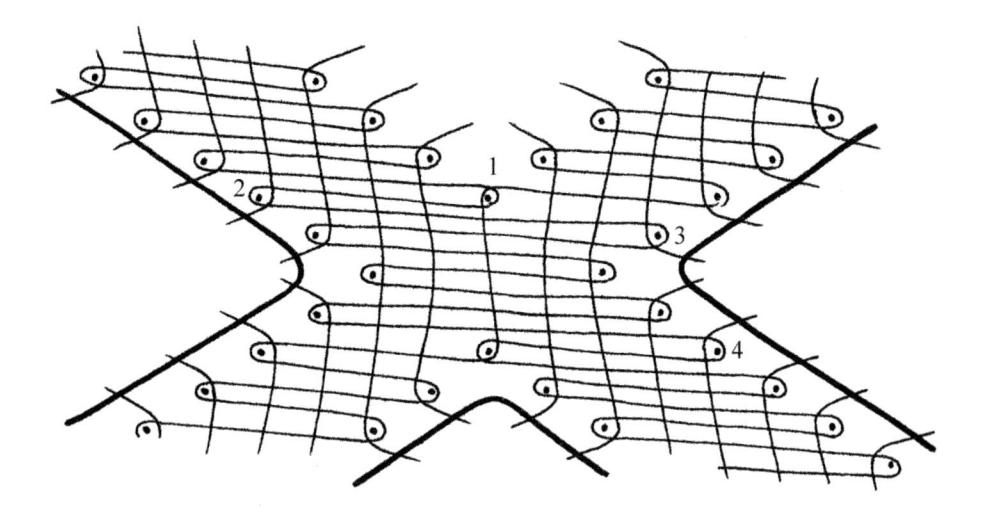

Figure 444 Combining wider trails

Dividing combined wider trails into narrow trails5&9

After combining the wider trails, continue until the first pin on each side, following the narrowest row have been set up, pins 2 & 3 (figure 445). Cloth stitch through half the passives plus one pair, the workers for the other trail, set up the pin and continue down the left trail, leaving out a pair at pin 4. The pair left out from pin 3 is the worker pair for the right trail.

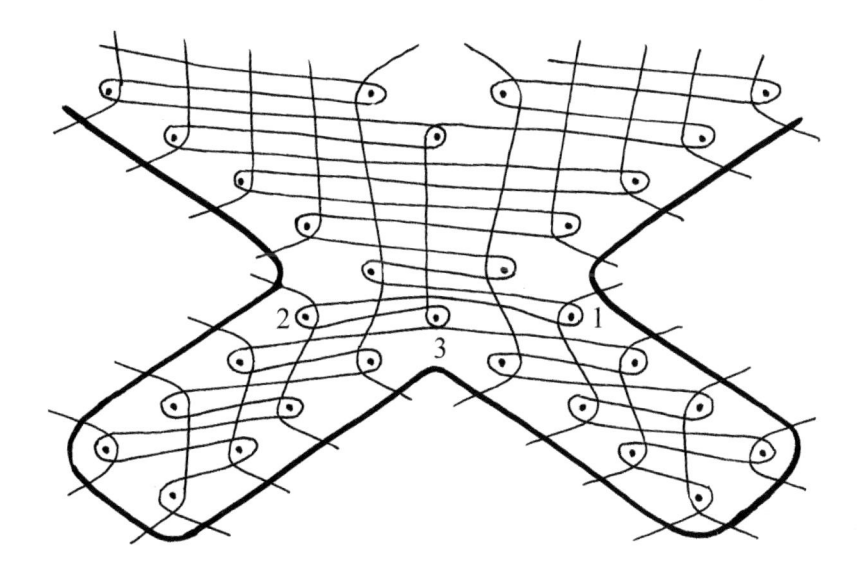

Figure 445 Wider trails combined then divided into narrow trails

Casting off along a diagonal footside[12]

At the corner pin, where the vertical footside becomes a diagonal footside -
1 Make up the edge at pin 2, i.e. cloth stitch the pair from the catch-pin, pin 1, (figure 446) out through the footside passives, set up pin 2, make the stitch about the pin, twist the pairs and return the workers through the passives and leave them to become the inner pair of passives.
2 *Work the ground pair from pin 3 through the three pairs of passives and make up the edge using pin 4. The pair returning through the three passive pairs to become a fourth pair. To avoid

177

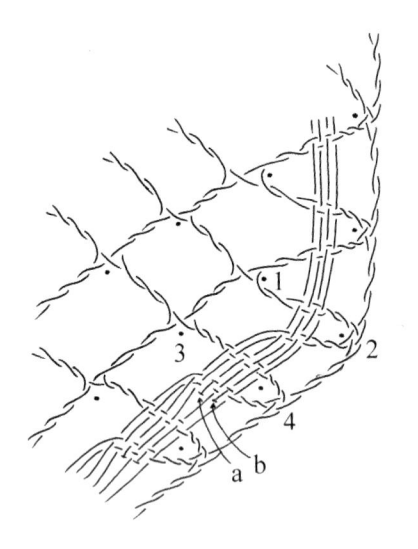

accumulating passive pairs along the edge, threads a & b*, the second and fourth threads, are laid back. Repeat *to* until only the pin at the point remains unused.

Figure 446 (left) *Casting off along a diagonal footside*

Finishing the footside at a point
Cut off all the bobbins except for the two edge pairs and six passive pairs, three pairs from each side, which need to be finished off.
1 Remove most of the pins leaving only those along the diagonals and three rows of pins inside them. Trim the pairs thrown out close to the work and push the ground pins down flush with the pillow.
2 Cover the lace with a cover cloth, lift the remaining six passive pairs and two edge pairs between the two central pins and, keeping them strictly in order, lay them back over the work until they are pointing in the opposite direction.
3 Turn the pillow through 180°, (the lace is now upside down).
4 Cloth stitch the two centre pairs, the original edge pairs, set up the pin at the point between them and twist them. Work each pair of workers through three pairs of passives, then cloth stitch the workers together and leave them.
5 Starting with those nearest the pins take one thread from each side and tie reef knot. Lay the bobbins back over the back, one to each side. Repeat with the next thread from each side and lay them out next to the first pair. Repeat until four threads from each side have been knotted with the corresponding thread from the other side (figure 447).
6 There are eight threads left, four each side. For each group of four threads, first knot the centre two threads, then the two other threads.
Make the knots carefully, avoiding any loose threads or straining the work.

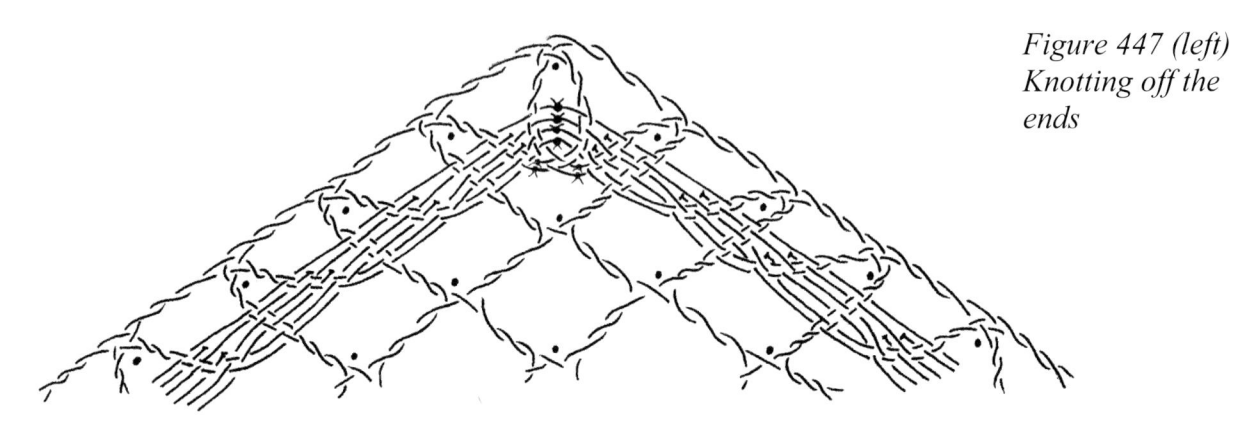

Figure 447 (left) Knotting off the ends

Making up the finger plate

Select a piece of paper or fabric for the background for the lace and cut to size using the card template in the fingerplate kit. Stick the background to the card and attach the lace, with several small stitches, using some of the lace thread. The remaining threads that were knotted off at the point can be sewn through to the back.

END NOTES

1 Drafting the pattern

1. Using Grid No 1, draw in the gimps (figure 448).
2. Remove a single vertical line of unwanted dots from the centres of the lozenges.
3. Remove single diagonal lines of dots from the centres of the wider trails
4. Remove unwanted dots from the honeycomb areas.
5. Adjust the footpins and catch-pins along both sides of the pattern draft. Adjust diagonal edge rows at the ends to allow for the passives but, since there are no catch-pins along the diagonals, the second row does not need adjusting (figure 248).

The narrow trails are worked across adjacent diagonal rows of dots and therefore no dots are removed.

Figure 448 (right) Draw the gimps (continue drawing the lower half to match).

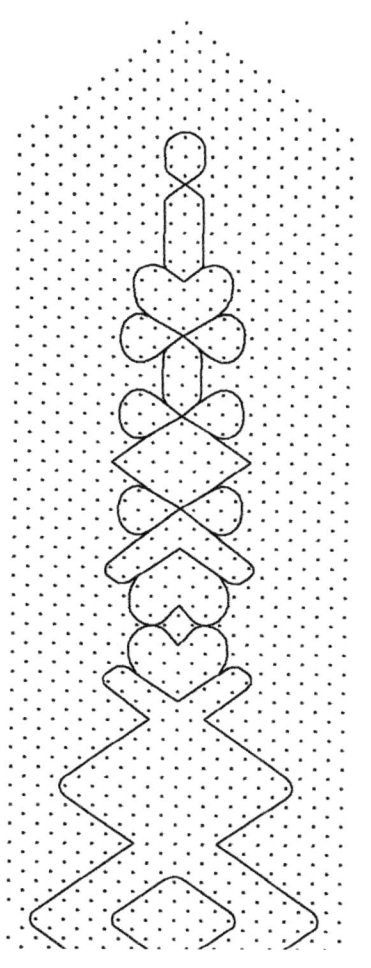

6. From the diamonds (figure 449), remove the three dots along the line across the centre (figure 450).
7. If the six dots in the centre are used, as they are, for the eyelet, the hole will be unpleasantly large; to make the hole smaller, add 6 dots within the remaining centre circle of dots (figure 451).
8. Remove the original circle of 6 dots figure 452).

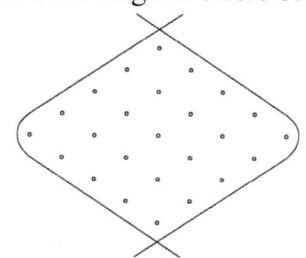

Figure 449 (left) Gimps drawn

Figure 450 (right) Three dots across the centre removed

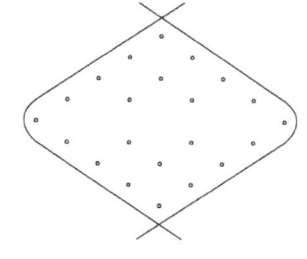

Chapter 13

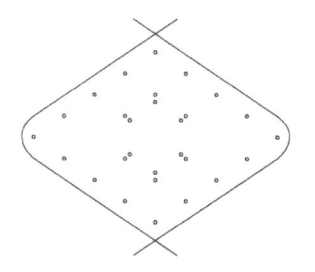

Figure 451 (left) Add a circle of six dots within the central circle

Figure 452 (right) Remove the original centre circle of six dots

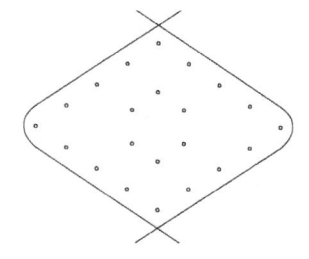

2 Working with colour[3]

The lace in the fingerplate (figure 433) was worked in green and mounted on ivory, so the background is lighter than the lace. Compare this with the sample worked in white that is mounted on a dark background (figure 434). One is the negative of the other. The clothwork of the sample is light, the way we usually see it; that of the fingerplate is dark, not the usual appearance of clothwork. The honeycomb of the sample shows as black spots, as we usually see it; that of the sample shows as white spots. These effects can be quite surprising, and unsettling, the first time you place a piece of lace on a lighter background. This effect should be taken into account when designing with colour.

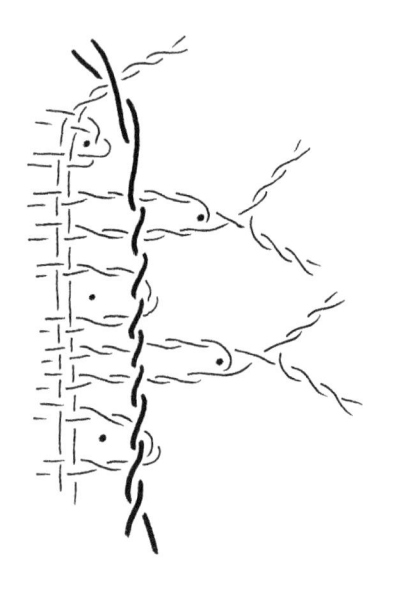

3 Binding on when using coloured gimps[2]

After working through the passives twist the workers and pin (figure 453). Pass the workers through the pair of coloured gimps, twist the gimps, pass the workers back through the gimps and twist the gimps again.

Figure 453 (left) Binding on coloured gimps

4 Catch pin by vertical gimp

If a lozenge is worked following the usual rules (figure 454) there would be only one pair of continuous passives, and the workers would be too widely spaced.

Figure 454 (right) Lozenge worked following usual rules

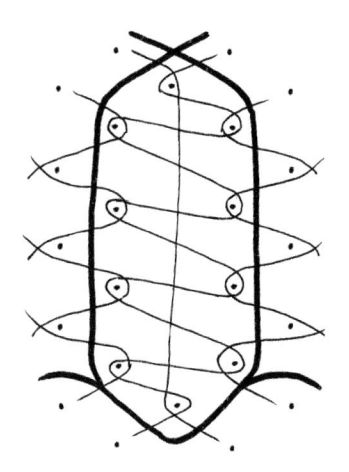

Chapter 13

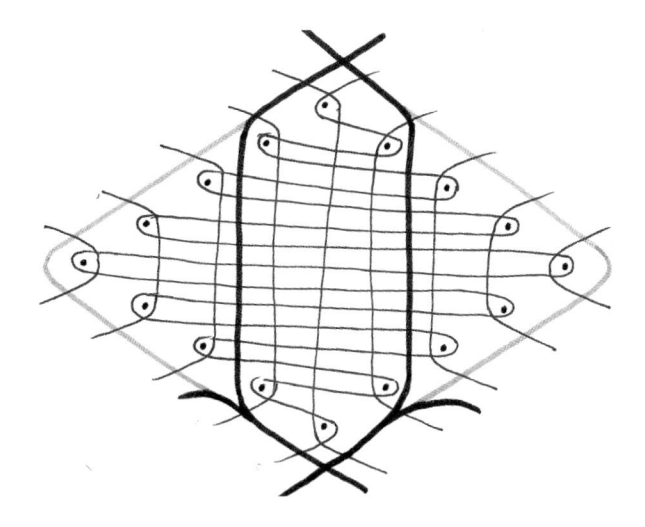

However, if we superimpose the lozenge on a clothwork diamond (figure 455) we see why it happens. Standard clothwork has pinholes at every dot along the diagonals. The lozenge (figure 454) only uses the pinholes that occur within in the vertical lines and they have double the spacing vertically, therefore there will be half the number of rows of clothwork across the lozenge than there would be across the diamond.

Figure 455 (left) Lozenge superimposed on a diamond

To repeat the spacing of the row of the diamond in the lozenge, extra dots are added (figure 456) so that there is one level with each of those of the superimposed lozenge (figure 455) and they are placed alternately inside and outside the gimp.

Figure 456 (right) Lozenge superimposed on a diamond with pinholes added

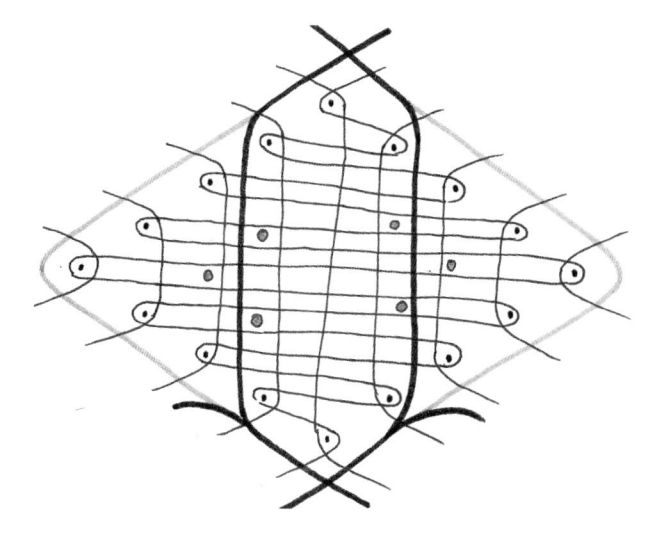

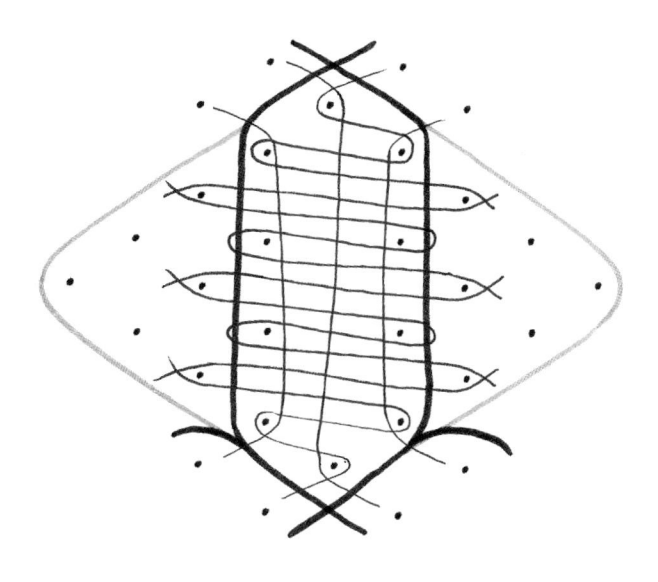

In order to make a lozenge using these extra pins, the workers cross the gimps to work catch-pin stitches in the ground and return (figure 457). Alternating with these rows are those using pinholes within the gimps. Since there is neither a pair entering across the gimp, nor leaving across it, the gimp would separate away from the clothwork. Therefore the gimp should be bound on.

Figure 457 (left) Working diagram for a lozenge

181

Chapter 13

Traditionally the workers remain untwisted when they pass across a gimp (figure 440) to make a catch-pin stitch, since the presence of twists would cause the gimp to be deflected. However, in some cases twists could possibly be used between the passives and gimp (figure 458 & 459).

Figure 458 (right) Twists between passives & gimp

Figure 459 (far right) Twists between passives & gimp

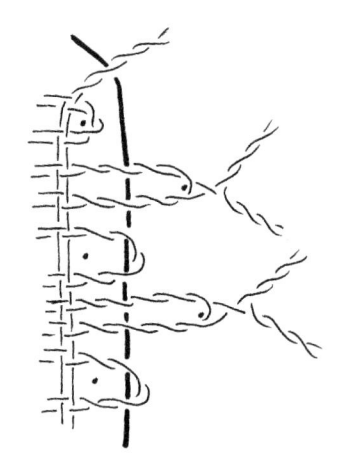

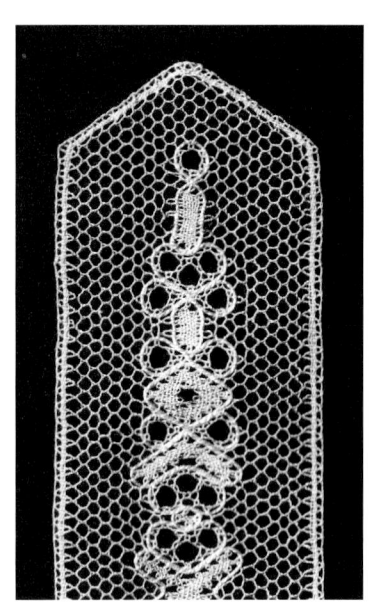

5 Dividing clothwork
When clothwork is divided it is traditional to twist the original workers before covering the pin; the passive pair is not usually twisted. Always firm up this stitch.

6 Combining clothwork
When clothwork is combined it is traditional to twist the pair that will become the new workers before covering the pin; the workers that become a passive pair are not usually twisted. Always firm up this stitch.

7 Winkie pin
Winkie pins are commonly found around the edge of an eyelet in cloth stitch. The workers are twisted two or three times as they pass around the pins to give the appearance of small picots, (figure 460). At these pins there is neither a pair entering the clothwork nor leaving it, pins 8,10, 13 and 15).

8 Dividing and combining for an eyelet in clothwork[5&6]

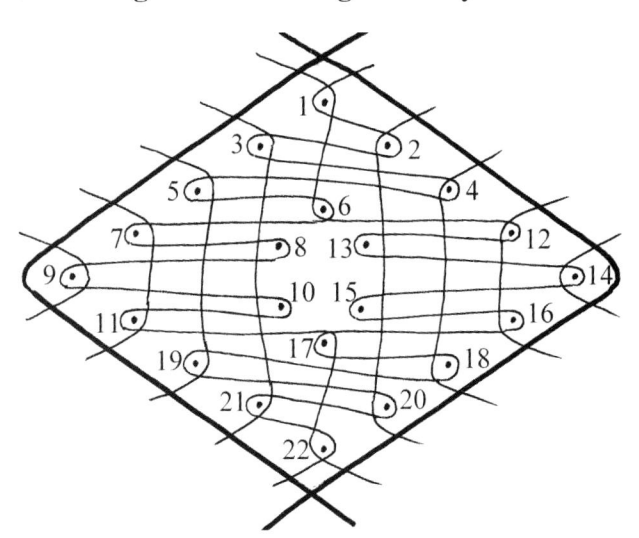

When there is an eyelet in a clothwork area, the paths taken by the workers depend on the position of the two pins either side of the centre of the eyelet. For this diamond pins 8 & 10 and 13 & 15 (Figure 460).

1 The worker on the left must travel from pin 8 to 10 via 9, and the one on the right from pin 13 to 15 via 14.
2 Tracing the path of the worker back from pin 8 it will have travelled from pin 7 and pin 6 and the worker at 13 from 12 and 6, the same

Figure 460 Dividing clothwork

182

centre point at the top of the eyelet, pin 6. From here the path of a single worker can be traced back to the top pin, pin 1.

3 Since there is the same number of pins on both sides (the top pin is counted for each side) of area above pin 1, the workers could travel in either direction. However, if there are other areas of clothwork they should ideally all have the workers starting in the same direction. In this piece we have already had a lozenge with the workers starting towards the right. Therefore this diamond should follow a similar path and the workers travel from the top pin, pin 1, towards the right. When all the pins above the top hole in the eyelet, pin 6, have been worked the clothwork divides.

4 From pin 5 the worker works through half the passives plus the next pair (the centre pair of passives of this row). This extra pair becomes the other pair of workers and is not included when working down the left side. Continue with the original workers down the left side of the eyelet, pins 7-11. Using the pair remaining at pin 6 as the workers, continue down the right side to pin 16.

5 With both workers work cloth stitch, pin 17. From here you can continue with the workers travelling in either direction. However, the top triangle appears to have an extra half row on the left, occurring where the workers doubled back from pin 6 to pin 7. To balance this we can work from pin 17 towards the right, pin 18, and on to the end of the diamond. The other worker, left at pin 17, remains untwisted as a passive pair.

9 Clothwork dividing into narrow trails[5]

The inverted 'V' of clothwork, (figure 461) is essentially a clothwork area dividing into two narrow trails. Theoretically it can be started with the workers travelling in either direction from the top pin unless, as in this case there are previous clothwork areas that, ideally, it should match.

1 The centre pin, where the trail divides, lies between pins 4 and 5. Start at the point with the workers travelling towards the right and work until all the pins up to, and including both those in line with the centre, pin 6, have been worked.

2 Work through half the passives of the next row plus the centre pair (the other workers), set up pin 6 and cover the pin. These two pairs both continue as workers, the original workers continuing towards the left and the original centre pair towards the right.

The completed trails will have the same density. However, in order to achieve this, the workers on the left lie at a slightly different angle. There is no perfect solution; a choice has to be made between the angle of the workers and the density of the trails. With narrow trails the density is probably more important.

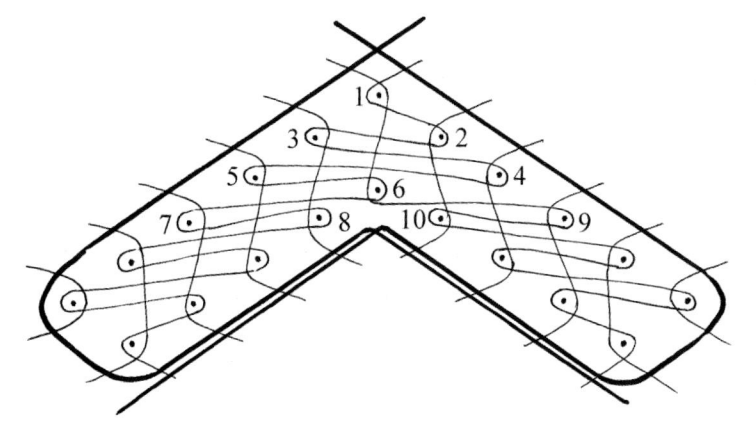

Figure 461 Clothwork dividing into narrow trails

Chapter 13

10 Narrow trails combining then dividing into wider trails[5&6]

When two narrow trails have been worked with the workers travelling inwards from the top pinholes to produce the maximum density, each trail is continued until the workers meet at the centre pin, pin 1 (figure 462). The workers make a cloth stitch, pin and cover the pin. The workers could continue in either direction unless, as in this case, there are other areas of clothwork to be taken into consideration. In this piece I have taken the workers towards the left, to match the lower part of the preceding diamond. This method of combining two narrow trails with the workers travelling in opposition results in one more row of clothwork, than would have occurred if both had been started in the same direction. There is no perfect solution; a choice has to be made between the angle of the workers and the density of the trails. With narrow trails the density is probably more important, the difference between two or three passives is substantial, but this is not necessarily true for wider trails.

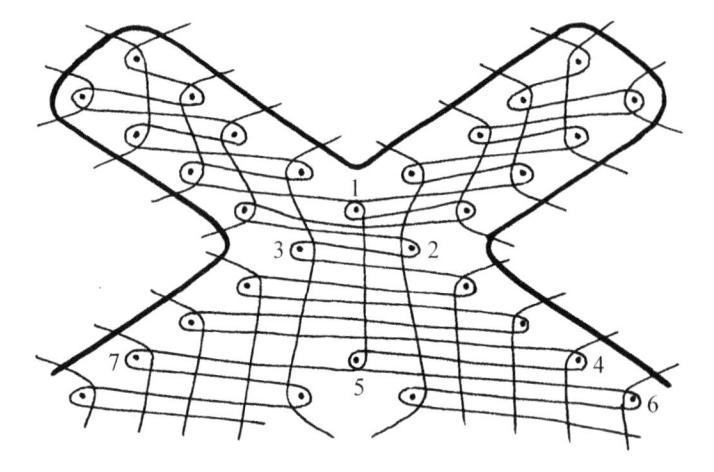

Figure 462 Narrow trails combining then dividing into wider trails

To determine where to divide the clothwork for wider trails look for the pins at the side of the clothwork that are on the horizontal line through the dividing pin, pin 5 (figure 462). In this case they are pins 4 and 7. Complete rows are worked as far as the beginning of the row through the centre pin, then the worker works through half the passives plus one more pair, the centre pair that will become the workers for the other trail. However, when the number of passives is counted it appears that there are eight pairs of passives, but this has not taken into account the pair of passives that will enter at the end of the next row on the left at pin 7. By including this pair we now have nine pairs of passives between pins 4 and 7. Therefore, after pin 4, they will work through half the passives, four pairs, plus the centre pair, making five pairs. After setting up the centre pin, pin 5, cover the pin. There are now two working pairs working away from each other. One trail, in this case the right trail, will have more pair than the other and this will change when the trail changes direction. Since each trail has a relatively large number of pairs, one less pair in one trail is not obvious. In this example the left hand trail starts off having four and five pairs in alternate rows. The right hand trail starts five and six pairs in alternate rows. When the trails change direction, and angle towards each other, they change and the left hand trail will have five and six pairs in alternate rows and the right hand trail will have four and five pairs in alternate rows.

11 Wider trails combining & dividing [5&6]

Work each trail until the workers meet (figure 463). At this point they make a cloth stitch and the central pin, pin 1, is set up. From here one pair continues as the working pair while the other becomes a passive pair. To determine which pair becomes the working pair check the alignment of the pins. By lining up through the centre pin and the last pin used on one side, then through the centre pin and the last pin the other side, it is clear that the next pin to be set up is pin 2. Therefore the pair on the right side of the pin will become the workers and continue towards the left. This produces an extra half row that will balance the half row that was made on the right side when the clothwork divided onto the two trails.

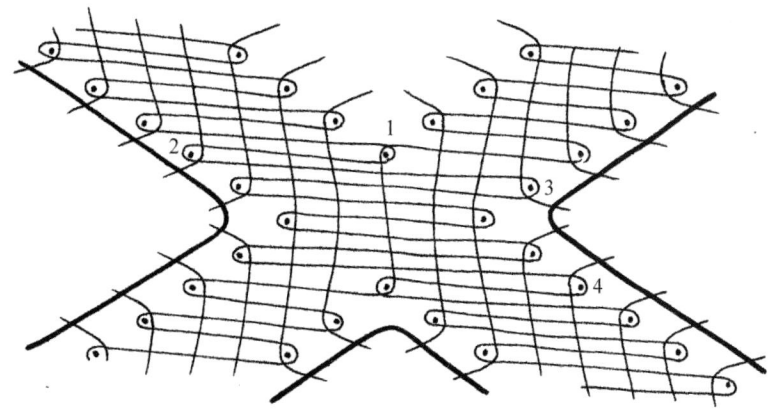

Figure 463 Wider trails dividing & combining

12 Alternative methods for casting off along a diagonal

(1) A more traditional approach to casting off is to stack by taking each pair approaching the edge through the passives to make up the edge, then cover the pin with a cloth stitch. When the number of passive pairs increases beyond an acceptable number the pair inside the inner pair of passives is thrown out (figure 464).

Figure 464 (right) Casting off by stacking and throwing out pairs

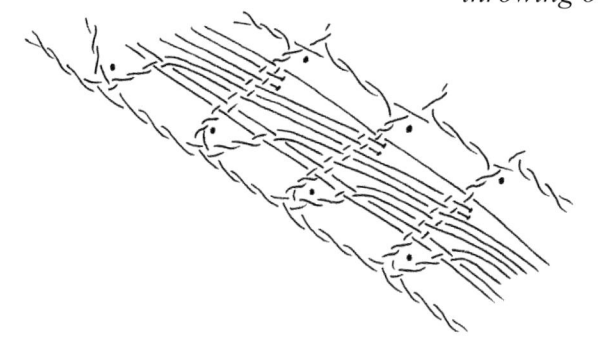

(2) A variation on this theme is to stack by taking each pair approaching the edge through the passives to make up the edge, then cover the pin with a cloth stitch. When the number of passive pairs increases beyond an acceptable number the second and third threads from the inner edge of the passives, are thrown out. Since these threads are from different pairs the finish is stronger (figure 465).

Figure 465 Casting off by stacking and throwing out threads from different pairs

Chapter 14

Chapter 14
PROJECTS 21-24 A HEXAGON IN DIFFERENT SIZES (Plate no 8)

Project 21 Glass cover
Project 22 Tray
Project 23 Plate
Project 24 Wine coaster

New Techniques for Projects 21- 24
  using a long loop
  hexagonal motif with point ground along
    the diagonals

Materials required for Project 21
  pricking (figure 468)[1]
  Egyptian cotton no 60
  gimp no 8 perle
  12 crystal beads 5mm dia.
  6 crystal beads 5 mm dia.

End Notes for Projects 21- 24
1 drafting the pattern
2 working a hexagonal shape with point
   ground along the diagonals and a
   central honeycomb ring
3 the effects of changing thread size
4 the effect of changing scale

Figure 466 (above) Glass cover

Figure 467 (left) Hexagon

186

Chapter 14

Figure 468 Pricking for the glass cover

Setting in[2]
Although hexagonal motifs are usually started along a diagonal or the line below the diagonal, it is not always the best position at which to join end to start. For this motif, the diagonal passes through an area of point ground; not a good place to join the lace. However, there are places where gimps travel the full width of the lace, namely through the centres of the sections (figure 469).

Chapter 14

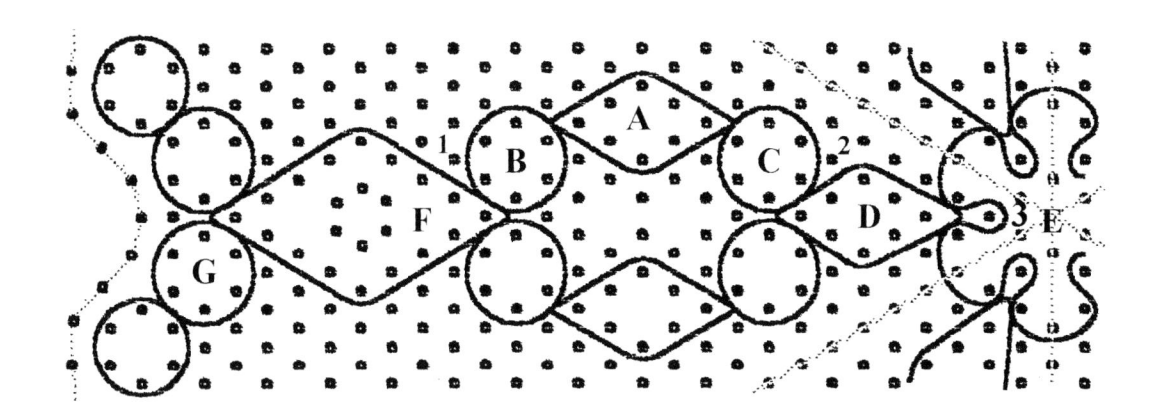

Figure 469 Setting in

1 Start with a pair of gimps over the upper small diamond A, and set in the diamond..
2 Introduce another pair of gimps below the diamond and cross with the previous gimps each side.
3 Set in the honeycomb ring each side, ring B, with a pair added at the point ground stitch outside the ring at pin 1, and ring C with a pair added at the point ground stitch, pin 2. The space between the upper and lower diamonds is an area of honeycomb stitches with pin-chain down the centre.

Note: More pinholes are in use than for normal honeycomb ground, this is to avoid holes in the corners, and all stitches are honeycomb stitches.

4 Set in the small diamond close to the centre, D. Add a single gimp and start setting in the centre snowflake, E , at pin 3.
5 Using the gimp from honeycomb ring B, set in the large diamond, F.
6 Add a pair of gimps, below the large diamond F, and set in the honeycomb ring at the headside, G.
7 Finally set in the headside. Extra pairs of passives will be required as the width at the headside increases, one for each extra vertical row of pins that occurs after this point (not counting the picots).

Two pairs of gimps will be thrown out as the central rings and diamonds of this section are completed.

When lace was made commercially speed was of the essence, and patterns were designed with this in mind. Today we make lace for enjoyment and the time taken is not important. Also, there are very few fully trained lace designers, and none that I know of, who design Bucks point. Those of us who are designing Bucks point do so to the best of our ability, but there may be certain shortcomings as far as ease of working is concerned. Also, today we are more concerned with the aesthetic effect than the time taken making the lace.

Long loops
One of the shortcomings concerns the use of gimps. Some modern designs have gimps that dip down below the working line, i.e. there is a stitch in the next row, around which the gimp must pass before the current row can progress. In this situation the stitch in the next row can be

Chapter 14

accommodated by making a long loop. This is a modern technique that has developed to deal with a situation that, because it slows progress, was avoided in traditional patterns.

In this pattern, each snowflake (figure 470), has four stitches, A-D, that require long loops and there are places where snowflakes overlap, X and Y. (X & Y are not always in these positions.)

Figure 470 (right) Snowflake

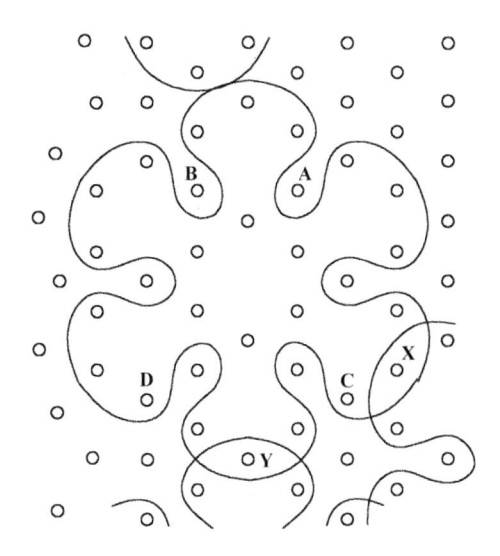

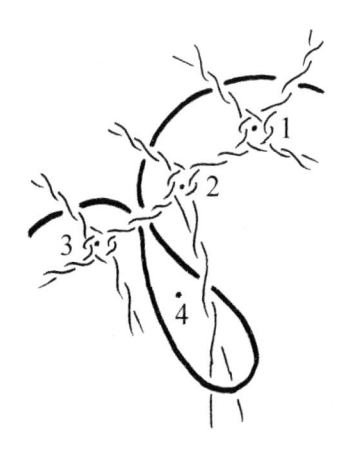

Figure 471 Preparing a long loop at A

Using a long loop at A

1 Work the top lobe of the snowflake, pins 1 and 2, (figure 471)
2 After completing the stitch at pin 2, pass the gimp through both pairs and twist the right pair.
3 The gimp then loops around pin 4, but the stitch at pin 4 cannot be worked until after the stitch at pin 3 has been made
4 Enlarge the loop until it is 7-10cm (3-4 ins) long and pin towards the right.

5 Lift the gimp bobbin, towards the left, over the right pair from pin 2, through the left pair from pin 2, and through the next pair on the left. The left pair from pin 2 bridges both the gimps.
6 Twist the pairs and work the stitch at pin 3.
7 Move the left side of the loop over the right thread from pin 3 (figure 472), and lift the left thread over the gimp and down through the loop and twist the pair.

Figure 472 (right) Passing pairs into the long loop at A

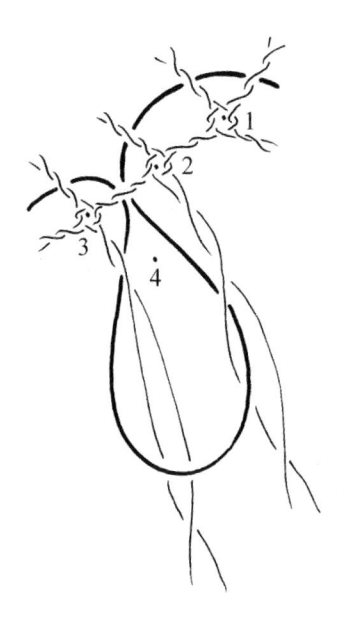

Chapter 14

8 Make the stitch at pin 4 (figure 473) and lift the left thread from each pair up through the loop.
9 Pull the gimp to reduce the loop (figure 474), twist the pairs from pin 4 and continue making the lace.

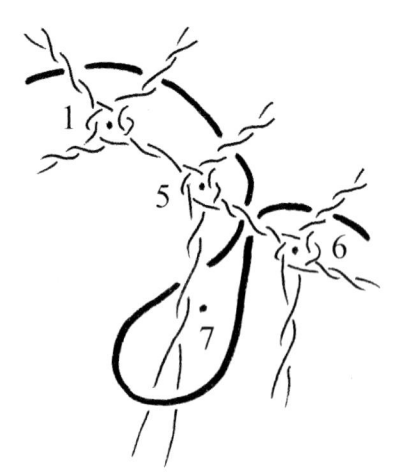

Figure 473 (left) The stitch in the loop and the pairs brought out of the loop at A

Figure 474 (above) The long loop at A reduced

Using a long loop at B
Complete the top lobe of the snowflake by making the stitch at pin 5 (figure 475). The gimp then loops round pin 7, but the stitch at pin 7 cannot be worked until after the stitch at pin 6 has been made.

1 After completing the stitch at pin 5, pass the gimp through both pairs and twist the left pair.
2 Pin a loop of gimp 7-10cm (3-4ins) long towards the left.
3 Lift the gimp towards the right over the left hand pair from pin 5, pass the gimp through the right hand pair from pin 5, and the next pair on the right, with the right pair from pin 5 bridging both gimps, and twist the pairs.
4 Work the stitch at pin 6.

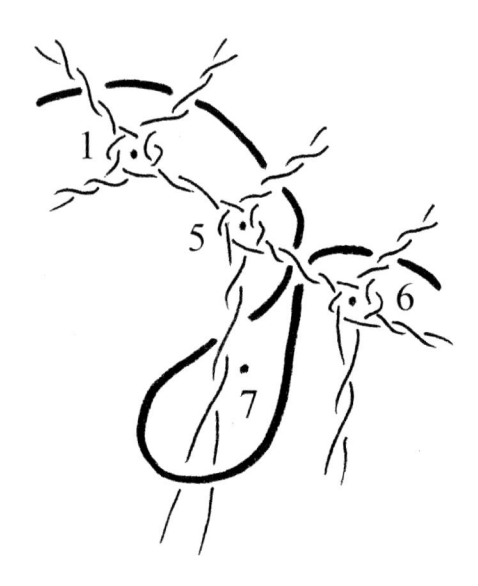

Figure 475 (right) Preparing a long loop at B

Chapter 14

5 Lift the left thread from pin 6 over the gimp (figure 476), pass it down through the loop and twist the pair
6 Make the stitch at pin 7 (figure 477) and lift the left thread from each pair up through the loop.

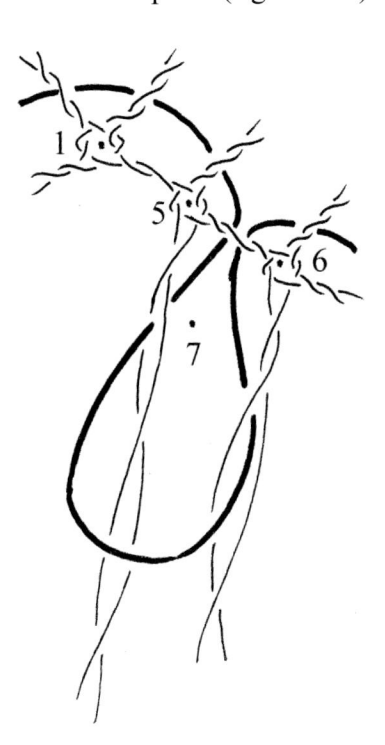

Figure 476 Passing pairs into the long loop at B

Figure 477 The stitch in the loop and the pairs brought out of the loop at B

7 Pull the gimp to reduce the loop, twist the pairs from pin 7 (figure 478) and continue as normal, crossing the gimps according to the indicator lines.

Figure 478 (right) Long loop at B reduced

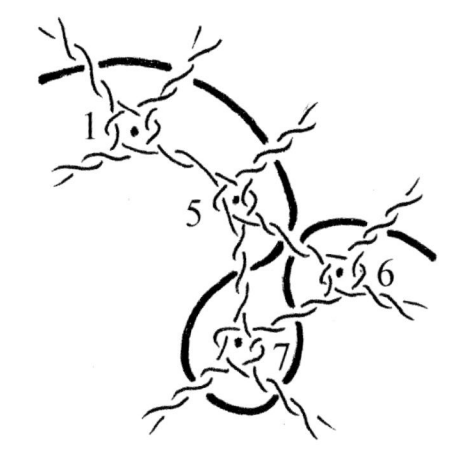

191

Chapter 14

Using a long loop at C
Work the lower right hand lobe of the snowflake as far as pin 8 (figure 479) and cross the gimps. The gimp then loops round pin 10, but the stitch at pin 10 cannot be worked until after the stitch at pin 9 has been made.

1 After completing the stitch at pin 8, pass the gimps through the pairs and cross the gimps.
2 Pin a loop of the gimp, (the gimp now on the left,) 7-10cm (3-4ins) long towards the right and lift the gimp towards the left over the left pair from pin 8.
3 Pass the gimp through the next two pairs on the left, twist them and make the stitch at pin 9.
4 Move the left side of the loop over the right thread from pin 9 (figure 480) and lift the left thread over the gimp and down through the loop. Twist both pairs that are inside the loop.

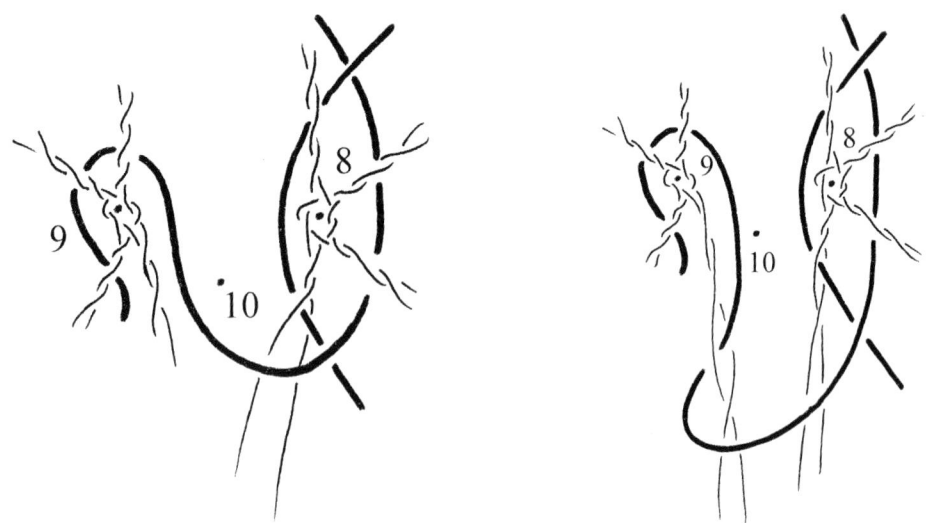

Figure 479 Preparing a long loop at C   *Figure 480 Passing the second pair into the loop at C*

5 Make the stitch at pin 10 (figure 481) and lift the left thread from each pair up through the loop.
6 Pull the gimp to reduce the loop, twist the pairs from pin 10 (figure 482) and continue making the lace

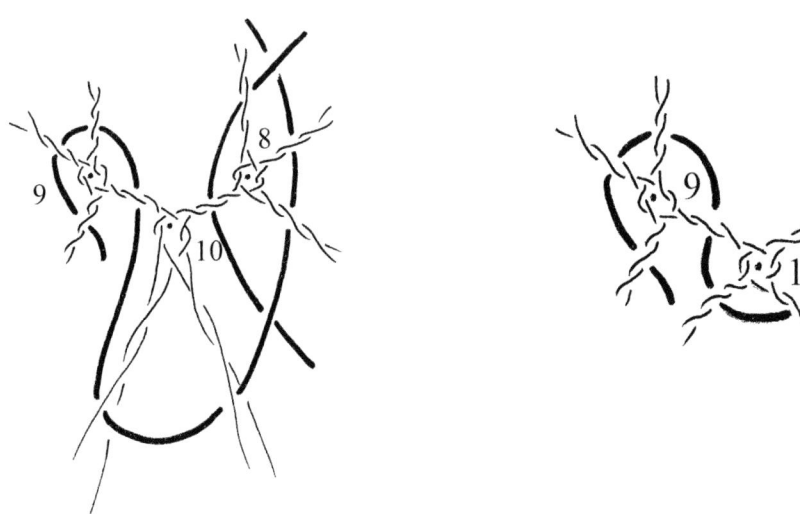

Figure 481 The stitch in the loop and the pairs brought out of the loop at C   *Figure 482 Long loop at C reduced*

Using a long loop at D

Work the lower left hand lobe of the snowflake as far as pin 11 (figure 483). The gimp around the snowflake then loops round pin 13, but the stitch at pin 13 cannot be worked until after the stitch at pin 12 has been made.

1 After completing the stitch at pin 11, pass the gimp through the left pair.
2 Pin a loop of gimp 7-10cm (3-4ins) long towards the left and lift the gimp towards the right over the right pair from pin 11.
3 Pass the gimp through the next two pairs on the right, twist them and make the stitch at pin 12.
4 Lift the left thread of the left pair from pin 12 (figure 484) over the gimp, down through the loop and twist the pair.

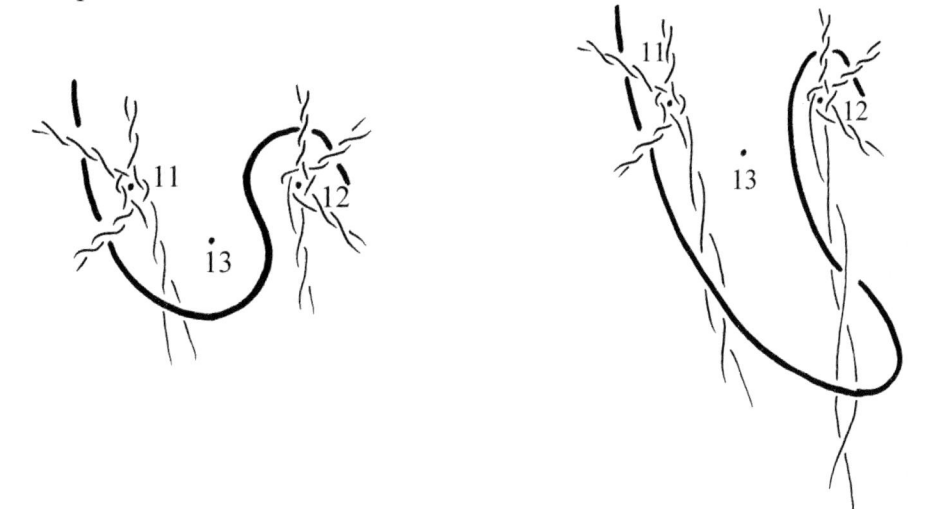

Figure 483 Preparing a long loop at D   *Figure 484 Passing the second pair into the long loop at D*

5 Make the stitch at pin 13 (figure 485) and lift the left thread from each pair up through the loop.
6 Pull the gimp to reduce the loop, twist the pairs from pin 13 (figure 486) and continue making the lace.

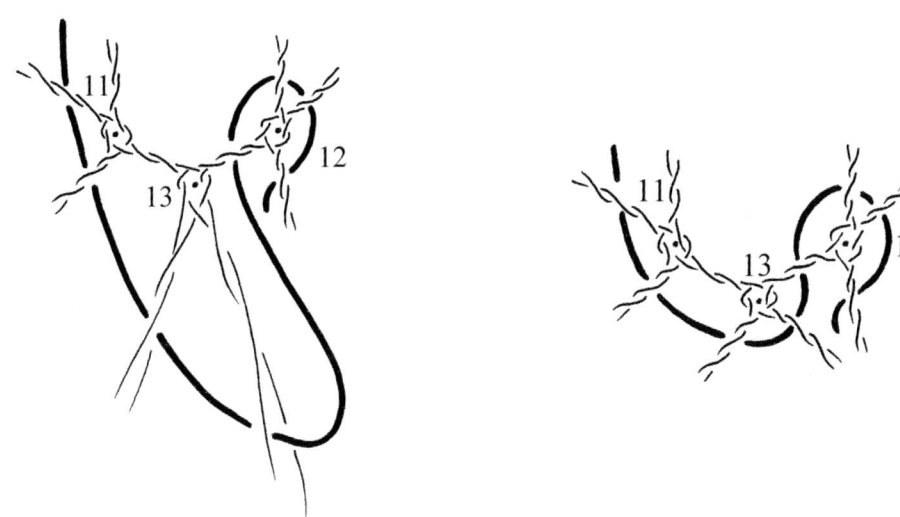

Figure 485 The stitch in the loop and the pairs brought out through the loop at D   *Figure 486 Long loop at D reduced*

Chapter 14

When the pin, where two snowflakes overlap one below the other, is reached, there are two ways of using the gimps. The gimps may be crossed before the honeycomb stitch between the gimps is made and crossed again after. The second method is to introduce a new pair of gimps before the honeycomb stitch and throw out those of the completed snowflake after working the stitch. The second method is the one used here; it preserves the line of the gimp and gives a better overall effect. However, the first method is quicker and stronger.

Passing from one section to the next[2]
When the row along the diagonal is reached, work it from the centre outwards, and make the picot at the corner, pin 2, and return through the first pair of passives (figure 487). At this point turn the pillow and rearrange the cover cloths. Since the remaining pair at pin 1 is required to complete the lobe, pin 4, it cannot be used for the next picot, pin 3. After making the corner picot, pin 2, the picot pair remaines in the headside making three passive pairs. One of these pairs can be used for the next picot. Not the edge pair, not the second pair, the pair that made the picot, so it must be the inner pair of the three pairs of passives that works outwards to make the next picot, pin 3. This pair then returns to cross the gimp and make the honeycomb stitch, pin 4, with the remaining pair from pin 1. These last two pins, pin 3 & 4, are the start of the first row of this section. Continue downwards towards the centre.

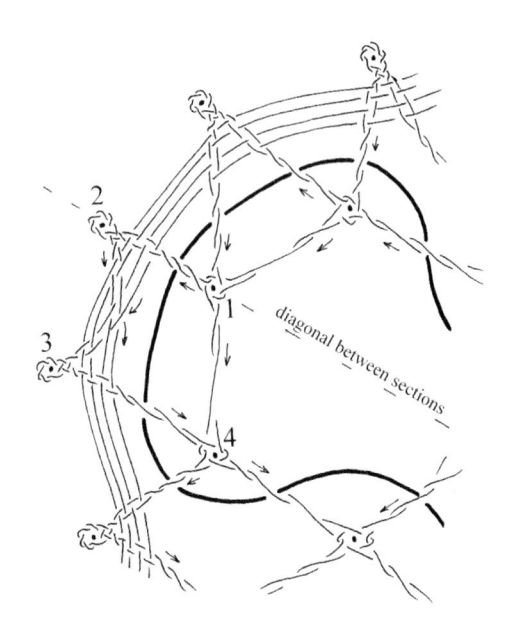

Figure 487 Starting the next section

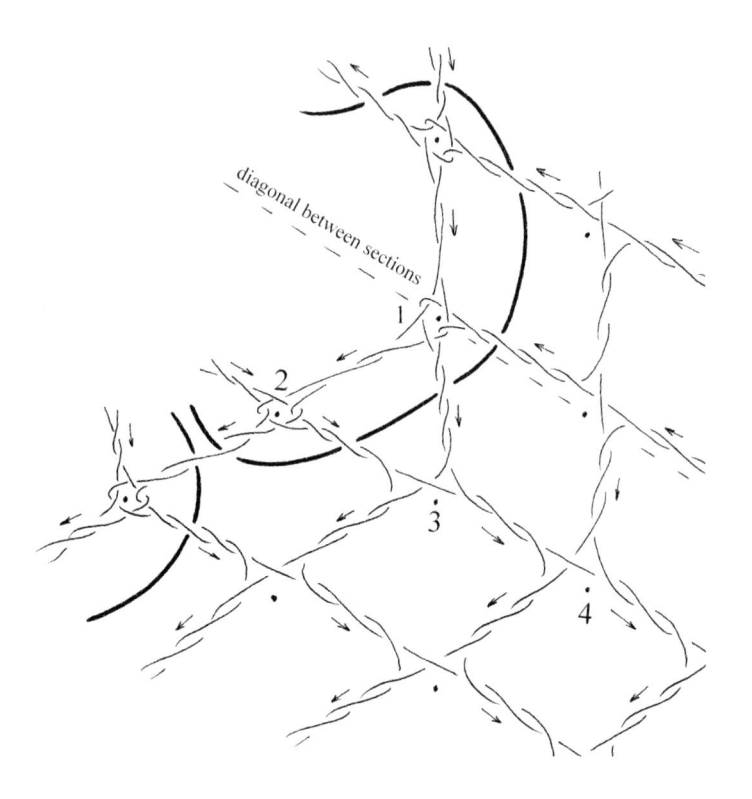

Starting the first line of point ground of the section[2]
The first line of point ground starts from the inner lobe of the inner snowflake of the cluster, and is worked downwards towards the centre (figure 488).

1. After completing the snowflake the first point ground stitch, pin 3, is made with the right pair from pin 2 in the lobe of the snowflake and the remaining pair from the centre pin of the lobe, pin 1.
2. The next point ground stitch is made with the next pair on the right, pin 4, and continue down the row.

Figure 488 (left) Starting the first line of point ground after turning at the diagonal

Chapter 14

Adding beads

To weight the glass cover, three beads are added at each corner; a 6 mm bead at B and a 5 mm bead each side of it at A and C. Since the pins are too close for the size of bead required to give the necessary weight, the beads are sewn on using a needle and thread. At each corner there are three beads A, B and C (figure 489). Each bead is sewn across a honeycomb ring with the needle passing through spaces 1 and 2 (figure 490)

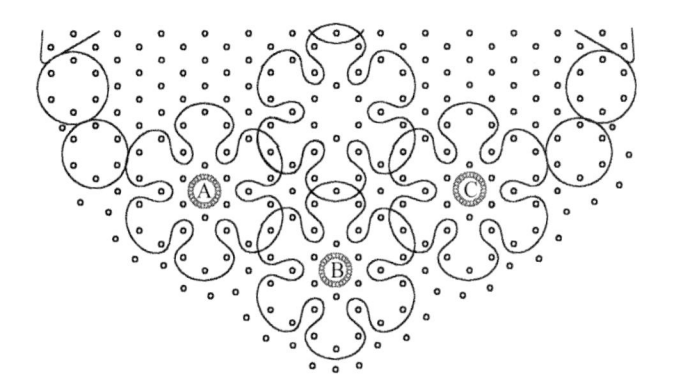

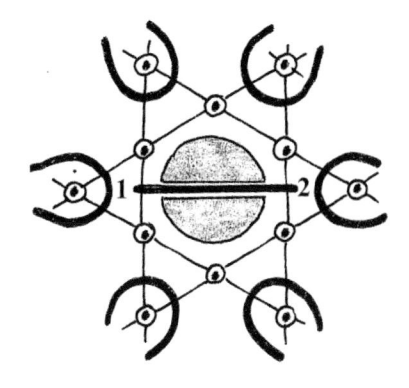

Figure 489 Positioning the beads

Figure 490 Sewing on a bead

PROJECT 22 LACE INSERT FOR A TRAY

pattern figure 492$^{1,3\&4}$
Egyptian cotton no. 90,
gimp no 12 perle
tray with 5¼in (135mm)
 diameter centre

Figure 491 (right) Lace insert for a tray

195

Chapter 14

Figure 492 Lace insert for a tray (figure 491)

PROJECT 23 LACE INSERT FOR PLATE
pattern figure 494[1,3&4]
Egyptian cotton no 100
gimp one strand stranded embroidery thread,
plate with 6in (150mm) diameter centre

Figure 493 (right) Lace insert for plate

196

Chapter 14

Figure 494 Pricking for lace insert for plate (figure 493)

PROJECT 24 WINE COASTER

pattern figure 496[1,3&4]
Egyptian cotton no 120
gimp one strand stranded embroidery thread,
plate with 10.5 cm (4¼ in) diameter centre

(Note: This is not the same photograph as figure 483, compare the relative sizes of the bases of the glasses!)

Figure 495 (right) Lace insert for coaster

197

Chapter 14

Figure 496 Pricking for lace insert for a wine coaster (figure 495)

END NOTES

1 Drafting the pattern
1 On Grid no 3 (for the tray), Grid no 8 (for the glass cover), Grid no 9 (for the plate), the one used here, or Grid no 10 for the wine coaster, draw the three intersecting lines to divide the area into six segments.
2 Draw the gimps (figure 497).
3 Remove the dots from outside the outer gimps, the honeycomb snowflakes, the honeycomb rings, the diamonds and two dots from the area between the small diamonds for the pin-chain. Add dots for the eyelet within the large diamonds and the line for the picots (figure 498).
4 Add the dots for the picots (figure 499).
5 Remove the picot line (figure 494).

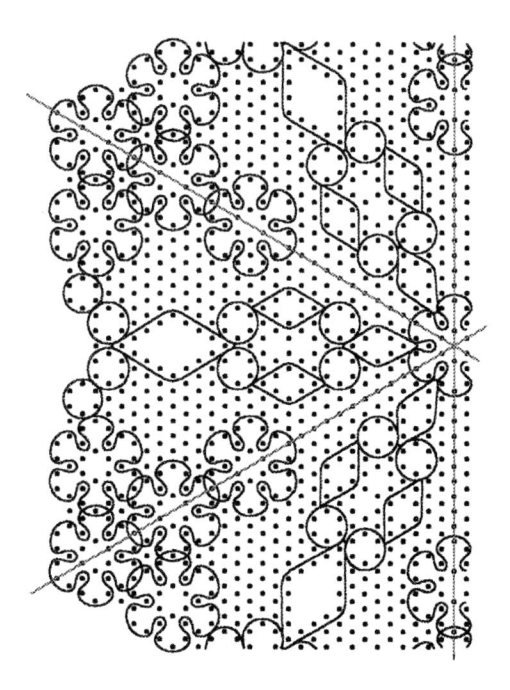

Figure 497 (right) Gimps drawn in

Chapter 14

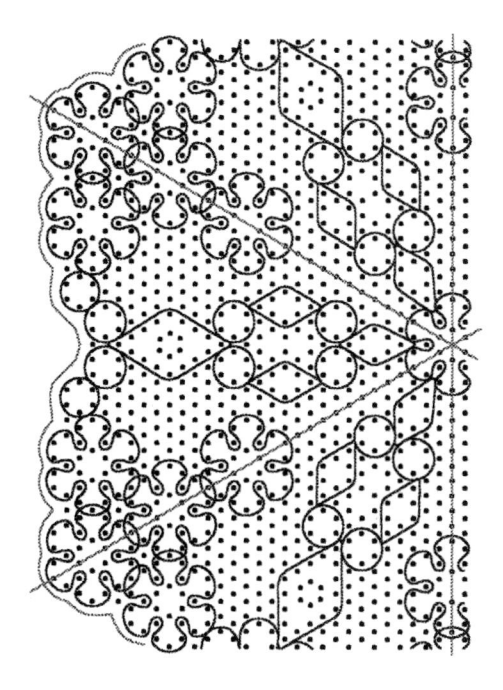

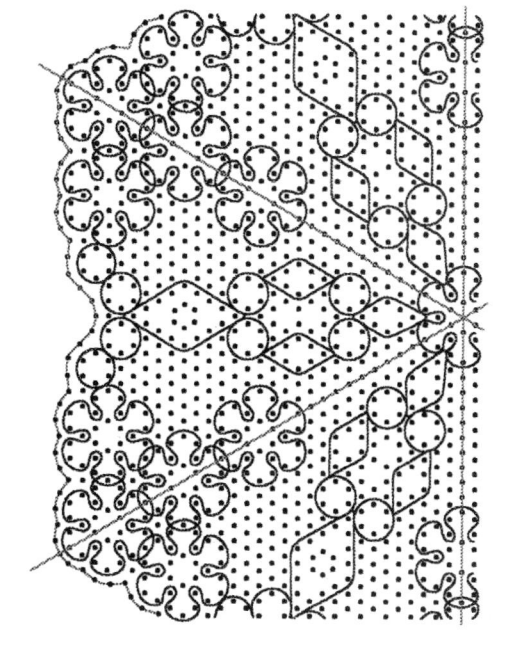

Figure 498 Unwanted dots removed   *Figure 499 Picots added*

2 Working a hexagonal shape with point ground along the diagonals and a central honeycomb ring

Hexagonal shapes are usually worked radially, i.e. the motif is usually worked in six sections and the work is turned through 60° when moving from one section to the next (figure 500). When there is a gap row of honeycomb along the diagonals the direction of working along the diagonal is irrelevant since there is no pair travelling along the row. However, when the row is point ground it must be worked from the centre outwards, otherwise the pairs will not be in the correct places for the next row.

In Figures 500 & 501 the diagonals are worked in point ground and the very centre of the motif is a six-pin honeycomb ring. The motif is normally worked in six sections.

1 Start the first section from the outside and work from A diagonally downwards towards the centre, to pin B. This is the first line **below** the diagonal between the sections, pin B, in the honeycomb ring, being the last pin of the row. Finish the section along the diagonal between the sections working **outwards** from pin B, in the honeycomb ring, towards C.

Figure 500 (right) Working a hexagonal shape with a honeycomb ring centre

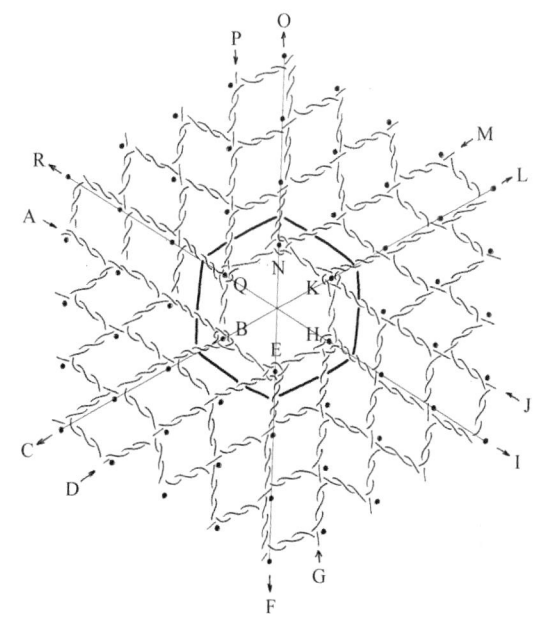

199

Chapter 14

2 At this point turn the pillow and rearrange the cover cloths.
3 Start the next section by working inwards from D to E and finish the section by working outwards along the diagonal between the sections E to F.
Continue around the hexagon.

Figure 501 (right) Working a point ground hexagon, with a honeycomb ring in the centre

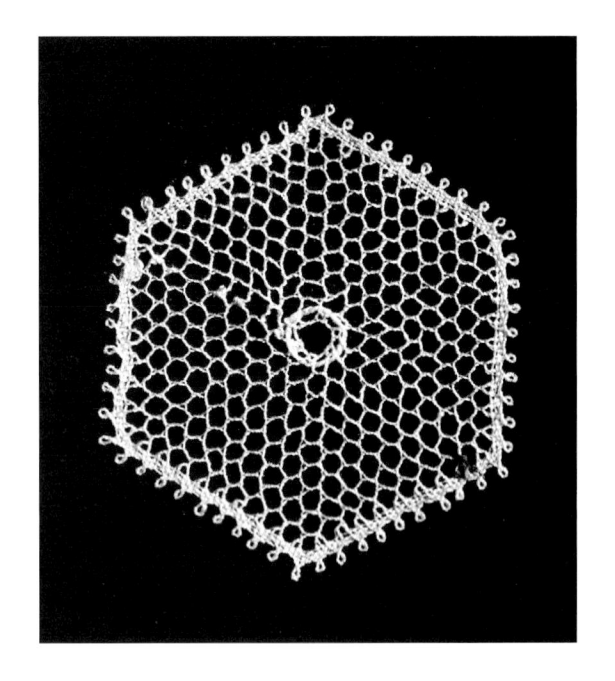

3 The effects of changing thread size
In order to achieve a very light appearance the pieces were made in a size finer thread than would usually be used with each grid. As the thread size is reduced it is the clothwork that is the first to suffer. This design contains relatively small areas of clothwork, the largest being the diamond with an eyelet. Here, the spacing of the pins opening the hole in the clothwork pushes the remaining threads closer, so minimising the effect of reducing thread size.

4 The effects of changing scale
Enlarging lace not only makes it bigger, it changes it aesthetically. Try looking at lace made to different scales. Use the actual lace made in the different sizes, looking at pictures does not give the same effect, and look at them from a distance of 70-100cm ($^3/_4$-1yd). Lace developed to be looked at from a distance! Start with the wine coaster motif. The general effect of the clothwork appears as plain white areas, honeycomb as a pattern of dark holes with the snowflakes making a decorative pattern. The gimps strengthen the outlines and the ground gives an all-over, non-descript background that supports the rest. As the scale increases first the stitches can be seen in detail and later even the texture of the threads. As these extra elements become apparent, the design becomes more busy and confusing and the eye can become distracted from the main picture, focussing on the detail, not the basic lines of the design. The pattern may be the same but the design is not the same, new design elements, namely the patterning of the stitches and the texture of the thread, have appeared and it has changed very subtly. From earliest times lace has been made on a fine scale and the techniques and fillings developed accordingly. There is no reason why lace should not be made on larger scales, but it may cause unexpected effects.

Chapter 15

PROJECT 25   CLOCK FACE (Pate 7 & cover)

Figure 501 Clock with lace insert made using 90 denier Piper's silk floss

New Techniques
motif with hexagonal footside

Materials required
pricking (figure 502)[1]
Piper's 90 denier silk floss, use 6 strands for gimp
or Egyptian cotton no. 60 with perle thread no. 8 for gimp
clock kit

End Notes
1 drafting the pattern
2 designing for a particular space
3 working with silk
4 setting in the footside when working from catch-pin stitch to footpin.
5 modified pin-chain no. 2

Chapter 15

*Figure 502 (left)
Pattern draft*

*Figure 503 (right) Lace insert made
using Egyptian cotton no. 60*

202

Chapter 15

Stiffening silk lace[3]
Before removing the pins, silk lace can be stiffened by spraying with a non-coloured, non-perfumed hair spray. Should you wish to do this, the pricking should be covered with a transparent sticky backed plastic film so that the spray cannot interact with the pricking and lift the colour from the pricking card or ink. Check the hair spray on some spare silk thread, to make sure there are no adverse effects, before using it.

Setting in[3]
The best starting line is usually the one crossing the least amount of ground, in this case the line immediately below the diagonal between the sections. As usual, there can be many different lines along which the piece can be started.

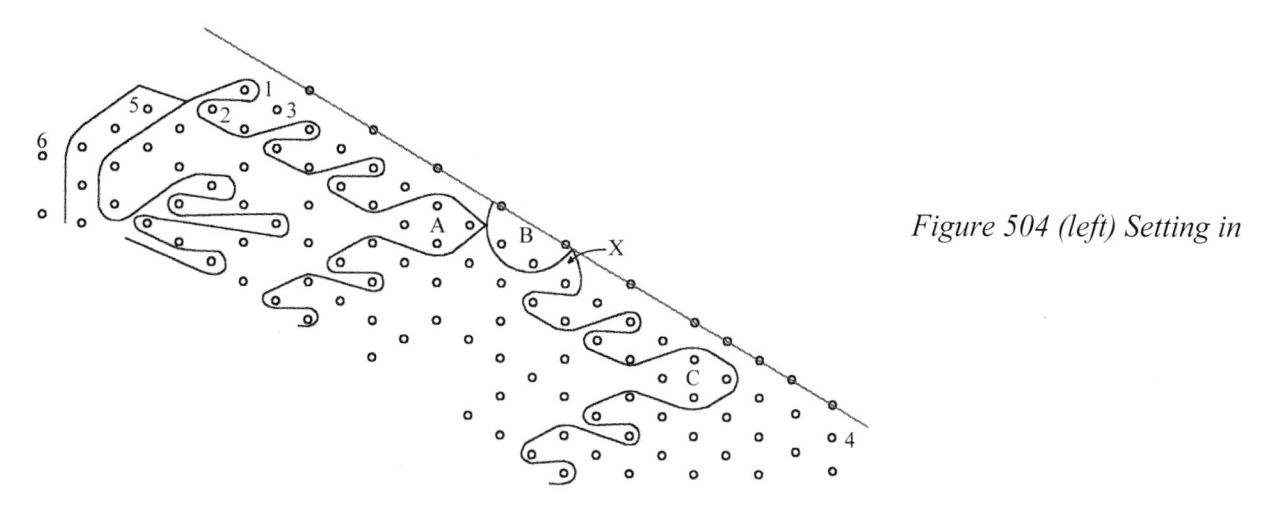

Figure 504 (left) Setting in

1 Start with a pair of gimps and two pairs at pin 1 (figure 504). Add pairs at pins 2 & 3, and at each pin down the diagonal, working the two lines of honeycomb, across which the gimp snakes in and out, as far as the cloth stitch diamond A.
2 Add a new gimp and work two pins of the honeycomb ring B. Support the gimp close to the division line; a new pinhole will be required at X.
3 Continue, using the same gimp, down to the next cloth stitch diamond at C.
4 Work point ground to the footside, pin 4 and make up the footside.

Setting in the footside when working from catch-pin stitch to footpin[4].

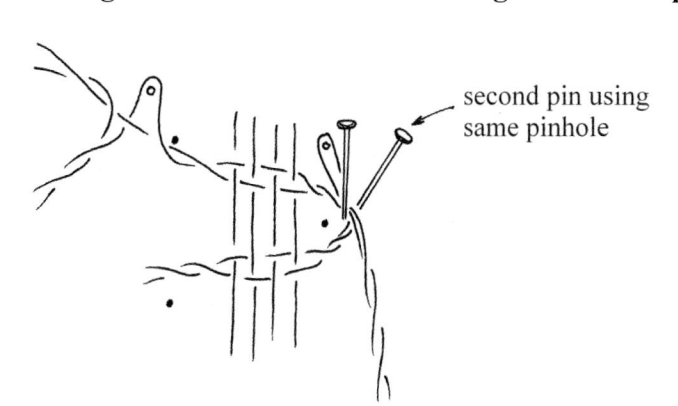

After working the stitch about the pin, insert another pin into the same pinhole as the footpin to prevent the edge pair slipping (figure 505).

second pin using same pinhole

5 Add another gimp before working the honeycomb stitch in the honeycomb stem, pin 5 (figure 504), and set in the headside using picot pin 6.

Figure 505 (left) Placing two pins in the same pinhole

203

Chapter 15

The valley
When the valley is reached there are three gimps coming together and, as usual, there are several ways of working them. My choice was to use the inner two to work around the triangle of honeycomb stitches, and to wrap the outer one around the outer gimp at the centre point (figure 506). Note that a pair from the upper honeycomb stitch of the triangle crosses the gimp to become an inner headside passive. It cloth stitches across the former inner headside passive, and the latter cross the gimp to make lower honeycomb stitch of the triangle.

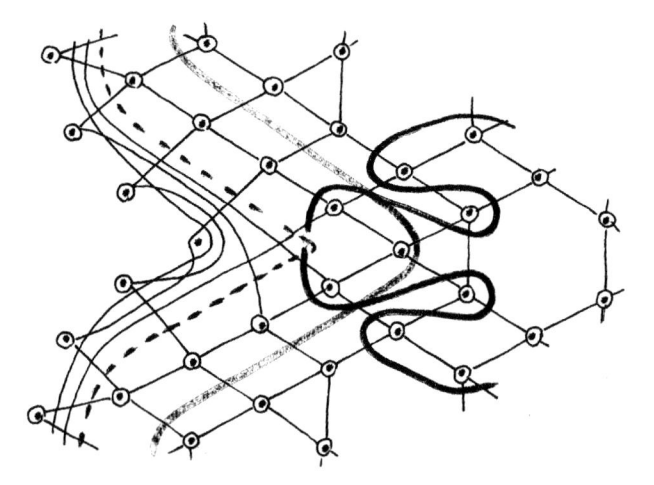

Figure 506 Gimps around the triangle

Modified pin-chain[5]
The pin chains leading into and out of the large cloth stitch diamond are modified, because the second pin of the first pin chain is also the first pin of the diamond, and the last stitch of the diamond is the first pin of the second pin chain.

The pin chain and first pin of the diamond can be worked -
    first half honeycomb stitch, pin, second half honeycomb stitch,
    cloth stitch, twist workers twice, pin, cloth stitch (figure 507)

The last pin of the diamond and the pin chain can be worked
    cloth stitch, twist workers twice, pin, cloth stitch, twist both pairs twice,
    first half honeycomb stitch, pin, second half honeycomb stitch (figure 508)

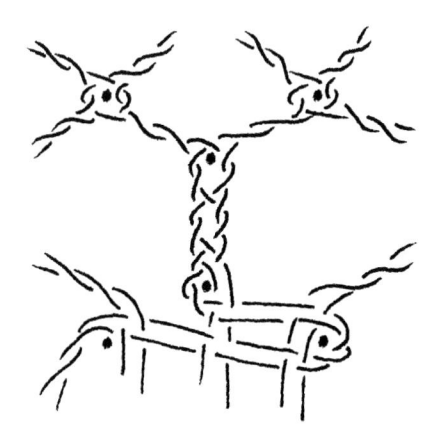

Figure 507 Pin chain above the diamond 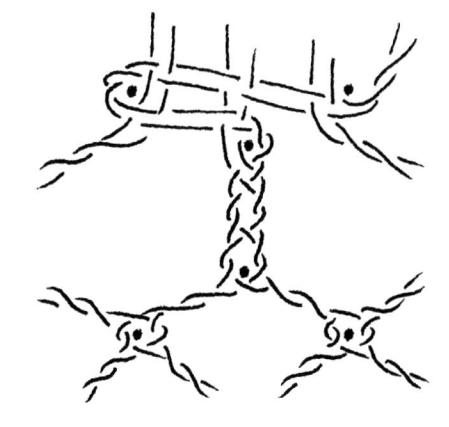   *Figure 508 Pin chain below the diamond*

Chapter 15

The last row of this section is worked outwards from the footside pin, pin 1, and its catch-pin, pin 1 2 (figure 509).

Complete the first of the six sections along the diagonal, between the sections, working outwards from the centre, pin 1, 2 etc. (figure 509), ending by working the picot on the diagonal and returning the picot pair through the headside passives and leaving them untwisted. figure 510).

Figure 509 (left) Completing the first section

Again there are several routes for the gimps at the outer honeycomb ring on the diagonal (figure 510).

Turn the pillow, rearrange the cover cloths and start the next section Continue by taking the second pair of passives out to make the first picot of the new section.

Figure 510 (right) Changing sections at the headside

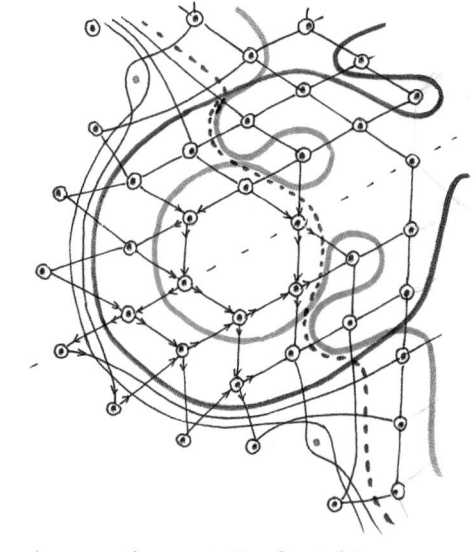

Changing sections at the footside

At the footside, the previous section ended by working the footpin at the corner, pin 1, and its catch pin, pin 2 (figure 509). After turning the pillow, the new section is worked downwards towards the centre to the stitch at pin 4 (figure 511). Now, cloth stitch the catch-pin pair from pin 2 through the footside passives and leave it untwisted. Cloth stitch the new centre pair of passives through the inner pair, set up the catch-pin, pin 5, twist them, and make up the edge, pin 6. Continue around the hexagon and join end to start.

Figure 511 (left) Changing sections at the footside

205

Chapter 15

Should you wish to stiffen the lace[3], first shield the remainder of the pillow with plastic sheeting. After checking that there will be no adverse effects, spray and leave to dry before removing the pins. For cotton lace spray starch may be used. Again check that there will be no adverse effects.

Mount the lace and make up the clock according to the manufacturers instructions.

END NOTES

1 Drafting the pattern
1 Using Grid no 3, draw the diagonals, trim the grid to the size required and draw the gimps (figure 512)
2 Remove unwanted dots, taking care above and below the diamonds where there are pin chains, and adjust the dots for the inner footside (figure 513). The footside dots on the diagonals are placed where the lines drawn through the footpins of each section cross. Dots adjacent to these may need adjusting.
3 Remove the dots outside the outer gimps, draw the picot line and add the picots (figure 513).
4 Finally erase the picot line (figure 502).

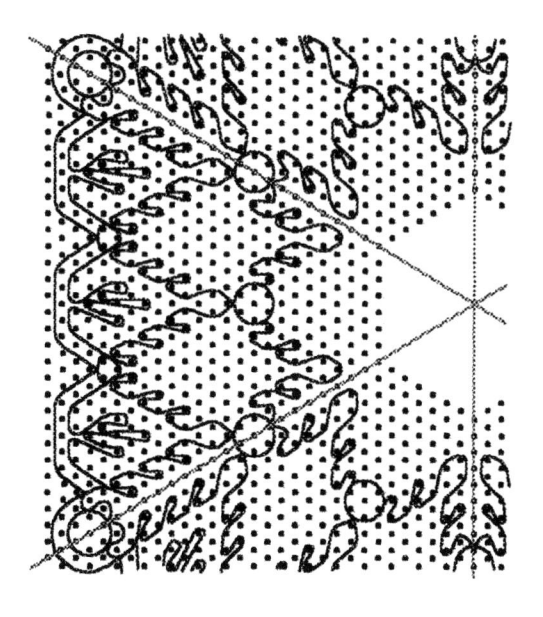

Figure 512 Draw the diagonals, trim to size and draw the gimps

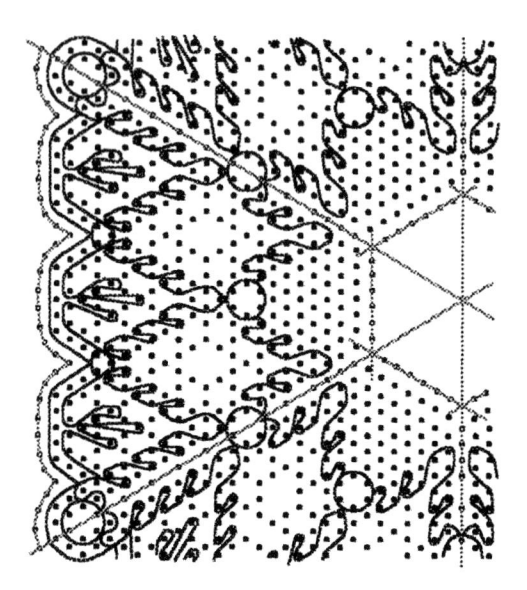

Figure 513 Dots on, and close to, the diagonals adjusted, dots outside the gimps removed, picot line and picots added

2 Designing for a particular shape
The space available for lace in this clock is strictly limited.
1 Select an appropriate grid; for this piece one having a 60° angle since it is to be worked hexagonally.
2 Trim the grid until it fits comfortably within the space available, in this case a centre hole is also required (figure 514).

3 Draw your design, modifying where necessary, so that it extends from the inner line of pins to the outer line. When the outer edge is curved a few of the outermost pins may extend slightly beyond the original line. Check by placing in position.
4 Trim the draft along the inner and outer lines of pins, and place in position. Stand back and judge whether it fits comfortably, if not, keep adjusting until you are satisfied with the result.

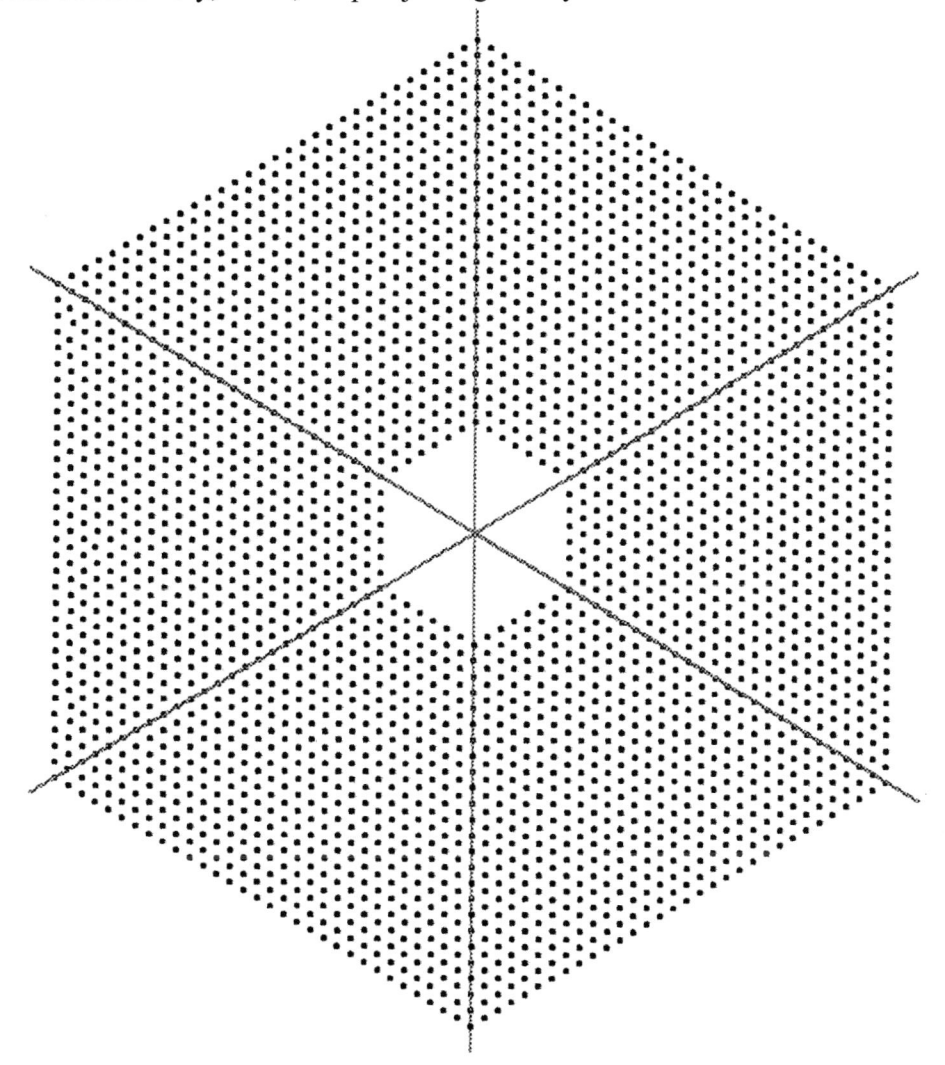

Figure 514 Designing for a particular shape

3 Working with silk
Silk, especially floss silk, has different properties from cotton. It is much stronger. Floss silk, is a continuous filament thread, (the fibres run the length of the thread) and there are only about four twists per 2.5 cm, resulting in a more shiny appearance. Because there are so few twists the fibres can spread out to fill more space in clothwork. Conversely, when the pairs are twisted they pack together closely. This means that a silk floss thread can replace a cotton thread several times its own thickness; the clothwork will be sufficiently full while the point ground and honeycomb appear very delicate. Unfortunately, the small number of twists allows fibres to escape, and the thread 'fluffs' easily when lace is continually done and undone. Sliding a moistened thumb and finger down the thread may control these errant fibres. Spun silk is made from shorter fibres and spun like cotton threads. It has, apart from its strength, properties closer to those of cotton and

linen. When knotting across a join, a reef knot with an extra twist may reduce the tendency for the knots to slip.

Silk thread is very slippery. Not only does it slip off bobbins more easily, but the passives, especially continuous footside or headside passives and the gimps, must have the pins surrounding them left in for much longer than when working with cotton or linen, to avoid unintentional gathering.

4 Setting in the footside when working from catch-pin stitch to footpin no 2

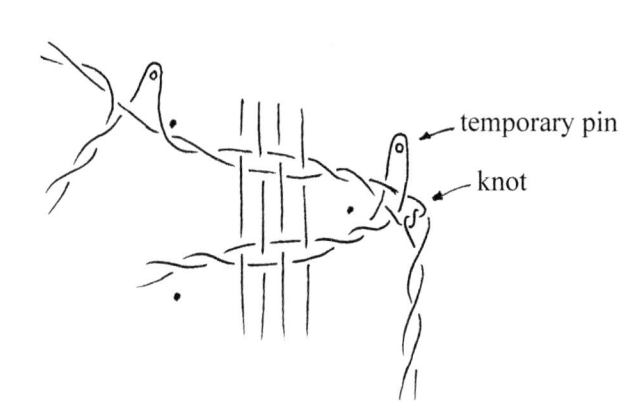

Place new pairs on temporary pins to the right of the work. Working from the catch-pin stitch, work through the passives, set up the edge pin and twist. From here, letting down the last pair, the ones that made the stitch about the pin, onto a support pin can be a problem; the pair added as the footside pair, to become the new workers crossing the passives, tends to pull around the footpin. To control this pair, the footside pair can be knotted, immediately after working the stitch about the pin, (figure 515).

Figure 515 Using a knot at the footside

5 Modified pin-chain no. 2
Other ways of modifying the pin-chains are

The pin chain and the first pin of the diamond can be worked
    first half honeycomb stitch, pin,
      cloth stitch, twist workers twice, pin, cloth stitch, (figure 516)

The last pin of the diamond and the pin chain can be worked
    cloth stitch, twist workers twice, pin, cloth stitch, twist twice,
    pin, second half of honeycomb stitch (figure 517)

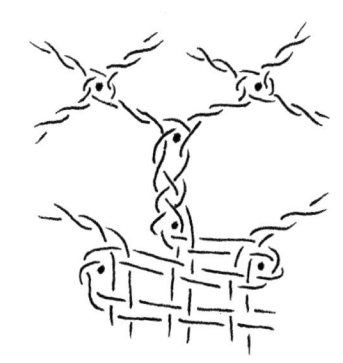

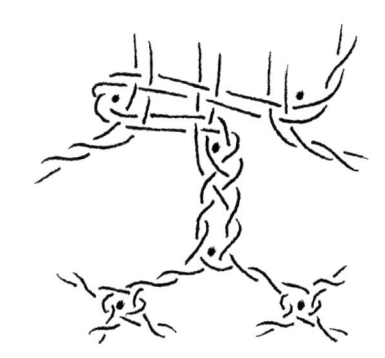

Figure 516 Pin chain above the diamond   *Figure 517 Pin chain below the diamond*

Chapter 16

Chapter 16

PROJECTS 26 & 27   LID MOTIFS FOR BOWLS

Project 26   Lid motif for crystal bowl, worked in white cotton (Plate 3)
Project 27   Lid motif for satin glass bowl, worked in black silk (Plate 4)

Figure 518 Crystal Bowl with lace motif

Figure 519 Pattern draft for motif in cotton

New Techniques for Projects 26 & 27
    clothwork workers making picots
    large honeycomb rings
    hexagonal motif with point ground centre

Materials for Project 26
    pattern draft (figure 519) [1&2]
    Egyptian cotton no. 100/2 (sample)
        or no. 120/2 (in the crystal bowl)
    gimp perle 12
    crystal bowl kit

End Notes for Projects 26 & 26
    1 drafting the pattern
    2 gimp route
    3 hexagonal motif with point ground centre
    4 colour coding when designing

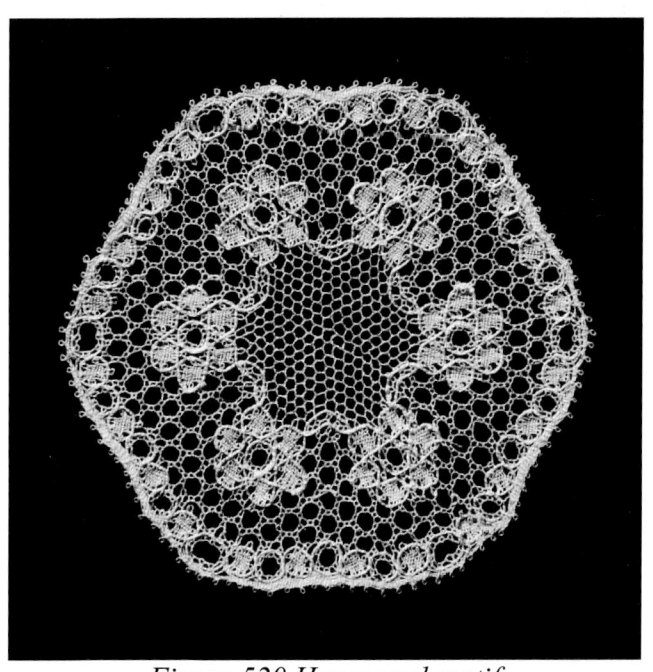

Figure 520 Hexagonal motif

Although this pattern has flower motifs it is not Floral Bucks; all the pinholes, except those for the picots, match the grid.

209

Chapter 16

Inventing indicators (not traditional, but very useful)
Indicators are reminders and there is no reason why we cannot invent our own for situations where we may otherwise make mistakes. We produce patterns for ourselves, and not for sale; therefore, if we wish to add our own hieroglyphics, why not? This pattern has six-pin rings worked in both cloth and honeycomb and it is very easy use the wrong technique! Also, there is a tendency to start some, particularly the outer rings, from the wrong position. To avoid the inevitable problems I used my own series of symbols (figure 521). In the honeycomb rings I drew a circle, with a line down the centre indicating the first and last stitches of the ring. For circles that cross the diagonals, the line changes direction as the order of working the pins changes. Where the area is to be filled with cloth stitch, I drew a zigzag, (not the complete path the worker takes; only a representation). However, after still making mistakes, I filled the cloth stitches rings with a strong colour. Where the worker passes across the gimp to make a loop round a pin, rather than work a honeycomb stitch, I drew a 'U' around the pin. If you have a pattern that causes this type of problem, draw in your own indicators. Drawing a 'key', on the pricking, avoids confusion next time the pricking is used. It is not traditional to invent indicators, but they can avoid a lot of 'reverse lacemaking'.

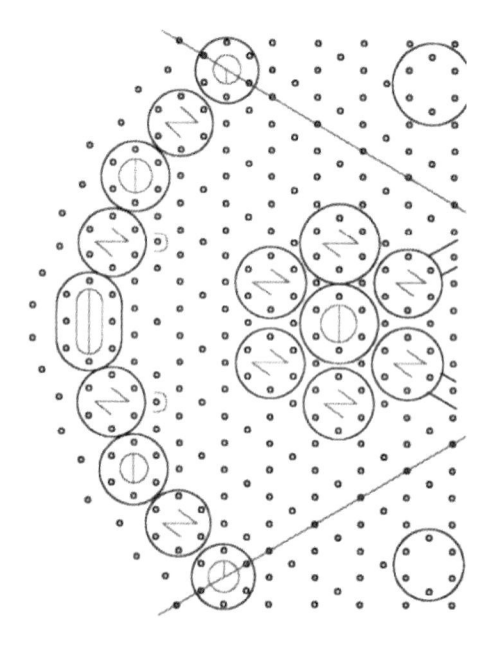

Figure 521 Indicators

Setting in[2&3]
With such large areas of point ground and honeycomb the starting line cannot avoid passing through them. By starting with two cloth circles of the flower, including the honeycomb stitch at the sides, pairs need only be added at three honeycomb stitches before the footside rings are reached (figure 522). The honeycomb stem is started and the pattern worked as far as the corner. As usual, this is only one of many possible starting lines. The point ground along the diagonal cannot be worked from the centre towards the headside, only from the headside towards the centre; hence the point ground is not added until the first row after the diagonal has been turned; the row being worked from the picot towards the centre.

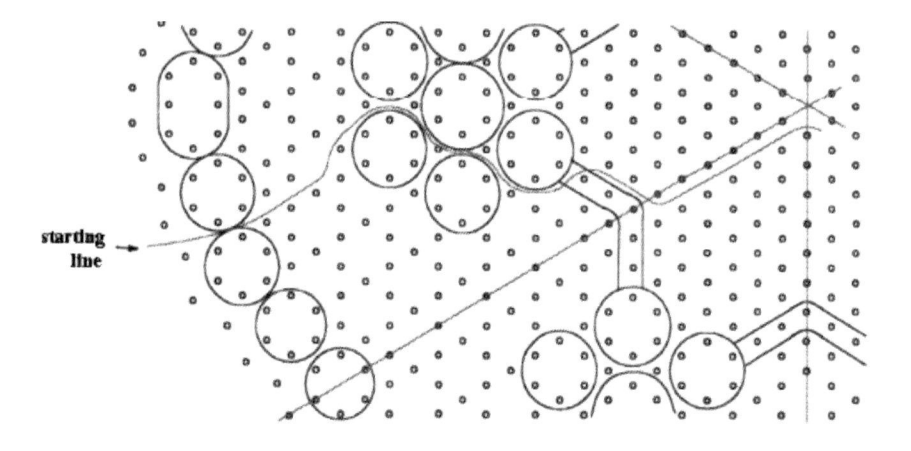

Figure 522 (left) Setting in

Chapter 16

The clothwork areas and honeycomb rings are not always in line with the honeycomb ground, causing some anomalies. When a pair leaves the upper side pin of a honeycomb ring an extra honeycomb stitch may be required to accommodate it. These are included in the pattern. As usual there may be more than one route for the gimps. The route used for the sample is explained in the End Notes[2].

Using an extra pin when a cloth stitch motif abuts honeycomb ground, also the same motif worker makes a picot

The three honeycomb rings at the center of the outer edge of each section at are worked in cloth stitch. In order to prevent the clothwork looking starved the pins outside the inner gimp at the widest parts are used, as are the picots of the headside (figure 523). After working the first three pins of the clothwork normally, cross the gimp to pin 4, where the workers are twisted twice, and return across the gimp. Cross the gimp at the headside, use the workers to make the picot, pin 5, and return to work pins 6-8 normally. As usual the workers are not twisted on the clothwork side of the gimp, but they are twisted outside the gimp in both cases.

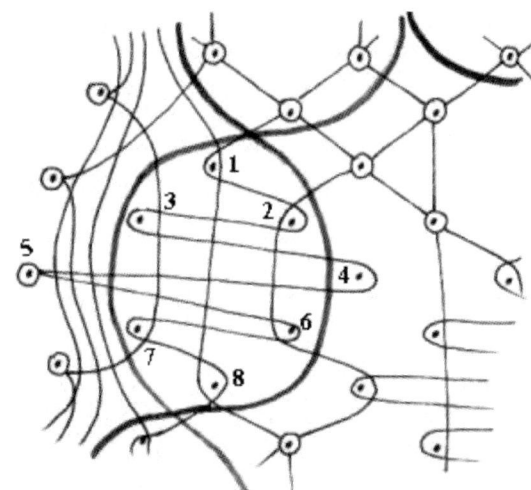

Figure 523 Working the clothwork areas at the headside

After turning the corner, the first continuous row of honeycomb working towards the centre continues as point ground with pairs being added as required, including one on the next diagonal. The pair on the diagonal starts the final row of the section[3], which must be worked from the centre to the headside. (figure 524).

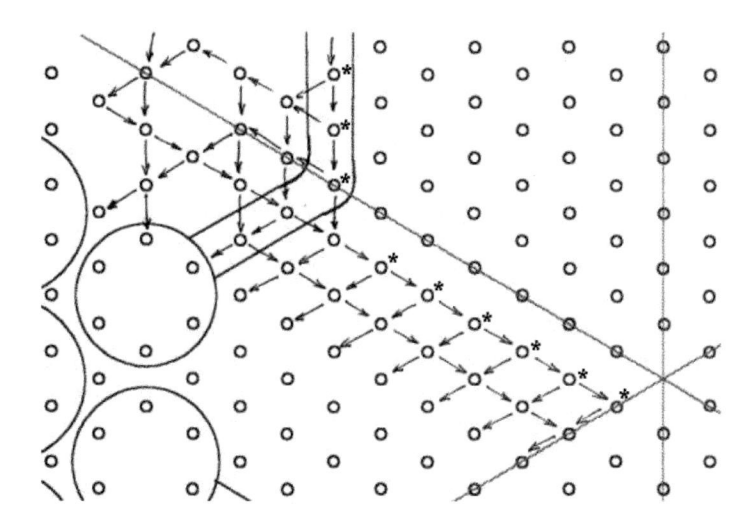

*Figure 524 (left) Adding pairs to the point ground, * indicates each new pair added.*

211

Chapter 16

Large honeycomb rings
Start as a six-pin honeycomb ring for the first five pins then, for each side, take a pair out to the next pinhole outside the gimp and make a stitch or picot. Return a pair across the gimp to make the next stitch of the ring on that side. Complete as for a six-pin honeycomb ring (figure 525). The usual twists are made both sides of the gimp.

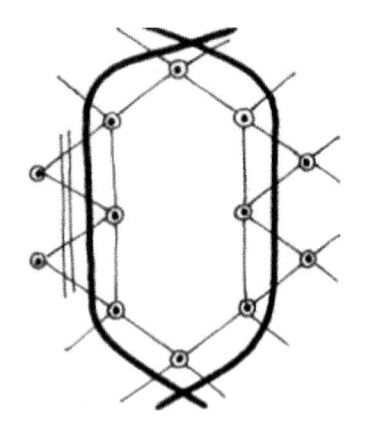

Figure 525 (right) Large honeycomb ring

Join end to start carefully checking that the sizes of the holes in the point ground, particularly the central hole, are the same.

PROJECT 27   LID MOTIF FOR CRYSTAL BOWL (worked in black silk)

Materials for Project 27
  pattern draft (figure 527) [1&2]
  Piper's no 4/20 twisted silk
  gimp 6 strands silk
  crystal bowl kit

New Techniques
  working with silk
  using black thread

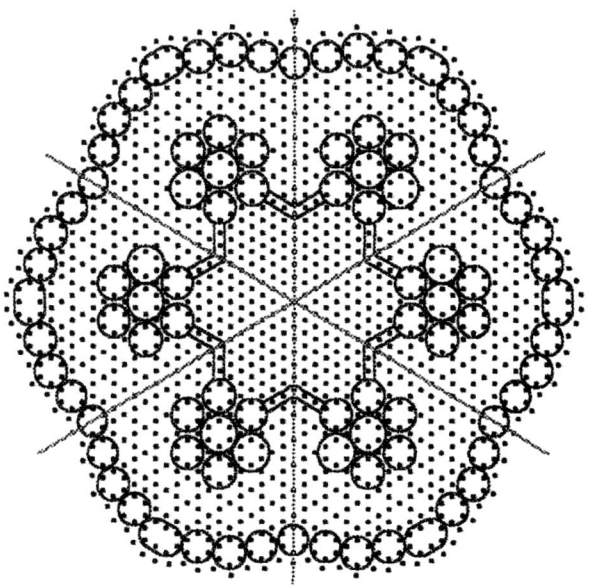

Figure 526 (above) Lid motif worked in black silk

Figure 527 (right) Pattern for silk motif

212

Chapter 16

Working with black threads
Use white or a pale colour, for the pattern and the cover cloths. so that the black threads show up. Draw the gimps, and indicators, in red; black gimp lines and black threads are easily confused. Traditionally, Black Bucks has areas worked in half stitch, rather than cloth stitch, because the half stitch is lighter and the same areas in cloth stitch would be very dense and heavy. To make the half stitch areas even lighter, a thread size finer than is usually used for that scale can be used. Working with black thread is more trying on the eyes, so make sure there is plenty of light.

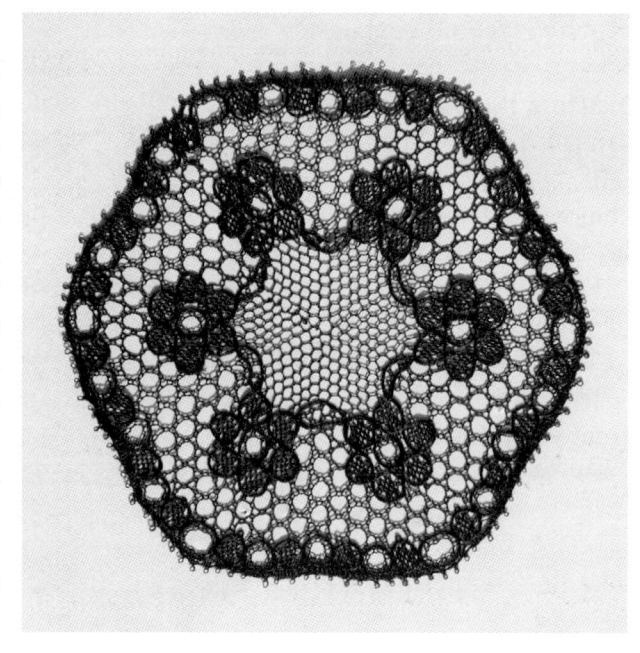

Figure 528 (right) Lid motif in black silk

Using silk floss
The filaments of silk floss compact more easily than cotton threads and the space for the headside passives should be reduced to compensate. Thus the pattern for use with silk (figure 527) has less space for the headside passives than the one for use with cotton (figure 519). Silk is also very slippery and firms up very easily; keep plenty of pins in use to prevent gimps, the headside and the footside from gathering.

Half stitch rings
These are worked as for cloth stitch rings but add a twist before the worker passes out of the ring to work the stitch, pin 1, or picot, pin 2, outside the gimp (figure 529). Similarly twist once after the worker returns across the gimp and before half stitching across to the other side.

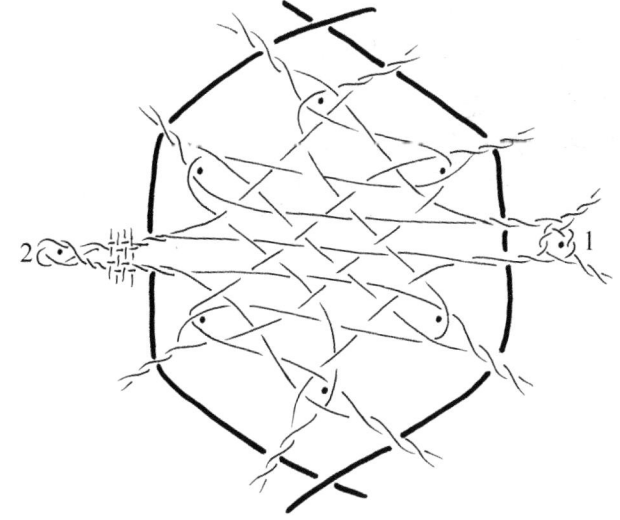

Figure 529 (right) Half stitch ring

213

Chapter 16

END NOTES

1 Drafting the pattern
1. Using Grid No 9, draw the gimps (figure 530)
2. Remove unwanted dots from the rings and the honeycomb area between the flowers and the border of rings. **Note:** The honeycomb inside the rings does not line up with the honeycomb outside the rings. (Check with the pattern figure 2).
3. Remove the dot in the very centre.
4. Remove all dots outside the outer gimps, draw the picot line, according to the thread to be used, add the picots and remove the picot line (figures 519 & 527).

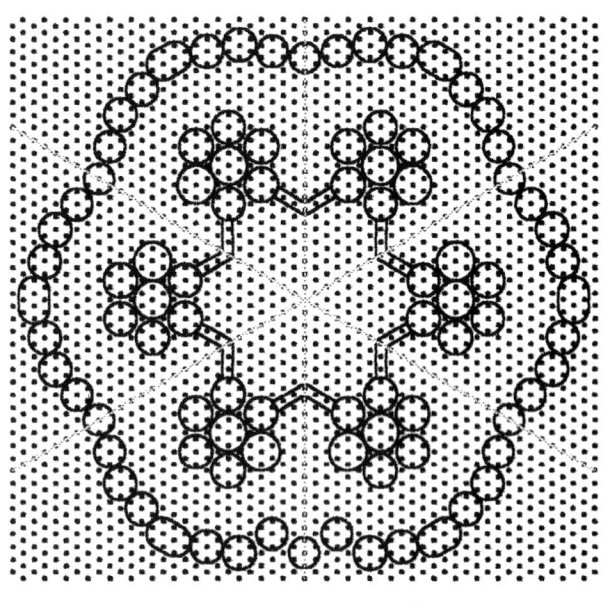

Figure 530 Gimps drawn

2 Designing
A pricking is only the part of a design; the remainder is the interpretation, and this can make or mar the final effect. To assist decision-making, when faced with the choice of cloth stitch or honeycomb for six-pin rings, try shading the dominant cloth stitch areas (figure 531), or filling in with a bright colour. Designs are easier to view critically from a distance; try looking at the pattern from a distance of about 1m (1 yd). Place the pattern where you will have time to study it. The little room is an ideal place for contemplation. Check the dominant features and how they relate to the balance of light and shade. Are there too many features cluttering the design? Is there too much ground or honeycomb causing the design to become bland, or insufficient so that the motifs and edgings are too close together? Always keep a copy at every stage. It is so easy to try a new idea and change the design, only to discover it is no better than the former, or even worse.

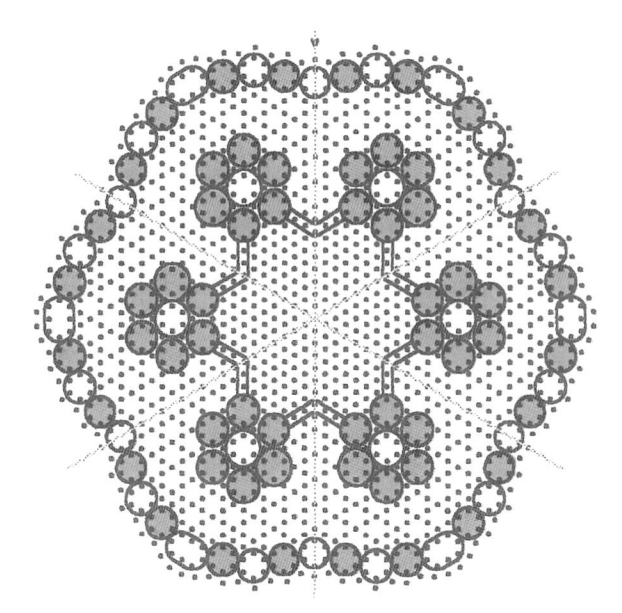

Figure 531 (left) The original design with clothwork shaded in

The following designs use the same pricking but with different interpretations. View them critically from a distance and make your own judgment. The original interpretation was based on the elements that required explaining and it is not, necessarily, the best as regards design.

Chapter 16

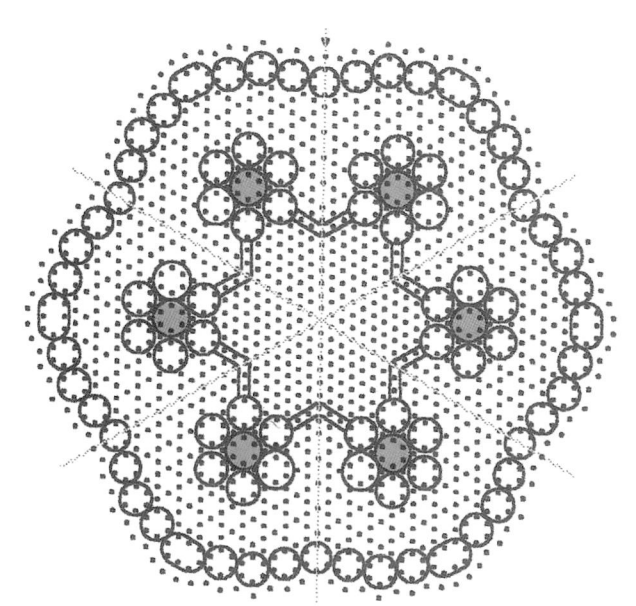

Figure 532 Pattern for honeycomb rings around outer edge, flowers with honeycomb ring petals and cloth stitch centre

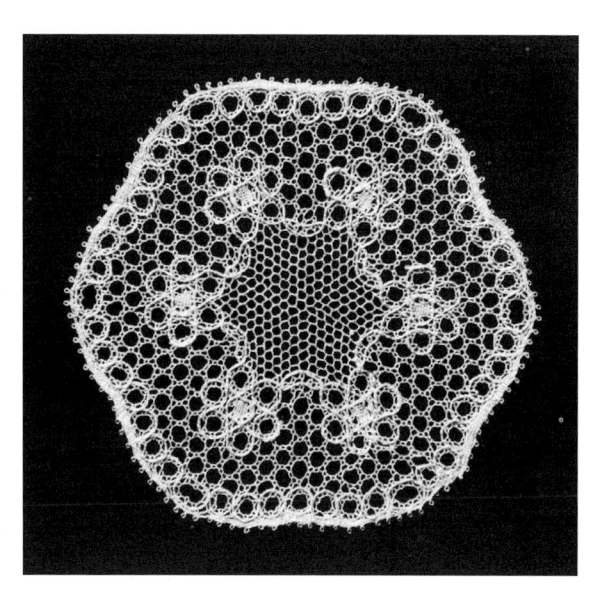

Figure 533 Lace with honeycomb rings around outer edge, flowers with honeycomb ring petals and cloth stitch centre

When working this motif (figures 532 & 533), the extra pin needed when a cloth stitch motif abuts honeycomb ground, is unnecessary, the gimp is bound on. The lower honeycomb stitch being made with the same two pairs as pair as the upper honeycomb stitch on that side.

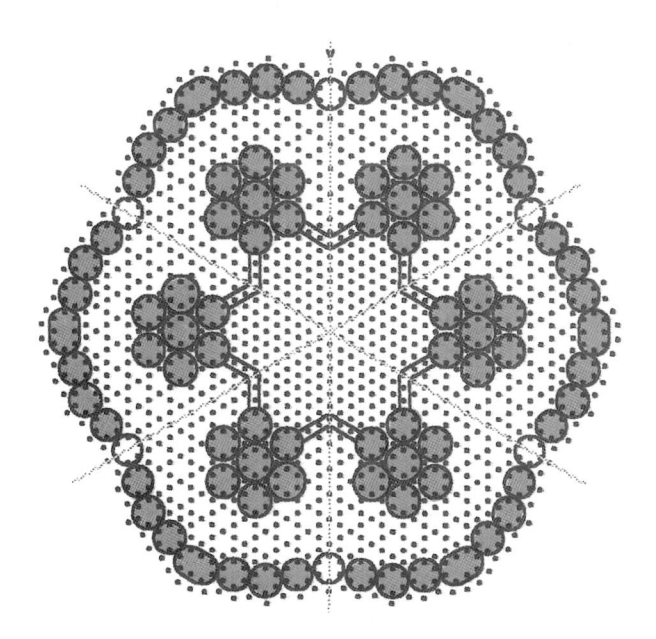

Figure 534 Pattern for cloth stitch rings around the outer edge, with a honeycomb ring across the diagonal, and cloth stitch flowers

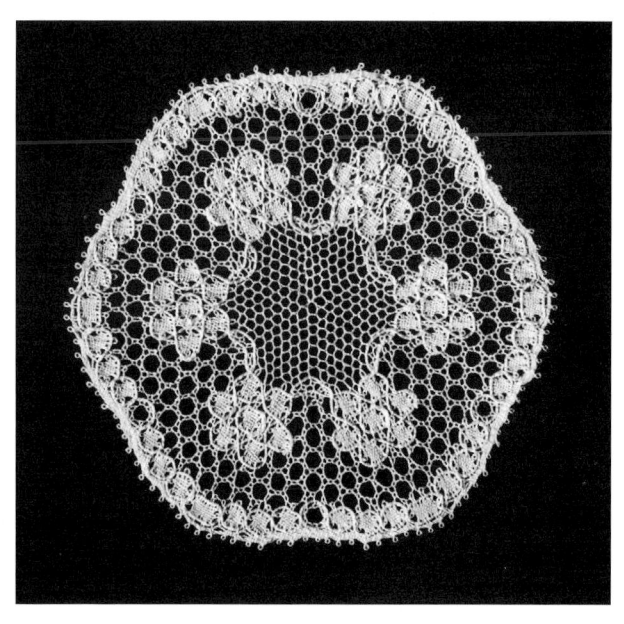

Figure 535 Lace for cloth stitch rings around the outer edge, with a honeycomb ring across the diagonal, and cloth stitch flowers

215

Chapter 16

Cloth stitch rings cannot be made all around the edge (figures 534 & 535); the rings on the diagonals cannot be made in cloth stitch unless they are fudged, and then they would not be geometrical Bucks point. The instructions for working the large oval cloth stitch ring are in Chapter 17.

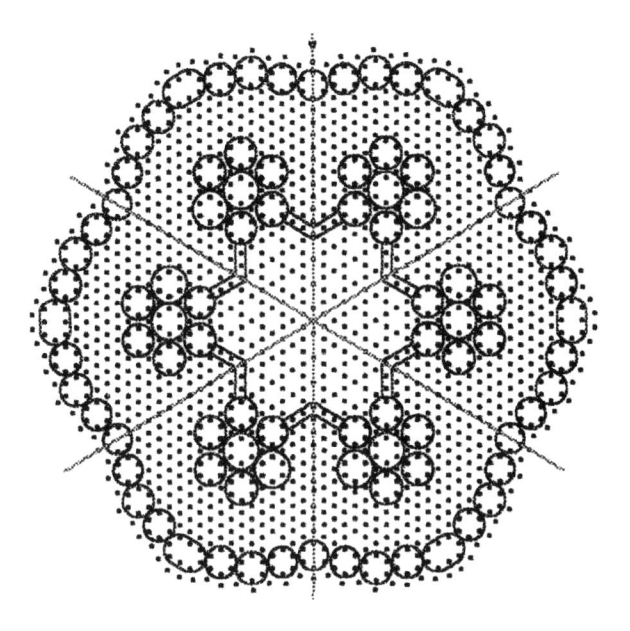

Figure 536 Pattern for cloth stitch flowers with a honeycomb ring centre, alternate cloth stitch and honeycomb rings around the edge and the grounds inverted

Figure 537 Pattern for cloth stitch flowers with a honeycomb ring centre, alternate cloth stitch and honeycomb rings around the edge and the grounds inverted

Inverting the grounds, i.e. exchanging the point ground and honeycomb (figures 536 & 537) has a striking effect on the final appearance.

3 Gimp route
Each new flower requires a new pair of gimps, together with the pair of gimps from the bar from the previous flower. Two gimps are cast off below the lowest petal when the flowe is finished. A separate pair of gimps is required for the central ring (figure 538).

Figure 538 (right) Gimp route used for the sample, * new pair of gimps added

Chapter 16

4 Working a hexagonal shape in six sections with a point ground centre
Hexagonal shapes are usually worked radially, i.e. the motif is divided into, and worked in, six sections, the work being turned through 60° when moving from one section to the next (figure 539). When there is a gap row of honeycomb along the diagonals the direction of working along the diagonal is irrelevant, since there is no pair travelling along the row. However, when the row is point ground, it must be worked from the centre outwards, otherwise the pairs will not be in the correct places for the next row.

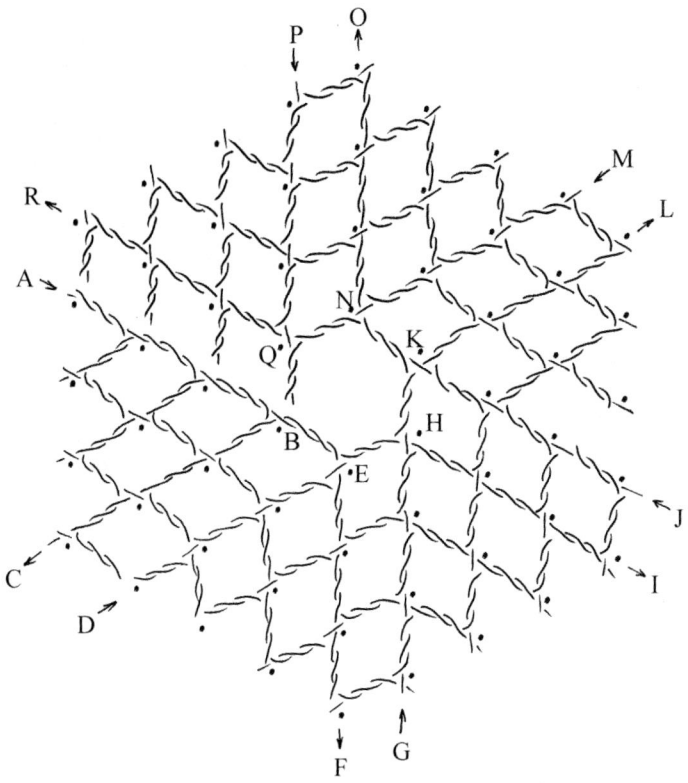

Figure 539 Working a hexagonal shape with a point ground centre

In figures 539 & 540 the motif is worked in six sections and the diagonals are worked in point ground.
1 Start the first section from the outside and work from A diagonally downwards towards the centre, to pin B. This is the first line **below** the diagonal between the sections, pin B being the last pin of the row. The last row of this section is worked along the diagonal between the sections, working outwards from pin B towards C.
2 At this point turn the pillow and rearrange the cover cloths.
3 Start the next section by working inwards from D to E, the first row under the diagonal, and finish the section by working outwards along the next diagonal between the sections E to F.
Continue around the hexagon.

Continue around the hexagon and join end to beginning. Tension the central mesh carefully to make it look the same as the rest.

217

Chapter 16

However carefully the centre of a radially worked hexagonal motif is made, the seam will usually show. Hence it may be preferable to work the motif from top to bottom, unless it its to be mounted on a backing. When a motif is mounted on a backing, the ends can be sewn through to the back and the knots can be carefully pulled into the backing, thus concealing the join (figure 533).

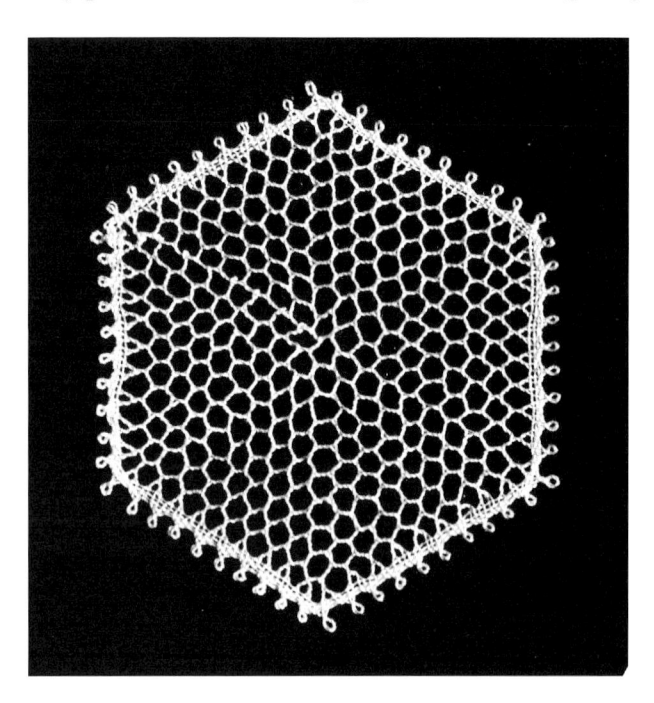

Figure 540 (left) A hexagonal shape with a point ground centre

Chapter 17

PROJECTS 28-30 LINGERIE SET (Plate no 5)

Project 28   Camisole
Project 29   Half-slip
Project 30   French knickers

New Techniques for Projects 28-30
using an extra pin when a cloth stitched motif
   abuts honeycomb ground
trail made with a gimp
spider
honeycomb adjacent to the footside
changing from a footside to a picot edge
changing from a picot edge to a footside
workers pass out to the footside and back
pin stitch

Materials required for Project 28
prickings (figures 542 & 547)[1]
dressmaking pattern for camisole
Piper's silk floss no. 90
   with 6 strands for gimp
or 60 Egyptian cotton
   with perle thread no. 8 for gimp
Piper's silk thread no. 420 to match lace for
   attaching lace to silk fabric
China silk, crepe de chine, batiste
   or lightweight crepe back satin
   according to dressmaking pattern
silk machine sewing thread to match
   fabric
1 m of 6mm muslin ribbon for straps
   to match fabric
10cm of 1cm muslin ribbon for bow
   or ready- made bow to match fabric
2mm pearl bead for bow

Figure 541 Camisole with lace made using Piper's 90 denier silk

End notes for Projects 28-30
1 drafting the pattern

Chapter 17

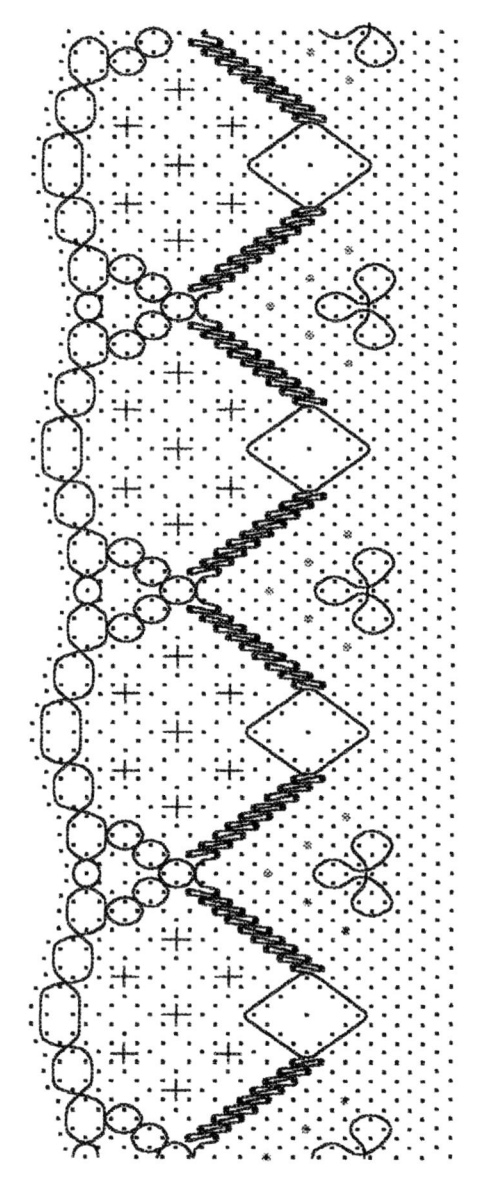

Figure 542 Pattern for wide edging to be made in silk

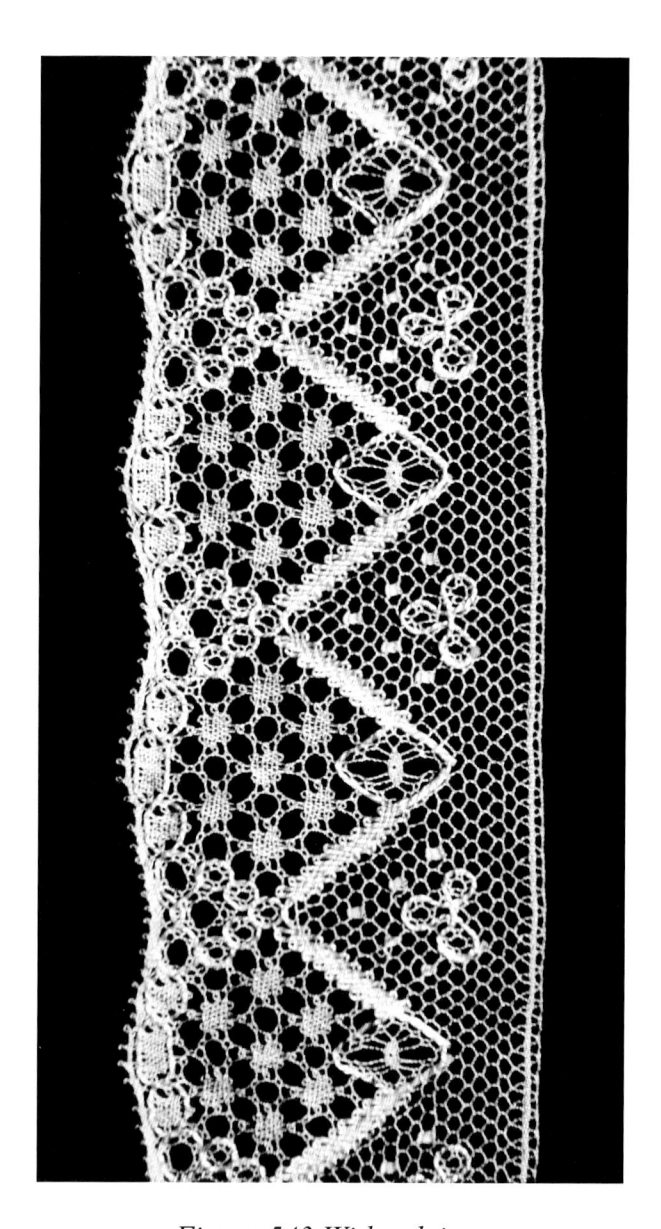

Figure 543 Wide edging made in no 60 Egyptian cotton

Using floss silk
Silk is very slippery and firms up very easily. **Take great care not to gather up the footside** by leaving in plenty of pins along the footside and tensioning the footside passives very gently. Always measure the length of the lace before turning corners or finishing etc. If it is shorter than expected work a little more lace.

Estimating the length of wide lace required
Measure the width across the upper edge of the camisole, and estimate the number of pattern repeats. Since the camisole looks better with the junction between two heads (repeats from one valley to the next equivalent valley) in the centre, an even number of repeats will be required across the top. Add a seam allowance of two repeats, one for each side.

Chapter 17

Setting in
The lace is mounted to the fabric before the item is made up, and the French seams go through the lace, therefore there is no special start or finish, and there is no need to wind the bobbins in couples. Just tie the bobbins in groups of eight, or more, to pins above the top of the pattern and start working.

Using a gimp to make a trail
The trails in this edging are made by passing a gimp along the path usually taken by the worker (figure 544). After the gimp passes through a pair the pair is twisted once, except when next to the pin where the pair may be twisted twice (figure 545). As with cloth stitch trails, there will be one more pair in the trail when it travels diagonally one way than in the trail when it travels diagonally the other way, unless, as in this pattern, the trails are not connected and each can be started in the direction that will give the desired result.

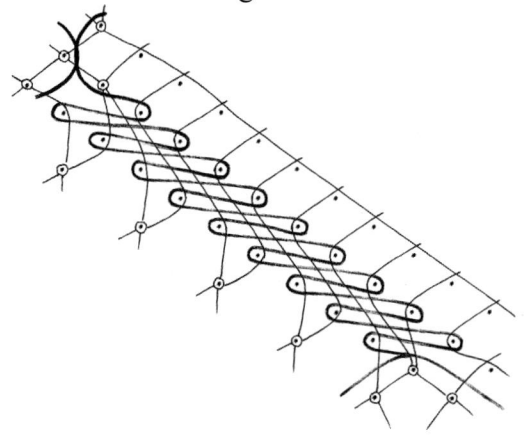

Figure 544 Trail path taken by gimp

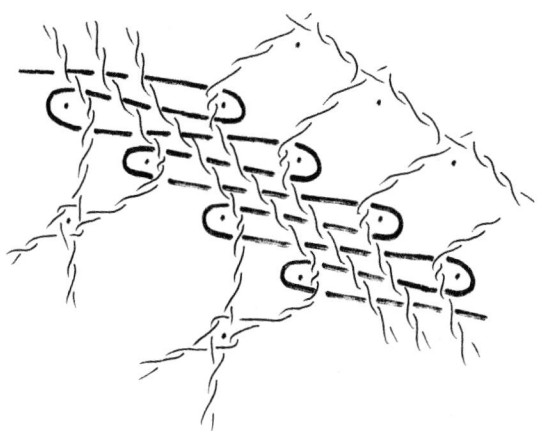

Figure 545 Passing the trail gimp through the pairs

Spider
A spider is made in an open diamond shape and it has one pin in the centre (figure 546). Each 'leg' of the spider is twisted a number of times, the basic number being the number of 'legs' per side, in this case three. However, this number may be increased or decreased as according to the situation. When working in silk I prefer to add an extra twist, it is optional.

The centre is worked by cloth stitching one set of 'legs', A, B and C across the other set D, E and F, setting up the pin in the centre and repeating the stitching. To do this, *cloth stitch the centre two pairs, 'legs' A and D. Using one of these pairs, A, as the workers, cloth stitch across the remainder of the other set, E and F. Take the next pair from

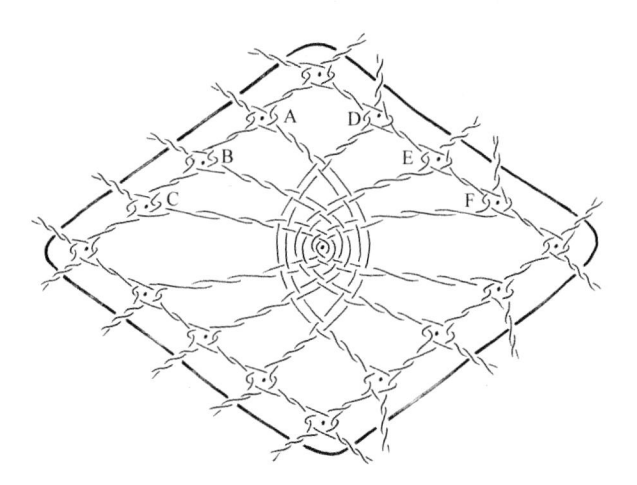

Figure 546 A spider

221

Chapter 17

the first set, B, and cloth stitch across the other set, D, E and F. Take the next pair of the first set, C, and cloth stitch across the other set, D, E and F*. Set up the pin between the two sets of pairs and repeat *to*. Twist the 'legs' the same number of times as before working the centre

When sufficient lace has been made cut off the bobbins. The lace has no special finish.

Narrow edging
For a camisole, with splits at the sides, the narrow edgings start and finish at points and have two corners.

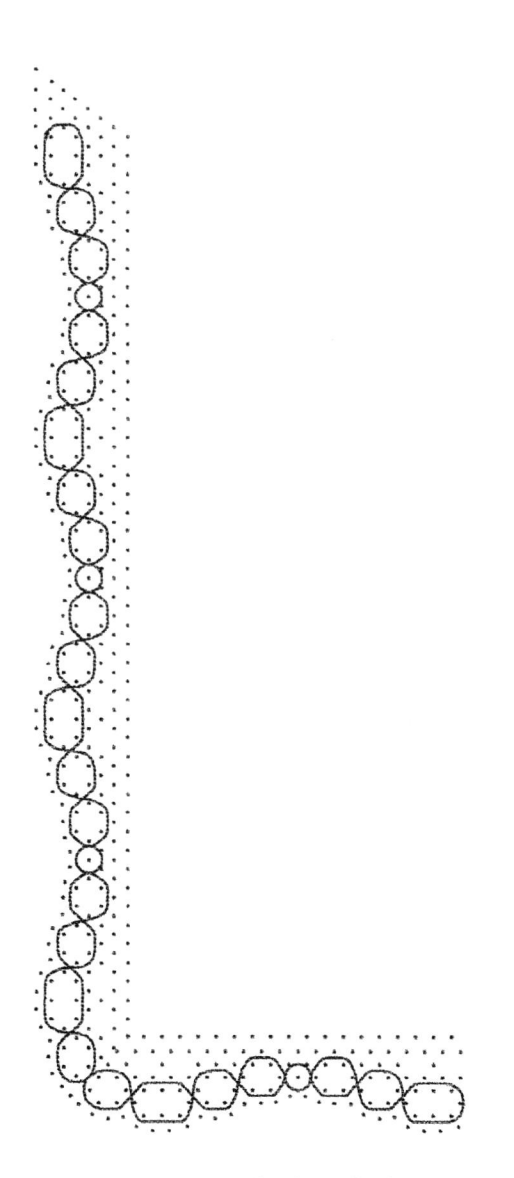

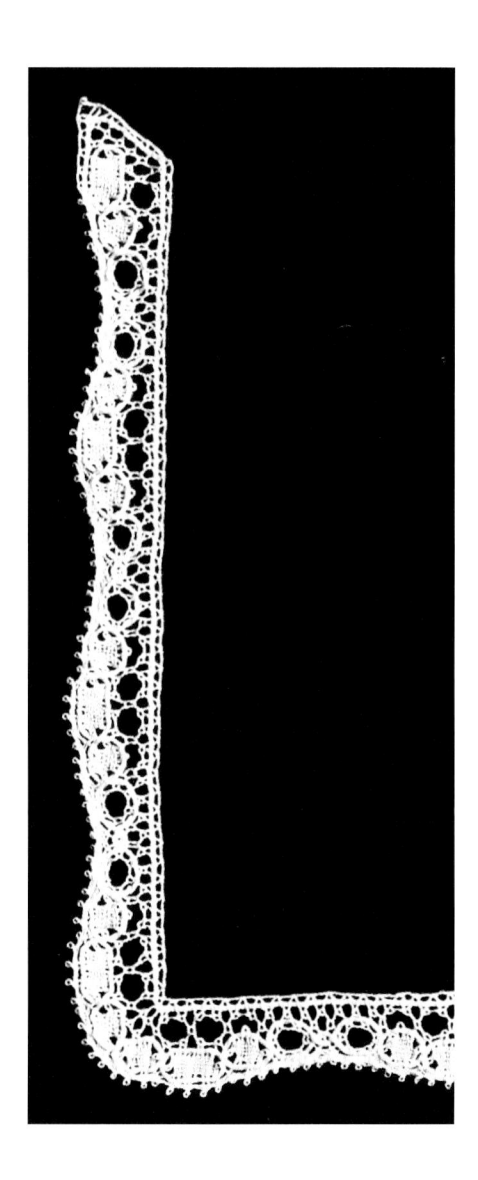

Figure 547 Pattern draft with sloping start to be made in silk

Figure 548 Narrow edging with sloping start

222

Estimating the length of narrow lace required
If there are to be no splits at the sides, discount the seam allowances and measure the distance around the lower edge of the camisole. Estimate the number of pattern repeats. If there are to be splits; discount the seam allowance and estimate the number of repeats required for each lower edge from corner to corner. For a 13.3 cm (5¼ in) split, two heads will be required between the point and the corner as in the patterns figures 547 & 549. The patterns are printed with the diagonal start and finish and sufficient edging to reach the corner at the lower edge of the camisole, but adjust as desired. Copy and repeat the straight section and dovetail the pieces.

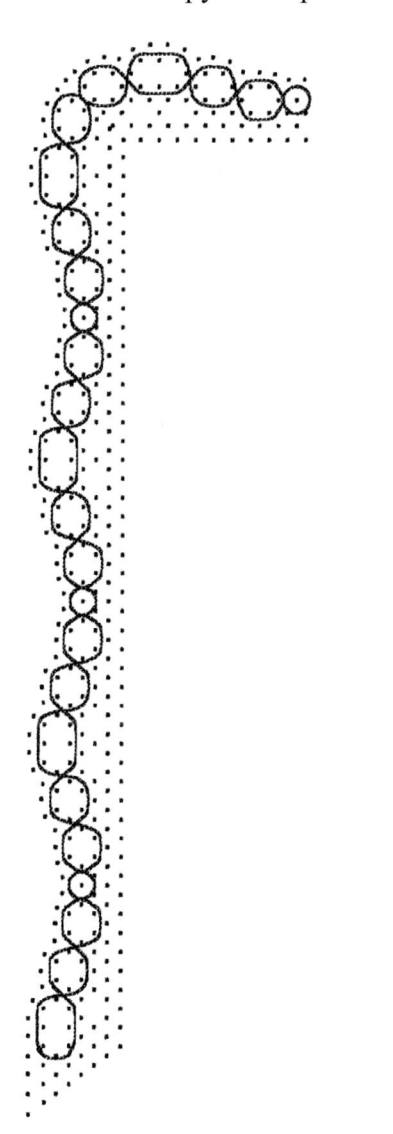

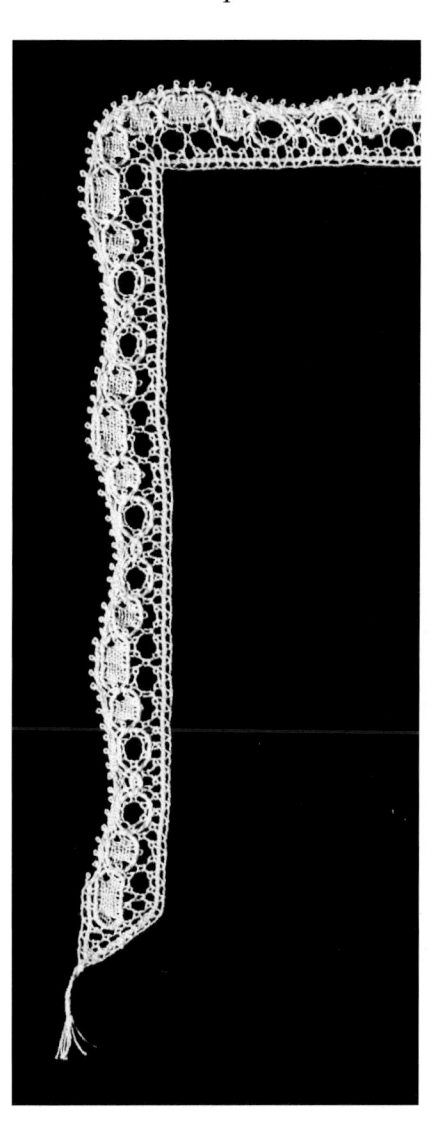

Figure 549 Pattern draft with sloping finish to be made in silk

Figure 550 Narrow edging with sloping finish

Chapter 17

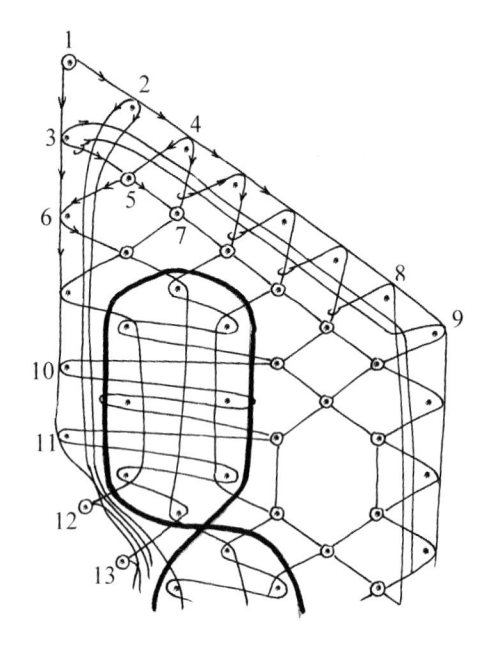

Figure 551 Setting in on the diagonal starting at a point

Setting in along a diagonal
1 Start with two pairs and make a whole stitch round pin 1 (figure 551).
2 Place two pairs straddled over a temporary pin, placed to the right of pin 1. Cloth stitch the right pair from pin 1 with the nearest new pair. Twist both and set up a pin, pin 2 between them, Twist the edge pair. Similarly add two pairs at pin 3 and two more at pin 4.
3. Cloth stitch the right pair from pin 3 through the two pairs from pin 2. Slip a new pair on second pair from pin 3, and cloth stitch this new pair through the two pairs from pin 2. There are now four pairs of footside passives, two pairs for each side.

The left side is a footside for the first five pinholes, then it changes to a picot edge.

4 Cloth stitch pair 2 (the slipped on pair is not counted) through two pairs of passives. Cloth stitch the left pair from pin 4 through the two passive pairs and make a honeycomb stitch with the pair from pin 3, pin 5. Return the left pair from pin 5 though the passives and make up the edge, pin 6.
5 Work the remaining pair from pin 4 through the passives and slip on a pair, and make the honeycomb stitch at pin 7.
6 Continue down the diagonal start and turn the corner at pin 9. When returning to the honeycomb stitch, after making up the edge at the corner, pin 9, see note 'Honeycomb adjacent to the footside' below.
7 When working the clothwork lozenge, the workers pass out to make up the edge at pins 10 and 11 and return to continue as workers for the lozenge. Complete the lozenge.
8 To change the footside to a picot edge, cloth stitch the edge pair (do not remove the twists), though the edge passive pair and leave as passives. Work the next two picots, pins 12 and 13, normally. However, only two pairs of passives are required when the lace is at its widest and adding in the edge pair results in three. Return to the usual number by removing a pair of passives.

Honeycomb adjacent to the footside
When honeycomb is worked adjacent to the footside there will be a lot of strain on the pair leaving the honeycomb stitch to become the footside workers. If this causes distortion of the honeycomb stitches, a modified honeycomb stitch may be used.

Chapter 17

1 When making the last large lozenge, the picot edge changes to a footside. Add a pair, by slipping a pair on the picot pair before making the last picot, pin 1 (figure 552) and making a cloth stitch with this pair and the edge passives.
2 Before working pin 2, twist the edge passives to become edge pair of the footside, and make up the edge as usual. Continue making the lozenge, casting off the gimps when it is complete.
3 Work the last row of honeycomb to pin 3.
4 Cast off pairs along the diagonal as far as pin 4.
5 Make up the edge at pin 5 and cloth stitch across the pairs between the pins, making up the edge at pin 6. Throw out the second and third threads from each side of the centre bunch.
6 Cloth stitch back to pin 7 and make up the edge. Cloth stitch the edge pair from pin 6, through the passives and use the edge pair and workers from pin 7 to make a bunch and tie.

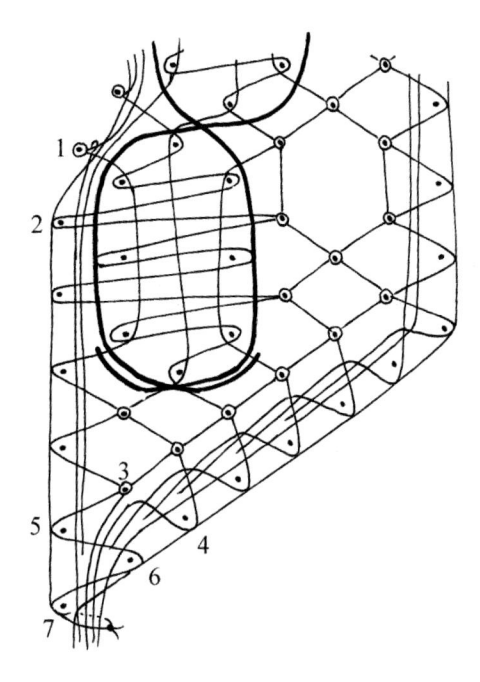

Figure 552 Casting off along a diagonal

Casting off along a diagonal
Measure the length of the lace along the lower edge before turning the corner and, if it is shorter than expected, work another head. If there is no split, join end to start and darn away the ends.

Galloon straps
A galloon is a strip of continuous lace with a scalloped edge down both sides. This one has a series of holes through the centre for a ribbon to be threaded through.

The galloon pattern (figure 553) has large holes down the centre where pairs are left out and, following the usual rules; these pairs appear to have no place to go

Figure 553 (right) Pattern for galloon, to be made in silk

Figure 554 (far right) Galloon

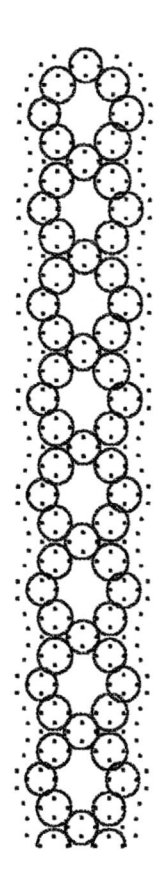

225

Chapter 17

1 When the first pair adjacent to the large hole, pin 1, (figure 555) has been worked, twist the pair twice, pass the gimp through, twist the pair twice and leave it.
2 After working the stitch at pin 2, twist the pair adjacent to the large hole, pass the gimp and the pair from pin 1 through at the same time, i.e. the pair from 2 bridges the gimp and the pair from pin 1. Twist the pair from pin 2 and leave both pairs. The pair left out from pin 1 is now adjacent to the gimp.
3 After making the stitch at pin 3, pass the gimp through the pair from pin 1, currently just outside the gimp, twist the pair and make a stitch. The pair adjacent to the hole bridges the gimp and the pair from pin 2, and is twisted twice. The pair from pin 2 now lies adjacent to the gimp. Leave both pairs.

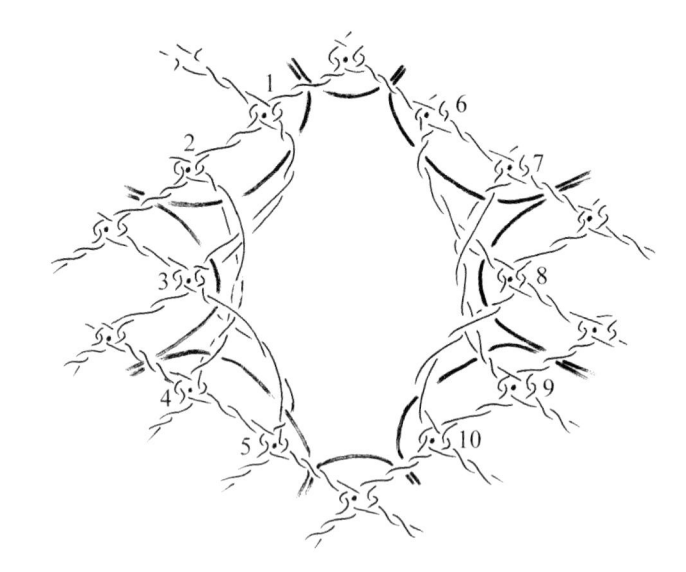

Figure 555 Working around the central hole

4 When pin 4 is reached, pass the gimp through the pair from pin 2, currently just outside the gimp, twist the pair and make the stitch at pin 4.
5 When pin 5 is reached, pass the gimp through the pair from pin 3, currently just outside the gimp, twist the pair and make a stitch at pin 5.
6 Work the other side to match.

Check the finished length of the straps, from edge of fabric to edge of fabric, and add 8cm (3 ins approx.). Make a neat start at the top of the pattern, but the end does not require a special finish as it will be turned in and sewn securely.

Attaching the wide edging
Attach the wide edging to the front before making up the garment. Tack the wrong side of the lace to the right side of the fabric, with the headside of the lace level with the finished edge of the garment, and the junction between two repeats at the centre front. Use a fine ballpoint needle and double thread. Attach the footside of the lace to the fabric, first with a foundation row then, for silk, with pin-stitch, pulling up the pin-stitches **very** firmly. Pin-stitch is not suitable for coarser fabrics. For cotton fabrics use four-sided stitch.

Pin-stitch
1 Fasten on the thread at the footside, just below the footside. Insert the needle at A and bring out at B. Pull firmly (figure 556).

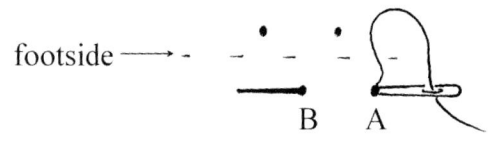

Figure 556 Starting pin stitch

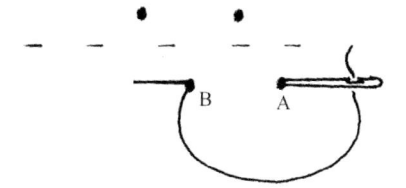

Chapter 17

2 Again insert at A and bring out at B. Pull firmly (figure 557).

Figure 557 (left) Making the first stitch

3 Insert at C, through a hole in the footside, and bring out at B. Pull firmly (figure 558).

Figure 558 (right) Making the second stitch

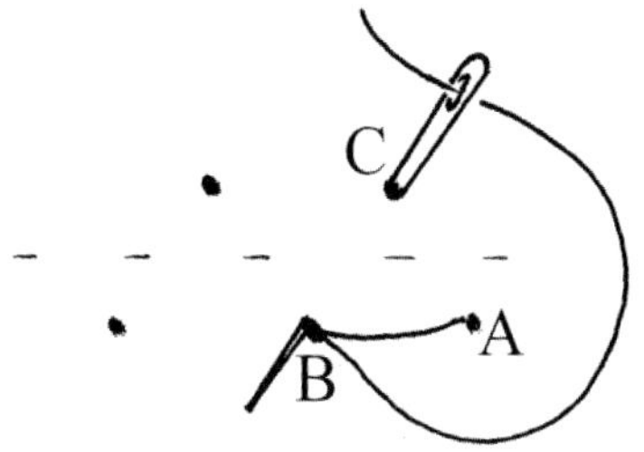

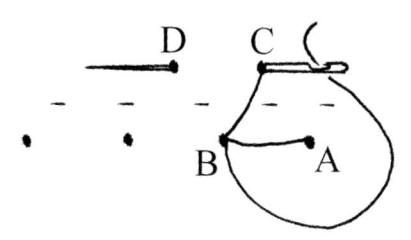

4 Re-insert at C and bring out at D, the next hole in the footside. Pull firmly (figure 559).

Figure 559 (left) Making the third stitch over the second

5 Insert again at C and bring out at D. Pull firmly (figure 560).

Figure 560 (right) Making the fourth stitch

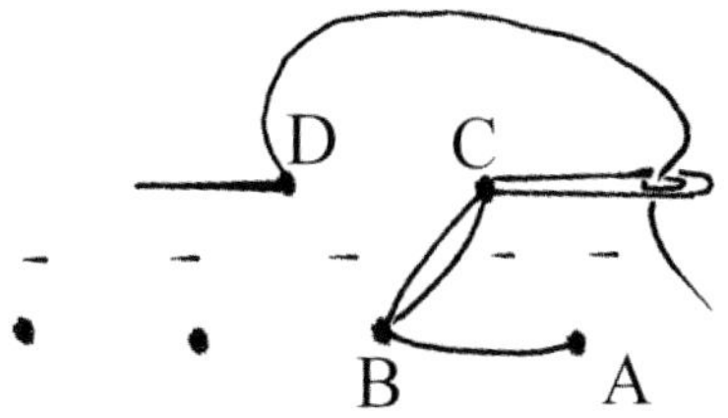

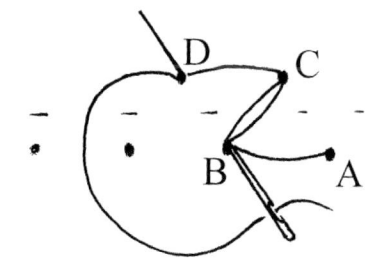

6 Insert at B and bring out at D. Pull firmly (figure 561).

Figure 561 (left) Making the fifth stitch

7 Rename B as A, and D as B and repeat from note 2 (figure 562).

Figure 562 (right) Making the sixth stitch over the fifth

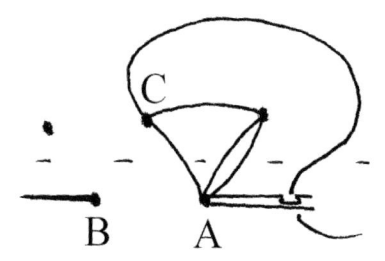

8 When all the stitching has been completed pull the fabric taught across the footside, to complete the tightening of the stitches, and trim off the excess fabric.

227

Chapter 17

Making up the garment
Make up the garment according to the pattern instructions. Use French seams down the sides and treating the lace across the upper edge as part of the fabric. Stop the French seams to allow for the lace at the splits (figure 563).

Attaching the narrow edging
Place the narrow edgings on the back and front, so that the headsides reach the lower edge of the fabric. The points of the lace should meet a short way above the end of the French seam (figure 565). The headsides along the split should meet at the side seam, and they are joined by oversewing them together (figure 564).

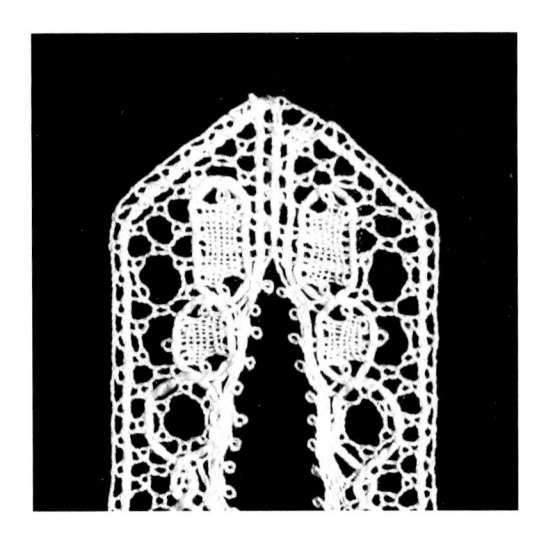

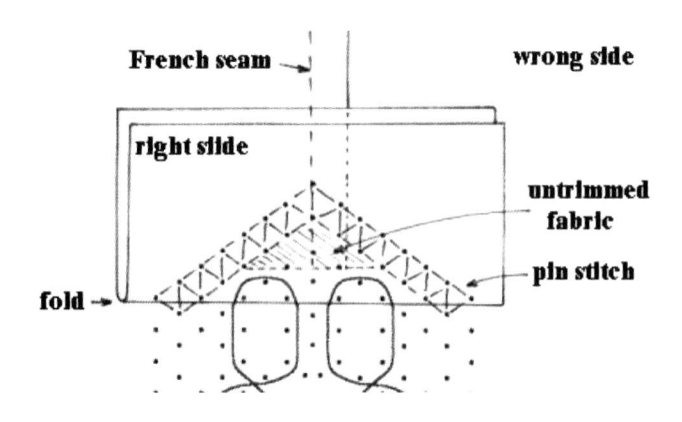

Attach the lace using pin stitch. Trim the excess fabric, leaving a small triangle, about 6mm (¼ in) deep below the stitching where the points meet, and cut across the French seam at right angles to its seam.

Figure 563 (above) Positioning the points of the narrow edging

Figure 564 (left) Joining the small sections of footside

Protecting the ends of the seams
1 Fold a piece of fabric 5cm x 10cm (2 ins x 4 ins) in half with wrong sides together and place on the wrong side of the fabric over the end of the French seam (figure 563 & 565). The fold should reach across the angles where the straight footsides meet the diagonal start and finish of the lace. Tack in place.
2 From the right side, work another row of pin stitch, over the existing row, stitching through the two layers of the reinforcing.
3 Stitch the small sections of footside together (figure 564).
4 Trim the excess fabric.

Figure 565 (right) Reinforced seam end

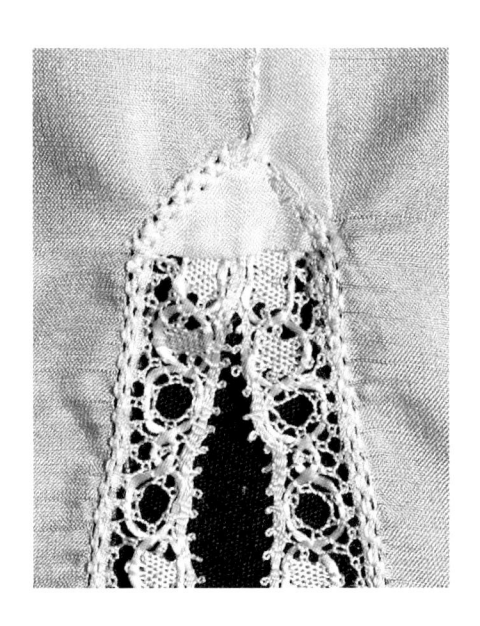

Chapter 17

Attaching the straps to the front of the camisole
Thread double ribbon, with the fold reaching the start of the lace, through the large holes of the galloon. Fold the lace across the widest point of the first repeat, move the fold of the ribbon to this line and tack the folds to the inside of the camisole along the pin stitch seam. From the right side, work a row of pin stitching over the existing row, working right through the lace and the ribbon. Allowing the ribbon to take the strain, tack, then stitch through the galloon and ribbon along the portion of the headside of the lace that they cross.

Before stitching the hem across the top of the back, check the length of the straps, and pin in place inside the back, with the pin very close to the edge. Fold end of the galloon and ribbon, tuck the raw end under the hem and tack in place. (It is easier to crease the lace before cutting to the required length.) Tack, then stitch the hem, continuing across the straps as they are met. Tack the strap to the top edge of the hem and work another row of stitching across the back, 3 mm ($1/8$ in) from upper edge of the back, again continuing across the straps.

Making the bow
1 Fold a 10cm (4 in) length of 6mm muslin ribbon in half and make a crease.
2 With double thread, make a row of running stitches down the crease from the upper edge, A, to the lower edge, B (figure 566).

Figure 566 (right) Crossing the sides and stitching

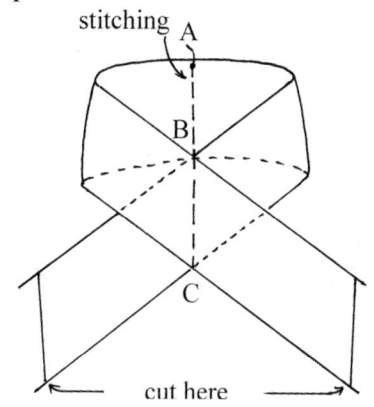

3 Fold each side, 8mm (5/16 in) from the centre crease, so that the sides cross at the end of the running stitches, B.
4 Continue the running stitches through both layers to the lower edge of the crossed sides, C.
5 Pull up the running stitches tightly and bind the double thread several times around the gathering.
6 Fasten off, but do not cut the thread, use these threads to stitch a pearl bead to conceal the binding threads (figure 567) and fasten off again. Do not cut the thread.
8 Use the remaining thread to stitch the bow to the centre front of the camisole.

Figure 567 The bow

Chapter 17

PROJECT 29   HALF SLIP

Figure 568 Half-slip

Materials required
pricking (figures 569, 571 & 574)[1]
dressmaking pattern for half-slip
China silk, crepe de chine, batiste or lightweight crepe back satin according to dressmaking pattern
silk machine sewing thread to match fabric
Piper's denier silk floss no. 90
with 6 strands for gimp
or Egyptian no. 60 cotton
with perle thread no 8 for gimp
Piper's 4/20 silk thread to match lace for attaching lace to silk fabric
10cm of 1cm muslin ribbon for bow, or ready-made bow, to match fabric
2mm pearl bead for bow
1 m 6 core elastic

New Techniques
honeycomb stitches along the diagonal through the corner

Chapter 17

Estimating the length of lace required
If the pattern does not have splits adapt it. If a split is required at centre back or front, where there is no seam, add a seam allowance down the centre fold line and cut two pieces. Join together as far as required. Calculate the number of pattern repeats required for around the lower edge and up the split. If there is no split choose a suitable starting line.

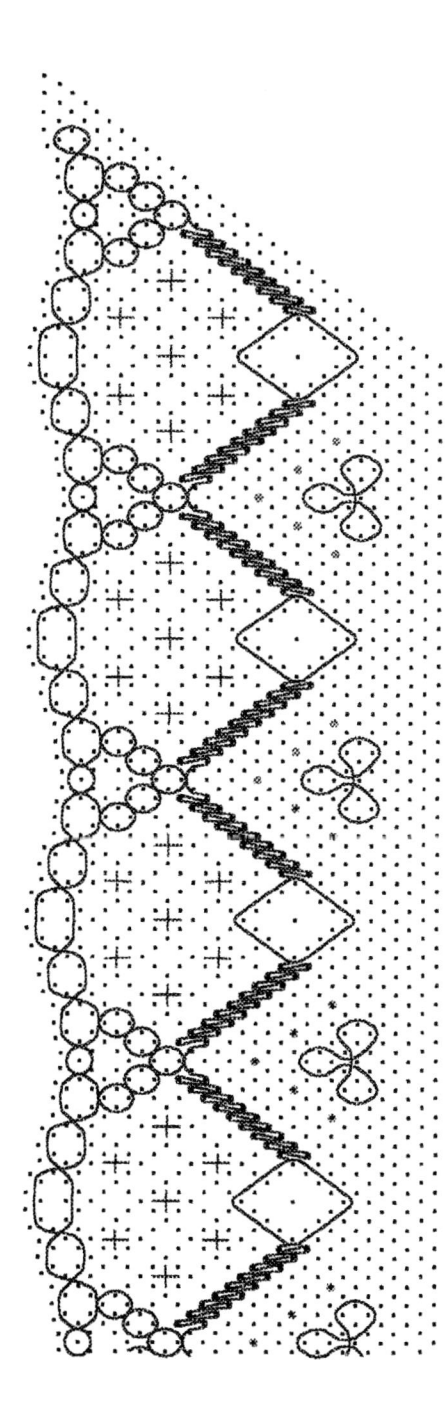

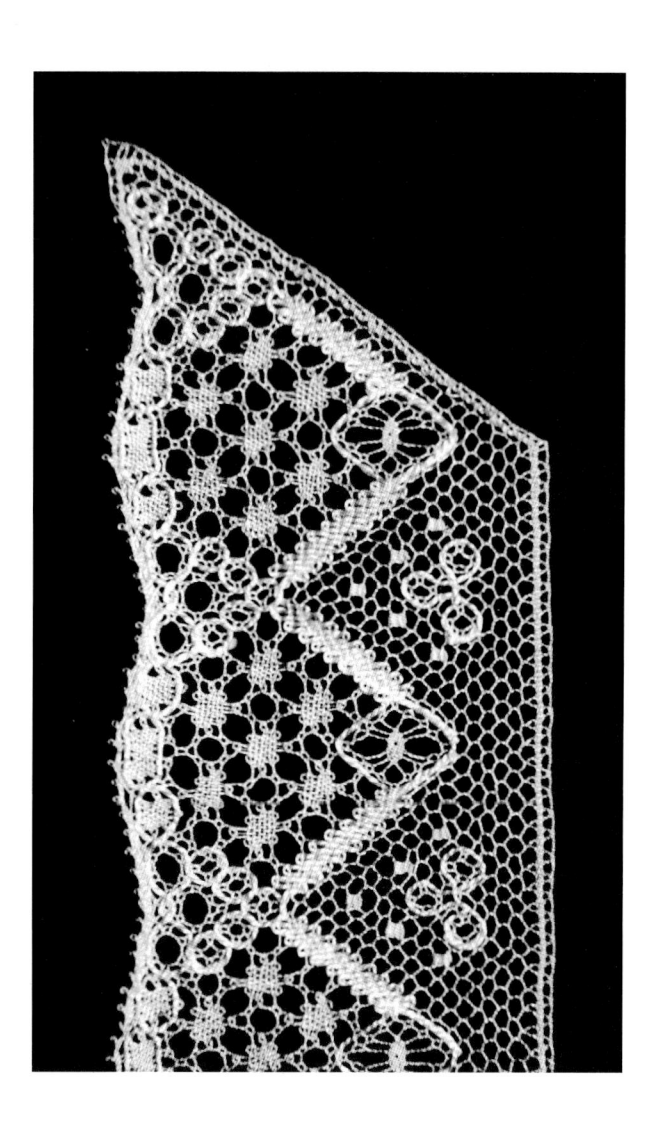

Figure 569 (left) Pattern for wide edging with a diagonal start

Figure 570 (above) Wide edging with a diagonal start

231

Chapter 17

Figure 571 Pattern for the corner of the wide edging to be made in silk

Figure 572 Corner for the wide edging

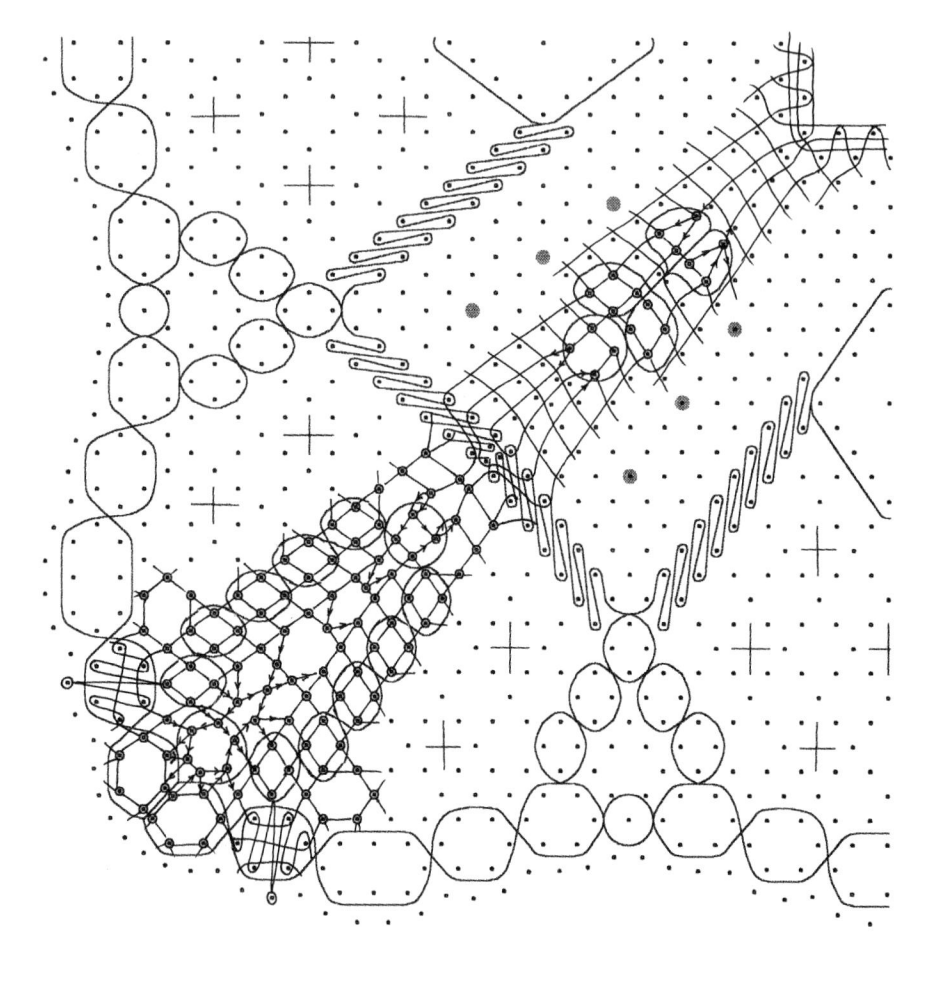

Figure 573 (left) Turning the corner

Chapter 17

Working the wide edging
Using pattern figure 569 start the edging at a point (570), as for the narrow edging of the camisole (figure 551). Work a corner (figures 571, 572 & 573) around the lower edge, another corner and finish at a point (figure 574 & 575) working it as for the narrow edging of the camisole (figure 552). If there is no split, join end to start and darn away the ends.

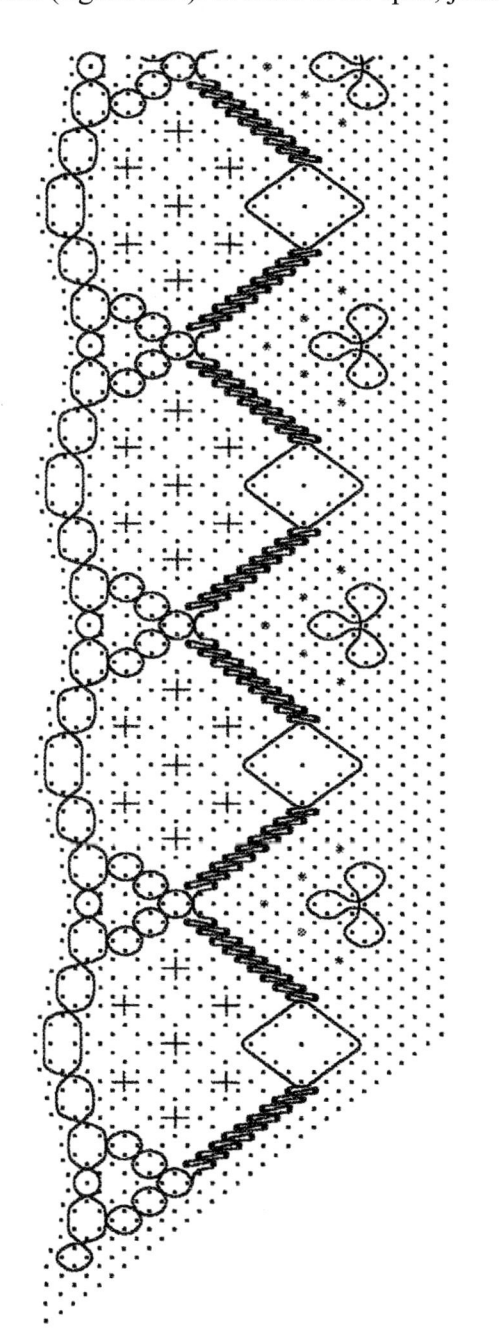

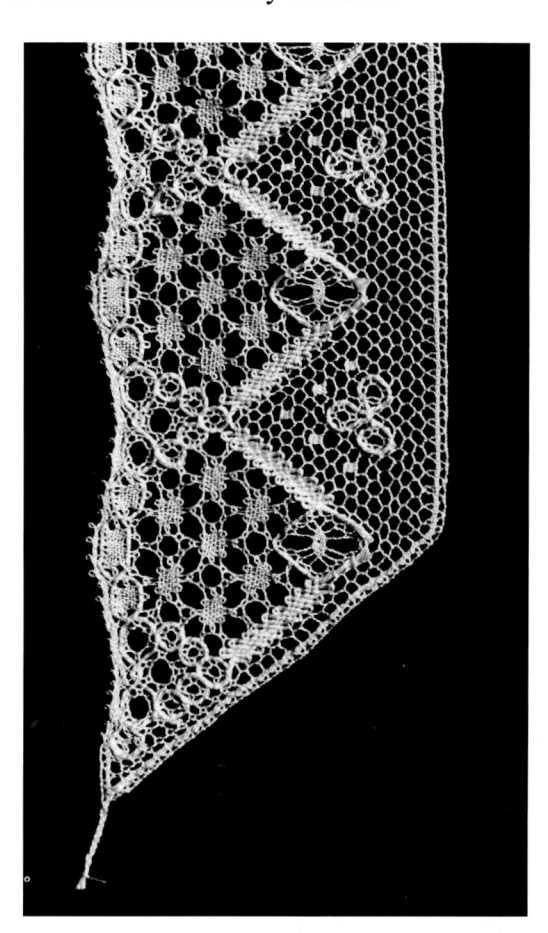

Figure 574 Pattern for the diagonal finish of the wide edging

Figure 575 Diagonal finish of the wide edging

Making up the half-slip
Make up the slip according to the instructions. Attach the lace as for the camisole, reinforcing the end of the seam at the split, if required. Attach a bow at the point of the split.

233

Chapter 17

PROJECT 30   FRENCH KNICKERS

Materials required
   prickings (figure 547, 549, & 577)[1]
   dressmaking pattern for French knickers
   China silk, crepe de chine, batiste or
      lightweight crepe back satin according to
      dressmaking pattern
   silk machine sewing thread to match fabric
   Piper's 90 denier silk floss
      with 6 strands for gimp
   or Egyptian cotton no. 60
      with perle thread no 8 for gimp
   Piper's silk thread no. 4/20 to match lace for
      attaching lace to silk fabric
   1 m 6 core elastic

Figure 576 French knickers

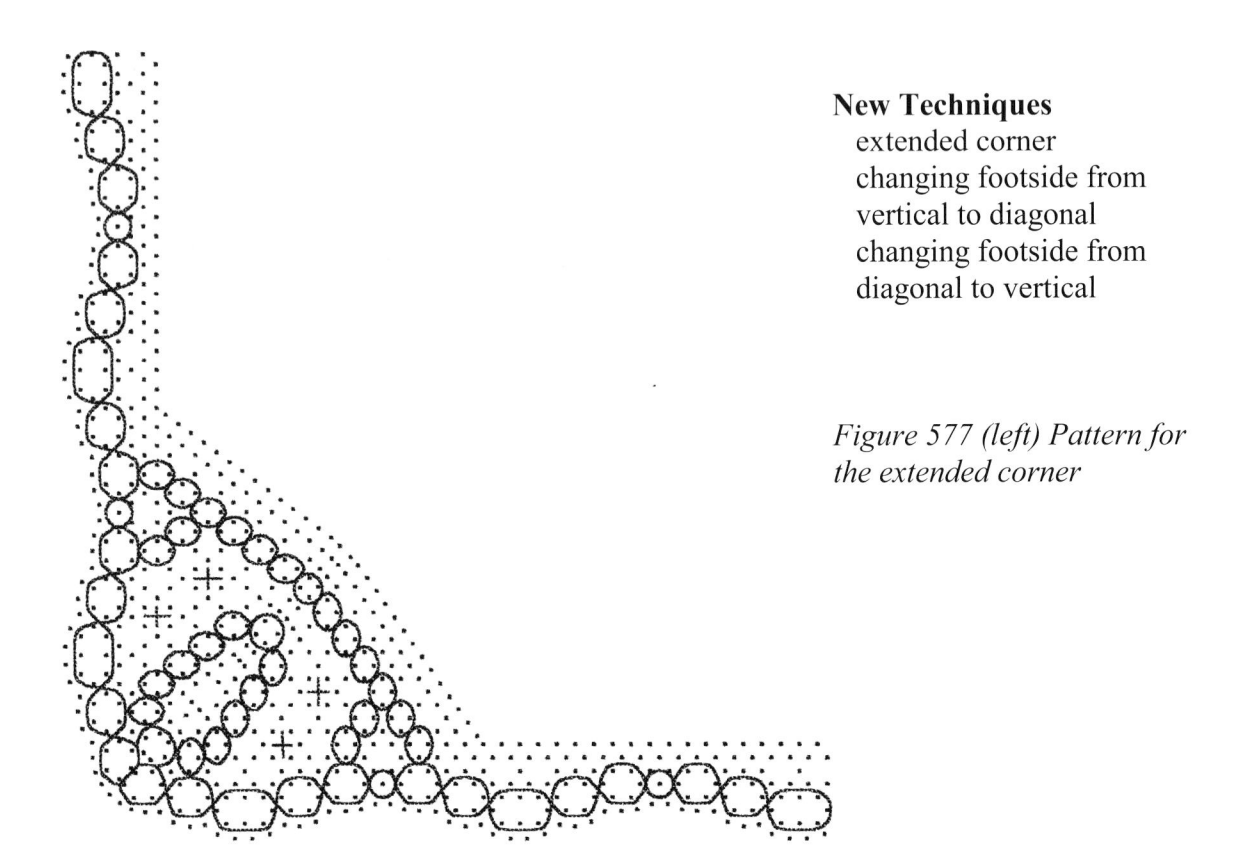

New Techniques
   extended corner
   changing footside from
   vertical to diagonal
   changing footside from
   diagonal to vertical

Figure 577 (left) Pattern for the extended corner

234

Chapter 17

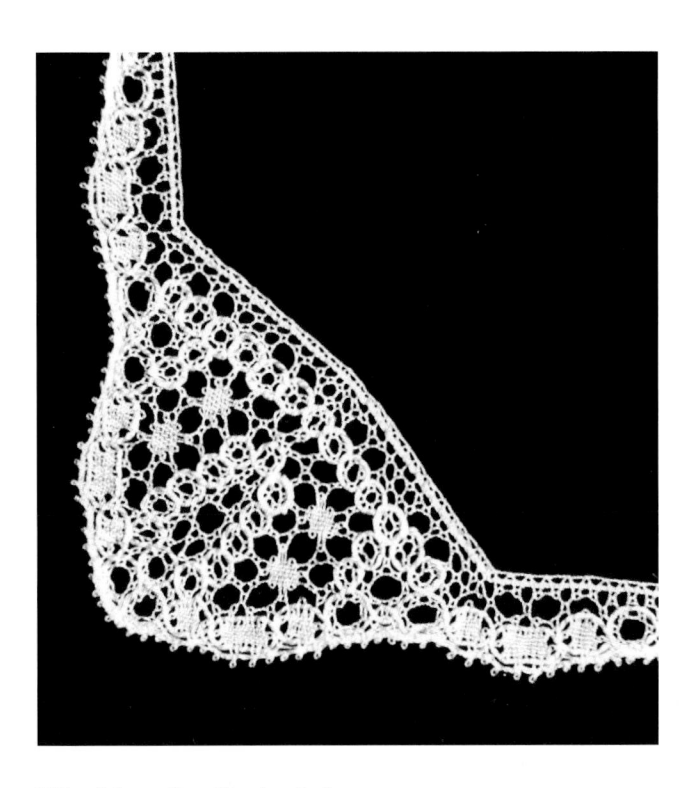

Estimating the length of lace required

If the pattern does not have splits adapt it if required. This split is shorter, one less pattern repeat, along the headside of the lace (ignoring the extended corner). Allowing for the extended corners at the front (figures 577 & 578), and narrow corners at the back, calculate the number of pattern repeats required around each leg opening. Also check the number of repeats required each side of the split.

Figure 578 (left) The extended corner

Working the first edging

Using pattern figure 547 start the edging at a point (figure 551) as for the narrow edging of the camisole. Work the narrow corner and around the leg opening. Working the extended corner is almost the same as for the wide edging, figure 573, the differences being at the inner 'footside' where pairs are added, by slipping on, as the lace widens along the diagonal through the corner (figure 579). Turn the corner, when the diagonal through it is reached, and work from the outside towards the inside, as for the corner of the wide edging. When the diagonal 'footside' is reached, and the lace narrows, pairs are thrown out instead of being added (figure 580). When the diagonal reaches the vertical footside (figure 581) the normal footside is resumed. Finish at a point as for the narrow edging of the camisole (figure 552).

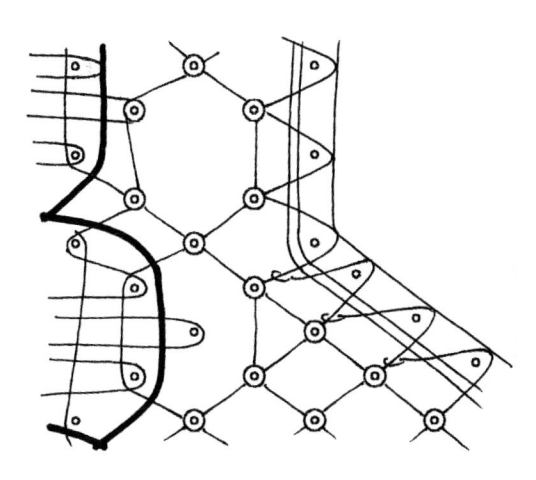

Figure 579 Progressing from the vertical footside to the diagonal

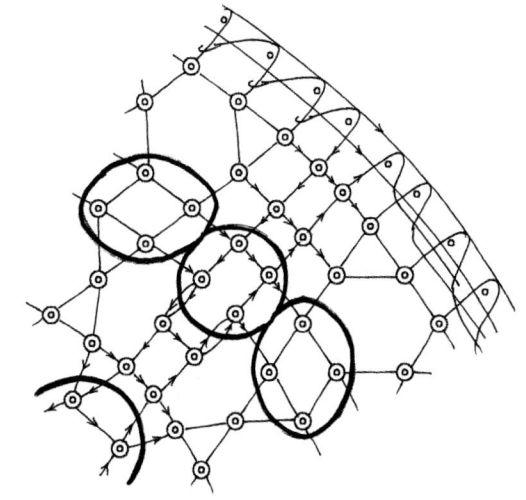

Figure 580 Inner part of the corner and throwing out pairs

235

Chapter 17

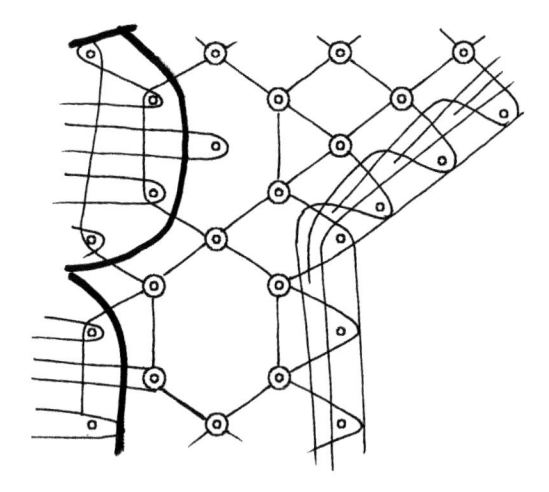

Figure 581 (left) Progressing from the diagonal to the vertical footside

The second edging
For the other leg opening, work the wide corner first, then the narrow corner. This will result in the lace having right sides out for both legs.

Making up the French knickers
Make up the garment according to the instructions, stopping the French seams at the sides to allow for the splits. Attach the lace as for the camisole, reinforcing the ends of the seams if there is a split.

END NOTES

1a Drafting the pattern for the wide edging[1]
1 Using Grid no 1, draw the gimps (figure 582)

Figure 582 (right) Gimps drawn in

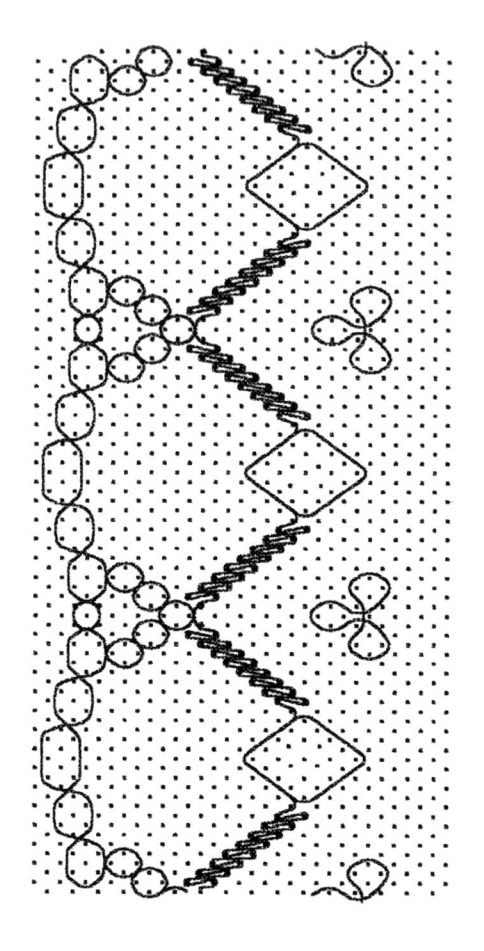

Chapter 17

2 Remove unwanted dots from the honeycomb areas, the diamond containing the spider, leaving the dot in the centre, and outside the headside gimp (figure 583)
3 Add the indicators for the Mayflower filling and the construction line for the picots. If silk is to be used the spacing for the headside pairs should be reduced.
4 Draw in the picots at the sides of the clothwork areas and the honeycomb rings, placing them half way between the dots in the motifs. It is not as critical for the picots adjacent to the honeycomb rings to be midway between the honeycomb stitches but, if those adjacent to clothwork are uneven, the clothwork will become distorted (figure 584).
5 Add the remaining picots, placing two, equally spaced, in each wide gap
6 Remove the construction line for the picots.
7 Finally adjust the footside (figure 542).

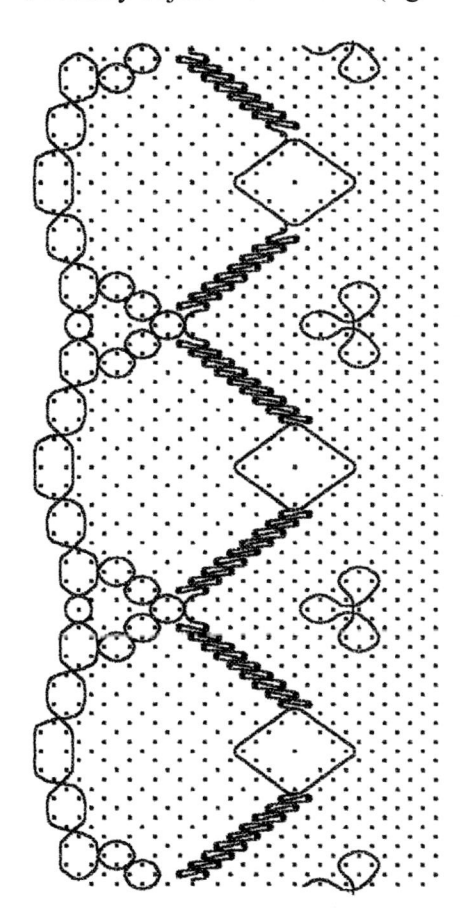

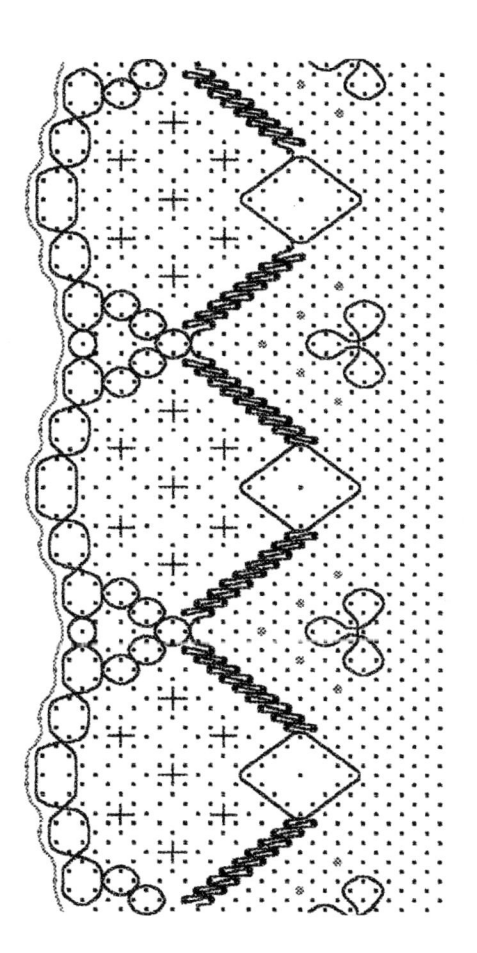

Figure 583 Unwanted dots removed

Figure 584 Unwanted dots removed indicators, picot line and picots adjacent to the clothwork added

1b Drafting the narrow edging with a diagonal start
1 Using Grid no 1, draw the gimps starting with the large honeycomb ring placed a little below the top of the grid (figure 585).
2 Remove unwanted dots from the honeycomb rings and the ground. Plot the picots as for the wide edging (figure 586).
3 For the diagonal start to the edging remove the dots above the two diagonal lines of dots above the top ring (figure 587).

Chapter 17

If silk is to be used the spacing for the headside pairs should be reduced.

5 Finally adjust the foot and catch-pins (figure 547). Only the outer line of pins along the diagonal start requires adjusting, making the gap between this and the next row slightly wider. There are no catch-pins along the second line.

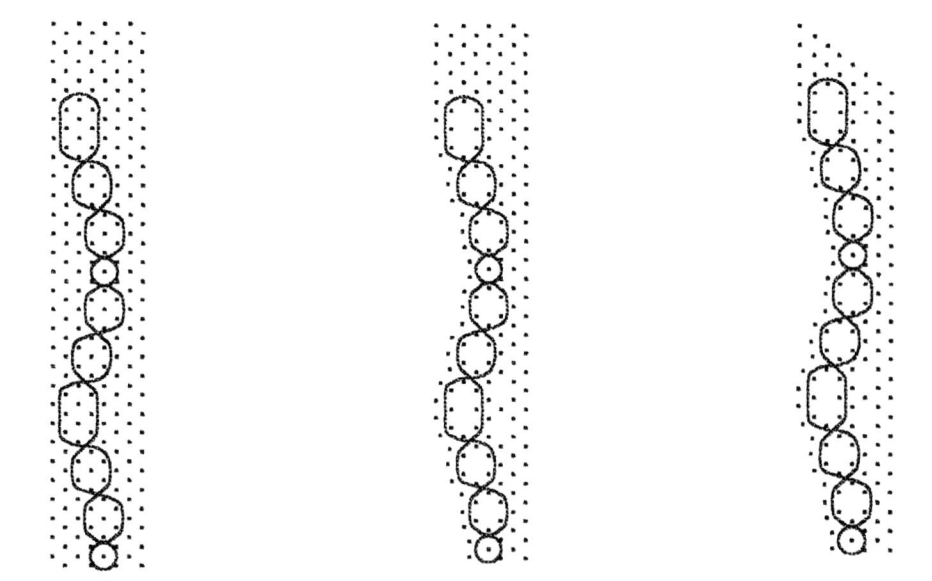

Figure 585 Gimps drawn   *Figure 586 Unwanted dots removed and picots plotted*   *Figure 587 Dots removed above the two diagonal lines of dots above the top ring*

1c Plotting the corner
Use a mirror placed at 45° to the footside to find a suitable position for the corner.

1 Draw the diagonal through the corner at 45° to the footside (figure 588) and remove all dots and lines beyond this line.

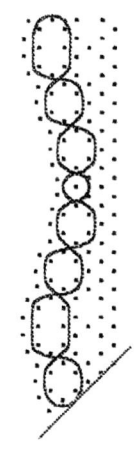

Figure 588 (right) Diagonal through the corner

2 Place this on another portion of edging so that they are at 90° to each other, and they match along the diagonal (figure 589).
3 Draw a curve through the picots at the headside and draw a dot where the diagonal and picot line meet (figure 590). Adjust the picots to give a good shape and spacing.

238

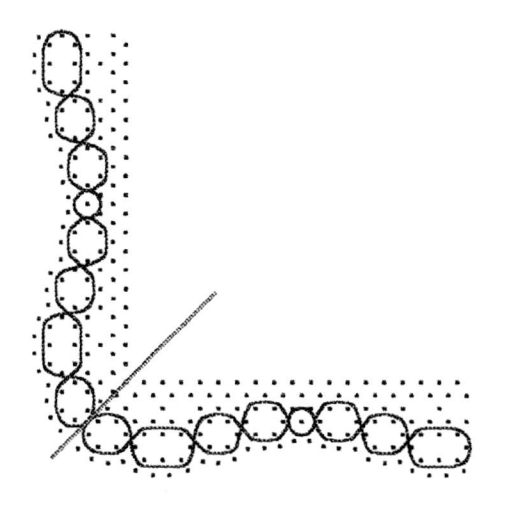

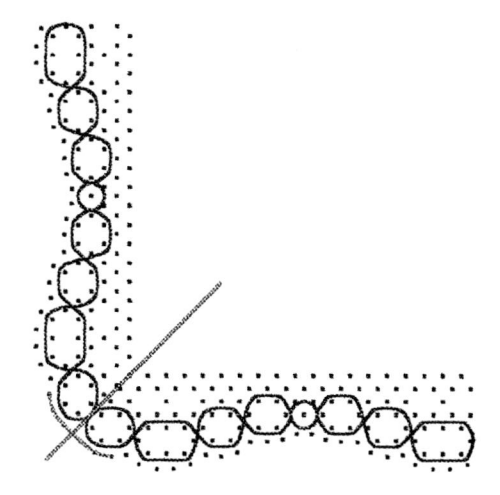

Figure 589 Two portions of the pattern meeting along the diagonal

Figure 590 Curve drawn through the picots

4 Erase the lines through the diagonal and the picots and adjust the catch-pins and footside (figure 547).

1d Drafting the galloon
1 Draw the gimps (figure 591).
2 Remove the dots from the central honeycomb rings, and the dots outside the gimps from both sides (figure 592).
3 Draw a picot line along both sides and add the evenly spaced picots. If silk is to be used, the spacing for the headside pairs should be reduced.
4 Erase the picot line (figure 553).

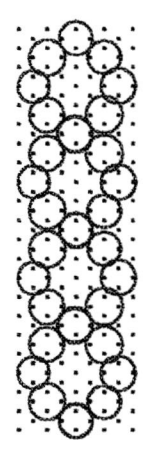

Figure 591 (left) Gimps drawn

Figure 592 (right) Unwanted dots removed, picot line drawn and picots marked

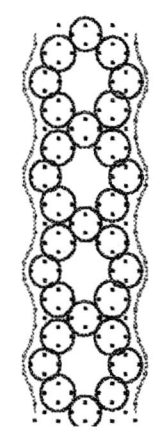

Chapter 17

1e Cornering the wide edging
Use a mirror placed at 45° to the footside to find a suitable position for the corner.
1 Draw the diagonal through the corner at 45° to the footside and remove all dots and lines beyond this line (figure 594).
2 Mirror across the diagonal by placing on another portion of edging so that they are at 90° to each other, and they match along the diagonal (figure 595).

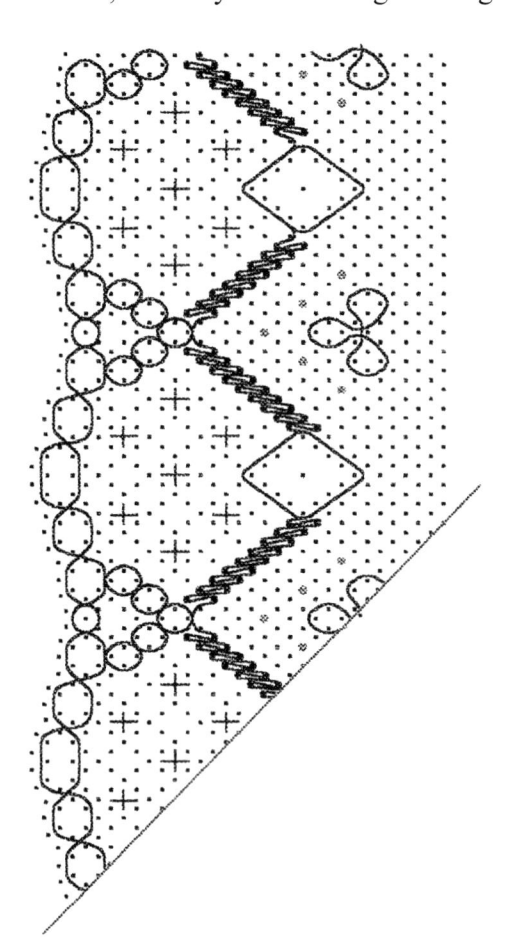

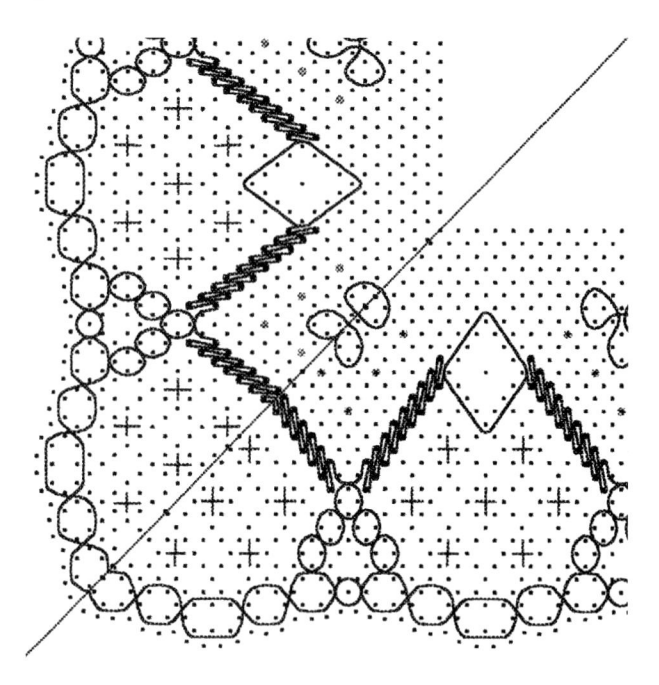

Figure 594 (left) Diagonal drawn, unwanted dots and lines removed

Figure 595 (above) Edging mirrored across the diagonal through the corner

Like this the corner may be workable, but is not aesthetically pleasing; the design requires modifying. Three disconnected rings, one of an unpleasant shape, have appeared in the ground. The zigzagging gimp needs to be properly connected and the area of honeycomb with mayflowers is too large and bland. The disconnected rings were joined and reshaped; some of the dots within the rings needed to be adjusted and. figures 574 and 575 show how I solved these problems, but there could have been other solutions. When extra design features are required to fill spaces, it is usually better to modify existing features than add completely new ones. An oval shape of four-pin rings, taken from the triangular motif between the honeycomb areas, has been used to break up the large area containing mayflowers. area and add interest., with another six-pin ring to add interest to the two rings already at the headside of the diagonal. The honeycomb within this oval has a gap row along the diagonal. To achieve this some pairs of dots across the diagonal were replaced by single dots; other dots also required adjusting to achieve a pleasing result. Some corners are easier than others, and most take several tries. After designing the corner, make a sample to check that the lace

Chapter 17

makes up as expected, and that you like the result. There were four aborted attempts, including their samples, before I was happy with this one

1f Diagonal start for the wide edging
Remove the dots leaving two rows along the top of a triangle of honeycomb stitches and continuing gimp trail (figure 598). Just drawing a diagonal through two rows above the large ring does not produce a pleasing result. The large ring has had be reduced to six pins, which brings the line nearer to the other rings on the diagonal. Also, by removing the top two dots on the left, and realigning the next dot at the headside, a more pleasing point is achieved (figure 596).

Figure 596 (right) Plotting the diagonal start

1g Diagonal finish for the wide edging
Plot the finish to match the start (figure 575).

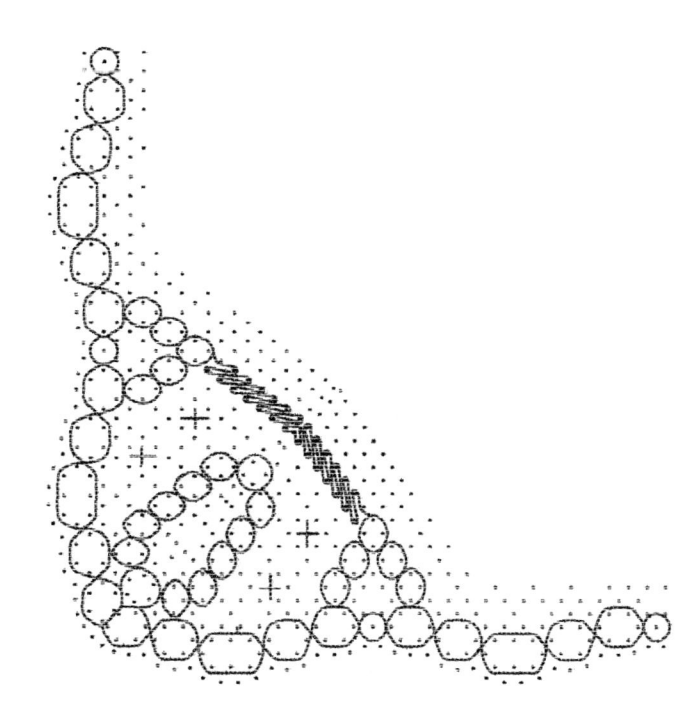

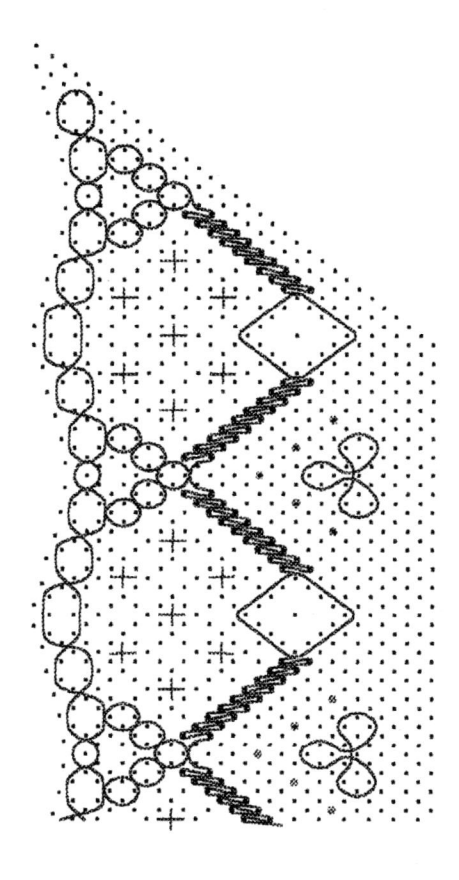

1h Extended corner
Usually a corner is extended when a narrow edging widens to a triangle across the corner. However, this one started as the corner of the wide edging that was reduced to a triangle with a narrow edging extending each side.

1 From the corner of the wide edging (figure 571), reduce the width of the sides to the width of the narrow edging and to within three rows of dots along the inner gimps (figure 597).

Figure 597 (left) Corner of wide edging reduced

241

Chapter 17

2 Change the trails to four-pin honeycomb rings (figure 598).
3 Add pins to complete the footsides of the narrow edgings, and the two rows along the diagonals that will form the 'footside' across the corner. Now the gap row sections of the honeycomb adjacent to the two diagonal 'footside' rows are unbalanced and need adjusting (figure 599).

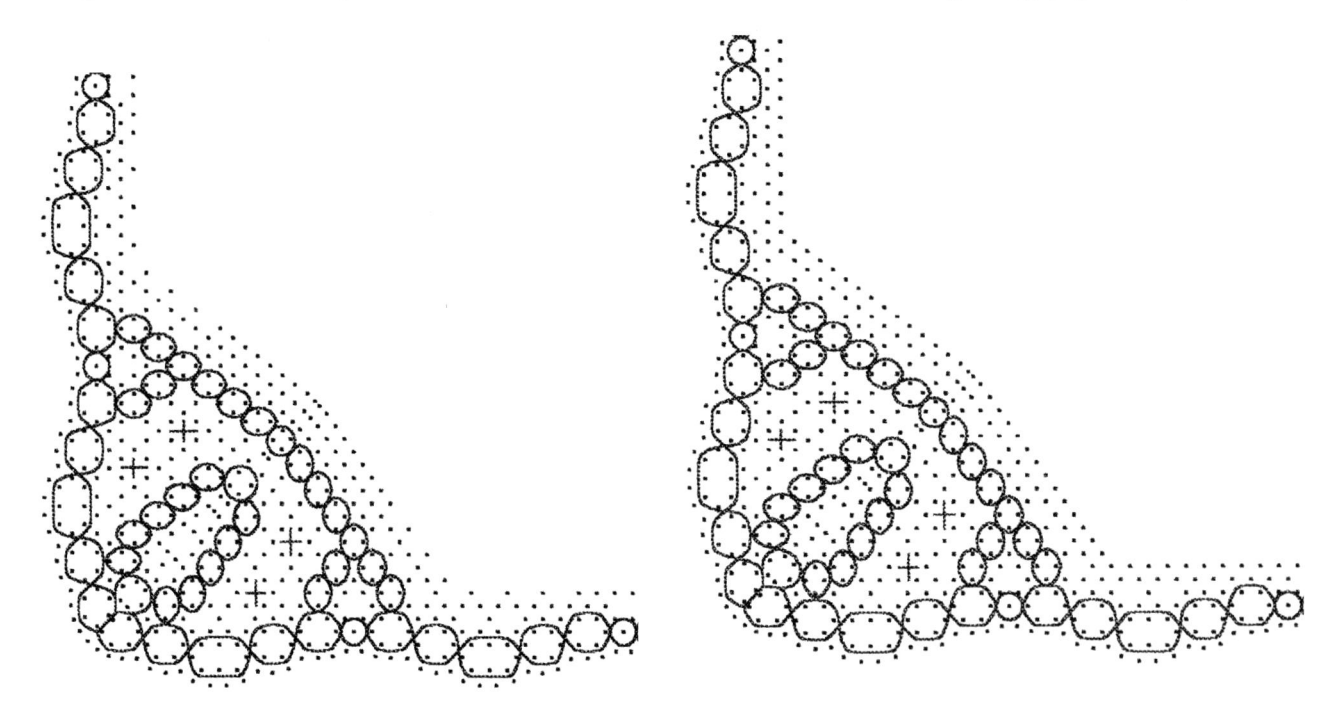

Figure 598 Trails changed to four-pin honeycomb rings

Figure 599 'Footside' rows completed and the 'gaps' adjusted

3 Finally adjust the diagonal 'footsides'. Along the section where pairs are added, move the pins slightly higher on the draft (figure 600), while keeping each in line with the diagonal line through the dots. Along the section where pairs are left out, move the pins slightly lower while keeping each in line with the diagonal line through the dots (figure 601).

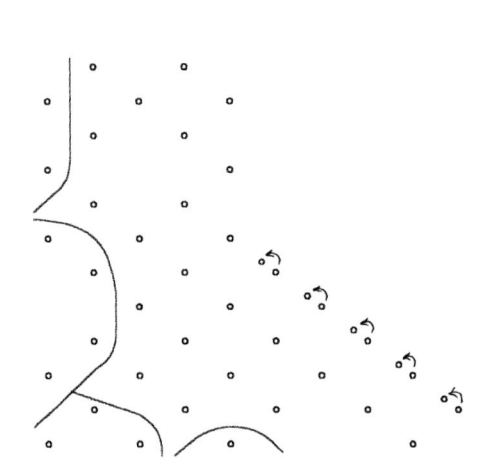

Figure 600 Moving the 'footside' dots 'up' along the first of half the corner

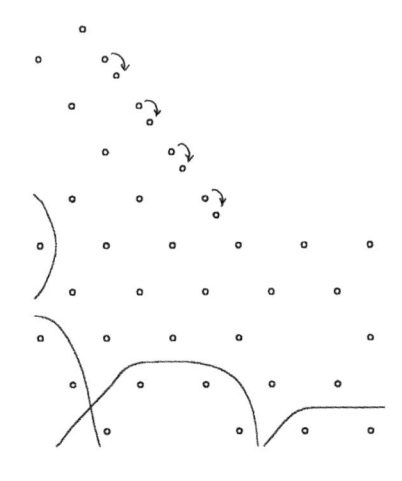

Figure 601 Moving the 'footside' dots 'down' along the second half of the corner

COPYING, ADAPTING AND DESIGNING BUCKS POINT PATTERNS
YOU DO NOT HAVE TO BE A TRAINED ARTIST TO 'HAVE A GO'!

Pattern drafting and Designing

Drafting the pattern for each project is included in the End Notes for that chapter and, as with the projects, they are a graded learning scheme with each building on the former chapters. Where appropriate, information on how the pattern was designed is included.

Most of us have the basic ability to design, but it is not until we try to use it that we realize it is there. It needs courage and practice to 'have a go'. Our first efforts are most likely to be very amateurish, mine certainly were, but that does not matter. It is only by practicing we get better. At first try changing patterns. When you have changed a pattern to the extent that the original is no longer recognizable you can claim to have designed a new one!

The easiest way to start is by copying[1] and then adapting patterns. The patterns, in the chapters with more than one project, develop a theme. Look at the way they change and try similar adaptations. The circular edging (Project 11) was altered by adding colour (Projects 9 & 11) and substituting beads for tallies (Projects 10 & 11). The small motif (Project 12) was elongated to make the pattern for the brush back insert (Project 13), on the way new motifs were required to make the longer shape interesting and the gimp decoration around the edge was changed at the start and finish; the latter dictated by the number of rows. The grid was reduced so that it would fit into the space available. (The grid was reduced from 50 to 53 pins per 10 cm). Using the original grid again, this was elongated for the ruler (Project 14) and the gimp decoration around the edge of the small motif was used, this time the choice was determined by the aesthetic effect rather than the actual space. Chapter 11 starts with a garter made from two edgings and an insertion (Project 15). These pieces are used again for the ring pillow, (Project 16), with both being gathered around corners; the lace does not turn the corner. The lace is turned for the corners and needs a side reverse for the photograph trim and the handkerchief, (Projects 17 & 18), the edging for the photograph frame being slightly narrower than that for the ring pillow. Making lace in a colour changes its character (Projects 20 & 27) and, traditionally, half stitch is substituted for cloth stitch when working in black. Both are the 'negative' version of their white counterparts. The hexagonal piece (Project 21) is reduced in size three times (Projects 22-24), changing the aesthetic effect. The lid motif, (Project 26), has been interpreted in several ways, each having its own character, see Chapter 16 End Notes. The negligee set starts with a wide edging, and a narrow edging that has corners and a diagonal start and finish (Project 28). The wide edging for the slip is cornered and is started and finished along a diagonal (Project 29) and the wide corner is adapted to an extended corner for the narrow edging (Project 30). At this point I thought I had reached the end of the possibilities but, with Maureen's permission, we have the wide edging adapted to make a square (figures 602-604).

Chapter 18

Figure 602 Using a mirror to produce a corner from an edging

Figure 603 Maureen's square made in Egyptian cotton no. 60

Chapter 18

Figure 603 Pattern for Maureen's square

When I first became involved in teaching the designing of lace I studied lace carefully in an attempt to understand what makes a good design. (I say attempt since I have not discovered any hard and fast rules only general concepts.) The majority of lace designs that I find pleasing, whichever the type of lace, have certain characteristics in common.

1 There is a distinct contrast in the density of adjacent areas e.g. cloth stitch against point ground and honeycomb. Honeycomb adjacent to point ground does not work as well, because they are similar in density, although they work better together when divided by a honeycomb stem.

2 There are usually four distinct elements that make a design.
    a) Dominant, comparatively dense areas, of cloth stitch (half stitch when made in black) These dense areas are usually relatively small in area so that they do not overwhelm the design and make it heavy.
    b) Areas where the texture is interesting. These include fillings, of which honeycomb is the most commonly used, and places where gimps are used to make designs.

    c) Parts a & b are embedded in an all-over background design that holds the different motifs together. This background should be light and unobtrusive as regards texture so that it does not detract from the dominant and textured areas, point ground in Bucks lace.

    d) Lines in a design 'lead the eye' from one part to another. Look at different pieces of lace and be aware of the parts you look at, and the order in which you view these parts. The eye follows lines, and is attracted to the more intricate parts of the design, as the brain attempts to understand the whole. Sometimes the eye continues to travel around a piece, for others it is drawn, or led, to a particular part of the design, the focus.

Good lace designs have the first three parts in balance, with the eye being led around the design to the focus of a piece, or travel along the design for an edging or insertion. Also there must be sufficient space between the motifs and fillings to avoid the lace looking 'cluttered'. There needs to be space for the design to 'breathe'.

Are you ready to have a go?
Start by copying patterns[1], then making a pattern from a piece of lace, but be aware that even if the pattern looks like a regular geometrical pattern, it may have had the rules 'stretched'. Try adapting patterns; increase the width and modify features to fit. Select the width, or shape, (e.g. brush back) and use features from patterns you like. Fit them together to make a pleasing design, keeping the basic shapes simple and the overall effect uncluttered. Stand back and view it from at least a metre (1 yard) away. At each stage take a copy if possible. It is annoying to modify a design only to prefer it as it was. Remember, tracing paper has two sides. Start drawing on one side then, when the design has progressed and there are many extra lines in the way, copy to the other side. Then it is easy to erase the mess without spoiling the design. Use tracing paper to mirror a design for a corner or side reverse. Trace part of the design, crease the paper and trace again to produce a corner, side reverse or square. Narrow erasers that work like propelling pencils are useful for removing dots and erasing in small spaces. An erasing guard, a very thin stainless sheet with holes and slits of various shapes and sizes, is very useful. The guard is placed over the design so that only the offending line or dot, showing through the sheet, will be erased. Place the pattern you are currently working on where you will constantly look at it (I have heard the little room is a useful site!); keep a pencil handy for modifications.

My designs are never right the first time, or even the second time I work on them. Many have taken several weeks with me going back to them over and over again; sometimes for just a few minutes at a time. The corner of the wide edging (Project 29) took four months and four aborted samples before I was satisfied. If you have sufficient bobbins, keep the ends when you finish a piece of lace then, when you have a design you like, tie the bobbins to a berry pin and work a sample of the design to test it; there is no need to start and finish tidily. When I am designing, I sketch in the workers for clothwork and half stitch, and draw circles in honeycomb to represent the holes etc., but even so I am often surprised with the finished lace. I have had designs that I was not impressed with turn out very attractive when made and others, that I thought would be beautiful, have turned out to be mediocre and I abandoned them. If you do not produce a beautiful design at your first attempt it does not mean you cannot do it. You will have learnt a lot and be more likely to succeed next time. Above all do not be in a hurry; learning to design is a continuous process.

Look at patterns critically. Not all current patterns are good design. Take your first impression of a piece of lace and examine what it is about the lace that makes you feel the way you do. Are the shapes in harmony, are they well spaced, are the areas balanced? Is the pattern too busy with too many small areas jarring against each other? Your eye will follow the pattern. Think about where it is being lead. Do you find you are being lead into the centre of the design or out of it? Is there an interesting focal point? Are there uncomfortable shapes? It helps to discuss designs with others; different people see designs slightly differently, but most enjoy the same ones. There is more than one way to learn, and learning to design is more a question of experience than knowledge acquired from someone else. Most of us have the basic ability to design, but it needs courage to 'have a go' and not mind if there is not a successful result. Most of our first efforts are likely to be amateurish; this is part of the learning process. It is only practice that makes us improve. Even if there is no apparent end result, the experience will mean there is a better chance next time. Be kind to yourself when the pattern does not seem to work, put it on one side and try something else for awhile; it may work out when you return to it. Patterns 'grow'. Abandoning a design that does not work is not admitting failure; it is accepting that designing is not always easy. The design you are attempting may be too advanced for the stage you have reached and you will not necessarily be aware of the fact. It is not possible to produce a successful corner for all geometrical Bucks point edgings, but you will not realize it will not work for a particular pattern until you try it. Pattern designing and drafting take time and patience. Enjoy puzzling out the problems, then the time taken becomes irrelevant, and more frequently the results are rewarding. Good luck and **above all, enjoy.**

GRIDS AND THREADS (numbers of pins per 10cm (4 in) are approximations)

The size of thread used for making lace is proportional to the spacing of the pins, which in turn is determined by the spacing of the grid. Experiment using threads on grids with different spacings and different angles. Build up reference samples by using up thread after finishing an item. Tie the remaining bobbins in bundles, pin to a pillow and, using any pattern, with a grid having a different angle or spacing, make a small sample. (There is no need for a neat start, just work with the bobbins as they lie on the pillow). Write the angle, number of pins per 10 cms (4 ins) and the thread, on a card tag, and attach to the sample and add to your collection. Making samples using different threads and grids will increase your ability to judge threads, and will prove very useful for comparison when making future decisions.

Equivalent threads

Increasingly we are experiencing problems with our favourite threads going out of production; several of mine disappearing whilst making the samples for this book, hence the need for a list of Equivalent Threads.

The following list of threads only gives suggestions for alternatives. There is much overlapping of the groups and there are threads that have not been included; simply because there are so many and there is little to be gained by trying many more. When you come across a new thread that looks interesting try it; you may prefer it. If you require a more solid or more delicate appearance (see Projects 21-24, a thread from the adjacent group may achieve a desired result, although this may be limited by the proposed use of the lace. Lace that is to be worn and washed usually requires a slightly thicker thread than is necessary for lace that will be protected by glass or other permanent transparent covering. The threads in each group vary slightly in thickness and also in texture. Threads that work up stiffer are more suitable for jabots; those that work up softer are more suitable for handkerchiefs. These properties can be added to the tags on your samples. Cotton is a natural fibre and varies according to the soil in which it is grown and also the weather when it grew. Hence even batches from the same manufacturer may vary slightly. Different brands have different properties, some are softer, others whiter. If you are mounting lace on fabric, check that they are the same colour. If the item is to be washed, check that they match after washing; some ivory threads wash up whiter.

To avoid forgetting the thread you are using, when making a piece of lace, write the name and number of the thread on the pricking together with the date. If a different thread is used, in the future, the date will distinguish between them. Making a note of the number of pairs used can also be useful.

NOTE. These are only suggestions. They are not the only threads that can be used with the listed grids, nor are they only to be used for the grids they are listed under.

Group 1; thread suggestions for use with grids having 40 pins per 10 cms (4 ins) along the footside.

Thread	Gimp
Egyptian cotton no 60	no 8 perle
Madeira Tanne no 50	
Finca no 60	
DMC machine embroidery no 50	
Mettler 60/2	
Finca no 50	
Madeira Catona no 50	
Egyptian cotton no 70	
Piper's 90 denier silk,	6-8 strands loosely twisted together

Group 2; thread suggestions for use with grids having 50 pins per 10 cms (4 ins) along the footside and 40 pins per 10 cms (4 ins) along the footside for designs requiring a delicate effect.

Thread	Gimp
Madeira Tanne no 80	no 12 perle
Madeira catona no 80	
Finca no 80/100?	
Egyptian cotton no 90	
Egyptian cotton no 100	
Brok 100/2	
Piper's 90 denier silk	4-6 strands loosely twisted together
Piper's 40 x 2 silk floss	Piper's 80 x 3

Group 3; thread suggestions for use with grids having 60 pins per 10 cms (4 ins) along the footside and 50 pins per 10 cms (4 ins) along the footside for designs requiring a delicate effect.

Chapter 18

Thread	Gimp
Egyptian cotton no 100	stranded embroidery thread, one strand
Egyptian cotton no 120	stranded embroidery thread, one strand
Piper's 20 x 2 silk floss	4-6 strands loosely twisted together

Group 4; thread suggestions for use with grids having 80 pins per 10 cms (4 ins) along the footside and some are suitable for grids having 60 pins per 10 cms (4 ins) along the footside for designs requiring a delicate effect.

Thread	Gimp
Egyptian cotton no. 100/2	stranded embroidery thread, one strand
Egyptian cotton no. 120/2	
Egyptian cotton no. 140/2	

Grid No 1. (Figure 605) 56° to the footside, 40 pins per 10 cms (4 ins) along the footside. Use for Projects nos. 1, 2, 4, 7, 15, 16, 17, 18, 20, 28, 29 and 30.

Grid No 2. (Figure 606) 56° to the footside, 50 pins per 10 cms (4 ins) along the footside. Use for Projects nos. 3, 12, 14 and 19.

Grid No 3. (Figure, 607) 60° to the footside, 50 pins per 10 cms (4 ins) along the footside. Use for Projects nos. 5, 22 and 25.

Grid No 4. (Figure 608) 54° to the footside, 50 pins per 10 cms (4 ins) along the footside Use for Project no. 6

Grid No 5, (Figure 609). Since this grid is circular the angle to the footside and number of pins per 10 cms (4 ins) changes for each circle of pins. Use threads suitable for grids with 40 pins per 10 cms (4 ins) for this grid. Use for Projects nos. 8, 9 and 10.

Grid No 6. (Figure 610) Since this grid is circular the angle to the footside and number of pins per 10 (4 ins) changes for each circle of pins Use threads suitable for grids with 50 pins per 10 cms (4 ins) for this grid. Use for Project no. 11.

Grid No 7. (Figure 611) 56° to the footside, 53 pins per 10 cms (4 ins) along the footside. Use for Project no. 14.

Grid No 8. (Figure 612) 60° to the footside, 40 pins per 10 cms (4 ins) along the footside. Use for Project no. 21.

Grid No 9. (Figure 613) 60° to the footside, 60 pins per 10 cms (4 ins) along the footside. Use for Projects nos. 23, 26 and 27.

Grid No 10. (Figure 614) 60° to the footside, 75 pins per 10 cms (4 ins) along the footside. Use for Project no. 24.

Chapter 18

40 pins per 10 cms (4 ins)   *50 pins per 10 cms (4 ins)*

Chapter 18

*Figure 607 Grid no 3, 60° to the footside,
50 pins per 10 cms (4 ins) along the footside.*

Chapter 18

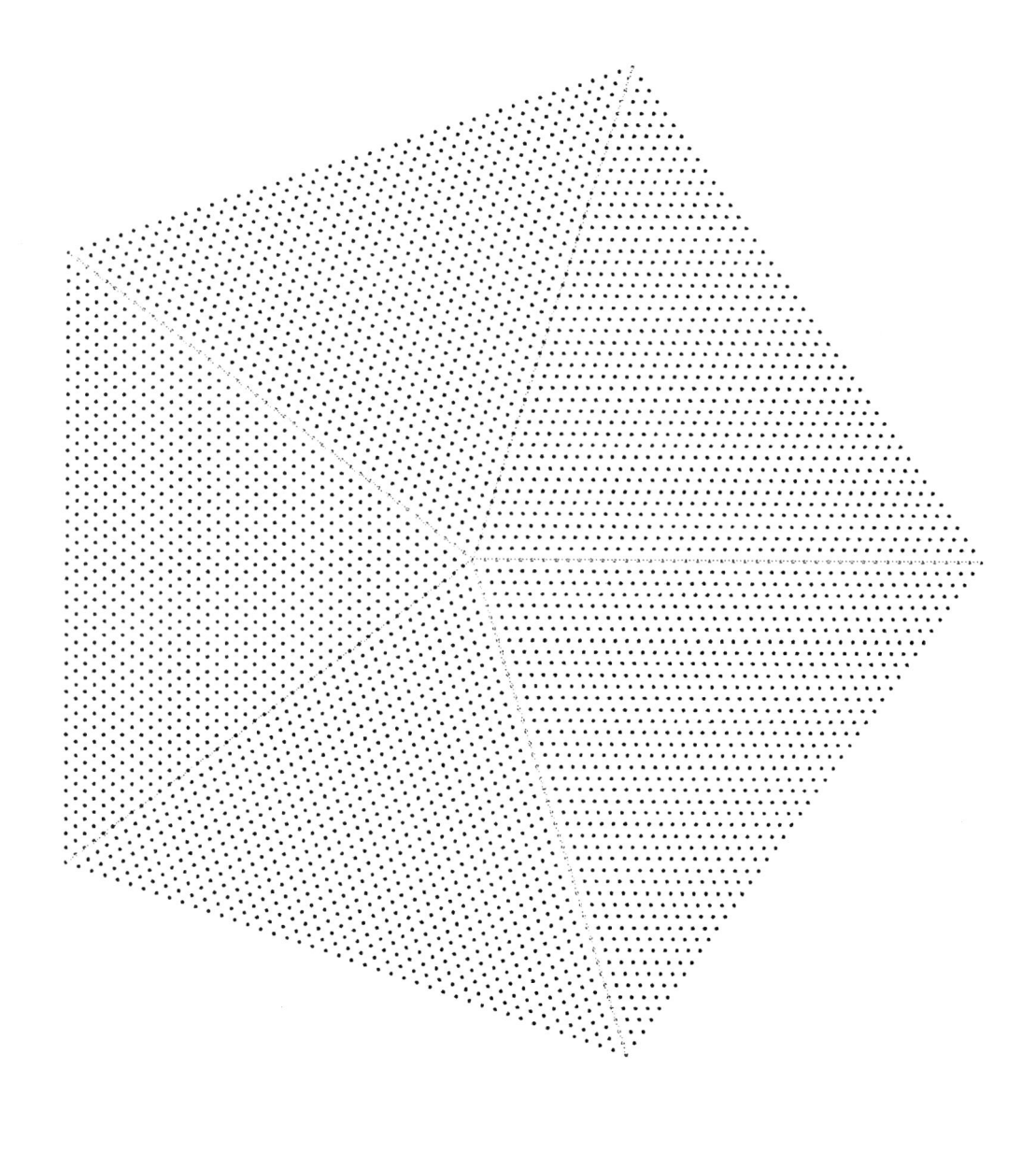

Figure 608 (above) Grid no 4, Pentagon
54°, 50 pins per 10 cms (4 ins)

Chapter 18

*Figure 609 Grid no 5,
Circular, equivalent to
40 pins per 10 cms (4 ins)*

*Figure 610 Grid no 6,
Circular, equivalent to
50 pins per 10 cms (4 ins)*

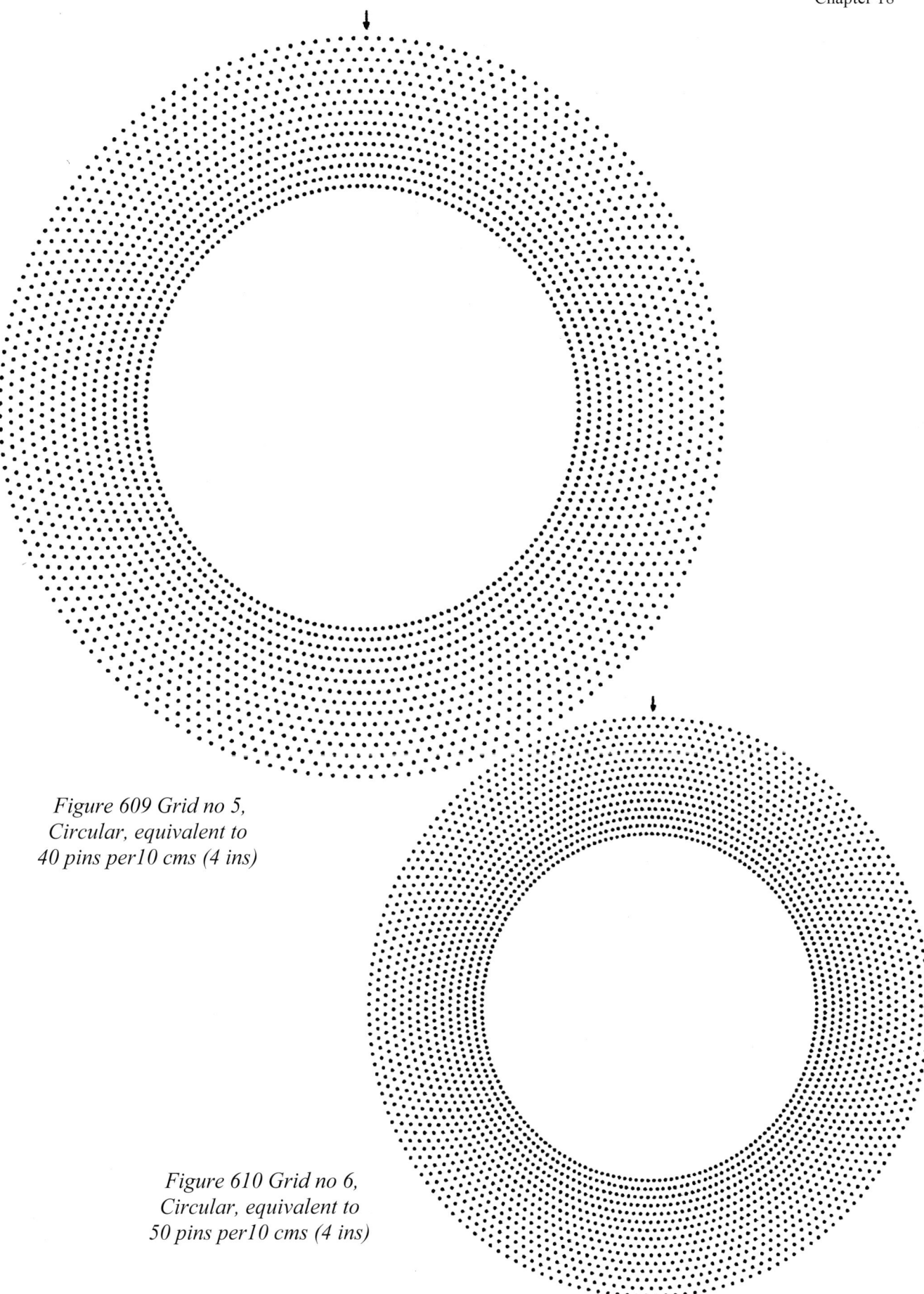

Chapter 18

Figure 611 (right) Grid no 7, 56°
53 pins per 10 cms (4 ins)

*Figure 612 Grid no 8, 60° to the footside,
40 pins per 10 cms (4 ins) along the footside.*

Chapter 18

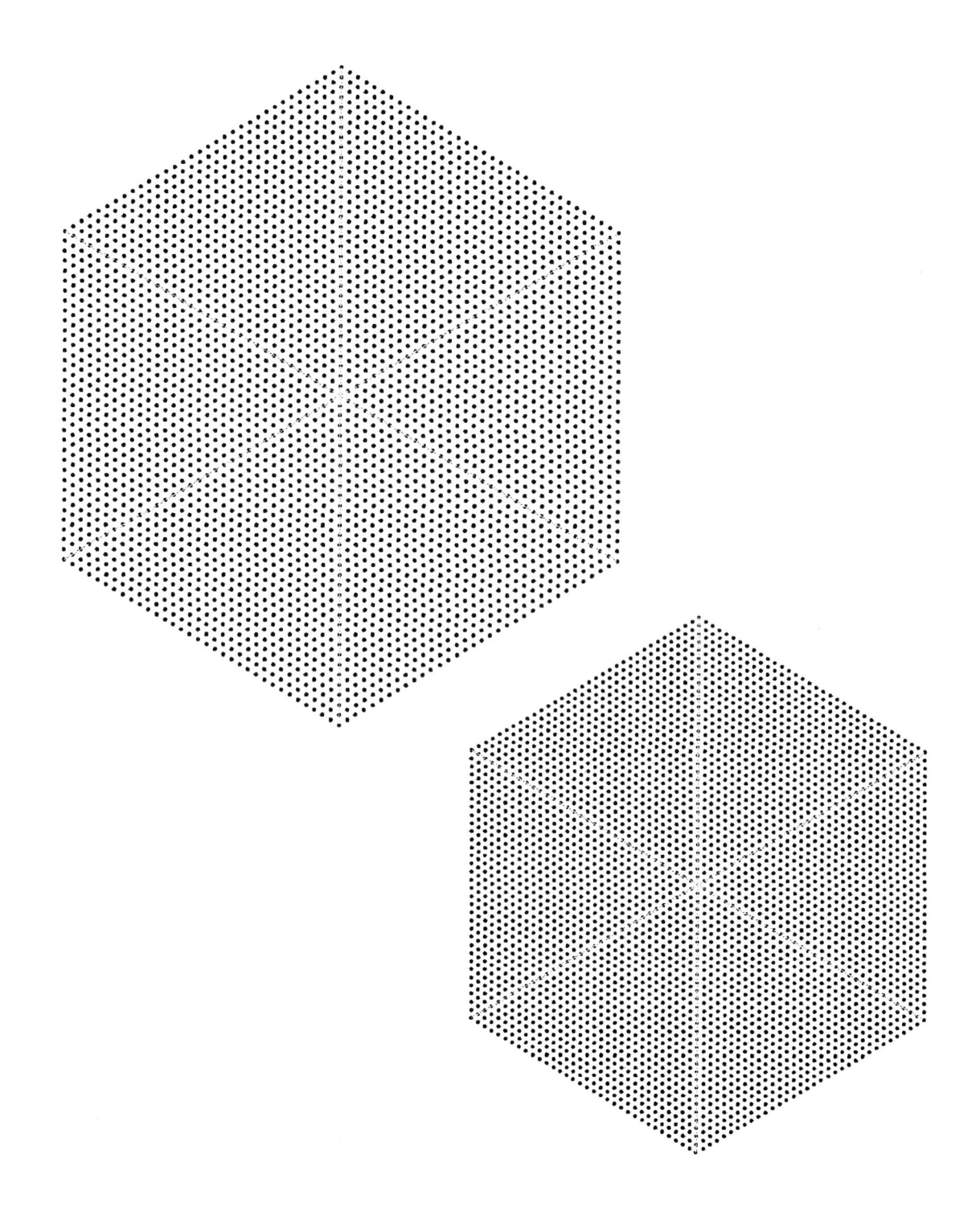

Figure 613 (above) Grid no 9, 60° 60 pins per 10 cms (4 ins)

Figure 614 (below) Grid no 10, 60° 75 pins per 10 cms (4 ins)

BIBLIOGRAPHY

ROBERTS, Georgiana, The Art of Making Buckingham Pillow Lace, Georgiana Roberts, 1926.

CHANNER, C.C., *Lacemaking, Bucks Point Ground,* Dryad Press, 1928.

WRIGHT, Thomas, *The Romance of the Lace Pillow,* Paul Minet, 1971.

MAIDMENT, Margaret, Bobbin Lace Work, Paul Minet, 1971.

NOTTINGHAM, Pamela, *The Technique of Bucks Point Lace,* Batsford, 1981.

COOK, Bridget, *Practical Skills in Bobbin Lace*, Batsford, 1987

LACE GUILD CARNEGIE FOLIO NO 4, Insight *into Bucks Point Lace,* Lace Guild, 1993.

STILLWELL, Alexandra, *Techniques used in the East Midlands to make the Footside of Bucks Point Lace,* paper submitted to 'Textile Journal', 1995.

STILLWELL, Alexandra, *Cassell Illustrated Dictionary of Lacemaking,* Cassell, 1996.

LUTON MUSEUM BOROUGH COUNCIL, *The Lace Dealer's Pattern book,* Luton Museum, 1998.

STILLWELL, Alexandra, *Techniques used to make Bucks Point Lace,* Lace Guild Bursary, 2000.

ORGANIATION INTERNATIONALE DE LA DENTELLE AU FUSEAU ET A L'AGUILLE, *Point ground Lace*, Organiation Internationale de la Dentelle au Fuseau et a L'Aguille,

INDEX
adding pairs 114, 124,
angle of the valley 68,
angle to the footside 4,5,
Alençon 1,4,
arrow 96,
attaching lace, see mounting
back stitch 86,
ballpoint needle 52,
bar 152, 153,
basic movements & stitches 15,
Bayeux 7,
beads 104, 105, 195, 243,
beeswax 10,
Beverse 7,
binding on a gimp 154, 174, 180, 181, 182,
black thread 10, 213,
blind spot 47,
block pillow 93, 94,
Blonde 7,
Blonde Catalana 7,
Blonde de Caen 7,
bobbin winder 14,
bobbins 8, 71,
bottom bead 8,
bow 133, 229,
bowing off 127,
breaking threads 13, 51,
bridge 48, 85,
broken thread – see breaking threads
Bucks Point   3
bulb 8,
bunching pairs 168,
button loop 41, 53,
buttonholed loops 52,
carbon paper (non-smudge) 10,
casting off 39, 87, 126, 160, 168, 177, 178, 225,
catch-pin 22, 27, 28, 58, 60, 174, 180,
catch-pin stitch 22, 28, 58, 60, 63,
central hole 226,
chain stitch loop 43,
changing sections 205,
Chantilly 7,
circular edging 97,
cloth stitch 16, 57, 63, 91, 92, 152, 153, 173, 211, 224,
cloth stitch bars and cucumbers 158, 165,

cloth stitch blocks 157, 159, 165, 165,
collar 9,
colour 101, 102, 103, 110, 111, 180, 243,
combining trails 176, 182, 184,
continuous row 38,
cord filling 155, 163,
cording 99,
corner 85, 86, 91, 138, 145, 173, 232, 235,
copying prickings   5, 249,
coupling bobbins 14,
cover cloths 12, 79, 80,
cross 15,
cucumber 158,
cucumber foot 97, 108, 158,
curved lace 32,
denser cloth stitch 152,
designing   6,
diagonal 'footside' 222,
diamond 57, 63, 119, 174,
dividing into trails 174, 175, 176, 177, 182, 183, 18, 4,
double picot- see picot
doubling up 39, 49,
doubling threads – see doubling up
down hill 63,
Downton 7,
Dressing a pillow 12, 79,
dovetailing 45,
East Midlands bobbins 8,
edge pairs 22, 97,
eraser 246,
erasing guard 246,
Erzgebirge 7,
extended corner 235,
eyelet 174, 179, 182,
false picot 114,
faulty stitch 49,
felt tipped pen 10,
fingers 85, 130, 136,
fillings 153-167, 244,
firming up 31, 32, 213,
floral Bucks 3, 4,
focus 244,
Fond Clair de Neuchâtel 7,
footside 4, 22, 28, 32, 50, 92, 132, 172, 203, 208, 224,

footside passives – see passives
foundation row 41,
four-pin honeycomb 115,
four-sided stitch 41,
French pillow 148,
galloon 225,
gap row 38, 63,
gate 109
gathering 34, 65, 220,
geometrical Bucks 3, 4,
Geraadsbergse Chantilly 7,
gimp 3, 37, 38, 39, 44, 46, 50, 57, 83, 85, 103, 115, 119, 132, 133, 154, 173, 180, 194, 221, 244,
grids 11,
ground 2,
half stitch 2,13,17, 91, 92, 213,
half stitch about the pin 130, 148,
half stitch laces 2,
half straddled 64,
head 8, 220,
headside (also see valleys) 4, 32, 38, 39, 46, 65,131,
headside passives - see passives
heel-ball 7,
heller 12,
hemstitch 142,
hexagon 74,77, 187, 194, 199, 205, 217,
hiding ends 25, 103,
hiller 12,
hitch 13,
hitch with two turns 13,
honeycomb 3,4, 38, 39, 44, 46, 63, 92, 211, 212, 224, 244,
honeycomb stem 98,109,
honeycomb with tallies 154,163,
indicators 10,11, 60,115, 153, 162,163, 164, 165, 210, 213,
insertion 131,
inverting grounds 216,
jabot 88,
joining lace 24, 103, 212,
joining threads 49, 133,
lace cloth 12,
ladder tally 98,
large honeycomb ring 212,
large hole 226,
lattice filling 156, 163,

layering 72,
Lazy Susan 111,
lengthening thread 15,
Libenau 7,
lifting 47,48,
lighter texture 153,
Lille 7,
long loop 188,
long neck 8,
lozenge 174, 180,
Macklin 2
making up the edge 177,
Malmsbury 7,
mayflower 63, 153, 162,
measuring the angle to the footside 249,
Mechlin 1,
Merletto aquilano 7,
modified honeycomb stitch 75, 80,
modifying filling motifs 155,
motifs 3,
mounting 39, 52, 59, 76, 99, 135, 141, 226,
mushroom pillow 9,
narrow trails 163,
neatening at a point 120,
needle threader 112,
non-smudge carbon paper 11,
number of pairs 122, 123, 124,
numbering 15,
off-set footside 26,
optical illusion 167,
overwinding 14,
pairs 148, also see couples
passives 16, 22, 28, 30, 50,
pattern draft 9,
pentagons 76, 78,
photocopying 11,
picot 4, 23, 31, 92, 114, 125,
picot edge 224,
pillow 9,
pillow cloth 12,
pin 9, 51, 79, 138,
pin chain 99, 107, 110, 204, 208,
pin-stitch 226,
Point Clair de marche-en-Femenne 7,

point ground 2, 3, 17, 18, 21, 22, 23, 27, 31, 92, 244,
Point Lace 3,
pricker 9,
pricking 10, 27,
pricking board 10,
pricking by eye 9,
pricking card 9,
protecting seam 229,
reef knot 160,
reef knot with extra turn 126,
reusing a pin 138,
right side 52, 127,
Rijsls e 7,
rim 9,
rings 211, 213, aslo see honeycomb
ringed holes 10, 11,
roller pillow 148,
sample 246,
scale 200, 243,
schematic diagrams 91,
sections 205,
selvedge 36, 39;
setting up 48,
seven-pin honeycomb ring 83,
shackle 9,
shank Tønder 7, 9,
short neck 9,
shortening thread 15,
shredding threads 13, 52,
side reverse 136, 147,
silk 203, 206, 212, 213, 220,
six-pin honeycomb ring 7,
sloping start - see diagonal 'footside',
South Bucks bobbins 9,
spangle 9,
spangle without shackle 9,
speed 52,
spider 159, 164, 221
square 245,
support pin 22, 57,
stacking 65, 68, 160, 168,
starting line 67, 96,
starved 93,
stiffening 203, 206,
stitch about the pin 22, 29,

stitch holders 47, 72,
stitch pins – see stitch holders
straddled 36,
symmetrical valley 69,
tail 9,
tally 97, 98, 108, 109, 118, 154, 163,
tassel 160,
temporary pin 18,
tension 52, 76, 87, 98, 220,
texture 244,
thread 9, 27, 49, 52, 200,
top beads 9,
tracing paper 246,
trails 86, 92, 175, 176, 177, 182, 183, 184, 221,
tram lines 10, 27,
transporting 47,
trimming ends 50,
trueing up 11,
Tulle du Pays d'Enhaut 7,
two twist net 2
Tylová cipka 7,
twist 15, 18, 29, 30, 31, 37, 45, 46, 60, 97, 174, 182,
tying off at point 116,
'U' shaped pillow 94,
uncovered pin 18,
uncovered ground 18,
up hill 63,
valley 65, 68, 69, 204,
valley pin 65, 68, 75,
Vanstena Finknyppling 7,
Vanha Rauman Pitsi 7,
vertical gimp 60,
Vlácka 7,
wax candle 10,
weakened threads 13,
weavers' knot 51,
whole stitch round the pin 21,
winder 13,
winding bobbins 12,
winding on 127,
winkie pin 175, 179,
wire 9
worker 16, 152, 153, 165, 213,
working cloth 12, 74, 75, 79, 80, 213,
working out of the valley 79,
wrong side 52, 127,